# Americans from Yugoslavia

Slovenian immigrants

*Photo courtesy*
*Brown Brothers*

Serbian gypsies
arriving in New York

*Photo courtesy*
*Brown Brothers*

Peasant women
from Croatia

*Photo courtesy*
*Brown Brothers*

Newly-arrived
Yugoslav refugees
in New York

*Photo courtesy*
*World Wide Photos*

# Americans
## from
# Yugoslavia

by
Gerald Gilbert Govorchin

Gainesville
**UNIVERSITY OF FLORIDA PRESS**
**1961**

TO

*My Mother and Father*

and the thousands of other Yugoslav immigrants
who have given their lives and labor
to create a better America

**A University of Florida Press Book**

*Copyright, 1961, by the Board of Commissioners
of State Institutions of Florida*

*Library of Congress Catalogue Card No.: 61-11312*

PRINTED BY PEPPER PRINTING COMPANY
GAINESVILLE, FLORIDA

# Preface

Wɪᴛʜ ᴀ ꜰᴇᴡ ᴇxᴄᴇᴘᴛɪᴏɴꜱ, the story of American immigrants has
been rather fully recorded. One exception is the Yugoslavs, who
have been slow to attract the attention of American scholars. There
have been character sketches and brief biographies of Yugoslav
personalities in newspapers, magazines, and books. Human interest stories dealing with these immigrants have appeared in
various publications. Particular aspects of Yugoslav American life
have been treated in a number of monographs. Broad outlines of
the South Slavic migration have been incorporated in many general
works on the subject. But the full story of the Yugoslav immigrants has not yet been told.

This lack of an inclusive narrative on the South Slavs has not
only constituted a serious lacuna in immigrant literature but it
has also served as a distinct barrier to a better acquaintance with
these citizens from the Balkans. Their place in American culture
can be correctly determined only through more intimate contact
with them. For a thorough understanding of them—their attitudes
and ideals, their hopes and ambitions, their struggles and accomplishments—a complete survey is necessary.

It is, therefore, with this specific need in mind that the writer
has embarked on the present project. His aim, however, is not to
produce an exhaustive account by giving a detailed description of
every aspect of Yugoslav immigration, but rather to provide a comprehensive study of its character as a whole.

In this book the author attempts to sketch the story of the Yugoslav Americans against a general background of immigration, so

that their role in America's making can be more easily assessed. The many phases of the immigrants' life in the United States are surveyed: their occupations, organizations, press, worship, education, and adaptation to the American environment, together with an evaluation of their principal achievements and most significant contributions. An effort has been made to write an account that will find general acceptance—a work that will be of use to scholars and of interest to the average reader. Such a compromise arrangement is difficult to effect, for many subjects do not readily lend themselves to this type of treatment. Whatever the result, it is hoped that this introduction will serve as a stimulus to further investigation.

The chief sources of information for this work have been books, periodicals, and people. The author consulted several hundred titles in the search for material, but he makes no pretense of having covered the entire literature on the subject. A number of references have been purposely omitted, while some important ones have undoubtedly been overlooked. Much material lies buried in basements and attics in this country, and there is a wealth of pertinent literature in the libraries of Yugoslavia. The numerous Yugoslavs interviewed have been virtually a mine of information. Conversations with Croats, Serbs, and Slovenes provided a valuable supplement to the printed word.

Many persons and organizations have helped in the preparation of this study, but the list is much too long to mention all by name. However, the writer wishes to acknowledge his indebtedness especially to P. D. Ostović, Yugoslav historian, teacher, and writer, who not only read the manuscript and offered invaluable suggestions but who also worked ceaselessly in helping to obtain much-needed and hard-to-get materials; to the librarians at Northwestern and Chicago universities, the Newberry Library, the John Crerar Library, the Chicago Public Library, and the Los Angeles Public Library; to the Office for Research and Education of the United States Immigration and Naturalization Service; to the Information Center and the Embassy of the Federal People's Republic of Yugoslavia; to the many Yugoslavs who responded so favorably to requests for information; to the members of the administration and faculty at the University of Miami (Dr. Jay F. W. Pearson, president; Dr. C. Doren Tharp, vice president and dean of faculties;

Dr. H. Franklin Williams, vice president and director of community affairs; Prof. Richard D. Kreske, chairman of the department of geography; and Dr. Charlton W. Tebeau, chairman of the department of history), whose understanding and generosity made possible the completion of the manuscript; to my secretary, Miss Marie K. Zerbey, who bore her typing chores most nobly; and to my daughter, Cherilyn Govorchin, who not only helped with the typing but also assisted in numerous other ways. Thanks are also due the publishers who so kindly gave their permission to quote from their works.

GERALD GILBERT GOVORCHIN

*University of Miami*
*Coral Gables, Florida*

# Contents

Modern Yugoslavia

# 1

# Causes for Immigration

W ITH THE YUGOSLAVS,[1]* as with other immigrants to the United States, there have been many reasons for leaving the warm familiarity of home and venturing on the long one-way journey across the sea. The early South Slavic[2] missionaries were intent on converting the American Indians; the peasants sought relief from the economic dilemma of overpopulation and land deprivation; lovers of liberty from farm and city alike shared the desire to escape constant political pressures; while the youths, of course, thought only of adventure.

Whatever their individual aims, the motley peoples who have come from all over the globe to call America their homeland have approached its shores with the common hope for a better future. Towards this beckoning promise they toiled, accepting the hardships of travel for an opportunity to labor in a strange, new, free land.

## SHIFTS IN IMMIGRATION

Unrestricted immigration to the United States passed through two fairly well-defined phases, which have been termed the "old immigration" and the "new." During the first phase most of our immigrants came from countries of northern and western Europe, principally the British Isles, Germany, the Scandinavian countries, France, The Netherlands, and Switzerland. During the second phase the majority were from countries of southern and eastern Europe, chiefly Austria-Hungary, Italy, and Russia. From 1820

* Notes to this chapter begin on page 283.

(when the government first began keeping records) to 1896 most of the immigrants were of the old strain; from 1896 to 1924 the new immigration held the lead over the old. With the adoption of the immigration restrictions in the 1920's, the tide was again turned in favor of northern and western Europe.

During the first decade of the twentieth century more than 70 per cent of the immigration was from the south and east of Europe, while only 20 per cent was from west and north of the continent. Twenty years before, the reverse had been true; 70 per cent of the immigration to the United States originated in the north and west of Europe and hardly 20 per cent came from eastern and southern Europe. Only a very small proportion of the immigrants came from countries of southern and eastern Europe until the late eighties. Not until 1887 did immigration from that section of Europe make up 25 per cent of the total immigration. A significant shifting of the source of immigration took place between 1895 and 1896. In 1895, 54.7 per cent of the immigrants came from northern and western Europe. In 1896 only 40 per cent came from those countries, while 57 per cent came from southern and eastern Europe. Thus, in a comparatively short period of time Austria-Hungary, Russia, and Italy surpassed the British Isles, Germany, and Scandinavia as the most important sources of immigration, an advantage they retained for a generation.[3]

The immigration of the South Slavs to the United States has also passed through a regular cycle. At first their immigration, like that of other southern and eastern European peoples, proceeded in a trickle. This continued with but little change until the closing decades of the nineteenth century. The movement then picked up tremendous speed as the swelling tide of new immigrants surged over the old. Finally, with the economic depression in the thirties, and the onset of World War II in the forties, the huge wave evaporated, leaving only a small dribble.

### WHY THEY LEFT HOME

The more important reasons for immigration to the United States have always been essentially the same: hard conditions at home (primarily economic) and the promise of greater opportunity in America (again primarily economic). The relative strength of expulsive and attractive forces has varied from country to country

2

and from time to time. That immigration has been mainly determined by economic motives is shown by the fact that variations in
economic conditions in the United States have exercised a considerable influence upon the number of incoming aliens. As shown by
careful investigations, with the exception of instances of unusual
disaster in the homeland, such as severe famine or political oppression, the time of arrival of immigrants has been influenced by conditions here. In other words, the "pull" has been stronger than the
"push." Moreover, there has been a fairly high degree of concur-
rence between periods of prosperity or depression in the United
States and the leading countries of emigration. Evidence clearly
shows that when prosperity has reigned, immigration has been
comparatively high; when depression has cast its shadow over the
land, the number of new arrivals has been relatively low.

The forces behind the immigration to the New World were
brilliantly set down by the well-known eighteenth-century French
American gentleman, farmer, scientist, and writer, J. Hector St.
John de Crèvecoeur. In his celebrated *Letters from an American
Farmer,* Crèvecoeur wrote:

> The rich stay in Europe, it is only the middling and the poor
> that emigrate. In this great American asylum, the poor of Europe
> have by some means met together . . . urged by a variety of
> motives, here they came. Everything tended to regenerate them;
> new laws, a new mode of living, a new social system; here they
> are become men: in Europe they were so many useless plants,
> wanting vegetable mould, and refreshing showers; they withered
> and were mowed down by want, hunger, and war: but now by
> the power of transplantation, like all other plants, they have
> taken root and flourished! Formerly they were not numbered
> in any civil list of their country, except in those of the poor; here
> they rank as citizens . . . his country is now that which gives him
> land, bread, protection, and consequence: *Ubi panis ibi patria,*
> is a motto of all emigrants . . . . Here the rewards of his industry
> follow with equal steps in the progress of his labor; his labor is
> founded on the basis of nature, *self-interest*; can it want a strong-
> er allurement?

The economic motive was undoubtedly uppermost in the immigrants' thinking, but other factors were also of consequence. Among
these may be mentioned: political and religious unrest and per-

secution; wars; military service; burdensome taxes; quest of adventure; stimulation by steamship ticket agents, land speculators, and industrial employers; books written by those who had lived in America; and personal letters from immigrants to relatives and friends in the old country. That the influence of these separate forces has not been the same at all times and in all places hardly needs stressing.

Among the South Slavs, as among the other emigrants, the most impelling motive for emigration was economic. The bulk of them were poor peasants occupying tiny plots of land. They were at a distinct disadvantage in trying to compete with a few great landowners, who held much of the land. The small holdings of the peasants led to overpopulation in some districts, giving rise, in turn, to further privations and sufferings. Wages were very low in the country and only a little better in the city. High rates of taxation were especially burdensome for the impoverished Slavs. It was no wonder then that they sought to escape from their misery and go to America to better their fortunes.

This was true of Slovenes, Serbs, Croats, and Dalmatians. Slovenes saw little opportunity for economic betterment in their mountainous country with its poor agriculture and little or no trade and manufactures. Serbians from Serbia emigrated but in insignificant numbers. Their emigration was mainly from those territories under the political control of Austria-Hungary, and included largely miners, farm laborers, and peasants, all of whom experienced difficulties in maintaining a bare existence. One of the principal economic reasons for the emigration of the Croats is to be attributed to the breaking up of the *zadruga* (a household cooperative), which in turn led to excessive subdivision of land. This is also one of the reasons why the Dalmatians left home, but added to it must be overpopulation, decline of the old commerce dependent on sails and piracy, the effects of competition of Italian wine merchants, especially after 1890, and the failure of the Adriatic fisheries.

Thought not as significant as the economic factors, political considerations should also be emphasized. Most of modern Yugoslavia was, during the decades of the great immigration to the United States, a part of the Austro-Hungarian empire, only the kingdoms of Serbia and Montenegro being independent. (See Appendix I for the history of the South Slavs.) Following the creation of the

Southern Slavic Peoples in the Austro-Hungarian Empire

Dual Monarchy in 1867 the Slovenes were placed under Austrian control, the Serbs (in Croat territories) under Hungarian, while the Croats were subject to both. Dalmatia and Istria, both Croatian provinces, were governed from Vienna. The "Kingdom" of Croatia, Slavonia, and Dalmatia occupied a rather unique position in Hungary, having its autonomy theoretically recognized in matters of administration, justice, public instruction, and cults. In practice, however, its financial system, coinage, weights, measures, commercial treaties, banking, exchange, patents, copyrights, maritime commerce, mining, customs, trades, post and telegraphs, railways, harbors, and shipping were all directed from Budapest. Thus, the Croats had little control over their own destiny. Bosnia and Hercegovina were transformed into an Austro-Hungarian condominium in the wake of the decisions of the Berlin Congress in 1878.

5

The Austrians and the Hungarians sought in every way possible to make good Germans and Magyars out of the Croats, Serbs, and Slovenes; but they failed utterly. The Habsburgs contemptuously called their Slavic subjects *Völkersplitter* (ethnic fragments) or *Völkerdünger* (ethnic manure). The Napoleonic occupation of Dalmatia and southern Croatia in the early nineteenth century had introduced the principles and ideals of the French Revolution which drastically altered the former social and political relations. These doctrines helped to keep the embers of national dissatisfaction burning in spite of all the efforts of the autocratic regimes to extinguish them. As education increased and agitation in favor of an independent Yugoslav state spread, the South Slavs became ever more conscious of the burdens they bore and the humiliation and injustices they suffered as the subjects of foreign rulers who were bent on maintaining the supremacy of their own separate nationality. Mounting political unrest was the natural outcome of this state of affairs. Some of the South Slavs sought to bring an end to the political oppression and indignities and to restore peace and order by plunging more deeply into the campaign for Yugoslav unity and independence. Many others found escape from the seething Balkan cauldron by leaving their homes and migrating to America, where they could pursue a freer and more peaceful life.

Conditions improved very little with the dissolution of the Dual Monarchy at the end of World War I. The majority of the South Slavs were incorporated in the new Yugoslav state (the Kingdom of the Serbs, Croats, and Slovenes), which, unfortunately, turned out to be nothing more than an enlarged Serbia. Thousands of Slovenes and Croats living in the region of Trieste became the subjects of Italy, which was designated as one of the heirs to the Habsburg possessions. Thus, it is clear, only the masters were changed, as Serbs and Italians replaced Austro-Hungarians. Political subservience to a Karadjordjević, a Mussolini, or a Habsburg was equally distasteful. Centralism was as abhorrent to the non-Serbs in Yugoslavia as Italianization was to the South Slavs in Istria. Accordingly, many Slovenes, Croats, Dalmatians, Bosnians, Hercegovinians, and Montenegrins continued to look upon emigration as a solution for their political problems. The free air in the United States acted as a huge magnet which drew them across the wide expanse of the Atlantic. The singular American liberties which have always been a source of attraction for oppressed nationals everywhere were brought into sharp focus by Stoyan Pribichevich, a Serb American writer who escaped from King Alexander's iron rule, when he stated:

> In this country I experienced for the first time the magnificent feeling of absolute personal freedom. No policeman could stop me in the street or in a restaurant and ask me to show him my papers. I could walk about without carrying an identity card in my pocket, change my address without reporting to the police, and slap a cop on the shoulder just because I was feeling fine. Only a European can appreciate the personal freedom a man enjoys in this country.[4]

As is well known, political liberties were not enlarged following the deposition of the Karadjordjevićes and the institution of the Communist regime under Tito in 1946. Some of the more unrelenting opponents of Communism refused to accept the new life and sought relief through flight. And so emigration by the freedom-loving Yugoslavs in the new Yugoslavia went on, though on a reduced scale, as it had in the old.

Political and economic reasons, however important, do not in themselves complete the list of causes for emigration from the native land and entry into the United States. Others must be included if the whole story is to be told.

Thus, religion was very important in bringing to American shores the early Slavic missionaries, who came to the wilderness primarily to convert the Indians. Strange as it may seem, however, the religious factor did not loom large in the general mass immigration of the South Slavs. This is explained by the fact that, although a subject people, they were allowed, generally, to pursue their religious beliefs and practices unhindered by their rulers.

Thousands of young men left Austria-Hungary and fled to the United States to escape compulsory military service. Droves of other South Slavs were influenced and assisted by relatives and friends who had gone to America earlier. Still others succumbed to the propaganda of steamship agents. Then too, among the Slavs as among any immigrant group, the desire for adventure and excitement in a new land lured countless numbers. Finally, it might be argued, not without some support, that the very policy of the

Habsburgs toward emigration was an influencing factor. The rulers at Vienna, regarding emigration as harmful to the empire, tried at first to repress it entirely and later to regulate and confine it within narrow bounds. Accepting humanity for what it is, one could readily conclude that such limitations may have perhaps led some of the bolder souls to defy authorities by emigrating.

It is thus evident that the causes and incentives for leaving the homeland and going to America are many and varied, simple and complex. Some of these, of course, are harder to understand fully than others and so require further amplification and elucidation.

## ECONOMIC CAUSES

It is not to be denied that a great motive for immigration to the United States has always been the desire for liberty. The majority, however, immigrated in order to improve their material status.[5] They came to America for jobs, for rich land, for an opportunity to better themselves. Their first and foremost concern was material gain. Konrad Bercovici, paraphrasing Crèvecoeur, underlined the importance of this fact when he stated that "the subconscious motto of the people is *ubi bene, ibi patria*: where it is well, there is my fatherland."[6]

The significance of the economic factor in the immigration of the Yugoslavs was clearly brought out in an explanation given the author by a prosperous Montenegrin living in Miami, Florida. In reply to the query as to why he had left home and come to America he stated in broken, but understandable, English:

> You ask me why I leave the old country and come here. That's no hard to answer. Over there I have nothing; here I got everything. I was in Crnagora for twenty-five years. I live on a small farm with my mother, father, six brothers, and four sisters. With such a big family, it was tough. I was hungry and barefooted most of the time; I was lucky to get a pair of *opanci* [sandals] in the winter time. You blame me I run away from all that? I come to this country and right away I get a good job in steel mill in Gary, Indiana. I made lots of money—more money for one pay than I saw in all my life in Crnagora—but I no like the factory. So I work couple years and I move to Florida and get a job with a small building construction company. I work hard and save my money, and pretty soon I become a partner in the

8

company. I make good. Then I buy houses and apartments and rent them. Today I have enough property to take care of me for the rest of my life and something left over to help my brothers and sisters in the old country.

Unable to earn a living at home, thousands of the South Slavs emigrated *trbuhom za kruhom* (literally, with belly after bread).[7] Political oppression was undoubtedly a great motive for emigration, but economic hardships (usually increased by political oppression) were a greater incentive still to mass emigration to a better economic environment.[8]

During a period of nearly thirty-five years, ending in 1910, about three and a half million people left the Austro-Hungarian empire, and about three million entered the United States.[9] The mass emigration "caused the empire to lose its most active, most courageous, most enterprising material."[10] For a long time freedom from Habsburg oppression semed impossible to the South Slavs, and reports of political and economic freedom in the United States had a great attraction for them.[11]

Earlier immigration to the United States was spurred by the availability of good land at a low price, and the desire for political and religious freedom. Soon, however, the good land was taken up; but the industrial expansion after the Civil War, with a call for cheap, unskilled labor, provided the masses of central, eastern, and southern Europe with an unusual opportunity to improve their condition. Presently, industrial and railroad companies from America and shipping companies from Europe set up their agencies all over the continent, promising to pay the fare of prospective immigrants in return for a contract for assigned work in mill or mine. Direct railroad connections between Vienna and the Atlantic ports of Hamburg, Bremen, Antwerp, and Le Havre aided the immigrant transport companies immensely. They utilized these cities as headquarters for their operations.

Thus, the post-Civil War boom in the United States helped to draw another wave of immigrants into the country: Italians and Slavs. In describing these new arrivals one eminent writer said:

> These newer groups of Slavic immigrants were mainly drawn from more primitive districts than earlier groups; districts where the population was less in touch with Western Europe. They

9

generally came, not intending to take up farms and settle, but hoping to earn money to send to their homes, to which they planned to return. To this end they sought the best paid work that they could find in mines, factories, foundries and elsewhere. A large proportion of both the old and the new comers were peasants, that is, small independent farmers; but among the new, the proportion of men possessing trades was less, and mere laborers were numerous.[12]

The United States Immigration Commission—created by Congress in February, 1907, for the purpose of making a thorough investigation of immigration—stated in its report (published in 1911) that whereas the old immigration (in the early nineteenth century) was made up of persons who intended to become permanent settlers, the new immigration (in the first decade of the twentieth century) was made up of a large proportion of individuals who apparently had no intention of settling in the country. Investigation showed that nearly 40 per cent of the new immigrants were returning to their European homeland, about two-thirds of these remaining there. A portion of these immigrants had made enough money to live on, but others returned because they had failed, or because they had contracted a disease which made them unfit for industry. Still others were widows and children of immigrants who had died in the United States.

Stressing strongly the economic factor, the Immigration Commission pointed out, "In practically every instance the Commission's query as to the cause of emigration was met by the answer 'to earn greater wages in America.' "[13] Lack of sufficient land for cultivation, primitive industrial development, low levels of production, lack of resources, and wide lack of opportunity for work spurred emigration in European countries.

In many cases peasants owned land which was too small to produce enough for subsistence. With twelve and one-half acres being the estimated minimum required for sustenance, the average small holding in Dalmatia, for example, was less than one and one-half acres. In the Lika-Krbava district of Croatia there were, in 1900, 268,000 persons and only 225,780 acres of arable land. In all of Croatia there were 400,000 farm properties, with only 209 large holdings and 930 medium-sized ones, the overwhelming remainder being small plots. The condition was very similar in the Slovene provinces. In Dalmatia 86 per cent of the population earned their living in agriculture and forestry; 72 per cent of the Croatians engaged in agriculture; and 75 per cent of the Slovenians worked on the farm.[14] With three-fourths of the South Slavs thus occupying such tiny strips, the great majority constantly faced starvation.

Not only was there a lack of land for cultivation, but the soil in many places was poor. This was especially true of the districts of the karst (a limestone topography characterized by caverns and sinkholes made by solution work of ground waters), which embraced southern Slovenia, western Croatia, the interior of Dalmatia, a portion of western Bosnia, the greater part of Hercegovina, and western Montenegro. Cultivation was virtually impossible in such areas. Added to these handicaps were many others. The methods of farming were extremely primitive. Unfamiliar with artificial fertilizers and crop rotation, the peasants rapidly exhausted the fertility of the soil. Moreover, farming implements were crude, agricultural machinery being practically unknown.

Life in the country was further complicated by the gradual disappearance of the *zadruge*. The dissolution of these communal households was brought about by the increased exhaustion of soil, plant diseases, laws forbidding the pasturing of goats (because they damaged the woods), laws requiring the partitioning of communal property, and the increased urbanization of life. By the end of the nineteenth century only a small fraction of the peasants remained in the *zadruge*, and the number steadily decreased. Following the disintegration of the cooperatives many of the former members found themselves orphaned, without home or farm, and some, as a consequence, chose to migrate to America in search of new opportunities.

In addition to the depressed conditions described above, the wages of farm laborers were exceedingly low. In its study of the economic causes of emigration in the Austro-Hungarian empire, the Immigration Commission reported:

> Of the eighty-one "national districts" reporting the average daily wages of farm laborers in winter, thirty-five paid from $.10 to $.16 and twenty-three paid from $.16 to $.20. The prevalent daily wage of women farm laborers in more than two-thirds of the districts reporting was from $.10 to $.16. In summer wages were higher both for men and women. The former were paid

11

from $.20 to $.30 in the majority of the districts reporting. The prevalent wage paid for women farm laborers was from $.16 to $.20. When food was not furnished wages were from $.17 to $.18 higher for men in winter and $.20 higher in summer. Women were paid from $.12 to $.14 more in winter and $.15 more in summer when food was not furnished.[15]

It was found that in the provinces where a large number of people emigrated the wages paid to laborers were relatively low. This is further witness to the fact that there was close relation between wages and emigration.

Industrially, too, the provinces surveyed by the Commission were found to be backward. As a result, the existing industries could not absorb the excess population from the farm districts. "Since industry affords no outlet for a population grown too large for the land to support, emigration has been the only alternative," the Commission concluded.[16] According to the census of 1900 only 26.8 per cent of the population of Austria were dependent on the manufacture of food, drink, and clothing.[17] In Hungary only 14.4 per cent of the population depended on mining and industry.[18]

As in agriculture, so in industry the wages were low and the hours long. In most places employees received little more for eleven or twelve hours of work than did the laborers on the farm.

It is true, of course, that the cost of living was low. However, it would be misleading to think that wages were low due to low living costs. To be sure, the amount of money spent by a peasant on food was low when compared with the proportion of earnings spent on food by American laborers and farmers. On the other hand, the European low-income peasants ate a poor diet, with meat served only rarely.

The Immigration Commission pointed out that "the staple food of peasants in Austria-Hungary is rye bread, potatoes, cabbages, corn meal mush, meat being rarely eaten," and that the "necessities of the American farmer would be luxuries for the peasants."[19] The wardrobes of the peasants were just as limited, with one outfit for the summer and another for the winter serving as the average quota. Materials for shoes were difficult to get, so that it was not unusual for two or three members of a family to share the same pair. And the dwellings of the peasants, primitive and inadequate, were in keeping with their low standards of existence. Most of them lived in one-room, windowless huts, with floors of bare earth.  Under-nourished and in unhealthful surroundings they became the easy victims of numerous diseases, especially tuberculosis, malaria, and typhoid.  It is no wonder then that these unfortunate souls emi-grated to the United States when they could, in order to better their circumstances.  The desire for improved living conditions for a time spread contagiously.

Besides the aforementioned economic factors which were at work throughout the South Slav lands generally, there were other forces in operation in certain specific areas.  These too should re-ceive some attention in order that a more complete account may be presented.

In Dalmatia, during the Italian control from the fifteenth cen-tury to the end of the eighteenth, the stripping of forests along the coast line (for the piles of Venice, for ships and masts, and for build-ings) had an adverse effect upon the economy of the region.  Fol-lowing this tragedy came the decline and disappearance of sailing vessels.  Dalmatian sailors, known around the globe as skilled navigators, became idle as the steamship replaced the sailing schooner on the high seas.  The once-thriving cities of Korčula, Orebić, Perast, and others lost their old glory as their harbors fell into disrepair, the result of neglect and abandonment.  With no railways connecting these ports with the rich hinterland to provide new employment, privation and suffering increased as the decline in shipping was accompanied by a diminution in commerce.

In the nineteenth century also, a plant pest known as phylloxera destroyed many of the vineyards in Dalmatia.  At the same time, competition from Italian wine producers forced the price of Dal-matian wine, which was the principal article of export, to sink to new lows.  To add to the distress the fish catch in the Adriatic drastically diminished, due chiefly to the failure of the fishermen to follow an effective policy of conservation.  Oppressive taxes and overpopulation increased the suffering.  At the opening of the pres-ent century the situation in Dalmatia was desperate.  Hundreds of villages lacked drinking water, while stagnant, polluted waters spread over the fertile valleys of the Imotski, Neretva, Sinj, Vrana, and Vrgorac.  The Habsburgs did not raise a hand to alleviate the lot of the unfortunate Dalmatians.  Seeking to escape from their distress and poverty, some peasants began the illicit raising of tobacco, while others, mainly fishermen, resorted to the shipment of contraband goods. The young and adventurous males, however, hearing of specific openings in the United States, departed for the New World, leaving behind them only the women, the children, the aged, and the infirm.

In Croatia, too, varied forces and conditions combined to stimulate emigration. The Magyar masters maintained a monopoly over Croatian farm products and compelled their transport through Budapest instead of permitting direct passage to their natural outlet in Vienna, using the absence of regular train service between Croatia and Austria as a pretext for the action. The consequence was agricultural as well as industrial stagnation. Many of the existing industries were transferred to Hungary. Timber plants in Croatia and Slavonia were placed under Hungarian control. In this way the commercial center shifted from Zagreb to Budapest.[20]

For many years Croatia served as a crossroad from Austria to the Adriatic. Croatian wheat and oaks and Hungarian tobacco made their way down the Danube, Sava, and Kupa rivers to Karlovac, from where they were carried by wagon trails to Rijeka and Senj. The population along this artery of transportation—mainly the inhabitants of Lika and Gorski Kotar—earned its livelihood through the handling of these articles of commerce. In 1873 the first railway from Karlovac to Rijeka was completed. Soon this railway, together with the one between Vienna and Trieste built nearly twenty years earlier, took over the transports. The large number of workers who had transported the goods by hand or with burros found themselves out of work. Within a decade many of the displaced freight handlers began to leave for America.

In these same years (about 1883) the vineyards in Croatia, as in Dalmatia and Slavonia too, were ravaged by the phylloxera plague. After a brief period of recovery renewed invasions followed in 1900 and 1901, resulting in widespread poverty.

The condition of the peasant continued to degenerate. Emancipation (effected in the middle years of the nineteenth century) had not brought any real relief. It had meant merely a change in masters—the gentleman of the city for the aristocratic landlord. Many peasants were left without land and were compelled to look for employment elsewhere. Bloody revolts occurred with increasing frequency as peasants fought against their masters over oppres-

14

sion and against one another over the common use of pasture land and woods. Adding to the difficulties of the rural population was the government regulation prohibiting goat raising. This caused the virtual disappearance of milk and milk products from the peasant's table, leading to a great loss of sustenance and consequent loss of vigor. Simultaneously, overpopulation increased.

Taxes bore heavily on the weak shoulders of the peasants. With industry and trade practically at a standstill, the government relied on the income tax as its principal source of revenue, much of which was taken from the pockets of the peasants by the tax collectors. In order to meet their obligations many were forced to go to a moneylender or a bank for a loan and pay usurious rates of interest, ranging from 12 to 40 per cent. Such high rates kept the borrower perpetually in debt.

The government in Budapest not only turned a deaf ear to the pleas of the Croats for relief, but actually cooperated with the moneylenders and bankers in stripping the peasants of their possessions. Public auctions of peasants' houses and lands were daily occurrences. The result of this development was forced migration of Croats from their homeland and their replacement by foreigners. In the thirty-four years from 1880 to 1914 more than half a million Croats left their country, with only about one-fourth of them returning. During approximately the same period (1840 to 1910, to be exact), the Magyar inhabitants in Croatia increased from 5,050 to 105,948 and the German from 13,226 to 136,221.[21]

Thus, the Croat peasant, oppressed by burdensome taxes and denied an opportunity to eke out a bare existence in the native land, looked toward greener pastures across the broad expanse of the Atlantic. Having just one member of the family in America often meant the difference between starvation and survival for those at home, as the immigrant sent back much of what he earned.

From the end of the fourteenth century onward the Serbs enjoyed certain defined rights in the Croat districts of Lika and Vojvodina to which they had fled before the conquering Turk. In agreements made with the emperors of Austria they obtained full title to the lands they occupied. They were exempted from taxes and promised religious and political freedom. In return, the Serbs agreed to arm all adult males (sixteen years of age and upward) and be ready to do battle whenever the Turks threatened. Immediately after the creation of the Dual Monarchy of Austria-Hungary in 1867, however, Emperor Francis Joseph abrogated the pledges of his predecessors. Destruction of their ancient privileges made life in the Habsburg realm unbearable for many of the Serbs, and so now they fled from their new oppressors just as they had from the old, five centuries earlier. Whenever the opportunity presented itself they emigrated to the United States.

Conditions in Slovenia were not far different from those in other South Slav lands. The Slovenes in Carniola, particularly, experienced difficulties in earning a livelihood because of the poor conditions in the country and the backward development of commerce and industry in the city. Consequently they departed in large numbers for America.

There was slight improvement on the economic front for the South Slavs following the creation of the Yugoslav state. Industry remained small-scale in scope, primitive in organization, and retarded in technique. Domestic capital, technology, and initiative needed for improvement were lacking. This opened the way for exploitation by foreign investors, who were mainly concerned with securing cheap raw materials for their own plants or for sale to their associated concerns, and who took no interest in investing their profits in the expansion and improvement of Yugoslav industry in general.

Under such conditions the lot of the industrial worker was poor, indeed. Security was unknown. Unemployment was common. Conditions of work were often intolerable. Hours were long and wages low. The peasant on the farm fared no better than the worker in industry. While the country as a whole was under-populated, the rural areas were overpopulated. Out of every 100 Yugoslavs, 77 worked on the land, much of which was of inferior quality. Then, too, of the approximately 2,100,000 peasant holdings, some 672,000 were of less than 5 acres each and had to provide livelihood for over 2,000,000 peasants and agricultural workers. Another 276,000 holdings, of from 5 to 10 acres, had to support 3,500,000 people. Altogether 5,500,000 peasants could not make a living on their farms and had to supplement their earnings elsewhere. Thus, unable to earn a living either in the factory or on the farm, thousands of Yugoslavs fled from the misery at home and entered the United States before the lowering of the gates of immigration. So desperate were some of the men to get to the Land of Promise that they were willing to pay interest rates of 60 per cent for money for their fares.

## INFLUENCE OF RELATIVES AND FRIENDS

In 1911 the Immigration Commission stated that one of the primary causes of emigration was the advice and aid given to emigrants by friends and relatives who had themselves emigrated at an earlier date. "Through the medium of letters from those already in the United States and visits of former emigrants, the emigrating classes of Europe are kept constantly, if not always reliably, informed as to labor conditions here, and these agencies are by far the most potent promoters of the present movement of population."[22] A similar observation was made by the eminent authority on immigrant labor, Isaac A. Hourwich. Writing in 1912, he said:

> The real agents who regulate the immigration movement are the millions of earlier immigrants already in the United States. It is they that advance the cost of passage of a large proportion of the new immigrants. When the outlook for employment is good, they send for their relatives, or encourage their friends to come. When the demand for labor is slack, the foreign-born workman must hold his savings in reserve, to provide for possible loss of employment.[23]

The late Louis Adamic, a well-known writer on immigrant affairs, and one who was himself a Yugoslav immigrant, thus vividly describes the influence of returning emigrants.

> As a youngster, eighteen or twenty years ago, back in my native village in Carniola . . . I experienced a thrill every time a man returned from the United States. Four or five years before he had quietly left for America, a poor peasant clad in homespun, with a bundle on his back, now, an *Amerikanec*, he usually sported a blue serge suit, buttoned shoes, with india rubber heels, a derby, a celluloid collar, and a loud necktie, made even louder by a dazzling horseshoe pin, while his two suitcases of imitation leather bulged with gifts from America for his relatives and friends in the community. . . . Thus in my boyhood the idea that the United States was a sort of paradise on earth—the Golden Country—the Land of Promise—was kept vigorously

17

alive by the *Amerikanci* in our village, and, of course, by tens of thousands of returned emigrants in other villages and towns in Eastern, Central, and Southern Europe, from which, until lately, American industries (notably mining and steel) drew much of their labor power. Thus the ambition to go to the United States was kindled in boys by men who had been there.[24]

Like Adamic, the author, too, had an opportunity to observe similar events and conditions in his native Dalmatia. He recalls clearly the rejoicing and celebrations attending the return of a native son from the fabulous land of America. The emigrant was wined, dined, and entertained, often until it hurt—the guest from overindulgence and the hosts from excess generosity. But it made no difference if the emigrant suffered from headaches and indigestion and the villagers killed their last fowl. Nothing was too good for the *Amerikanac*, especially if he happened to be an eligible bachelor who might marry one of the unwed young ladies in the village and take her back to America with him.

Evidence, therefore, seems to support the fact that the two main stimuli for emigration in the early years of the twentieth century were visits from the United States by former emigrants and letters from this country to friends and kinsmen in Europe. Of the two, according to the Immigration Commission, letters were of far greater importance. It goes without saying that more letters than visitors reached Europe. "In fact," reported the Commission, "it is entirely safe to assert that letters from persons who have emigrated to friends at home have been the immediate cause of by far the greater part of the remarkable movement from southern and eastern Europe to the United States during the past twenty-five years."[25]

This writer had the good fortune to be able to examine several letters of emigrants to their kinsfolk and friends back home. One of these, though not belonging to the era of unrestricted immigration, nevertheless appears fairly representative of the emigrant letters. It was written by a young man who arrived in the United States in the immediate post-World War I period. In this letter (dated September 14, 1922) the emigrant wrote to a younger brother in a small village in Dalmatia:

You ask me whether I still long for the old homestead. Yes, I do, very much. I miss you and all our other brothers and sisters, our mother and father. I miss the joyful Sunday activities in our village, particularly the morning chat sessions in front of our church, the afternoon unions of the men in the harbor tavern and the evening folk dances in the village courtyard. I recall with much pleasure also the gatherings of our neighbors around our hearth every evening to exchange tales of our daily experiences. I miss all of those things, young brother, and many others which seemed so important in my life over there. But I am willing to sacrifice much of what I had at home for the new life that has become mine in America. Here I have found new friends and new pastimes. I have a good job as a rigger in a cement plant. I get 40 cents an hour, and I have something left from each paycheck to put in the bank. I already have enough saved for your passage if you should change your mind about coming to this country. . . .

The above letter is undoubtedly similar to thousands sent from America to Europe, for emigrants naturally kept in close touch with relatives and friends in the homeland. The role of the missives from the United States was effectively brought out by the Immigration Commission, which observed:

It was frequently stated to members of the Commission that letters from persons who had emigrated to America were passed from hand to hand until most of the emigrant's friends and neighbors were acquainted with the contents. In periods of industrial activity, as a rule, the letters so circulated contain optimistic references to wages and opportunities for employment in the United States, and when comparison in this regard is made with conditions at home, it is inevitable that whole communities should be inoculated with a desire to emigrate. The reverse is true during seasons of industrial depression in the United States. At such times intending emigrants are quickly informed by their friends in the United States relative to conditions of employment, and a great falling off in the tide of emigration is the immediate result.[26]

A few emigrants who returned to their homeland went back because they had failed to establish themselves successfully in the new environment, or had lost their health. The majority, however, were able to return for a visit to their former homes because they had prospered, and they told of their success. It was such visitors as these who stimulated further emigration to the United States. The government investigations emphasized that:

Knowledge of conditions in America, promulgated through letters from friends or by emigrants who have returned for a visit to their native villages, creates and fosters among the people a desire for improved conditions which it is believed can be attained only through emigration. Unfortunately, but inevitably, the returned emigrant, in a spirit of braggadocio, is inclined to exaggerate his economic achievements in America. In consequence, some whose emigration is influenced by these highly colored statements, accompanied perhaps by display of what to them seems great wealth, are doomed to disappointment. The latter, however, naturally hesitate to admit their failures, and consequently there is little to disturb the belief prevailing in southern and eastern Europe that success awaits all who are able to emigrate to the United States.[27]

The successful immigrants in the United States sent loans or gifts of money to their friends in the homeland, materially helping them to emigrate. "It is impossible to estimate with any degree of accuracy what proportion of the large amount of money annually sent abroad by immigrants is sent for the purpose of assisting relatives or friends to emigrate, but it is certain that the aggregate is large," stated the Immigration Commission.[28] The governmental agency went on to point out that "in the calendar year 1907, 27.6 per cent or 64,384 of the 233,489 steerage passengers embarking at Naples for the United States were provided with prepaid tickets. In all probability this is a fair average for all European ports."[29]

The Commission estimated that perhaps one-quarter of all immigrants admitted to this country had their passage paid in advance by previous arrivals in the United States.[30]

### PROPAGANDA BY STEAMSHIP TICKET AGENTS

A significant influence in the Slavic immigration of the twentieth century came in the form of agents sent abroad by steamship companies and mine owners. Pennsylvania mine owners, for example, are known to have dispatched unofficial representatives to encourage immigration of laborers. The Irish mine workers had proved unruly and dissatisfied with the existing pay rates, and mine owners looked for workers who could be handled more easily and who would be satisfied with the prevalent wage levels. "In a number of places these raw recruits of industry seem to have been called in as the result of a strike, and there probably were plenty of instances of sending agents abroad to hire men or of otherwise inducing labor to immigrate either under contract or with an equivalent understanding."[31] The recruiting of foreign labor was made illegal by the law, passed in 1885, which forbade the immigration of labor under contract.

If advice from relatives and friends already living in the United States was a primary factor in stimulating emigration in European countries, the propaganda spread by steamship ticket agents was not far behind. These agents operated in every country in Europe from which people were emigrating, even though such activities were against the laws of many of the countries. Emigration laws were everywhere being violated, not by steamship companies directly, but by their agents and subagents who operated locally. In its exhaustive report, the Immigration Commission stated, "Selling steerage tickets to America is the sole or chief occupation of large numbers of persons in southern or eastern Europe, and from the observations of the Commission it is clear that these local agents, as a rule, solicit business, and consequently encourage emigration, by every possible means."[32]

There are no figures available as to the number of steamship ticket agents who were engaged in selling steerage tickets during the first decade of the twentieth century, when emigration reached a new peak. There is no denying, however, that the total number of such agents was large. The lines operating passenger ships considered the steerage business as a very important source of income, and competition among companies for a share of this business was keen. It was noted that an agreement existed among the larger steamship companies, whereby unrestricted competition was diminished and traffic was distributed more evenly. This agreement nevertheless did not deter the ticket agents in their work of soliciting passengers and encouraging emigration, particularly in Austria, Hungary, and Russia.

Added, therefore, to the economic and political incentives for immigration to the United States was another important reason: "the blandishment and trickery of the steamship agent."[33]

## OTHER REASONS

Though perhaps less important than the causes already discussed, there were other urges behind the great wave of immigration to the United States. One of these was a desire to escape from the exceedingly stratified society and the inequality engendered by it. Two principal classes existed in Croatia, Serbia, and Slovenia, the *gospoda,* or masters or gentlefolk, and the *narod,* or common people, each with its own modes of existence, economies, sets of customs, and moral codes. With feelings of superiority, honor, and arrogance exhibited by the upper class and resignation, fatalism, and fierce resentment by the lower, the natural outcome was bitter strife between the two opposing groups.

Countless thousands came to America in search of adventure. The adventure motive was particularly strong among the younger immigrants. This was stressed by numerous Yugoslavs in personal interviews with the author. For example, out of 200 persons polled in Chicago, Illinois, including Slovenes, Croats, Dalmatians, Serbs, and Montenegrins, 118, over one-half, gave adventure as one of the attractions that drew them to America. In Los Angeles, California, 100 Yugoslavs were interviewed, with 57 stressing adventure among the reasons for immigration.[34]

The desire for excitement and new experiences is picturesquely painted by Adamic.

> By the time I was fourteen, I had not only listened to dozens of *Amerikanci* but had read such books, translated into the Slovenian, as *The Last of the Mohicans* and dime novels dealing with the adventures of bold Yankees in Indian territories; and when I finally induced my parents . . . to let me go to America by flunking in school and otherwise demonstrating my unfitness for life in Carniola, my chief motive in emigrating was not the hope of economic betterment, but a desire for excitement and adventure.[35]

Other reasons were indirectly related to economic necessity, so that the individuals who were influenced to emigrate did not see the larger principle underlying their personal reasons. The Immigration Commission clearly pointed this out.

> While it is undoubtedly true that economic necessity is the underlying motive of emigration it is often obscured by particu-

lar incidents which are only the expression of the principle. For example, the United States tariff law of 1890 is said to have destroyed the pearl-button industry in Bohemia, thereby throwing many out of work and giving impetus to the emigration movement. In certain districts of Carniola and Croatia the vineyards have been destroyed by phylloxera. The peasants, barely able to eke out subsistence under ordinary circumstances, have been unable to cope with this new difficulty and have been forced to emigrate.[36]

It is certain that most of the peasants who emigrated did not realize what it was that had made it impossible for them to earn a livelihood in their native provinces, but emigrate they did. Thus, in Dalmatia, as already noted, many emigrated as a result of steamships taking the place of sailing vessels, and later more left for America because Dalmatian wine producers could not sell their product at the same low price as the Italians, who, by a treaty signed in 1890, got their wine admitted into Austria-Hungary free of duty. These forces behind the exodus, however, were not clear to many of the emigrants, who only saw that they could not make a living at home and therefore lent willing ears to the voice of opportunity in America.

Another important reason for emigration was compulsory military service. In the Dual Monarchy, military service was three years, with few exemptions. Discipline was very strict and those guilty of violating regulations were dealt with severely. The pay was extremely low, an ordinary seaman in the navy earning fourteen kronen, or less than three dollars, a month and an army private getting only about one-half as much. The life of a serviceman was a hard one during normal times, in times of peace and comparative tranquility, but it became practically unbearable during periods of diplomatic crisis and war. And there was more of the latter than the former. Strife was eternal in the Balkans, becoming especially acute in the last decades of the nineteenth century and in the early years of the twentieth as Austria-Hungary, Germany, Turkey, and Russia fought for spoils in the peninsula. Furthermore, it should be noted that men subject to compulsory military service in Austria-Hungary were forbidden to marry. Such interference in private life was as hateful as the long interruption of vocation by induction. There is no question but that military service worked a serious hardship on numerous South Slavs. As a consequence, many of them fled from their homeland and rushed to America. This military motive was brought into sharp focus by a Congressional survey. "Unsuccessful merchants, advanced in years, young clerks, and young men of all conditions of life, who cannot pass the examination which is required to limit military service to one year instead of three are anxious to avoid the drudgery of a common soldier's life and escape to the United States without asking leave of the Government."[37]

The burning desire to leave the native land and emigrate to America has been uniquely described by a writer of the old school who made a lengthy study of the native environment of central and eastern European immigrants. He expresses his views in this manner:

> Today Austria-Hungary no longer exists. It has become Czecho-Slovakia, Hungary, Austria, a part of Poland, a part of Rumania, a part of Yugo-Slavia. The inhabitants of these new divisions of an old empire have as little in common as they had before the war; but the few things which they have in common have grown during the last few years. They hate one another even more passionately than they hated one another in 1914; they are even more dissatisfied with their governments, for the most part, than they used to be; and their longing to go to America is so violent and poignant and all-pervasive that they would willingly permit themselves to be kicked all the way from Warsaw to Danzig or from Belgrade to Paris—both of which trips would require a vast amount of kicking, to say nothing of a frightful amount of wear and tear on the garments of the kickee —if the final kick deposited them aboard a ship bound for America.[38]

Another authority on Slavic immigrants put it this way, "Men emigrate to avoid family frictions, to escape a scandal, to see new scenes, to join relatives, because others have gone, and for a thousand other unclassifiable reasons."[39] Generally, it may be said, few emigrants realized that there were larger general causes for movement to America. Each person thought only of his personal reasons.

# 2

# The Vanguard

YUGOSLAV IMMIGRANTS, undoubtedly, formed a part of the new immigration which had its beginning in the 1880's and reached its peak in the early years of the twentieth century. Nevertheless, immigration of the South Slavs must not be regarded as being solely confined to that late period. Yugoslav names dot the pages of American history from the earliest times.

## FACT OR FABLE?

Croatians and Dalmatians, particularly Ragusans, were among the leaders in the arts of sailing and navigation in early modern times. Being excellent seamen, they were hired as crew members on ships of all seafaring nations, making trips to all parts of the then known world. Marco Polo, the famed thirteenth-century Venetian traveler in China, was born on the island of Korčula along the Dalmatian coast and obtained his first taste of the sea on the waters of Dalmatia. Dubrovnik (Ragusa) was one of the great seafaring powers during the Middle Ages, competing with Venice and Genoa for supremacy on the Adriatic and Mediterranean. (See Appendix I.) Many writers on South Slavic affairs are convinced that there were Croatian sailors on the ships of Columbus.[1*] Tradition has it, also, that one of the sailors returned from the great adventure with much treasure, and built a palce in Dubrovnik.[2] Although these authors have mustered much circumstantial evidence in support of their arguments, they have not offered any tan-

* Notes to this chapter begin on page 284.

25

gible data as yet. Until such a time, therefore, as more substantial evidence is uncovered, the claim must of necessity remain weak and ineffectual.

Another questionable claim concerns the fate of the lost Roanoke colony founded by Sir Walter Raleigh. This English settlement, it may be recalled, was established on Roanoke Island in 1587 with John White as governor. Immediately after their arrival it became evident that without outside help the colonists could not long survive. Their store of supplies was dwindling fast; moreover, the Indians were hostile and dangerous. Under the circumstances it was thought best that White should at once return to England for additional supplies.

When the governor made his way back to Roanoke Island three years later, he found not a sign of the colonists. Houses were in ruins and covered with vines. Around the doors grew vegetation which indicated that for a year at least the colony had been abandoned. Before leaving for England it had been agreed between White and the colonists that should it be found necessary to abandon the settlement before his return they should leave a mark on a tree by which he might know where they had gone. It was understood that a cross would be the sign that they had left the settlement in distress. He searched over the island and at last upon a tree he saw carved in capital letters the word "CROATAN."[3] There was, however, no cross to indicate that they had left in distress. After a rather desultory search of the neighborhood White returned home, reporting that the colony was lost.

Historians have offered varying solutions regarding the mysterious end of this early colony. Some dismiss the episode as the result of a sudden and disastrous Indian raid. Others maintain that the remnants of White's colony, on the verge of starvation, sought the hospitality of the Croatan Indians, the only Indians in that region who were friendly to the English. Transplanted to an Indian culture, they intermarried and gradually lost their English identity.[4]

However, some South Slavic writers argue that since a record exists of a Croatian ship named "Croatan" that set out on a voyage to North America in the 1580's, it is possible that the members of the crew contacted the colonists on Roanoke. How? When? and Why? are questions that are not and cannot be answered. One author attempts to explain the matter in this way:

It can be *conjectured* [italics are mine] that a Croatian ship calling at this first permanent settlement in America left its imprint on the tree, or even salvaged the entire settlement from the destruction that was taking place and hurriedly left only the name of their ship, the Croatan, on the tree, as a guide, but that it met destruction either by the elements or some other way later, as no trace was ever found of the colonists in question.[5]

Whether this is accepted or not, there seems to be, in any event, sufficient cause for exploration of the American continent by South Slavs. Suffering under the oppressive rule of the Turks, many of the Croats and Dalmatians sought an avenue of escape through emigration. Some, it is believed, sailed to America in the middle of the sixteenth century in the hope of finding a haven in the New World. But apparently all did not go well and the ships returned home, with the exception of one which was wrecked off the coast of the latter-day North Carolina. The surviving seamen from the destroyed vessel, it is asserted, made their way to one of the nearby islands and presently intermingled with the aborigines, who subsequently became known as Croatan Indians. Their name was given to the island upon which they lived, as well as to Croatan Sound, which links Pamlico and Albemarle sounds. Their descendants exist to this day in Robeson County, North Carolina, and in Maryland, Virginia, and West Virginia.

Here again it must be admitted that primary evidence is at best tenuous. Nevertheless, the fact exists that the name "Croatan" has been well preserved in southeastern United States.

Along with these speculations concerning Croatian sailors there have been similar ones in regard to Slovenian soldiers in the American revolutionary forces. In the roster of George Washington's army appear such names as Cherne, Gorshe, Vavtar, Vertnar, and Vidmar. These are all good Slovenian names and, although not specifically designated in the records, it would not be illogical at all to conclude that a number of Slovenes, no matter how insignificant, fought with the American colonists in their struggle for independence.

## HOLY MEN AND HEATHENS

Though one must proceed with caution when dealing with these early quasi-historical characters, he is on surer ground when he turns

27

to the missionaries, who were among the South Slav pioneers in America. They began coming in the seventeenth century and continued right on through the eighteenth and nineteenth. These holy men not only brought the Scriptures and an advanced culture to the natives of the American wilderness, but made this country better known to the plain people in the Croatian and Slovenian lands.

One of the earliest of the ecclesiastical representatives in America was Baron Ivan Ratkay, a young Croatian nobleman. After receiving his holy orders, Ratkay joined the Society of Jesus and soon thereafter received appointment as a missionary among the Indians of New Spain. Prior to his dispatch on his assignment, he was given intensive training in Rome and Madrid. Arriving in America finally in 1673, he took up his work among the Taramuhari tribe in the southwestern section of the country. During the next decade he instructed and baptized hundreds of the pagans. While performing his many missionary duties and functions, which took him to some of the wildest parts of the continent, he had an opportunity to study and become acquainted with the physical geography of the area. His explorations, especially in New Mexico, a record of which he kept with great care, proved of invaluable assistance to the pioneer settlers who followed him into this corner of the country. Unfortunately, his remarkable career was cut short (at the age of 36) when in 1683 he was seized and scalped by Indians who opposed his missionary activities.

About a half century later another Croat won wide acclaim for his work in California and Mexico. This was Father Ferdinand Konšak, who is better known in Spanish colonial history as Padre Consago Gonzales. Konšak, like Ratkay—in fact, to a higher degree —was extremely versatile, performing brilliantly as an anthropologist, astronomer, botanist, geographer, zoologist, illustrator, linguist, and writer. The son of an army officer, he was born in 1703 at Varaždin, Croatia.[6] He studied at the Jesuit college in Budapest, Hungary, and entered the Society of Jesus in 1719.

Manifesting an early predilection for the Indian missions, Konšak was sent to Mexico in 1730. After two years he was transferred to California, where he became one of the most prominent missionaries. During the first five years he assisted at various missions, and then for twenty-two years, until his death in 1759, he attended the San Ignacio Mission in the San Vicente Ferrer Valley, first as superior and later as visitor. From San Ignacio he made frequent tours of exploration into the wild maritime territories between the Gulf of California and the Colorado River. One of the more practical results of these excursions was the discovery that Lower California was a peninsula and not an isle, as it had been previously believed. Another important consequence was a highly accurate map of Lower California which for several centuries was the only dependable guide to that little-known region. Copied in 1770 by J. Baegert in his *Nachrichten von Kalifornien,* the map became well known among the geographers and explorers of the West. It would be impossible to state, even approximately, the number of miles that Father Konšak traversed while in California. As a superior he had to visit every mission; but, when his attendants and their beasts took needed rest, this tireless Croat missionary would devote himself to prayer on his knees.

When he was not engaged in explorations or in ministering to the needs of his wards, Father Konšak was busy writing. Among his most popular literary works are his *Historia de las Misiones de la California* and *Diario de California,* the latter a revealing record of his activities published posthumously in Spain. For his many and varied contributions he won the plaudits of his superiors and contemporaries as well as of scholars of all ages. Writing in the second half of the eighteenth century, the famous Italian author, Clavigero, stated in his *Storia della California,* "It is hardly possible to tell all that this zealous man accomplished notwithstanding his delicate health. . . . On account of his exemplary virtues and apostolic labors, the name of Consag deserves to be placed among those that have become illustrious in California."

Continuing along the same path of conspicuous achievement was Josip Kundek, also a Croatian missionary, who arrived in America in 1838. Assigned to a vast parish in the Midwest extending from St. Louis, Missouri, to Pittsburgh, Pennsylvania, he gave his life and labor to the improvement of the spiritual and material well-being of the Indians and immigrants and the transformation of the desolate prairies into flourishing communities. Not only did he strive to save the souls of the numerous savages in the Midwest, but he served as father-confessor to the section's German and Swiss Catholic immigrants—in whose records, incidentally, he appears as a German and Swiss cleric.

The talents and achievements of Father Kundek were diverse, indeed. Besides being a successful missionary and priest, he was a gifted poet and musician. In 1854 he established the Benedictine Abbey of St. Meinhard, Indiana. He was also instrumental in founding a number of towns, outstanding of which were Ferdinand and Jasper in southern Indiana, where he spent most of his time until his death in 1857.[7]

It is important to point out that the work of these missionaries in America was supported by collections made in the churches of the South Slavs at home. According to the records kept in the archives of the provincial government, Croatia alone contributed toward the support of churches and schools 57,400 florins (about $10,000) in the decade 1830-1840.[8] This in itself should be testimony enough that not all Yugoslavs came to the United States to make money to send back to the family and relatives. Some of the funds, at least, traveled westward.

Like the Croats, the Slovenes also sent many prominent missionary leaders to America. Among them were Bishops Baraga, Mrak, Stariha, Trobec, and Vertin; Monsignori Buh, Plut, and Stibil; Abbot Locnika; and Fathers Pirec and Skolla. Standing head and shoulders above all these churchmen was Bishop Frederic Baraga, who devoted his energies to an extension of the Christian way of life among the Ottawa and Chippewa Indians in the Midwest. His work and career are exceptionally interesting and serve as a fine illustration of the everlasting impression made upon America by the Slavic ecclesiasts.

Frederic Baraga was born in 1797, the scion of an aristocratic family in lower Carniola, a Slovene province under Austrian rule.[9] In 1809 he entered the gymnasium at Ljubljana, and at the age of nineteen he was admitted to the University of Vienna, where he pursued courses in languages and law. Legal studies, however, did not appeal to him, and so he changed to a program that would prepare him for the priesthood. Soon after graduation Baraga received a small parish in his native Slovenia. When the Leopoldine Society was founded in Vienna in 1829 with the purpose of supporting North American missions, he promptly sent in an application for an assignment. The society replied by appointing him as it first missionary.[10]

Selling his property and bringing the proceeds with him, Father Baraga landed in New York at the end of December, 1830. Five months later he reached Arbre Croche, Michigan, where he was to begin his life work among the Ottawa and Chippewa Indians. His radiant personality helped to ingratiate him in the favor of the tribesmen from the very beginning. He learned their language. He eagerly participated in many of their activities. He respected them as human beings and treated them as equals. As a consequence, he was able to win their complete confidence and support. His success seemed to be assured by his personable character and his piety and zeal as well as by his marked ability for planning and organizing construction projects and the ready assistance of his host of warm friends in Europe.

Baraga saw immediately upon his arrival that the pressure of the whites upon the red men was tremendous, and that it would crush them before long unless steps were taken to correct the conditions. This meant changing the very customs and habits of a people, certainly not an easy thing to do. Nevertheless, toward that goal the holy man directed his best efforts. He worked ceaselessly to get the Indians to give up their nomadic ways of life and to establish permanent settlements and to expand their economic functions beyond the uncertain pursuits of fishing and hunting so as to include agriculture and other fundamental activities. He prevailed upon them to learn trades, such as carpentry, which he taught them himself, being a first-rate carpenter. As added buttresses to this strong economic foundation Father Baraga encouraged his Indian friends to build churches and schools, some of which he helped to erect with his own hands, even after he became bishop in 1854. He sent a barrage of letters and leaflets to his old acquaintances in Carniola in appeals for money to support his projects, besides making several trips himself to solicit funds personally in his native land. He not only wrote to friends in the old country, but carried on an extensive correspondence in America as well. Most of his letters show his concern for his charges, his determination to carry on his work, as is illustrated by the following excerpt taken from a letter written from Grand Rapids to Bishop Friedrich Rese in Detroit:

> It is true, Sir, that the erection of the new Mission was very costly, much more than I expected; but you know, Sir, that all the money you gave me, was sent to your hands expressly for me, and that it came from my relations and friends without any prejudice to the Vienna Society. . . . Although I have a strong

31

right to some portion of the money that the Vienna Society sends over for the support of our Missions, being the first Missionary sent by this Society, and furnishing to the same continually materials for publication; still I don't ask any support out of the money of the Society, but pray only to send me without delay the amount that will soon arrive to your hands, expressly destined for me. . . . I am here in a very unpleasant situation indeed, but still I am determined to live for ever with the Indians, when it is the will of God and your will, and when no other Missionary should supply me in this place; because I have pity on the poor Indians, who would soon return pagans when they were destitute of Missionaries.[11]

Outstanding achievements of Baraga among the Indians are, undoubtedly, in language and literature. He wrote a book of poetry in the Ottawa language. For the Chippewas he prepared a grammar and dictionary, and translated the Bible. In addition, he wrote, in Chippewa, a prayer book, a life of Jesus, and a sermon book which included the Epistles and Gospels of all the Sundays and holy days of the year as well as a brief Bible history of the Old Testament and instructive extracts from the four Gospels, the Acts of the Apostles, and the Epistles. For the enlightenment of Europeans he wrote *The History, Character, Life and Manners of the North American Indians.*

The eternal vigilance, tireless activity, and ineffable suffering of Father Baraga in carrying on his missionary work are well noted by his official biographer. He writes:

As bishop we find him indefatigable in promoting the cause of religion and virtue in the extensive territory committed to his care, which for many years embraced not only the Upper Peninsula of Michigan, but also a great part of Lower Michigan, Northern Wisconsin, Eastern Minnesota, and parts of Ontario. Every year he visited almost all the missionary stations and congregations of this extensive territory, often suffering untold hardships and miseries, traveling in winter on snowshoes, sleeping under the open air or in some wretched Indian wigwam, shivering with cold, living on a little bread, cheese and tea.[12]

Despite his most strenuous efforts, however, Baraga could not succeed in attaining his cherished goal: that of saving the soul of the Indian. Time and tide were against him. Greed of the mining and timber interests, whisky of the traders, corruption of the Indian agents, and indifference of Washington were too much for one man and so combined to spell defeat. Notwithstanding, during the thirty-seven years (he died in 1868) he toiled among the Indians, he made a profound impression. Today his Indian policy forms a part of the federal government's program. Baraga County in Michigan and the Baraga Association in Illinois also help to perpetuate the name of this Slovene pioneer in America.

On his visits to Carniola, Baraga induced to accompany him to America numerous Slovenians, all able men and anxious to do what they could for Roman Catholicism. The result was that by the middle of the century nearly all the missions in Michigan north of the present Traverse City and also northern Wisconsin as well as eastern Minnesota were in the hands of Slovenes: Baraga at L'Anse, Pirec at Grand Portage, Mrak at La Croix, and Skolla at La Pointe.[13]

Among the Slovene apostles, next to Baraga stands the Reverend Francis Pirec, who is generally known in American missionary history under the name of Pierz. Father Pirec was born in Godić, Carniola, in 1785. He attended school in Kamnik, and then entered, like Baraga, the gymnasium in Ljubljana. In 1813 he was ordained and assigned to a parish in Kranjska Gora.[14] In 1830, when Pirec was already forty-five years old, Baraga tried to persuade him to leave Carniola and go to America with him, but he refused, feeling that he was too old for the adventure. Baraga, however, continued to plead with him to devote himself to the American Indian. Finally, after five years, Pirec succumbed to his friend's entreaties.

Father Pirec arrived in Detroit in September, 1835, and started his missionary work at La Croix. Four years later he moved to Arbre Croche, where he worked among the Ottawas for thirteen years. In 1852 he began his work among the Chippewas.[15]

Aside from converting the Indians, Pirec established schools for them, and taught them how to farm and trade. The success of his methods is seen, for example, at Arbre Croche, where in one year his charges sold 400 barrels of fish and 8,000 pounds of maple sugar.[16]

Pirec did not retire until he was eighty-six years old, when he went to Rich Prairie in 1871. He died in 1880, at the age of ninety-four. A worthy appraisal of Father Pirec is made by the biographer of Baraga:

Pirec was indefatigable in his missionary work. At an age at

33

which the energies of many are on a decline, he appears as vigorous and strong as in the first years of his ministry in Carniola. Frequently he was in need of the necessaries of life, always engaged in the work of traveling, instructing, or administering the sacraments, still his energies seemed to be inexhaustible.

Not only was he a spiritual Father to the Indian, ministering to the needs of the soul, he was likewise interested in the betterment of the temporal condition of the Red man. His knowledge of agriculture and horticulture, his personal experience with everything pertaining to successful farming, made him a valuable advisor to the ignorant children of the forest. Pirec in all the settlements taught the Indian how to render the soil fertile; procured seeds for them, mostly from the gardens and farms which he himself cultivated. He instructed them how to build comfortable homes, exhorted them to abandon the wigwam of the savage and to build habitations of civilized man. . . .[17]

Another Slovenian priest whom Bishop Baraga lured to America was Father Mrak. Appointed as vicar-general for the missions in the lower peninsula of Michigan in 1859, Mrak succeeded to the see of Marquette ten years later.[18] He tried to take up where Baraga left off, and did succeed, in spite of many obstacles, in maintaining many of the high standards set by his predecessor, thus carving for himself an important niche in the missionary hall of fame.

Not all of the men who joined Baraga, however, were able to transform a savage wilderness into civilized Christian communities. In this category the most notable example is Otto Skolla, also a Slovene, who joined Baraga's missionary protégés in 1841.[19] Father Skolla, though a competent, sincere, and ardent servant of the church, made little headway in his attempts to bring Christianity and civilization to the Indians. He failed to win the confidence of his superstitious wards, many of whom believed that he performed rites of black magic. Despairing after sixteen years of seemingly fruitless effort, Skolla returned to his native Carniola in 1857.

Though not always successful in reaching their goals, the Croat and Slovene missionaries, nevertheless, occupy an important place in Yugoslav immigration to the United States. They not only attracted other ecclesiastics but in addition acquainted laymen in South Slav territories with America, thus giving stimulus to a movement that eventually grew into an avalanche.

## TRAIL BLAZERS ALL!

The missionaries, without question, were important South Slav pioneers in the United States, but numerically they were an insignificant group. The first large colony to reach American shores arrived early in the eighteenth century. The beginning of this story, however, goes back several hundred years.

By the end of the sixteenth century the Croatian and Slovenian provinces were seething with rebellion. To their earlier feudal burdens and oppression in general were added at this time the frightful persecutions accompanying the Catholic Counter Reformation. Those Slavs who dared to listen to the German Protestants, chiefly Lutherans, were caught in the dragnet of the fanatical Catholic Austrian Archduke Ferdinand and punished mercilessly. Oppression and persecution were too much, leading the Croats and Slovenes to break out in open rebellion in 1573. The revolt was put down with little difficulty, but the Slavs could not be cowed so easily.

In the years following the explosion thousands of the industrious Croats and Slovenes emigrated to Prussia at the invitation of the Hohenzollern rulers, who were anxious to build up the strength of their state on a par with that of their Habsburg rivals in Austria and therefore welcomed workingmen, especially the skilled. Though they did not suffer from want and were allowed to worship their Lutheran faith unhampered, the South Slavs were not entirely happy in the Prussian home. They longed for greater opportunities and for enlarged liberties. In time they learned of the riches and freedom in the New World, and decided to search for a haven in America. But many years passed before they could translate their dreams into realities.

Finally, through the efforts of the foreign members of the board of trustees of the Georgia colony, they, together with large numbers of the persecuted Lutherans from Salzburg, Austria, were invited to make their homes in Georgia. A bargain was struck. They were to assume citizenship in the colony, settle in one city, and obey the laws. In return they were to be granted fifty acres of land for each person, comprising a garden plot and farm land, tools, seed, a year's support, free transportation to America, and all the rights of Englishmen in the colony. Much of their expense in coming was borne by the Society for the Promotion of Christian Knowledge and the German Evangelical Lutheran Church, to which they belonged.

The elated emigrants left the continent for Dover, England, where they obtained passage in January, 1734, reaching first Charleston and, finally, Savannah. There were fifty-six persons in the party with their two pastors, Christian Gronau and Martin Bolzius.[20]

James Oglethorpe, the founder of the Georgia colony, welcomed the new arrivals heartily, as they were a valuable addition to his settlement. He ordered that they be cared for in Savannah until a place should be found for them to settle—for, speaking a different language, they wanted to live in a group by themselves. They wanted a hilly country away from the sea, a region as nearly as possible like their old home. Hence, Oglethorpe chose a site about thirty miles inland at the confluence of the Savannah River and a crooked, sluggish little stream. Both the stream and the town were called Ebenezer (the Stone of Help) in remembrance of God who had brought them safely to their new home.

Inured to hardships and poverty, industrious, and intensely religious, these hardy South Slavic pioneers of Ebenezer soon cleared the woods and brush and laid out their town. Discontent, however, arose among the settlers not long after they had moved to Ebenezer, for their dwelling site proved inaccessible and unhealthful because of the surrounding marshes. They consequently begged for a new location. Though Oglethorpe considered it unnecessary, feared trouble with the Indians, as the land desired was reserved for them, and advised against it, yet he finally consented. Accordingly, in 1736, they transferred to a new site, at Red Bluff on the Savannah River, which they called New Ebenezer. Here they made a fresh start. They built their homes, a church (a quaint old house of worship which still stands), and a school, and established a thriving community. Others of their harried kinsmen soon joined them. By 1751 they numbered 1,200, which increased to 1,500 the following year. Though they maintained no court of justice, order and decency prevailed among them. Hard workers, used to simple living, they made excellent frontiersmen.[21]

The settlement prospered, and the organized congregation accumulated in its own name property sufficient to pay the pastor's salary and provide for the orphans and unfortunates. As in Europe, the South Slav settlers in New Ebenezer devoted their time and energies principally to agricultural pursuits. It was, indeed, in the economic sphere that they made their most significant contribution to American life. They introduced the cultivation of the silkworms into Georgia, an industry engaged in by their ancestors before migrating to Prussia. Each of the colonists was presented with a mulberry tree in 1736, and instructed in the art of reeling. They began immediately to use both gift and knowledge. Pastor Bolzius was always at hand to encourage and help. He bought worthless silk bolls to spur men on; he purchased hundreds of mulberry trees; he erected a machine in his own home for manufacturing raw silk. The profit, to be sure, was small, and the wages amounted to scarcely a shilling a day. However, had it not been for these thrifty, industrious, and persevering settlers the industry would have died in its infancy.[22]

Neither in silk culture nor in any of their other enterprises did the South Slavs use Negro slaves. Being God-fearing, freedom-loving, and hard-working men and easily adaptable to pioneer conditions, they felt no particular need for slave labor, and unanimously opposed the holding of human beings in bondage. For them, the climate was not as pictured: too hot for white men to work.[23]

With the coming of the Revolution the settlement at New Ebenezer received a serious setback. The people suffered much, even though some of them took the oath of allegiance to the British Crown after the English troops took possession in 1779. Those (the majority) who refused to take the oath had their property confiscated and destroyed. Although they produced no outstanding leaders, the Croats and Slovenes of New Ebenezer did their small bit in helping America gain its independence, and it is very likely that some of them fought against the English in the Revolutionary War.[24]

Never fully recovering from the disaster of the Revolution, New Ebenezer continued to lead a precarious existence for nearly another century. Then followed the fatal blow which spelled the end of this unique South Slav settlement in the South. During the Civil War it became a part of the battleground between the Union and Confederate armies. The colony was destroyed by General Sherman's forces in 1864, and the inhabitants, who were fortunate to escape, scattered throughout the country, never again to unite. And so New Ebenezer, too, joined the ranks of the dead towns in young America. As a consequence, today hardly more than a cemetery with Croat and Slovene names on gravestones remains as a monument to this earliest South Slav community in America.[25]

Besides the missionaries and oppressed peasants, there were other South Slavs who also came at a comparatively early date. In the 1840's and 1850's there arrived a number of Croat and Slovene immigrants who had learned about America while earning a living in the outside world. These men were simple peddlers who had traveled through most of eastern and central Europe in selling their wares—gems, jewelry, rosaries, religious medals, reliquaries. In America they pursued the same trade, many of them using the growing town of Chicago as a base of operations and disposing of their goods in Illinois, Iowa, Nebraska, Michigan, Wisconsin, and Minnesota. Branching out in other lines, a few managed to amass small fortunes. One of these, a Slovenian by the name of John Gorshe, invested every cent he could spare in real estate in Chicago and subsequently became one of the wealthiest of the South Slavs in the Midwest. An authority on Slavic immigration points out that "in Calumet, Michigan, there is a flourishing department store owned by the descendants of the Slovenian who came with a fellow countryman as early as 1856 as a peddler or traveling dealer."[26]

These businessmen, in turn, encouraged their relatives and friends in the old country to leave and come to the United States. Thus, in the 1860's and 1870's they sent many letters to Europe, telling about the copper and iron mines then opening up in Michigan and Minnesota. This brought an influx of immigrants from Croatia and Slovenia into the mining territories, stimulating the growth of population and towns, some of which, such as Brockway, Minnesota, sprang up largely as a result of the efforts of the Slavs.

The Slovenes, in particular, established a number of important settlements in these years before the beginning of mass immigration. In Calumet, Michigan, they settled as early as 1856; they first appeared in Chicago and Iowa about 1863; and in 1866 they founded their chief farming colony in Brockway. They arrived in Omaha in 1868, and in 1873 they founded their present huge colony in Joliet, Illinois. Their earliest settlement in New York was toward the end of 1878.

In the meantime, indeed since the beginning of the nineteenth century, Dalmatian sailors had brought their strange-looking windjammers to America with considerable regularity. Some, according to several prominent writers, made the journey indirectly by way of India and the Pacific; in fact, it is claimed that one of the Ragusan ships had reached the Pacific Coast by this route as early as the beginning of the eighteenth century, at a time when most of the area had been under Spanish control and long before many Americans across the continent had even heard about it.[27] Members of the Ragusan crew, it is said, settled south of the present city of San Francisco. In any event, it is an established fact that Dalmatians were old-timers in California by the time the first Yankees got there. It has also been claimed that a boatload of Dalmatians arrived in New York about 1790 in another vessel from Dubrovnik. Throughout the nineteenth century many more of them arrived by the same means. They stopped off not only in San Francisco and New York but in Boston, Philadelphia, and New Orleans as well, the latter being the favorite port of call for many years. Comparatively large numbers of the sailors left their ships before the middle of the century, married, and settled in and around New Orleans, where they worked at trading, shipping, and fishing, securing in time control of the oyster industry.

Other Dalmatians preferred California, where the Mediterranean type of climate, sea, and configuration of the land strongly appealed to them, reminding them of their homes in the old country. Increasing numbers poured in as news of the gold strike of 1848 spread contagiously. However, as the gold disappeared from the hills and the excitement of the rush subsided, many settled down, engaging in farming and fruit growing. They literally took over the famed Pajaro Valley, which was subsequently labeled "New Dalmatia," and transformed its untilled, desolate acres into a virtual paradise of orchards, where figs, grapes, apples, plums, and apricots were raised in abundance.

Among the California Dalmatians the names of Mark Rabasa and Steve Mitrovich stand out. Rabasa introduced the apple industry to northern California when he went into business in Watsonville in the 1870's. Mitrovich gave a strong impetus to fig growing in the 1880's when he imported the Dalmatian brand into Fresno. The variety of fig known as the Adriatic, developed by Mitrovich, brought its producer first prize at the Columbian Exposition in Chicago in 1893.[28]

The Dalmatians who made their homes in California did not all go into agriculture and fruit raising, but some, like their kinsmen in New Orleans, went into shipping and fishing. From small beginnings the fishermen expanded their holdings and area of operations from the Mexican border to Alaska, seriously challenging the supremacy of the Italians and Japanese who had got a head start on them.

In addition to those enterprising individuals already mentioned, there were other daring souls who struck out alone, and by initiative, persistence, and unending toil managed to win for themselves a place in the "Who's Who Among Yugoslav Immigrants." Included in this group are the Volks of New York. The brothers Abraham and Thomas Volk, Slovenian immigrants, married English and Dutch girls, settled in New York in the late eighteenth century, and became quite prominent in New York circles. About a century later one of the grandsons of Thomas, Leonard Volk, established a widespread reputation as a sculptor.

Another conspicuous figure among the early comers was George Černić, a Slovenian who settled in Chicago about 1849. Černić for many years ran a saloon in Chicago which served as a meeting place for the Slovenes of the region.[29] Desiring to assist his countrymen with everything within his restricted means and capacities, he often acted as banker, lawyer, confidant, interpreter, and secretary (writing letters for the illiterate).

High also on the list of eminent Slovene Americans in the years before mass immigration is Jacob Zupančić, who arrived in 1868 and settled in Illinois. Equipped with a fine intellect and an education above average, he rose from a lowly clerk to postmaster of Chadwick in 1874, a position he continued to occupy until 1888.[30]

Arriving a little later—in the eighties and early nineties—were several Croatian trail blazers, outstanding of whom were Josip Subašić, A. G. Skrivanić, Nikola Polić, Zdravko Valentin Mužina, and Josip Marohnić. All these men attained prominence in their communities and among their fellow nationals. All of them, moreover, played an important role in the founding of the Croatian Society, which later became the National Croatian Union and finally the Croatian Fraternal Union. (See Chapter VI.) Subašić, born in Vukova Gorica, near Karlovac, first settled in Millvale, Pennsylvania, and then moved to neighboring Allegheny City. A machinist by trade, he was one of the very few skilled workers among the early South Slavic immigrants. Skrivanić was a leader of the Croats in Hoboken, New Jersey, where he edited and published *Napredak* (Progress), one of the earliest newspapers of the South Slavs in America. (See Chapter VII.) A former member of the Croatian legislature and a journalist, Nikola Polić became the founder and editor of the newspaper *Chicago* in the Windy City. Like Skrivanić and Polić, Mužina was a pioneer journalist, serving first as assistant editor of *Chicago* and then becoming editor and publisher of *Danica* (Morning Star), the first Croatian newspaper in Pittsburgh. Another intellectual was Josip Marohnić. A native of Hreljin, Dalmatia, he emigrated to Chicago in 1894 and then the following year moved to Allegheny City. Not satisfied with his trade as a printer, he studied accounting for a brief time at Wheaton College in Illinois. After moving to Allegheny City he set up there America's first Croatian bookstore, importing and publishing Croatian books for the immigrants. As an aid to his readers he edited the first English-Croatian and Croatian-English dictionary. In 1899 he began the publication of the humor magazine *Brico* (Barber), and in 1908 he launched the weekly *Hrvatski Glasnik* (Croatian Herald).[31]

Of the Serb pioneers in America the best known are the famous scientists and inventors, Nikola Tesla and Michael Pupin, whose careers are treated in detail in later chapters. Not as prominent, but nevertheless to be counted with the early arrivals, are Nikola and Ilija Dabović, two brothers who left their native village of Sasovici, in the district of Herceg Novi, and who settled in San Francisco in the middle years of the nineteenth century. Ilija became the father of the late Archimandrite Sebastijan Dabović, the first American-born priest, the first Serbian Orthodox missionary, and the first head of the Serbian Orthodox Mission in America. Among the pioneers of the eighties were Nikola Vujnović, Milenko Maravić, and Petar Vignjević and his wife Simica, who it is claimed was the first Serbian woman to reach American shores (1888). One of the more distinguished arrivals of the nineties was Sava Hajdin, who became the founder and the first president of the Serb Orthodox Federation Serb Sentinel, the parent of the future Serb National Federation. Hajdin remained for many years a leading figure in the organizational and social life of the Serb Americans. Other pioneers of the nineties were Petar Bolarin, Krsto Gopčević, and Sava Radaković, who were very active in the fraternal movements among the Serbs in Chicago in the last years of the nineteenth century and in the early years of the twentieth.

Postman, peddler, and priest; fisherman, farmer, and fruit-grower; sailor, saloonkeeper, and silk cultivator; coming early and late, settling in city and country in the North and South and East and West, all contributed their skills to a rising young nation, and helped to form an important vanguard that paved the way for the legions that followed.

# 3

# Atlantic Caravan

As NOTED EARLIER, immigration to the United States changed radically in character during the last two decades of the nineteenth century and the first decade of the twentieth.

## THE GREAT TREK

The new immigration flowed from southern and eastern Europe, displacing the earlier immigration which had come predominantly from the northern and western countries of the continent and the United Kingdom. Of this new immigration one eminent authority writes:

> The 30 years 1880-1909 brought us over 17,000,000 immigrants as against less than 10,000,000 in the preceding 40 years. Not only did the numbers thus increase, but during this period three new elements have come to be of main importance among our immigrants; namely Italians, Jews, and Slavs. It is not until 1899 that it is possible to get the necessary data, but in the eleven years since these three groups have made nearly six out of every ten immigrants, Italians being about a quarter and Slavs over one-fifth of our total immigrant body for that period.[1]*

The three new elements in American immigration mentioned above came principally from Italy, Austria-Hungary, and Russia. During the period from 1820 to 1930 Italy sent 4,651,195 immigrants to the United States, Austria-Hungary contributed 4,132,351, and

* Notes to this chapter begin on page 286.

43

Russia furnished 3,341,991, 44 per cent of whom were Jews. These three countries together were responsible for 86.9 per cent of the total immigration from southern and eastern Europe in the years 1820-1930.[2]

It is thus clear that, next to Italy, Austria-Hungary was the most important source of the new immigration. In the first half of the nineteenth century Austrian emigration was unimportant, amounting to less than one thousand a year. Following the discovery of gold in California there was a sudden increase in emigration in the period 1851-1855. The Czechs from Bohemia formed the largest segment within this movement. Subsequently, other Austrian stocks also were drawn into the current and at the beginning of the 1880's Austria joined the ranks of the important emigration countries. The number of 20,000 emigrants was first passed in 1880, that of 50,000 in 1891, 100,000 in 1903, and 175,000 in 1907. With the beginning of Austria's real emigration the importance of Bohemia, which had contributed three-fourths of the earlier emigrants, diminished, and the Tyrol, Carinthia, and Galicia took the lead in the great trek across the Atlantic. In the decade 1901-1910 the Poles and Jews constituted the largest contingents; during that time there were 926 emigrant Poles and 683 Jews per 100,000 of the specified stock in Austria. The corresponding rates of the other nationalities were: Croatians and Slovenians, 692; Czechs and Slovaks, 494; Italians, 226; and Germans, 219.[3]

The emigration from Hungary, Austria's partner in the Dual Monarchy, also began to rise rapidly in the 1880's. The total flow increased in volume year by year until in 1903 the number exceeded 100,000 and in 1907 reached nearly 200,000. Emigration from Hungary was almost entirely Slovak during the early years, but soon included other stocks, first Magyars, and then Germans, Croats, and Serbs in comparatively large numbers. From about 1905 on, the Magyars furnished the largest contingent, though it was lowest in relation to population, the emigration rate amounting to about one to five per thousand. Next came the Rumanians and after them Croatians and Serbs with emigration rates corresponding to the average for the entire population. The emigration rates of the Ruthenians and the Germans were higher but did not reach the level of the Slovak rate, which in each year was the highest of all. In the total number of emigrants, however, the order was somewhat different. According to Hungary's prewar statistics for the period 1899-1913, the various groups lined up as follows: Magyars first, with 401,123 emigrants; Slovaks second, with 300,432; Germans third, with 232,591; Rumanians fourth, with 184,512; Croatians fifth, with 137,266; Serbs sixth, with 64,181; and Ruthenians seventh, with 54,980.[4]

Evidently South Slav, alongside the general southern and eastern European, immigration to the United States increased by leaps and bounds. In the ninety years from 1820 to 1910 Austria-Hungary contributed 3,172,461 immigrants, with 367,239, or 12 per cent, coming from Croatia and Slovenia—two-thirds from Croatia and one-third from Slovenia. During the first decade of the twentieth century, out of a total of 2,332,583 new immigrants, 401,300, or 17.2 per cent, were South Slavs.[5]

Mass immigration of the South Slavs may be said to date from about 1880, though from some districts in Croatia and Slovenia the caravan across the Atlantic got underway somewhat earlier. The kingdoms of Serbia and Montenegro, at the time, sent over few immigrants, which was also true of Macedonia. The majority of the South Slavic immigrants were from provinces then under the control of Austria-Hungary. Thus, most of the emigration of the Serbs was from Bosnia, Hercegovina, Dalmatia, and Croatia, especially the Croat districts of Lika and Vojvodina, where their Serb forebears had found refuge from the Turks after the disastrous defeat by the Asiatic conquerors in 1389 at Kosovo. Croatian emigration was from Dalmatia, Istria, Bosnia, Hercegovina, Slavonia, and Croatia. Much of it originated in the Lika-Krbava district after the eighties. Slovene emigrants were mainly from southwestern Austria, from the provinces of Carniola, Carinthia, and Styria, as well as from Resja and Videm in northeastern Italy, and the Coastland of Austria-Hungary.

Emigration from Croatia-Slavonia in fairly large numbers began in 1873, upon the completion of the new railway connections to the seaport of Rijeka, when some of the more adventurous Croats departed for the United States. The race across the Atlantic gained rapid momentum as others caught the fever. Becoming alarmed, the Croatian government sought to regulate the movement by issuing an ordinance on emigration in Croatia and Slavonia in 1883 and by organizing a special service in 1891. But the tide could not be stemmed; it continued unabated. Some towns became virtually depopulated. In one Croat village, for instance, the population dwindled from 3,400 to 1,600 because some 1,800 left for America—with the great bulk of them settling in Calumet, Michigan. In 1899 just the two districts of Zagreb and Modruš-Fiume lost more than 1,000 emigrants who went to the United States, but by 1907 there were eight districts in Croatia which showed a loss of more than 1,000 people through emigration. From a few thousand in the seventies the emigration figure total rose to 22,800 in 1907.[6]

In the 1890's, emigration from Carniola to America became so marked that the governor of the province in 1893 made an investigation of the movement. This merely confirmed an already-known fact: emigration was steadily rising. In the single year of 1903 more than 6,500 persons left Carniola for the United States. In the ten-year period from 1890 to 1900, 12 per cent of the population in the districts of Littai, Gottschee, and Černomelj departed.[7]

In Dalmatia there never was the same mass movement out of the country as in Slovenia and Croatia, but emigration, as Emily Balch says, was more like "a long-continued dripping of individuals." Many of the emigrants, as earlier, were sailors, who simply deserted their ships when they arrived in an American port. The number of emigrants from Dalmatia going to the United States jumped from 367 in 1899 to 4,812 in 1910.[8]

Though Serbs had dribbled into the country for some years prior to the period of mass immigration and had established a number of settlements scattered over the continent, with one of the most important of these located in the San Francisco Bay area, a steady flow of Serbian immigrants did not really commence until the last decade of the nineteenth century. In 1892 several hundred Serbs and Montenegrins came with a group of Dalmatians and settled in California. From then on there was a small but continuous influx of Serb arrivals. The stream began to increase in 1903 and reached its highest point in 1907.

Of the total immigration to the United States of Croatians, Slovenians, Dalmatians, Bosnians, and Hercegovinians in the period from 1899 to 1910, about 98 per cent of each came from Austria-Hungary, while only some 40 per cent of the Bulgarians, Serbians, and Montenegrins were from the Dual Monarchy. This would appear to contradict what has been said earlier about the origins of the majority of the Serb immigrants. The seeming contradiction, however, is easily cleared away. It is necessary to note several pertinent facts; first that there were very few Montenegrins and even fewer Bulgarians in the Habsburg empire, and second that these two peoples were not separated from the Serbians in the United States immigration statistics. Therefore, a high percentage of Serb emigrants from Austria-Hungary is markedly reduced when combined with the low percentages of Montenegrin and Bulgarian emigrants from that country. The table below presents a summation of the South Slavic immigration (including the Bulgarian) during the years under consideration, 1899 to 1910.[9]

TABLE 1

IMMIGRATION OF SOUTH SLAVS, 1899-1910

| Race or People | Total Number of Immigrants | Immigrants from Austria-Hungary | |
|---|---|---|---|
| | | Number | Per Cent |
| Bulgarian, Serbian, and Montenegrin | 97,391 | 39,099 | 40.1 |
| Croatian and Slovenian | 335,543 | 331,154 | 98.7 |
| Dalmatian, Bosnian, and Hercegovinian | 31,696 | 31,047 | 98.0 |

This situation may perhaps be explained by the fact that these people were minorities in Austria-Hungary, politically without voice and economically depressed. Where South Slavs were politically autonomous, emigration was not as great.

IMMIGRATION AND LEGISLATION

Before continuing with the discussion of the Yugoslav immigrants themselves, something must first be said about legislation affecting immigration. It is essential for comprehension of the modifications of immigration and of the regulation and shift of the tide to limit the overflow and restore the balance in favor of northern and western Europe.

The sheer magnitude of immigration after 1880 is a source of amazement. The tidal wave starting in 1880 reached a height of 788,992 in 1882, with 563,213 coming from northern and western Europe and 84,973 from southern and eastern Europe. In 1886 the number of arrivals dropped to 334,203. In the next seven years, from 1887 to 1893, they varied from a little above to a little below 500,000 each year, but changes were taking place in the class of immigrants coming. In 1888 out of 546,889 immigrants, 397,123, or 72.6 per cent, were from northern and western Europe, and 141,281, or 25.8 per cent, from the southern and eastern portions of the continent. Greater change came in 1892, when out of a total of 579,663 immigrants, 300,792, or 51.9 per cent, were from northern and western Europe and 270,084, or 46.6 per cent, from southern and eastern Europe.[10]

From 1894 to 1901 immigration fell below 500,000 each year. The year 1896 is important, however, in the story of American immigration, for in 1896 for the first time southern and eastern Europe furnished more immigrants than northern and western Europe, 195,684 coming in that year from the former areas and only 137,532 from the latter.[11]

In 1901, out of 487,918 arrivals, the number of representatives from northern and western Europe was down to 115,728, or 23.7 per cent of the total, while those from southern and eastern Europe climbed to 359,291, or 73.6 per cent of the total.[12] For over two decades, from 1896 on, each year the number of new immigrants exceeded that of the old.

Immigration went above the 500,000 mark in 1902. In 1907 it reached the highest point in any year, 1,285,349, of which number 979,661, or 76.2 per cent, were from southern and eastern Europe and 227,958, or only 17.7 per cent, from northern and western Europe. In each of the years 1905, 1906, 1907, 1910, 1913, and 1914 immigration was above 1,000,000 and did not drop below 750,000 in any intervening year. The year 1914 saw the second highest point in immigration, when the number arriving was 1,218,-480, of which 915,087, or 75.1 per cent, were from southern and eastern Europe and only 165,100, or 13.6 per cent, from northern and western Europe.[13]

With the coming of the war in 1914 immigration from Europe was appreciably reduced. In 1917, however, 105,399 immigrants came from British North America, and 42,380 from Mexico, Central and South America, and the West Indies.[14]

In 1920 a new wave of immigration began from Europe. That year the total number of immigrants reached 430,001, with 162,595, or 37.7 per cent, from southern and eastern Europe and 88,773, or

48

20.7 per cent, from northern and western Europe, with the countries of North and South America furnishing most of the remainder. The next year, 1921, saw 805,228 immigrants reach United States ports, including 520,654, or 64.7 per cent, from southern and eastern Europe and 143,445, or 17.8 per cent, from northern and western Europe.[15]

Accompanying the general rise was, of course, the rapid increase in South Slav immigration. Added to the nearly half million immigrants who came in the first decade of the twentieth century were the 199,309 who followed from 1911 to 1920.[16] The preponderant majority of the latter, 185,922, came over in the years 1911 to 1914, while only a handful, 13,387, came during the war and the years immediately following, 1915 to 1920.[17]

Thus, in the two decades from 1901 to 1920, 16,531,197 foreigners of all kinds entered the United States. Out of this total, 9,605,107, or 58.1 per cent, were from southern and eastern Europe.[18] The South Slavs alone contributed 636,783, or 3.6 per cent, of the total.[19]

The swelling tide of immigration from eastern and southern Europe hastened the adoption of a new national policy toward all incoming aliens and the passage of restrictive legislation. Indeed, sometime after the Civil War the conviction had grown that, with the dwindling of free homesteads in the West and the formidable problems raised by the herding of immigrants in cities, national self-protection necessitated measures of selective immigration. As early as the 1880's there were expressions of hostility toward the recent arrivals by native Americans whose patriotism had been aroused, often taking the form of organized, political movements, as seen in the American Protective Association. Prejudiced persons everywhere attacked the newcomers, some asserting that they were inferior, and others declaring them a menace to the American way of life. There were Protestants who considered the masses of Italian and Slavic Roman Catholics as threats to their supremacy. Organized labor complained and urged that steps be taken to safeguard native workers against unfair competition. Congress responded to these different influences with legislative measures of increasing severity.

In 1882 laws were passed prohibiting immigration from China and excluding various undesirables, mainly the insane, convicted criminals, and persons likely to become public charges.  This was followed in 1885 by the alien-labor-contract law which forbade employers to import foreign workingmen under previous contract.  The restrictive legislation increased until by 1903 the prohibited classes embraced physical, mental, and moral defectives of all kinds, as well as assisted immigrants, professional beggars, polygamists, and anarchists.

Strong sentiment developed during the 1890's for special devices to discriminate against the new immigration without discriminating against the old.  Some favored a literacy test, pointing out that more than 35 per cent of the more recent comers were illiterate as compared with 3 per cent in the case of the older alien elements. But this proposal met with vigorous opposition on the part of individuals who insisted that ability to read or write was a test not of mental capacity or social usefulness but of youthful opportunity. For precisely those reasons Presidents Cleveland, Taft, and Wilson vetoed bills seeking to set up literacy requirements.  In spite of opposition, however, in February, 1917, Congress succeeded in passing, over Wilson's objections, an act excluding, with certain exceptions, aliens over sixteen years of age who were illiterate.

The 1920's witnessed the passage of the most rigorous legislation. In 1921, 1924, and 1929 Congress enacted laws which set up limits for immigration from Europe.  In 1921 the annual quota of persons from a European, Near Eastern, African, or Australasian country was established at 3 per cent of the number of immigrants from that country who were in the United States in 1910.[20]  The act of 1924 changed the quota to 2 per cent of the number of immigrants from a country who were in the United States in 1890.  In 1929, an amendment to the 1924 act being adopted, the quota for any nationality was set at a number which bears the same ratio to 150,000 as the number of inhabitants in the United States in 1920, but the minimum quota of any nationality was to be 100.[21]  Under the provisions of the immigration act of 1924, and as amended in 1929, all countries were made subject to quota limitations, with the exception of Newfoundland, Canada, Mexico, Central and South America, Cuba, Haiti, and the Dominican Republic.  The Immigration and Nationality Act of 1952, usually known as the McCarran-Walter Act, which aimed at the codification of all previous immigration measures, retained the quota principle.

## EFFECTS OF RESTRICTIVE LEGISLATION

The adoption of the policy of restriction has had most profound effects upon immigration to the United States. It has materially reduced the number of immigrants from the areas to which it applies, and at the same time it has stimulated the movement from Canada, Mexico, and other countries that are exempt from quota limitations. Moreover, as designed (out of the quota of approximately 150,000 allotted to Europe by the 1924 and 1929 acts, about 126,000 went to the northern and western countries and about 24,000 to the southern and eastern), it has turned the tide once again in favor of immigrants from northern and western Europe. Thus, from 1921 through 1950, a total of 5,670,679 immigrants arrived in the United States, with 1,204,760, or 21 per cent, coming from Canada and Newfoundland; 826,797, or 14 per cent, from Mexico, the West Indies, and Central and South America; 1,961,933, or 34 per cent, from northern and western Europe; and 1,476,913, or 26 per cent, from southern and eastern Europe. Yugoslavia furnished 56,475, or less than 1 per cent, of the total, or 3.8 per cent of the number from southern and eastern Europe.[22]

Restrictive legislation, it is evident, has had its effects upon Yugoslav immigrants also. In the period from 1901 to 1910 over 400,000 South Slavs arrived in the United States. From 1911 to 1920 the number, however, dropped to 199,309. And in the following decade the plunge was sharper when only 48,053 came, with the overwhelming majority, 38,651, coming in the years from 1921 to 1924.[23] During these same years, it is interesting to note, nearly 15,000 "Istrians" (Slovenes and Croats from the Istrian Peninsula) fled from Mussolini's oppressive rule and migrated to the United States.

Reduction in numbers, however, was not the only effect of restriction upon Yugoslav immigration. Other profound results were manifest. A notable transformation, as, of course, was expected, occurred in the intellectual character of the immigrants. In one of the last uninterrupted years of immigration, 1913, out of a total of 56,106 South Slav immigrants, 14,039, or 25 per cent, were unable to read or write.[24] The year 1921, representing the peak of postwar immigration, however, presented a different picture. Out of 19,865 arrivals only 740, or 3.7 per cent, were illiterate, a reduction of 21.3

per cent in a period of eight years.[25]  In succeeding years illiteracy was reduced to a neglible fraction.

Simultaneously, there was an accompanying modification in the occupational character of the Yugoslav, as well as of all other, immigrants.   Unlike other changes, this one often seems to be overlooked or ignored, but it is, nonetheless, important.   In the pre-World War I years the unskilled immigrants totally submerged the skilled (mechanics, farmers, professional and business people).   As an illustration, of the 367,239 Croatians and Slovenians who reached American shores up to 1910 only 270 claimed to have a profession and an insignificant 17,601 listed themselves as skilled workers.   In the period from 1899 to 1910, according to the investigations of the Immigration Commission, only 5.9 per cent of all the South Slav immigrants belonged to the skilled labor class.[26]   The legislation of the twenties, however, completely reversed this situation.   Thus, by 1947, 79.8 per cent of the arrivals possessed skills.[27]   And this trend has continued to the present with only slight variations.   It is necessary to note, moreover, that most of the unskilled immigrants of the era before restriction came to seek industrial employment, while the later arrivals were largely domestic servants and service workers, with a sprinkling of farm and nonfarm laborers.

Like those coming in, the immigrants already in the country were affected by, and reacted, quite sharply in some instances, to the national policy of restriction.   In the main, South Slav immigrants before the quota laws had come to the United States with a view of remaining here for a number of years (until such a time as sufficient savings had been accumulated) and then returning home with their American gains.   This attitude and purpose, as well as general habits and practices, however, were radically modified by the restrictive measures of the 1920's.   The bars on immigration induced the large majority to remain permanently in their new homes, thus slowing down the parade from America to Europe too.   This, in turn, led to a stabilization of every aspect of existence.   The changes took place first among the Slovenes, then the Croats, and finally the Serbs.   Of course, the desire to return to their home country some day still remained, but it was seldom carried out, for the general conditions in their native land were rather discouraging.

With their minds made up to stay in America, the Yugoslavs began to buy farms and real estate, and to establish handicraft shops, in which they increased their invested capital from one million to five million dollars.[28]   Whereas, as a rule, they had formerly been engaged in unskilled employments, in the twenties they began to learn skilled trades in order to establish themselves in better-paid occupations.

Formerly the immigrants had seemed to take little or no interest in the English language, but with the coming of restriction they began to study it with unending enthusiasm.   English clubs, composed of young and old alike, were organized in many of the South Slav communities to teach the aliens, some of whom were completely illiterate, the language of their adopted land as well as to stimulate general interest in American culture and civilization.   Many flocked to the evening adult education classes and swamped publishers with orders for Yugoslav-English dictionaries.   The foreign-language newspapers began to add English sections.

Similar zeal was likewise displayed in the acquisition of citizenship papers.   This phenomenon is amply borne out in official data. Thus, while in 1920[29] only 25.2 per cent of the Yugoslav immigrants were naturalized, 46.3 per cent were citizens in 1930[30] and 61.3 per cent in 1940,[31] more than doubling the citizen body in two decades. During the succeeding ten years another 47,711 of the aliens became American citizens, leaving a dwindling minority without their certificates.

## TYPES OF IMMIGRANTS

Although sporadic reference has already been made to the character of the South Slav immigrants, the subject, important as it is, requires more systematic treatment and elaboration.   To begin with, some light can, perhaps, be thrown on the subject by the following interview which the writer had with a Dalmatian American in San Pedro, California:

Q. When did you come to this country?
A. I arrived in New York in June, 1906.
Q. How old were you at the time?
A. Nineteen.
Q. Were you married?
A. No.
Q. Did you make the trip alone?
A. Yes.

Q. Had you done any traveling before?

A. I had never before left my native island of Olib.

Q. Did you pay for your own passage?

A. Not at all. In fact, my family had to sell half of our stock of goats, sheep, and pigs in order to raise enough money for my passage—even for third class.

Q. Were you coming to anyone in the United States?

A. Yes, I had a cousin in Seattle.

Q. Did you go to him upon your arrival?

A. Yes, at once. You see, I did not know any other language than Croatian, as I had had only four years of grammar school, and I wanted to be among our people, at least until I learned to speak English. I went to Washington and my cousin got me a job on one of the fishing boats.

Q. Since you were so young at the time and inexperienced in travel, were you not afraid to leave your family and undertake such a long journey alone?

A. I guess I must have been a little, but I was too excited to think of anything else but the new adventures that awaited me. I do recall, however, how when I made ready to leave our village, my grandfather, who had never been out of Dalmatia nor seen any city larger than Dubrovnik, called me to him for a bit of last minute advice. "You must remember," he cautioned me, "that you are going to a strange country which is ten times larger than Olib [an isle about the size of Terminal Island in San Pedro harbor], and a land full of godless and dangerous people; so carry with you at all times a scapular around your neck and a knife in your pocket."

These statements of a simple peasant immigrant are quite revealing, but alone they are incomplete and do not tell the whole story. It is necessary to go to official government data for enlargement and clarification of the picture.

Immigration records reveal that most South Slavs who were married emigrated without their wives. In the case of every group male immigrants outnumbered female, but the Slavs show the most marked difference in the proportion of the sexes. For the years 1899 to 1910 figures relating to the sex of the immigrants are shown in Table 2.[32]

The South Slavs who entered the United States during this period came, as seen earlier, with the idea of making as much money as they could in as short a time as possible and then return to their old homes. In such cases they did not bring their wives with them. Moreover, there were many immigrants who were still unmarried, and they came to find opportunities which their homeland did not provide. Married men, in many instances, did not bring their wives with them simply because they did not have the funds, they themselves frequently borrowing to pay for their passage. Some planned to send for their families after they had accumulated enough in savings to buy tickets.

TABLE 2

SEX OF SOUTH SLAV IMMIGRANTS, 1899-1910

| Race or People | Total Number of Immigrants | Number Male | Female | Per Cent Male | Female |
|---|---|---|---|---|---|
| Bulgarian, Serbian, and Montenegrin | 97,391 | 93,200 | 4,191 | 95.7 | 4.3 |
| Croatian and Slovenian | 335,543 | 284,866 | 50,677 | 84.9 | 15.1 |
| Dalmatian, Bosnian, and Hercegovinian | 31,696 | 29,252 | 2,444 | 92.3 | 7.7 |

That the average Yugoslav immigrant had little or no education is quite evident in the official statistics. Illiteracy among the South Slavs who entered the United States in the years 1899 to 1910 was rather high, as is shown by the accompanying table.[33]

TABLE 3

ILLITERACY AMONG THE SOUTH SLAV IMMIGRANTS, 1899-1910

| Race or People | Number, 14 Years of Age or Over, Admitted | Unable to Read or Write Number | Per Cent |
|---|---|---|---|
| Bulgarian, Serbian, and Montenegrin | 95,596 | 39,903 | 41.7 |
| Croatian and Slovenian | 320,977 | 115,785 | 36.1 |
| Dalmatian, Bosnian, and Hercegovinian | 30,861 | 12,653 | 41.0 |

Other investigations point to the same general conclusion. Frequently, however, there has been confusion between intelligence and illiteracy. Thus, Clifford Kirkpatrick, who made a study of intelligence among immigrant servicemen in World War I, concluded that the English-speaking countries, with the exception of Ireland, ranked highest in intelligence and exceeded the white draft taken as a whole, and the non-English-speaking countries of northern Europe also made a good showing, while Italy and the Slavic countries made a poor record.[34]  The scores compiled by Kirkpatrick are not necessarily an indication of a lack of intelligence of the Italians or Slavs, but may be more accurately a reflection of their illiteracy and lack of knowledge of the language and ways of the Americans.

Most of the South Slavs who were illiterate were so simply because they had been denied educational opportunities in the old country.  Illiteracy at home was high, but it was gradually decreasing.  In 1900, 61.4 per cent of the population over six years of age were able to read and write, whereas in 1880 the rate had been 49.4 per cent.  In some of the provinces, however, the level of intellectual development was extremely low.  Thus, in 1900 in Dalmatia 72.6 per cent of the population were illiterate and in the Coastland 35.5 per cent.  In Hungary conditions were no better.  In 1900, in the kingdom proper, 61.2 per cent of the population over six years of age could read or write, while in the subject province of Croatia-Slavonia the percentage was only 44.1.  Of all the South Slav areas the lowest rate of illiteracy was found in Carniola, where 21.7 per cent of the population over six years of age could neither read nor write.[35]  Although conditions improved after 1918, illiteracy still remained at a high level.  In 1931 Slovenia, with 5.54 per cent of illiteracy, had the best record.  For the country as a whole the per cent of literates, defined as persons ten years of age and over who could read and write, was 54.83.  Among men it was 67.31, and among women 42.9.[36]

There is no doubt that the high rate of illiteracy put the South Slavs in America at a disadvantage.  In the first place, the lack of knowledge of reading and writing almost automatically placed the bulk of them in the large unskilled labor pool; and secondly, it hindered them in their progress toward assimilation in the new environment.  Nevertheless, it did not prevent them from earning a livelihood, from getting employment in railroad and other construction work, copper mining and smelting, iron and steel manufacturing, iron ore mining, slaughtering and meat packing, bituminous coal mining, leather manufacture, and oil refining.  A subsequent chapter will cover more extensively the kind of work the Yugoslavs engaged in.

The years 1913 and 1921 were those of the heaviest South Slav immigration in the prewar and postwar periods and probably furnish as good a picture of the type of immigrant that was being admitted into the country as any that could be selected. Statistics clearly show that both in 1913 and in 1921 the majority of the immigrants were males in the age group from 16 to 44, with only a small minority in the lower and upper age brackets.[37] There were very few who belonged to the professional or skilled classes, most of them falling in the unskilled laborer category. Although a large number received financial assistance from relatives or friends, the majority paid for their own passage, leaving themselves usually less than fifty dollars to begin life in the new country. The literacy of the immigrants in the two periods, as already seen, varied considerably. In 1913 the number of illiterates admitted was comparatively high; by 1921 the figure had dwindled down to an insignificant proportion, due, in no small measure, to the literacy law in effect. Thus, the average South Slav immigrant has been a poor, illiterate peasant, without profession or skill, paying a fare which left him with nothing more than pocket money as he set foot on American soil to join his relatives or friends.

### EMIGRATION

Much has been made of the increases of the new immigration over the old in the early years of the twentieth century, but little has generally been said of the comparative rates of emigration. Unfortunately, immigration records did not take into account the aliens leaving the United States until 1907. However, a study of data in the years following discloses that the proportion of new immigrants leaving the country is far greater than that of the old immigrants. This is corroborated by findings of the Immigration Commission as well as by private investigations, such as those of Jenks and Lauck. In their joint work, these two authors state:

> The European emigration . . . in the year 1907 showed 22.7 per cent of the old immigration and 77.3 per cent of the new, whereas the difference between the immigrants of these two classes leaving the United States was still more striking, those

of the old immigration numbering only 8.9 per cent, while the new formed 91.1 per cent. . . .

It appears that taking a number of years in succession, 1908, 1909, 1910 (the later figures of 1911-14 indicate the same tendencies), the number departing for every 100 admitted varies greatly among the different races, and the distinction between the new immigration and the old in this regard was very striking. Not less than 56 per cent and over of the North Italians and South Italians, Magyars, Turks, Croatians, Slovenians, and Slovaks were returning to Europe in those years, whereas of the Hebrews and Irish only 8 per cent and 7 per cent, respectively, returned.[38]

In the years from 1908 to 1930 a total of 12,419,216 immigrants from all parts of the world arrived in the United States. Northern and western Europe contributed 4,606,358, or 37.2 per cent, while southern and eastern Europe sent 5,430,036, or 43 per cent. During the same period the total emigration was 4,015,381, with 699,561, or 17.4 per cent, of the emigrants of northern and western European origin and 2,611,101, or 64.9 per cent, of southern and eastern European background.[39] The balance sheet, accordingly, shows the northern and western Europeans with a gain of 3,906,797, or 84.9 per cent, in immigration over emigration, and the southern and eastern Europeans with a net gain of 2,818,935, or 47.9 per cent.

Over the same period of years the South Slav immigrants numbered 377,713, which was 3 per cent of the grand total or 6.9 per cent of the immigration from southern and eastern Europe. The emigration at the same time was 232,080, comprising 5.7 per cent of the total or 8.8 per cent of that from southern and eastern Europe.[40] That the ratio of emigration to immigration among the Yugoslavs is comparatively high is plain. While they contributed, as seen above, only 3 per cent to the total immigration, they made up 5.7 per cent of the whole emigration. The result was that they had, according to official data, a mere 145,633, or 38.6 per cent, excess immigrants over emigrants.

Undoubtedly, the above figures belie the true status, especially in the case of the Yugoslavs. The government statistics do not, and cannot, take into account undetected stowaways, deserting seamen, and others of that kind. It is well known among Yugoslav Americans that countless numbers of Dalmatian sailors skipped their ships as soon as they touched an American port. Although some of the illegal entrants were apprehended, it is also true that many escaped. Then also there are a number who came from Canada and Latin America, where they first settled and became citizens in order to ease their passage into this country. Such immigrants, as a rule, are not listed under the Yugoslav heading but rather under the banner of those nations whence they set forth. Therefore, the records of the government, particularly as regards immigration, are not as complete or as exact as they might appear.

As in the case of immigration so in emigration, there were varied reactions among Americans. There were some who were glad to see the southeastern Europeans depart, feeling that they were unassimilable and a liability to the nation. But there were others who thought quite differently. The immigrants, they pointed out, had come in as unskilled laborers but in America they had received excellent training and, therefore, when they departed, the country lost the full benefit of their added experiences, improved skills, and stimulated spirits of enterprise. They deplored the emigration, believing it was a definite loss to the nation, and advised that America offer inducements to the aliens to remain in the country.

### RECENT IMMIGRATION

That the immigration of Yugoslavs to the United States has dropped drastically is quite plain. The number of arrivals during the period of the depression was slight, as the following table reveals:[41]

TABLE 4

SOUTH SLAVIC IMMIGRATION, 1931-1939

| Race or People | 1931 | 1932 | 1933 | 1934 | 1935 | 1936 | 1937 | 1938 | 1939 |
|---|---|---|---|---|---|---|---|---|---|
| Bulgarian, Serbian, and Montenegrin | 429 | 184 | 92 | 98 | 173 | 172 | 301 | 431 | 397 |
| Croatian and Slovenian | 668 | 299 | 117 | 109 | 193 | 351 | 365 | 506 | 457 |
| Dalmatian, Bosnian, and Hercegovinian | 69 | 51 | 20 | 29 | 35 | 54 | 75 | 84 | 73 |

From these figures it is evident that Yugoslav immigration to the United States is insignificant in recent times. Indeed, during the years noted above more departed from the country (6,996) than entered it (5,832), as is shown by Table 5.[42]

TABLE 5

South Slavic Emigration, 1931-1939

| Race or People | 1931 | 1932 | 1933 | 1934 | 1935 | 1936 | 1937 | 1938 | 1939 |
|---|---|---|---|---|---|---|---|---|---|
| Bulgarian, Serbian, and Montenegrin | 927 | 954 | 582 | 302 | 289 | 201 | 185 | 114 | 195 |
| Croatian and Slovenian | 382 | 781 | 367 | 216 | 197 | 148 | 114 | 141 | 107 |
| Dalmatian, Bosnian, and Hercegovinian | 119 | 238 | 140 | 84 | 65 | 54 | 35 | 43 | 16 |

During the war years, 1940 to 1945, the number of arrivals exceeded the departures, but the net gain was slight. There were 1,309 immigrants and only 249 emigrants, leaving a favorable balance of 1,060.[43] With the coming of peace there followed a considerable increase in the number of arrivals. In 1946, 676 came, 1,117 in 1947, 1,190 in 1948, 1,384 in 1949, 9,154 in 1950, and 8,254 in 1951. After hitting a peak of 17,223 in 1952, the number of immigrants took a sharp downward plunge in 1953, with only 1,272 newcomers. In 1954 the climb upward was resumed, with 1,432 arriving in that year, 2,567 in 1955, 8,723 in 1956, and 9,842 in 1957. In these same postwar years the number of emigrants has remained comparatively low. Only 93 departed in 1946, 88 in 1947, 192 in 1948, 82 in 1949, 74 in 1950, 64 in 1951, 77 in 1952, 158 in 1953, 168 in 1954, 240 in 1955, 147 in 1956, and 135 in 1957.[44] This means that during the twelve-year span from 1946 through 1957, there were 62,834 immigrants as against 1,518 emigrants, or an excess of 61,316 immigrants over the emigrants.

Several other groups of postwar arrivals among the Yugoslavs should be mentioned. These include the so-called displaced persons (popularly known as d.p.'s) and refugees. They have been allowed to enter the country in relatively large numbers. For example, in the period from June, 1948, to June, 1955, 33,174 displaced persons reached American shores, while 2,453 refugees arrived in the three years from 1955 through 1957.[45] Thus, it is necessary to keep in mind these two classes of newcomers in order to get a comprehensive and accurate picture of recent Yugoslav immigration.

In spite of the postwar immigrant increases, the quota limits have been seldom reached. While the 1924 immigration act gave the Yugoslavs an annual quota of 671, the 1929 measure raised it to 845. Ostensibly, even the latter quota allotment is low, but that to the contrary, it has been infrequently filled. Most of the arrivals since 1945 belong to the nonquota categories, including nonquota immigrants, displaced persons, and refugees.

The new immigrant is well exemplified by Chedo Chuckovich, a Serb American oil dealer of Pacific Palisades, California. Chedo was born in Belgrade of a fairly well-to-do family. His father was part owner of the Serbian-American National Bank. He went to schools in France and Switzerland, with an eye on a diplomatic career. But all such plans were interrupted by the German invasion of Yugoslavia in 1941. Chedo fled with his family into the hills and joined the guerrillas. His father and brother were killed. Chedo himself was wounded and taken prisoner, and then starved for several years in a Nazi concentration camp. Two weeks before the end of the war he was freed by the Canadian forces. But upon his release he found that his family was dead or scattered and the family property had been confiscated by the new Communist regime in Yugoslavia. Chedo became a man without a country—but not for long. It was his fortune to gain admission into the United States as a displaced person. Chedo took up his abode in southern California and soon afterwards set up his own business.

The recent immigrants, it is thus apparent, are quite different from their ancestors of the days of mass immigration.[46] They are not illiterate and unskilled peasants and laborers, but a very select group, highly intelligent and well-trained, predominantly professional and semiprofessional people, farmers and farm managers, proprietors, clerical and sales workers, operatives, craftsmen, foremen, and managers.

It is plain that the days of mass immigration to the United States by Yugoslavs, as well as by most Europeans, are over. Restrictive measures, the depression of the thirties, and World War II with the uncertain conditions following in its wake have greatly discouraged the flow of foreigners into the country.

# 4

# Portrait in Statistics

THE SEVENTEENTH CENSUS of 1950 presents a very incomplete picture of the Yugoslavs in America. Besides listing the total number of immigrants (143,956) at the time of the enumeration, the report throws little additional light on this foreign element. Only a number of selected groups are treated in full. Considerably more inclusive and complete is the sixteenth census of 1940, wherein the many racial and national minorities are not ignored. The 1940 census will, therefore, serve as the basis for the discussions which follow.

## NUMBERS

According to the sixteenth census the total foreign white stock in the United States in 1940 was 34,576,718.[1]* Of this total, 11,-419,138 were foreign-born white and 23,157,580 native white of foreign or mixed parentage. The Germans ranked first in the number of foreign white stock with 5,236,612, or 15.1 per cent; and in native white of foreign or mixed parentage with 3,998,840, or 17.3 per cent; but stood second in foreign born with 1,237,772, or 10.8 per cent. The Italians, on the other hand, were second in foreign stock, numbering 4,594,780, or 13.3 per cent; and in native white of foreign or mixed parentage, totaling 2,971,200, or 12.8 per cent; but first in foreign born with 1,623,580, or 14.2 per cent. Close behind the Italians were other representatives of the new immigration. The Poles had 2,905,859 (8.4 per cent) foreign stock, 993,479 (8.7 per

* Notes to this chapter begin on page 287.

62

cent) foreign born, and 1,912,380 (8.3 per cent) native white of foreign or mixed parentage; the Russians 2,610,244 (7.5 per cent), 1,040,884 (9.1 per cent), and 1,569,360 (6.8 per cent); the Austrians 1,261,246 (3.6 per cent), 479,906 (4.2 per cent), and 781,340 (3.4 per cent); and the Hungarians 662,068 (1.9 per cent), 290,228 (2.5 per cent), and 371,840 (1.6 per cent). Somewhat lower down the ladder were the Greeks, who had 326,672 (0.9 per cent) foreign stock, 163,252 (1.4 per cent) foreign born, and 163,420 (0.7 per cent) natives of foreign or mixed parentage; the Rumanians 247,700 (0.7 per cent), 115,940 (1 per cent), and 131,760 (0.6 per cent); and the Bulgarians 15,688 (0.05 per cent), 8,888 (0.1 per cent), and 6,800 (0.03 per cent).[2]

The Yugoslavs occupied a midway position among the new immigrants. They had a foreign stock of 383,393 (1.1 per cent), a marked drop from the 1930 figure of 469,395 (1.2 per cent). Out of the total foreign stock, 161,093, or 1.4 per cent, were born abroad; while 222,300, or 1.0 per cent, were native of foreign or mixed parentage.[3] Considered by mother tongue, 37,640 persons were reported as Serbian, 115,440 as Croatian, and 178,640 as Slovenian,[4] a total of 331,720. Further refinement of the figures into foreign born, native of foreign or mixed parentage, and native of native parentage shows the Serbians with 18,060, 18,300, and 1,280; the Croatians with 52,540, 58,980, and 3,920; and the Slovenians with 75,560, 97,300, and 5,780,[5] each of the three groups having less of the foreign born and of the native of native parentage than of the native of foreign or mixed parentage. It will also be observed that there is a difference of 51,673 between the totals given for the Yugoslavs and for the Serbians, Croatians, and Slovenians combined. The difference, in part, may be accounted for by the designation of some Yugoslavs as Dalmatians, Bosnians, Hercegovinians, and Montenegrins, regional groups not listed in the census.

There are a few who disagree with the official census data and place the total number of Yugoslavs in the country at a higher figure. In the mid-1920's, Mirko Kosić, then a professor at the University of Belgrade, estimated that there were approximately 500,000 Yugoslavs in the United States.[6] About ten years later, another Slav investigator, Jurica Bjankini, by adding American-born children to the total number of immigrants in the United States born in Yugoslavia, arrived at the grand total of 700,000.[7] Still a higher estimate was presented by the well-known Croatian journalist and author Ivan Mladineo, who placed the figure at 1,000,000. He explained that the original immigrants made up a little less than one-third of the total, while the second and third generations represented a little more than a third each. Of the total of 1,000,000, Mladineo gave the Croatians approximately 500,000, the Slovenians about 300,000, and the Serbians some 200,000.[8] According to an investigation in 1929 of the Senate Committee on Immigration, which sought to determine immigration quotas based on national origins, Professor Kosić was closest to the true figure. The Senate Committee placed the total number of persons of Yugoslav stock at 504,203, of which 220,668 were listed as immigrants, 265,735 as children of immigrants, and 17,800 as grandchildren and later generations.[9] A more recent writer, Dragutin Kamber, dealing with only the Croats, figured their number at 500,000.[10] He says nothing of the other groups.

There is no doubt that the census figures as regards the Yugoslavs are not absolutely correct. They are somewhat misleading. The census of the foreign born takes into account simply the country of origin. With the great bulk of the South Slav immigrants coming from Austria-Hungary it goes without saying that many of them must have been classified as Austrians and Hungarians. Some of them, mainly Slovenes, came from Italy and have been designated as Italians. Others, principally Croats, entered as citizens of Canada and countries of Latin America and appear under headings other than Yugoslav. Even the subsidiary statistics based on mother tongues do not offer a reliable source of information. This is evident from the fact that these statistics show more Slovenians than Croatians, while the reverse is true as shown by other sources.

A closer estimate of the Yugoslavs in the United States can be obtained from the many and varied Croat, Serb, and Slovene organizations (political, economic, social; fraternal, cultural, recreational; national, state, local), branches of which are found wherever these groups have settled and which include the great majority of the immigrants. Eleven national mutual benefit federations alone, for example, have a combined membership of approximately 350,000, which, in conservative estimates, is not more than one-fourth of the total number of Yugoslavs in the country. A careful study of the membership of these federations and the other organizations, allowing for inevitable duplications, will show that there are about 700,000 South Slavs in the country, counting only the foreign born and the second generation, but about 1,000,000 if the third generation is also added, with the original immigrants accounting for less than a third. Of this grand total, the Croatians number slightly over 500,000, the Slovenians somewhat under 300,-000, and the Serbs about 200,000.

Inaccurate computations are due in part to pure negligence and in part to unfamiliarity with the prevailing conditions. As noted above, many of the South Slavs from the Dual Monarchy are classified as Austrians and those from Italy as Italians, and failure to account for these groups results in underestimates of the aliens. In a similar fashion, errors creep into calculations of numbers of the second and third generations through oversight or ignorance of the factors of marriage, divorce, and fertility. The immigrants have a higher proportion in the ages at which most persons marry, and this raises the proportion of those married. Not only do more of them get married but more of them stay married, a result of their early training, high morals, and religious beliefs. They have a considerably lower proportion of divorced persons than the native-born whites, only about two-thirds as many. Since larger numbers of the Yugoslavs are married, it would logically follow that more children are born among them. As a matter of fact, the birth rate among them, as among all the immigrants in the United States, has always been much higher than among native Americans. The Yugoslav women in America have shown the same high fertility as their sisters in Europe, and families of ten and twelve children have not been unusual. At the same time it must be admitted that the death rates among the aliens have also been higher than among the native-born whites, owing in part to the higher proportion of the immigrants in the upper-age groups and to their greater concentration in cities where death rates are higher. However, the death rates are not of such proportions as to nullify the gains by birth. The numbers born are more than sufficient to offset the loss of the immigrants by death; enough to leave a very favorable balance.

## SEXES

As among most of the immigrant classes from southern and eastern Europe, so in the population of the Yugoslavs the males exceed the females. This preponderance of males is a factor of considerable social significance. In 1940 there were 209,761 males in the total foreign stock of the Yugoslavs and only 173,632 females.[11] This gave a ratio of 120.8 males to 100 females, which was much higher than the ratio of 103.3 to 100 for the total foreign white stock of all immigrant classes. Since males tended to outnumber the females among immigrants, this ratio was slightly higher for the foreign born. Here the Yugoslavs, with 97,781 foreign-born males and 63,312 foreign-born females, showed a ratio of 154.4 to 100, in comparison to 111.1 to 100 for all foreign-born aliens.[12] Although there was a pronounced disparity between the foreign-born males and females of the Yugoslavs, it was no more marked than among the Danes, with a ratio of 154.2 to 100, or among the Greeks, with the highest ratio of all, 255.5 to 100.[13] On the other hand, the number of females exceeded the number of males among each of the nationality groups whose country of origin was Scotland, Ireland, France, Hungary, or Canada. These differences are closely related to variations in the ratio of males to females at the time of immigration.

The distribution among the nationalities in the second generation also showed differences between the sexes, though not as sharp. In general, females outnumbered the males in the second generation of those groups represented in the old immigration, while males outnumbered females in those belonging to the new immigration. The ratio for all groups was 99.6 males to 100 females. Among the Yugoslavs, as among the other new immigrants, males exceeded the females, but there was more balance between the two sexes of the second generation. With 111,980 males and 110,320 females, their ratio in this category was 101.5 to 100.[14]

## AGES

Recency of immigration is a factor that is also reflected in age differences by country of origin among the foreign-born white. Thus, the bulk of the immigration from the British Isles (with the exception of Scotland), the Scandinavian countries, Switzerland, and Germany antedated that from other European countries. The foreign-born white originating in these countries were, generally, older than the foreign-born white of any other European country, the average age being 55.1. In contrast, the foreign-born white of new immigrant groups such as the Rumanians, Greeks, and Italians, with an average age of 47.9, were younger than the foreign-born white of any other European nationality group. The Yugoslav foreign born, with a median age of 50, were, obviously, between the former and latter classes.[15]

Similar differences in age composition were likewise apparent among the native white of foreign or mixed parentage. Second-generation English, Irish, French, Swiss, and Germans had median ages between 40 and 46; whereas Russians, Rumanians, Greeks, and Italians ranged from 15 to 24. With their median age of 20.4, the Yugoslavs evidently fell in with the second group.[16]

## DISTRIBUTION

One of the most conspicuous facts about the distribution of the immigrants in the United States is their concentration in the Northeast, Midwest, and the far West. These three sections have shown the most marked increases since 1900 in the number of both foreign born and native born of foreign or mixed parentage. The increases in the Northeast and the Midwest are attributable to the industrial development of those regions and a relatively stable farm population, while those in the Rocky Mountain and Pacific Coast areas are due to the expansion of agriculture and mining.

The southern states, on the other hand, have never been able to attract many immigrants. There are numerous reasons for this. One of the most fundamental factors was the backward industrial development of the South. Important also was the prospect of Negro competition which discouraged the settlement of those aliens who wished to become farmers or wage earners. It has been generally believed that the South was traditionally hostile toward foreigners, especially Roman Catholics and Jews. Before the Civil War and during the period of Reconstruction prospective immigrants were warned not to go to the South through letters from immigrants in the North and through the foreign-language press. It has also been held that the laws in the southern states did not give adequate protection to the workingmen and did not guard against child labor. Before the Civil War the South boasted of its pure American population, a select group uncontaminated by the rabble from abroad. This attitude has not been entirely eliminated.

Many of the studies of the distribution of the immigrants stress

67

the predominant importance of economic opportunity in their settlement. In the latter half of the nineteenth century, when land settlement offered a real opportunity for economic betterment, vast numbers of the newcomers went to the land directly or within a few years after their arrival. But after 1900 settlement on land held attractions for very few. This was an important reason for the slackening of immigration from northern and western Europe and the coming of eastern and southern Europeans, poorer peoples who had not the means for settling on land no matter how much they may have preferred to do so. Because these later arrivals had to work for wages, they stayed in cities where wage jobs could be found, the capital being supplied by the employer.

In addition to the economic factor there have been others that have influenced the distribution of immigrants. Included among these are proximity to the major ports of entry and the availability of transportation, which account for the concentration along the Atlantic and Pacific coasts and the westward movement following the development of railroads; the recency of immigration, which is a factor in urban settlement; the tendency of peoples to cluster in ethnic and national units and to occupy contiguous territory; and subsidiary factors, such as climate, which, for example, exerted an important influence on the Yugoslavs in their settlement of California.

While immigrants have always been heavily represented in the cities, the tendency toward urban settlement has been especially pronounced in the case of the recent immigrants. The most highly urbanized ethnic groups are the new immigrants, primarily because the city offers greater opportunity than the country. During the days of abundant cheap land the immigrants settled mainly in rural areas. Because of the great industrial expansion beginning at the end of the nineteenth century more opportunity has been offered in the urban centers, and so the new immigrants have been flocking to the cities. Not only have they settled in cities, but they have tended to locate in the larger ones. This is also true, to some extent, of the children of the immigrants, who likewise demonstrate preference for life in the metropolis.

Study of the geographical distribution of the Yugoslavs shows that they conform fairly well to the general immigrant pattern. Though they have a few important colonies in the South, they have settled largely north of the Mason and Dixon's line, in communities extending from the Atlantic to the Pacific. Census reports reveal that by far the greater number of the South Slavs preferred the North to any other section of the country. There, in 1940, lived 317,497 of them. In contrast, there were only 55,625 in the West and a mere 10,271 in the South.[17]

Classification by mother tongue reveals the same general pattern of distribution in the major regions and in the main divisions thereof. Thus, there were 33,260 Serbians in the North, 1,420 in the South, and 2,960 in the West.[18] Of the Croatians, 102,700 were in the North, 3,080 in the South, and 9,660 in the West.[19] Some 146,020 Slovenians were located in the North, 3,860 in the South, and 28,760 in the West. The numbers of each of the three groups in the various divisions of the country are shown in the table below.[20]

TABLE 6

DISTRIBUTION IN DIVISIONS

| Division | Serbian | Croatian | Slovenian |
|----------|---------|----------|-----------|
| New England | 220 | 260 | 2,240 |
| Middle Atlantic | 12,900 | 36,280 | 49,920 |
| East North Central | 17,180 | 53,700 | 76,980 |
| West North Central | 2,960 | 12,460 | 16,880 |
| South Atlantic | 1,320 | 2,740 | 2,380 |
| East South Central | 20 | 260 | 400 |
| West South Central | 80 | 80 | 1,080 |
| Mountain | 1,280 | 3,460 | 10,920 |
| Pacific | 1,680 | 6,200 | 17,840 |

In looking at the distribution in the states it is seen that the state with the largest number of Yugoslavs was Ohio, followed by Pennsylvania, Illinois, Michigan, California, Minnesota, Wisconsin, New York, Indiana, Colorado, and Washington.[21] Serbians were found in significant numbers in but a few of the states. There were 11,240 in Pennsylvania and 6,000 in Ohio.[22] The bulk of the Croatians were in Pennsylvania (31,900), Illinois (20,400), Ohio (17,080), Michigan (6,700), and Wisconsin (5,820).[23] Slovenians lived chiefly in Ohio (38,500), Pennsylvania (37,100), Illinois (17,420), Minnesota (13,920), California (13,840), Wisconsin (10,-120), New York (8,440), Michigan (7,920), and Colorado (5,480).[24]

69

The distribution of the Yugoslavs in cities of 500,000 or more inhabitants, according to the 1940 census, is shown below.[25]

TABLE 7

DISTRIBUTION IN CITIES

| City | Serbian | Croatian | Slovenian |
|------|---------|----------|-----------|
| Baltimore, Md. | 140 | 80 | 220 |
| Boston, Mass. | 20 | — | — |
| Buffalo, N. Y. | 20 | 40 | 100 |
| Chicago, Ill. | 2,480 | 12,540 | 7,320 |
| Cleveland, Ohio | 640 | 5,780 | 24,720 |
| Detroit, Mich. | 3,360 | 2,100 | 2,340 |
| Los Angeles, Calif. | 240 | 1,220 | 3,640 |
| Milwaukee, Wis. | 300 | 2,400 | 4,100 |
| New York, N. Y. | 540 | 1,960 | 4,260 |
| Philadelphia, Pa. | 60 | 360 | 500 |
| Pittsburgh, Pa. | 1,340 | 3,740 | 2,480 |
| St. Louis, Mo. | 440 | 1,860 | 400 |
| San Francisco, Calif. | 180 | 240 | 2,100 |
| Washington, D. C. | — | 80 | 60 |

The census data clearly show that the Yugoslavs, though coming from a rural environment in the old country, flocked to the cities in the United States, as did most of the other new immigrants. Thus, 277,095, or 72.2 per cent of the total, were to be found in urban centers, whereas only 77,388, or 20.2 per cent, and 28,910, or 7.6 per cent, lived in rural-nonfarm and rural-farm regions, respectively.[26]

Of those living in cities, 237,895 were in the North, 4,097 in the South, and 35,103 in the West. In the rural-nonfarm regions there

TABLE 8

URBAN AND RURAL DISTRIBUTION BY DIVISIONS

| Division | Urban | Rural-Nonfarm | Rural-Farm |
|----------|-------|---------------|------------|
| New England | —— | —— | —— |
| Middle Atlantic | 61,287 | 27,131 | 4,976 |
| East North Central | 149,539 | 21,534 | 11,754 |
| West North Central | 25,556 | 9,214 | 4,455 |
| South Atlantic | —— | 4,052 | —— |
| East South Central | —— | —— | —— |
| West South Central | —— | —— | —— |
| Mountain | 10,123 | 8,495 | —— |
| Pacific | 24,980 | 5,689 | 3,856 |

were 58,365 in the North, 4,839 in the South, and 14,184 in the West. The distribution in the rural-farm regions showed 21,237 in the North, 1,335 in the South, and 6,338 in the West.[27] (See Table 8.)[28]

An overview of the Yugoslavs in the states for which figures were available under the heading of country of origin of the foreign stock is contained in the table below.[29]

TABLE 9

URBAN AND RURAL DISTRIBUTION BY STATES

| State | Total Foreign Stock | Urban | Rural-Nonfarm | Rural-Farm |
|---|---|---|---|---|
| California | 25,050 | 19,098 | 3,349 | 2,603 |
| Colorado | 7,099 | 3,469 | 3,101 | 529 |
| Illinois | 51,881 | 42,316 | 8,357 | 1,208 |
| Indiana | 11,622 | 10,275 | 1,002 | 345 |
| Iowa | 3,246 | 1,174 | 1,228 | 844 |
| Kansas | 5,793 | 4,386 | 804 | 603 |
| Michigan | 27,157 | 19,280 | 4,397 | 3,478 |
| Minnesota | 22,430 | 14,174 | 5,983 | 2,273 |
| Missouri | 5,236 | 4,140 | 879 | 217 |
| Montana | 5,934 | 2,968 | 2,008 | 958 |
| New Jersey | 4,936 | 3,992 | 791 | 153 |
| New York | 17,923 | 15,375 | 1,748 | 800 |
| Ohio | 73,584 | 63,924 | 5,780 | 3,880 |
| Pennsylvania | 70,535 | 41,920 | 24,592 | 4,023 |
| Washington | 7,059 | 4,218 | 1,953 | 888 |
| Wisconsin | 18,583 | 13,742 | 1,998 | 2,843 |

The states in the above table have the largest numbers of Yugoslavs, but there are others not included in the list that have important South Slav settlements, such as Louisiana and Texas with their colonies of fishermen on the Mississippi Delta and in Galveston, respectively.

According to the government data for the states arranged according to mother tongue (which, apparently, are as incomplete as the statistics under country of origin of the foreign stock), the Slovenians held first rank in the numbers living in the urban centers as well as in rural-nonfarm districts and in rural-farm areas. Their urban total of 104,360 was far above the 59,700 of the Croatians and the 12,540 of the Serbians. In the rural-nonfarm classification the Slovenians had 37,040 in comparison to the Croatians 18,080 and

71

the Serbians 3,960. Finally, on the farms the Slovenians led with 11,340, followed by the Croatians with 4,120 and the Serbians with 740. There were only two states showing Serbian inhabitants, five Croatian, and nine Slovenian. The figures for these states reveal that the Serbians had 7,760 inhabitants in cities in Pennsylvania and 4,780 in Ohio; the Croatians had 19,580 in Pennsylvania, 14,500 in Ohio, 16,680 in Illinois, 4,560 in Michigan, and 4,380 in Wisconsin; and the Slovenians had 6,500 in New York, 14,920 in Pennsylvania, 34,160 in Ohio, 13,260 in Illinois, 4,640 in Michigan, 7,980 in Wisconsin, 9,160 in Minnesota, 2,940 in Colorado, and 10,800 in California. In the rural-nonfarm areas, there were 3,100 Serbians in Pennsylvania and 860 in Ohio, 11,040 Croatians in Pennsylvania, 1,680 in Ohio, 3,300 in Illinois, 1,340 in Michigan, and 720 in Wisconsin, 1,220 Slovenians in New York, 19,500 in Pennsylvania, 2,800 in Ohio, 3,820 in Illinois, 1,720 in Michigan, 740 in Wisconsin, 3,440 in Minnesota, 2,240 in Colorado, and 1,560 in California. On the farms, the Serbs had 380 in Pennsylvania and 360 in Ohio. There were 1,280 Croatians on farms in Pennsylvania, 900 in Ohio, 420 in Illinois, 800 in Michigan, and 720 in Wisconsin. Of the Slovenian farmers, 720 lived in New York, 2,680 in Pennsylvania, 1,540 in Ohio, 340 in Illinois, 1,560 in Michigan, 1,400 in Wisconsin, 1,320 in Minnesota, 300 in Colorado, and 1,480 in California.[30] A comparison of the above totals for the states given with the totals for the divisions, regions, and the nation will readily reveal how incomplete the statistics are. Be that as it may, the figures do provide a fairly clear picture of the distributions of the three major groups of South Slavs in the urban, rural-nonfarm, and farm areas.

### PRINCIPAL SETTLEMENTS

A question frequently raised in regard to immigrants is, "Why did not these aliens scatter indiscriminately throughout the population and thus more speedily merge into American life?" The fact of the matter is that they could not even if they so desired. They established, instead, immigrant islands of isolation surrounded by seas of American society.

Of the many factors contributing to this development the two most important were: (1) the bonds of language and culture that held them to those of their own group, and (2) their low economic status. The newcomers soon discovered that they were complete

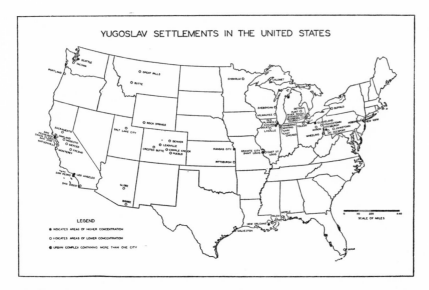

strangers in their newly-found wonderland. There was nothing familiar; the buildings, the roads, and even the farms were different from those at home. Everywhere they went they heard a strange new language, totally incomprehensible to them. They were just as baffled by American customs. Their shawls, babushkas, coarse dresses, and short embroidered coats were conspicuous and in glaring contrast to the dress of the people about them. It was no wonder that they were bewildered and that they clung together with those of their own minority group. Suspicious of the many strangers about them, they found comradeship and self-assurance with those who spoke their language and were familiar with their ways of living. A small settlement grew into a larger community, and a little Italy or a Slavia soon came into being.

The second important factor in the creation of the immigrant colony was economic in nature. Very few of the immigrants had money enough to delay permanently locating until they could make a choice. The great majority had hardly more than a few dollars. They consequently had no choice, for immediate employment was imperative, and the low wages that they received forced them to make their first home in the poorest sections. If they brought their families, they soon found it necessary to take in boarders to supplement their incomes, and thus added to the crowded condition of their tenement flats. If they left their families abroad, they sought cheap rooms in order that they might be able to save enough either to return home or to bring their wives and children to them. Thus, by accident, there sprang up throughout the country thousands of isolated immigrant communities, each resistant to the forces of assimilation, clinging to its own language and customs, finding the security of social status within its own group, and held in economic bonds permitting little more than a bare existence.

It was in the manner described above that the Yugoslav colonies, which are located in practically every industrial center in the United States, were founded. They are largely an outgrowth of the attempt made by these immigrants to adjust themselves to the strange environment in America. Ties of race or kinship, language and culture, and the need for social security inevitably led the South Slavs to settle in the same neighborhood. Adjustment was much easier where the immigrants from the same village or district could settle together and speak their own language, sing their own songs, eat their native food, and follow their old customs. Without his own ethnic community, the average immigrant would be lost.

Several decades ago Ivan Mladineo placed the number of Yugoslav communities in the United States at 1,077.[31] This estimate, including large and small colonies alike, appears to be a fairly logical one. Omitting the tiny scattered settlements, the Yugoslavs are now found in the following locations:

1. New York City and surrounding sections, particularly Hoboken, New Jersey.

2. Buffalo and vicinity and upstate New York.

3. The hard-coal districts of eastern Pennsylvania and western portions of New York.

4. The steel and coal districts of western Pennsylvania, including Johnstown, McKeesport, and Pittsburgh, and adjacent regions of West Virginia (Wheeling) as well as Ohio (Youngstown). A large group of Yugoslavs is located in Pittsburgh and Allegheny County, which, like Chicago, is an important Croatian center.

5. Wheeling, Benwood, and the coal-mine and lumber sections of West Virginia.

6. Cleveland and Akron, Ohio. Cleveland has more Slovenians than any other American city.

7. Detroit and other automobile production towns in Michigan.

8. Calumet and the copper-mining and agricultural communities of northern Michigan.

9. The industrial sections of northern Illinois and Indiana, including Chicago, Joliet, La Salle, East Chicago, and Gary.

10. Milwaukee and environs, extending to Sheboygan, Wisconsin.

11. St. Louis County in the iron-mining areas of northern Minnesota.

12. East St. Louis, Illinois, and St. Louis, Missouri.

13. Kansas City and Pittsburg, Kansas.

14. Denver, Pueblo, Leadville, and the mine districts of Colorado.

15. The mining districts of Wyoming, Montana, and Utah, including Rock Springs, Butte, Helena, and Salt Lake City.

16. Seattle and Tacoma, Washington.

17. Portland, Oregon.

18. San Francisco, Oakland, Fresno, Sacramento, Santa Clara, Merced, Modesto, Monterey, Los Angeles (including San Pedro), San Diego, and the entire coast of California.

19. The copper-mining areas of Arizona, such as Bisbee and Globe.

20. Galveston, Texas.

21. New Orleans, Olga, and Empire, Louisiana; Biloxi, Mississippi; Mobile, Alabama; and most of the Delta region.

The above merely embraces the more important Yugoslav settlements. There are many others, to be sure. Indeed, as one authority states, "Yugoslavs can be found in every state and territory of the Union. Settlements sufficiently numerous to allow the formation of organized groups exist in over 800 towns, cities, or hamlets, there being over 5,000 local organizations of various kinds all over the continent. By far the largest proportion of Yugoslavs live in Pennsylvania, Ohio, Illinois, Michigan, New York, Minnesota, California, Wisconsin, and Indiana. The Chicago area has the greatest number of Yugoslavs of any urban area, estimated at between 40,000 and 60,000. Pittsburgh is the most important Serb colony. Cleveland and its surroundings is the most important Slovene colony, with some 50,000 Yugoslavs."[32]

The early Slovenians, who were mainly farmer folk, settled as homesteaders in agricultural sections of the country, especially

Michigan, Minnesota, and the Pacific Coast. In Minnesota the Slovenes founded their own town, Kraintown, named after their native Kranjska (Carniola). The descendants of these pioneers live there at the present time, carrying on the work and traditions of their forefathers. In Michigan also they founded a town of their own, a farming community called Traunik (a name which means "meadow" in Slovenian).

Immigrant Slovenians who came after the disappearance of the frontier and cheap land went to the copper- and iron-mining districts, establishing colonies in Colorado, Montana, Wyoming, Idaho, and Utah. Thousands of others swarmed into the mines and industries of the Ohio Valley, founding important settlements like that in Cleveland, "the metropolis of American Slovenes."[33]

Croatians, settling in areas where there were opportunities for work in mines, furnaces, rolling mills, and factories, have relatively large colonies in New York, Pittsburgh, Allegheny, Cleveland, Detroit, Chicago, St. Louis, Kansas City, New Orleans, and San Francisco. Smaller groups are to be found in Great Falls, Anaconda, and Butte, Montana; Crested Butte and Cripple Creek, Colorado; and Calumet, Michigan. The leading communities of the Serbians are Pittsburgh, Cleveland, Chicago, East Chicago, and Gary.

Among the earliest Yugoslav settlements established by the new immigrants was that of the Croatians in Allegheny County, Pennsylvania (mainly Allegheny City, Pittsburgh, Millvale, Rankin, and Braddock). The first Croats arrived in Allegheny City (now a part of Pittsburgh's North Side) in 1882. During the years that followed, an increasing stream of the immigrants flowed into Allegheny City, Pittsburgh, and the neighboring towns. By 1894 the settlements in Pennsylvania had grown sufficiently to warrant the importation of a Croatian priest (Dobroslav Bozić) and the building of a church (*Sveti Nikola*) in Allegheny City. In 1900 there were some 13,000 Croats in Allegheny County (about 7,000 in Pittsburgh), most of whom were employed in the industries of the area.[34] Additional immigrants continued to pour in during the following decades, but the tide was stemmed by the restrictions of the 1920's.

Another of the early South Slav communities in the eastern part of the United States was that of the Dalmatians in New York City. Beginning with a handful of men in 1888, the colony grew rapidly until by 1912 it had between 2,500 and 3,000 persons.[35] As the settlement expanded it spread along Eleventh Avenue from Thirty-fourth to Forty-eighth streets and on the adjacent streets between Tenth and Eleventh avenues. There they have remained, working as stevedores, freight-handlers, and railroad employees.

Although the South Slavs were employed in the copper mines of Michigan as early as 1890, Detroit had few of these immigrants until the eve of World War I. As late as 1905 there were only forty or fifty Croatians in the city and still smaller numbers of Serbians. Most of the early comers had been in other industrial cities first. The earliest South Slavs in Detroit were employees of the American Car and Foundry Company, and they lived close to their place of work. According to one writer "this colony extended north and south from Hancock to Perry Avenue and east and west from Dequindre to Beaubien Street. A little later Croatians and Slovenians from the Upper Peninsula of Michigan began to move to Detroit to work in the automobile factories."[36]

A great influx of South Slavs moved into Detroit in 1914, at a time when a strike was going on in the copper mines to the north. There were some also who had been attracted a little earlier by the high wages offered by Henry Ford. Although nearly all immigration was stopped by the war, the flow was resumed after the cessation of hostilities. As more and more came into the city and with the passage of time, the status of the Slavs was considerably altered, as is so ably described by the same investigator, who writes:

> The decade following 1920 brought many changes to the original settlement on Russell Street. The better financial condition of many had made it possible for them to buy property away from the noise and dirt of the city. The old colonies have broken up and moved north, east and west, and down the river beyond Wyandotte. A group composed mostly of Croatians, but including a few Serbians and Slovenians also, is now living north of McNichols (Six-Mile) Road between Woodward Avenue and Dequindre Street. The majority own the houses in which they live, some of which are valuable properties.
>
> Another group, composed of both Serbians and Croatians who formerly worked at the Ford factory in Highland Park, invested in real estate there on Cottage Grove and Victor Avenue, and Pasadena Street, mostly east of John R. Street, also along Davison Avenue east of John R. as far as Dequindre Street. Many Serb-

ians and a few Croatians and Slovenians have recently moved to the new Fenkell Avenue district in the northwest part of the city. Clairepointe Avenue and adjacent streets, south of East Jefferson Avenue, are peopled almost entirely by Serbians. A few Serbians also live east on Centerline Road north of Harper Avenue.[37]

The Slovenians are scattered through Detroit in small groups, nowhere forming a large and compact community. In 1928 a number of Yugoslavs moved to Dearborn, Ecorse, and River Rouge, when the Ford factory was moved to Dearborn. There are other Yugoslavs now in Wyandotte, and they work in the plants of chemical and engineering firms.

An interesting, though small, group is that of the Moslem Yugoslavs. These people are Bosnians, whose ancestors were converted to Islam by the Turks. They do not associate with the Catholic or Orthodox Slavs but rather with other Moslems, particularly Turks, the bond of religion being stronger than race or language.

Another large settlement of Yugoslavs is in Cleveland. After World War I there were an estimated 40,000 in the city, and that total has decreased but slightly in recent years. The Slovenians were the first to arrive, settling near the steel mills, railroad terminals, and brick yards, where they found employment. Their chief location is along St. Clair Avenue, where they live all the way from east of East 30th to East 78th streets, with probably the largest number east of East 55th Street.[38]

The Croatians came to Cleveland at the end of the nineteenth century and later, as did the Slovenians. Their main residence district is along St. Clair Avenue, and its intersecting streets from about East 25th Street to East 70th Street. Dalmatians have their own community between Scoville Avenue and Woodlawn Avenue, East 26th Street and East 31st Street, as well as their own benevolent society. Immigrant Croatians worked as laborers in the steel and iron mills and shops, but many acquired skill in carpentry, welding, and other trades.

The Serbians are the minority group among the Cleveland Yugoslavs. Before World War I there were an estimated 2,000 Serbians in the city, but of these many migrated to Detroit, Akron, and other industrial centers, so that the federal census of 1940 showed less than a thousand of them in Cleveland.[39]

In Chicago there are said to be about three hundred Serbian homes.[40] This old colony was settled originally by natives of Lika (a district of Croatia where many Serbians took up their abode after the Turkish conquest of their homeland). In addition, Montenegrins settled in this city in not too small numbers, having in the years between 1905 and 1912 their own benefit lodge (Love of Montenegrins) with seventy members. Most of the immigrant Yugoslavs were employed in the Chicago iron foundries. They lived near the Carnegie steel plant, forming a compact community.

Chisholm, near Duluth, Minnesota, is also a center of a large Yugoslav settlement. Here the most important element consists of Slovenes, some of whom arrived in the last years of the nineteenth century and in the early years of the twentieth. The town has a distinctive Slavic flavor and could almost pass for one of the internal towns in old Carniola or Styria. Every phase of life in this little Yugoslavia has been affected, if not actually dominated, by the immigrants. According to one source, "there are two Yugoslav churches in the village and fifteen Yugoslav mutual benefit societies. Two banks, and twelve groceries and meat markets are owned by persons of Yugoslav stock. There are no less than thirty-four teachers in Chisholm of Yugoslav birth or descent. Of the village officials, the mayor, the treasurer, the district attorney, three of the aldermen, the school superintendent, truant officers, etc., are all of Yugoslav birth or descent."[41]

Though not as large or as old as some of the settlements described above, an interesting and flourishing new Yugoslav colony is that in Miami, Florida. For years there were very few South Slavs in Miami and other neighboring towns of Dade County. Florida was always considered a rich man's playground and therefore held no appeal to the destitute alien. However, in more recent times, after the retirement of some of the prominent Yugoslav leaders from the North in the area and visits by servicemen, businessmen, and prosperous industrial workers, the attitude was greatly modified. Florida came to be looked upon as being apart from the real South, a state offering tremendous opportunities. It was not long, as a consequence, that the movement south commenced.

Today, Miami has a Yugoslav colony of some three hundred families, and it is steadily growing. The new Floridians did not take long to find a place for themselves in the economic life of the community. Many took jobs in the building industry, some went into real estate, others opened up shops of their own, and several became members of the faculty at the University of Miami. Soon a Yugoslav-American club was organized, and now there is a good deal of enthusiasm expressed for the erection of a club house. A number of the fraternal federations, such as the Croatian Fraternal Union, have shown their interest in the group by proposing the establishment of their branches in south Florida. The Miami Yugoslavs do not as yet have their own place of worship, but have a Croat priest at the new Church of the Epiphany in South Miami.

Three thousand miles away from Miami, on the opposite coast of the United States, the Yugoslavs have one of their most prosperous settlements in the country. This is San Pedro, the port of Los Angeles, California. The Dalmatians predominate here. Some of the immigrants came to the town in the last decade of the nineteenth century, but the majority arrived in the years following World War I, most of them finding employment in the tuna fishing industry. During the 1920's between 5,000 and 6,000 Dalmatians arrived in San Pedro and vicinity, over 2,000 of whom came directly from Yugoslavia. In the 1930's the number increased to about 12,000.[42]

San Pedro is a typical Yugoslav fishermen's town. If a stranger cannot sense his whereabouts by the odor of the fish, he can do so by the fish lingo (much of it in a dialect of the Dalmatians) that he hears in the harbor or on the sidewalks in front of the cafes, taverns, and shops along Sixth Street and Pacific Avenue. At the waterfront one sees piers overcrowded with fishing vessels, many proudly bearing such names as "Agram," "Adriatic," "Alexander I," "Volga Boatmen," giving the harbor a Slavic flavor and reminding the observer that a large percentage of the fishermen are Yugoslav. Here also is "cannery row," near which are the houses of the less fortunate families whose heads earn their comparatively meager livelihoods as cannery workers and wharf laborers. As one, however, climbs to the hills beyond Gaffey Street and westward to Point Fermin and the ocean, he looks upon beautiful gardens of geraniums, carnations, and palms and pretentious homes, chiefly of Mediterranean architecture with pale-tinted stucco walls and tile roofs, attesting to the success and affluence of the more blessed boat owners and fishermen of this lively, thriving, noisy fish metropolis of southern California.

# 5

# At Work

INVESTIGATIONS have clearly shown that the immigrants in the United States have gone to work in those industries in which opportunities for employment have been most numerous, as well as in those into which, because of the handicaps of language and lack of money and experience, or because of national characteristics, they have best fitted. The aliens' unfamiliarity with American conditions, the lower standards of working and living conditions in the European countries from which they came, and their eagerness to earn money made them frequently willing to accept employment here under conditions below the general level in the United States. Accordingly, immigrants were employed in large numbers in sweatshops and in industries where working standards were low. They were given the hardest, dirtiest, and poorest-paying jobs. That was the price most of the immigrants had to pay in making their adjustment to the American industrial environment.

### TYPES OF OCCUPATIONS

Immigrants have been principally employed in manufacturing and mechanical industries, in occupations where little skill or technical training was required, where the work was unattractive, or where physical strength was a primary qualification. Many of them also found work in mines and in domestic and personal service. Few, however, went into agriculture, professional service, or into clerical pursuits.

The South Slav immigrants have been no exception to the estab-

81

lished tradition that the newcomers start at the bottom of the employment ladder. In the old country, under the Habsburgs, they had been employed as laborers in agriculture and forestry. Similarly, when they came to the United States, they went to work as unskilled laborers, though seldom in the country. In the years 1899 to 1909 inclusive, out of a total of 295,981 Croatians and Slovenians who arrived in the country, 146,278 were common laborers, and 80,167 were farm laborers.[1]* Reports of the United States Immigration Commission show that only 1 per cent were common laborers, and 27.1 per cent farm laborers.[2] These proportions also held for other Yugoslavs.

As previously seen, some of the South Slavs signed labor contracts in order to get across the Atlantic. Once in the United States, the immigrants were herded together by their traveling agents and sent to their assigned employers. They were generally employed in the coal mines of Pennsylvania and West Virginia or sent to Cleveland and Chicago, from which points they were distributed throughout the heavy industries and the copper, iron, and coal mines of Illinois, Michigan, Minnesota, Colorado, Arizona, Wyoming, Utah, Idaho, and Montana. As a rule, they were divided into brigades of a hundred men and compelled to labor under conditions imposed by the employers—conditions which even under the best employers could only be described as severe. Most of them lived in company dwellings—usually ramshackle, dilapidated wooden houses which were like furnaces in the summer and icebergs in the winter—and bought their necessities of life in the company stores—at prices far above the market. Whatever they had left over from their paychecks after taking care of the rent, food, and clothing they turned over to their employer in payment for their passage. As a consequence, few of these contract laborers were able to show any real benefit to themselves during their first years of hard toil in America.

The immigrants who came over without obligation of contract sought, and found, employment in scattered sections of the country. In the decades of the seventies and eighties most of them went to work in the dangerous copper and iron mines of northern Michigan and Minnesota, earning as little as $1.25 a day for twelve to sixteen hours of labor. Without benefit of modern safety devices, hundreds

* Notes to this chapter begin on page 289.

lost their lives and many more were crippled in accidents. Nevertheless, most of them survived, though some were minus an arm, a leg, or a lung. After several years of this type of work, a number of them returned to the old country, the more fortunate ones with enough savings to pay off debts on their farms. Others chose to live in America and sent for their wives or sweethearts to join them here.

Some of the South Slav immigrants entering the United States in the last three decades of the nineteenth century, instead of proceeding to the mines of the upper Great Lakes region as planned, stopped in New York, where they became dock workers and tugboat crews. Others found industrial employment in Cleveland, Chicago, Joliet, and Milwaukee. In later periods some of the immigrants originally destined for Cleveland or Chicago stopped instead in Pittsburgh or in the Pennsylvania anthracite coal region or in the bituminous towns of West Virginia and southern Ohio. Others went into the coal mines of Illinois and Kansas or into the copper mines of Montana and Utah. Still others found work on the highways and railroads all over the continent.

Though the majority of the early South Slav immigrants remained in the mines and factories, some of them shifted to other pursuits as time went on. They became masons, carpenters, lumbermen, longshoremen, farmers, and businessmen.

Not all of the immigrants, of course, began their labor in America in the pits and mills. Some, as already observed, went to the land and raised fruit, especially in California. Others turned to the sea for a livelihood. They became fishermen in New Orleans, Louisiana; Galveston, Texas; San Diego, San Pedro, Monterey, and San Francisco, California; along the coasts of Oregon and Washington; and on the Columbia River.

Table 10 shows the kind of work, as well as the percentages, engaged in by the Yugoslavs in 1921.

From the figures in Table 10 it is seen that the bulk of the Yugoslav Americans in 1921, at the outset of immigration restrictions, were employed in mines and industries, while a comparatively small number were found in agriculture. The tabulation of the Immigration Commission disclosed a similar distribution of South Slav workers.[4]

In his survey in 1937 Ivan Mladineo found a relatively small number of Yugoslavs in the professions. In Mladineo's list there were 604 professional people divided as follows: clergymen, 181; teachers, 163; physicians, 93; public officials, 78; lawyers, 68; and dentists, 21.[5]

TABLE 10

PRINCIPAL OCCUPATIONS

| Industry | Per Cent |
|---|---|
| Steel, iron, and zinc mines, smelters, refineries and works | 42.0 |
| Coal mining | 12.0 |
| Lumber industry | 6.5 |
| Stockyards | 6.0 |
| Fruit growing | 5.0 |
| Chemical works | 4.0 |
| Railroads | 4.0 |
| Electrical manufacturing | 4.0 |
| Farming | 3.0 |
| Copper mining | 3.0 |
| Fisheries | 2.0 |
| Automobiles | 2.0 |
| Sailors and longshoremen | 1.5 |
| Business | 1.0 |
| Oyster industry | 0.5 |
| Professions and other activities | 3.5 |

Today the Yugoslavs are in the same vocations as they were in the earlier periods. But, in addition, they have found new types of employment. The tremendous growth of the automotive and aviation industries has provided them with opportunities unheard of earlier. In these industries the majority of them, to be sure, hold positions requiring little or no real skill, but some have become engineers, designers, and pilots. And an even more select few are playing a part in the advancement of the space frontier through their contributions to missiles, satellites, and other space instruments and devices. The initiative, industry, and ambition of the Yugoslavs have sometimes led them into rather strange pursuits. One of them, for example, became the head of a firm engaged in salvaging cargoes from ships which had been sunk in the Caribbean Sea during World War II. It would thus appear evident that the Yugoslavs are earning their living in work on the land, in the earth, in the air, on the sea, and under the sea.

Because the great majority of the South Slav immigrants have filled unskilled positions in America, there has been a tendency to look upon them, as upon all unskilled alien workers, as inferior. That such thinking is fallacious and shallow has been conclusively demonstrated many times over by serious students of immigration. In his monumental work on immigrant labor Hourwich emphasized:

> An invidious distinction is drawn between the old and the new immigrants by reason of the fact that the bulk of the latter are incapable of any but unskilled work. A comparative statistical study of immigration shows that the old immigrants, like those of the present generation, were mostly unskilled laborers and farm hands. The proportion of skilled mechanics has at no time within the past fifty years been as high as one-fourth of all immigrant breadwinners, for the very obvious reason that the demand in the American labor market has been mainly for unskilled laborers. Invention of machinery has had the tendency to reduce the demand for mechanical skill, and most of that demand has been supplied by native Americans. . . . It is a misconception of modern industrial organization to confuse lack of "skill," i.e., ignorance of a trade, with "low efficiency." If every immigrant were a skilled mechanic, most of them would nevertheless have to accept employment as unskilled laborers. The special skill of the engineer would give him no superiority at loading coal over a common laborer, nor would the ability to read Shakespeare in the vernacular assure higher wages to a mule-driver.[6]

## MILL AND MINE

The South Slavs, as already noted, were introduced to American heavy industry in the period of reconstruction and expansion following the Civil War. This era saw the expansion of communication and transportation, the shift of manufactures from the domestic workshop to the factory, the development and perfection of machinery, the increase in size of business units, and the inauguration of the corporation, all of which marked the dawn of a new day in America. The country was transformed from an agricultural to an industrial—and with the phenomenal growth of cities to an urban—nation. At the same time demand for skilled labor declined while that for unskilled labor increased immensely. Invention of mechanical devices and processes eliminated the skill and experience for-

85

merly required in a large number of occupations, including those in steel and iron plants, foundries, textile mills, and mining.

The revolution in industry brought in its wake a host of problems. One of the more serious of these was presented by the old skilled workers, who believed they should share with the employers the benefits of the new age. They sought better working conditions, shorter hours, and higher wages, and formed trade unions to gain acceptance of their demands. With both the workers and employers determined to hold their ground, strikes broke out periodically.

In order to escape from their dilemma the employers began a search for new sources of labor supply. That they soon discovered in central, eastern, and southern Europe, which henceforth became the chief provider of cheap labor for American industry. Armies of these new immigrants, including South Slavs, made their way across the Atlantic. Arriving with only a few dollars in their possessions, they were forced to accept any job offered to them. They had been accustomed to a low standard of living and were, therefore, willing to accept low wages and unsatisfactory conditions of employment. Docile and manageable, they became easy victims of exploitation. At a result of the competition of this cheap labor supply the old labor force was subjected to unsafe and unsanitary working conditions, displacement from certain occupations and industries, and weakening of its labor organizations.

Thus, the newcomers were welcomed with open arms by the industrialists, who regarded them as a perfect weapon to combat the demands of the labor unions, but they were greeted with conspicuous hostility by their opposite numbers, who saw in them nothing more than the degradation of their ideals. Consequently hatred, distrust, and tension sprang up between the organized and unorganized workers. Evidence of this ill-feeling between the two sections of American labor was provided by developments and conditions in many of the industrial centers of the country. One of these was Pittsburgh. Here, the Amalgamated Association of Iron and Steel Workers, after its victory in the Homestead strike in 1889, signed a contract which excluded from its benefits all unskilled workers. By this maneuver the new arrivals (mainly Slavs and Italians) were relegated to a position of inferiority. First of all, they had to work for wages considerably lower than those obtained by the union for the skilled and the English-speaking workers.

Secondly, they were compelled to work from twelve to fourteen hours a day, receiving no extra pay for overtime. Finally, they had to accept the worst dwellings in the city or pay twice as much rent for the same apartment as their English-speaking neighbors.

Such is the story of the early South Slav immigrants in American industry. Yet in spite of all their hardships, they were far better off than they had ever been in Europe. And so their numbers in the factories continued to swell. By 1900 most of the 13,000 Croats living in Allegheny County, Pennsylvania, found employment in the plants of Pittsburgh and vicinity. When World War I ended in 1918, officials of the United States Steel Corporation estimated they had in their employ throughout the country some 25,000 South Slavs. Today, there are thousands of Yugoslavs working in steel mills and iron and steel foundries of the Pittsburgh district and the industrial complex of northern Illinois and Indiana, extending from Chicago, on through Hammond, East Chicago, and Gary, Indiana. Beginning as laborers, many of them have advanced to positions of skill and responsibility. A few of them are foremen and superintendents. Most of the others are employed as riggers, crane operators, rollers, machinists, electricians, boilermakers, blacksmiths, carpenters, patternmakers, molders, coremakers, burners, and welders. The immigrants also hold similar jobs in the large Sinclair and Standard Oil refineries in nearby Whiting, Indiana. During World War II Yugoslav women, like those of other nationalities, rushed to the plants to replace the men at the front and helped to win the battle of production.

A close-up of the immigrant in an American factory is provided by Pribichevich, a Serb American who despite his doctoral degree in political science felt no humiliation in working in a machine shop in Cleveland. Of his experiences in the plant, he says:

> We were only twenty in our group in the Assembly Room, but we were of fourteen different nationalities: Serbs, Slovenes, Croats, Italians, Hungarians, Rumanians, Czechs, Germans, Poles, Swedes, Englishmen, Scotchmen, Irishmen—even Americans. . . . The workers cast curious glances at the newcomer. They were amused at my clumsy attempts to punch the clock and showed me a vacant locker along the left wall where I changed clothes. Then, at four o'clock, the note of the factory bell sounded in my ears, and our shift started off like a regiment toward the ma-

chines in the center. Holding our tool boxes in our hands, we waited in line for the foreman to assign us our jobs. I did rough work on that first night. I swept the floor and picked up waste and dirt with my bare hands. I carried heavy machine parts in my arms or on my shoulders. I screwed big pipes together. A compassionate worker showed me how to hold a file, and with it I smoothed off the edges of five push-button plates. Within fifteen minutes my hands were blistered, my arms impregnated with black metal dust and machine oil, and my mouth full of grease. When I was through at midnight the muscles of my feet, legs, fingers, hands, arms, and back ached terribly. I dragged myself home and slept like a dead man. "How do you feel?" the foreman asked me as we washed up the following night. I shrugged my shoulders. He winked at another worker and laughed: "It'll do him good; in three weeks he'll have muscles like Popeye the Sailor."[7]

The present writer, having spent several years in steel mill, foundry, and oil refinery work in the northern Indiana industrial center, went through a similar experience. The work was sometimes hard, usually dirty, and often dangerous, with electric cranes operating overhead, furnaces spitting out their molten metal on one side, and machinery of all types grinding away on another. One, however, hardly gave thought to any of these things as he went about the many tasks assigned to him. Along with the hard work and serious application went a good deal of "horseplay," an uninitiated newcomer generally being the butt of the jokes and pranks of the oldtimers. But it was all in fun, as "Bohunks," "Dagoes," and "Hunkies" laughed at each other's failings.

It is interesting to note that nearly three-fourths of the total Yugoslav immigrant population is dependent upon the metal and coal industries. In the iron mines of Minnesota, which produce most of the iron ore in the United States, 50 per cent of the employees, it was estimated in the 1920's, were Yugoslavs.[8] In the coke industry the picture was pretty much the same. During the same period it was reported that 40 per cent of the workers in the coke ovens of western Pennsylvania were Yugoslavs.[9] These proportions have been altered very little in the succeeding years.

The account of the Yugoslavs in the coal mines is similar to their background in the factories, also an interesting though not altogether a flattering one. In the southern Pennsylvania coal fields before 1880 nearly all the workers were native Americans or old immigrants, predominantly English-speaking. To improve their conditions, in 1868 these miners had organized the Miners' and Laborers' Benevolent Association. Constant friction between the union and the employers, however, led to the sale of the mines to the railroads. The new owners determined not to yield to demands of the union, but, instead, to fight it by bringing in a new immigrant labor supply, like their fellow employers, the industrialists. This resulted in an invasion of the mines by thousands of southeastern Europeans, among whom were numerous South Slavs. The older workers were practically driven out, for they could not compete with the new arrivals who were willing to work longer and for less pay.

In the northern Pennsylvania fields where the Slavs began to press around the turn of the century, the old miners were more successful in holding their own. By shrewd political maneuvers they secured the passage of a law providing that a person had to be a laborer for two years before he could become a miner and also pass an examination in English. Just about this same time the English-speaking miners began to join the United Mine Workers of America, which had only recently come into the area, as a weapon against the Slavs. Conducting a successful strike in 1900, the miners secured a sizable wage increase, benefiting both groups of workers. Becoming more cognizant of the values of unity and cooperation by this experience, the Slavs fought side by side with the old miners in the strike in 1902. The mutual cooperation of the two groups of workers spelled success, resulting not only in higher wages and improved working conditions, but also in lessened competition and strife between the English-speaking miners and the Slavs.[10]

Investigations show that the first South Slavs to find work in the bituminous coal mines of Illinois were also hired because of labor trouble in the mining industry, which ended in the general strike of 1894.[11] The workers lost the strike, and the mine owners hired immigrant Yugoslavs because they were willing to work for lower wages. The South Slavs "gravitated . . . to the mining, metal-working, and packing centers, where there is a demand for unlimited quantities of raw labor, provided always it is cheap."[12] Wages for the hard work were extremely low, as was pointed out by the able writer and authority on American labor, the late John R. Commons:

Outside Pittsburgh, in the mills and yards, 16½¢ an hour seems to be the prevailing rate for the kind of work done by the Slav immigrant, but in Pittsburgh proper 15¢ is more generally paid for such labor. Jones and Laughlin, on the South Side, can hire Slavs at 15¢ when Homestead and the mill towns pay 16½¢. The difference is due to the greater congestion of immigrants in Pittsburgh, the place of their first arrival, and to their preference for the city with its agencies for employment and its fellowship and support when looking for employment.[13]

The Yugoslavs have also been important in the zinc mines of Illinois, but more so in the copper-mining districts, as in the Calumet region of Michigan, in Montana, and in Arizona.

## LUMBERING

In the lumber industry, as lumberjacks, Yugoslavs are found in every section of the country. They seem to possess a certain ability of their own in this particular occupation. Their rugged character, their strength and endurance qualities, enable them to stand the hard life of a lumberjack as few others can. In the Gulf states of the South, there is a small colony of Dalmatians that is widely known for its production of French claret staves, an undertaking which had its beginning in 1895. These staves are manufactured exclusively by the Yugoslavs, and are exported to European countries, mostly to France. They are made by hand and in the same manner as in the old country.[14]

## STOCKYARDS

Many of the South Slavs who came to the United States with the first waves of the new immigration found employment in the stockyards and packing houses of Chicago and Kansas City. They have had an especially difficult time in bettering their lot. Not possessing any special skills in the trade, they merely filled an urgent need for unskilled workers, and became absorbed in a system that, because of its utter lack of sanitation and disagreeable conditions, smelled across the continent, arousing the sympathy of humanists everywhere and causing liberal writers like Upton Sinclair (*The Jungle*) to attack vigorously the evils of the industry. In the course of time, with the spotlight turned upon them by the "Muckrakers," the employers improved conditions. As the work became more

90

tolerable, hours were reduced, wages increased, and better jobs opened to them, some of the Yugoslavs built homes near their places of employment. There they have remained to this day.

## AUTOMOBILE AND AIRCRAFT

The Slovenes, in particular, are employed in the automobile industry as skilled mechanics. In a speech before the Paris Peace Conference in 1919, the distinguished Yugoslav American inventor and professor, Michael Pupin, stated that "the work of the skilled Slovene mechanics in the factories of Detroit, Toledo, Cleveland, and Pittsburgh contributed towards the winning of the war as much as an army of 25,000 fully equipped soldiers."[15] Other Yugoslavs besides the Slovenes have also found employment in the automobile industry. Most of those in Detroit work in the auto factories. There have been some, too, who have opened up their own garages and gasoline stations. With the rise and spread of airplane plants, especially during World War II, many of the South Slavs were able to transfer their skills from the automobile to the aircraft production lines.

## CLOTHING

A small number of the immigrants find work in the garment industry in New York. In fact, most of the Slovenes in New York are employed in the manufacture of hats. They are highly appreciated and much sought-after workers because they are skilled and experienced, having learned the trade in their home country. Included in this group are both men and women, with many of the latter being employed as foreladies. Yugoslavs in general have shown high capacity in needlecraft, with some finding employment in the clothing industry while others have established their own tailor and dressmaking shops.

## AGRICULTURE

As previously seen only a small percentage of Yugoslavs chose agriculture as an occupation. A majority of those who did go into farming were Slovenes, who located chiefly in the Great Lakes region.

It may be surprising to hear that in America the majority of the Yugoslav, like many other, immigrants became engaged in work in mill and mine rather than on farm, whereas in Europe they had been employed chiefly as agricultural laborers. The reasons the immigrants went to town instead of country are clearly explained by Jenks and Lauck, noted immigration authorities:

> They do not wish to become separated from members of their own race, upon whom they depend for an expression of their wants and to whom they want to turn in times of emergency. As a consequence, the alien seeks colonies of his own people in cities. . . . The recent immigrant does not intend to remain permanently but wants to get as much money as possible in a short time. . . . Furthermore, the necessitous condition of the present-day immigrant when he arrives in the United States makes it imperative for him to seek work at once under any conditions which may be offered. He has no money with which to purchase land. In consequence the southern and eastern European farmer or farm laborer becomes transplanted to a new industrial environment.[16]

Most of the Yugoslavs in California are engaged in either fruit-growing or fishing. The part that these people have played in making California a great orchard state is noteworthy. In raising young trees, which is the very foundation of the fruit-growing industry, they have been exceptionally successful. In the nineteenth century, before many of America's finest orchards were planted, a little colony of Yugoslavs settled near Watsonville in the beautiful Pajaro Valley. They planted many fine apple trees, which bore fruit that was unsurpassed. The descendants of those early settlers are continuing in the same high tradition. Jack London, in *The Valley of the Moon,* described Pajaro Valley as an agricultural paradise, referring to the area as "New Dalmatia," and praising the Dalmatians for their industry, skill, and thrift.[17] Shortly after the Yugoslavs had settled in the region around Watsonville, others of their kinsmen from the old country took up the old Spanish land grants in the Santa Clara Valley. There also they planted many fruit trees, but chiefly prunes and apricots. Universally known, these delicious fruits are dried and marketed as Santa Clara prunes and apricots. Further south, near Fresno, the Yugoslavs, virtually inundating the area, devoted their energies and interests to the grape and raisin industries. In the Sonora and Sacramento valleys they turned chiefly to the cultivation of pears. A fair and sincere appraisal of the contribution of the Yugoslavs is made by the Jugo-slav Section of America's Making, a group which made one of the earliest studies of the immigrants:

> The value of any race to any country depends directly on what the race can produce. There can be no finer or better manner of producing than that of turning a barren plot into a bearing orchard. The orchards of California testify to the industry and patience of the Jugoslavs.[18]

## Maritime Pursuits

From the earliest times Yugoslavs from the littoral have been known throughout the commercial world as mariners, sailors, and shipbuilders. First among the Yugoslav immigrants to America, the Dalmatians settled along the Atlantic, Gulf, and Pacific coasts, where they followed their ancient customs in all industries pertaining to the sea. Many of them continued to follow the sea, hiring them-selves out as crew members on American vessels. Hardly a clipper sailed the high seas without some Yugoslavs among the crew. After the disappearance of the sailing ships, most of the Yugoslav marin-ers remained on shore and engaged in longshoreman trades. There are still several thousands of the old sea wolves employed along the Hudson and East rivers of New York, a great many of them com-posing the crews of tugboats, large scows, and ships used in harbor works. Most of the large shipbuilding yards on the Atlantic employ thousands of Yugoslavs while hundreds more are engaged in the yards of the Pacific Coast, especially Oakland, California, and the Puget Sound. Yugoslavs were among the first makers of shipmasts in the pine forests of Oregon.[19]

Early Dalmatian immigrants settled on the Gulf Coast and be-gan the development of the fisheries. Lucien Burman, who is well known for his folksy good-natured novels depicting life on the Mississippi and other rivers, describes in romantic fashion the origin and growth of the Yugoslav settlements in the South. He writes:

> Some years after the Civil War a Dalmatian fisherman, weary of his beautiful but troubled land, came to America and chanced to reach the region where we are now traveling [Mississippi Delta]. So cursed was the country with the mosquitoes . . . so hostile was it in every way to humanity that no one would remain

93

except the wandering hunter or hardiest Cajun. But the newly arrived fisherman was accustomed to hostility and difficulty. Day and night he worked without resting. Oyster and shrimp were plentiful and after a time his long-empty pockets were filled with money. Other Dalmatian men came to join him. Soon their wives followed, and their children, and then pretty girls for their sons to marry. They all thrived in the new country for they were all expert fishermen and knew the ways of the water. And some of them began settling on the shores where they could grow oranges . . . and ferment the fragrant orange wine. They were a gay, happy people, and they brought their gaiety with them, and their legends and their superstitions. And to the rare whites and Negroes who lived along the banks, they became known simply as "the Austrians."[20]

The oyster industry on the Delta today is largely operated by the Yugoslavs. The towns of Olga and Empire in Louisiana, which are centers of that industry, are almost entirely inhabited by Yugoslav oystermen and their families. They began on a small scale, gradually expanded their interests until today they not only own their own fleets but canneries as well, and some have gone into the insurance business to safeguard their widespread holdings.

A parallel development has taken place on the Pacific Coast. There, however, it is the salmon, tuna, and sardine that draw the Yugoslavs to sea. In the north, particularly around the Columbia River and the nearby bays, salmon is most important, whereas in the south, near San Francisco, Monterey, San Pedro, and San Diego, tuna and sardines constitute the largest proportion of the total catch. The progress of the fishing industry on the Pacific Coast is in large measure due to Yugoslav inventive genius. In 1917 Martin Bogdanovich virtually revolutionized commercial fishing by introducing the relatively simple practice of putting ice on board ships to keep the catch fresh. Some years later John Zuanich began successful experiments in preserving fish in brine. Today, most of the new vessels carry huge brine tanks (250-ton capacity on the ultramodern "St. Helena"), which are frozen after the catch has been placed in them and then thawed when ready to unload. In recent years also, Nick Bez, a leading Dalmatian fisherman from Seattle, has been carrying on experiments with the processing of sea food on board large floating canneries which accompany the fishing boats, with an eye toward reduction of costs and wastage.

Although there are many hazards, the life of the fisherman is filled with excitement, adventure, and all the romance found upon the sea.[21]  During the spring and summer months the salmon is the main attraction in the north.  At the same time the prized tuna (like the albacore, the finest of its species, known as the "chicken of the sea" and priced at over $400 per ton) lure the men (usually in groups of three or four boats to reduce risks) into the waters far to the south of the border—some as far as Peru.  In pursuing the sardines during the fall and winter, they remain closer to home, oftentimes returning with a load after a night out.  Watching a purse seiner (so called because its big net or seine closes at the bottom by pulling strings, just like a purse or money bag) at work is a most fascinating and educational experience.  The boat cruises about until it reaches sardine grounds.  The motor is then promptly cut off and the net lowered into the sea.  While most of the men are engaged in spreading the seine in the water and trapping the school of sardines, one man stands aside and pounds on the deck with a wooden mallet to scare wandering fish from under the boat into the net.  When the catch (ranging anywhere from several to fifty tons or more, which, at $60 a ton, is not bad for a night's work) is safely aboard, the boat heads straight for the cannery. The scene that follows is inimitably described by John Steinbeck:

In the morning when the sardine fleet has made a catch, the purse-seiners waddle heavily into the bay blowing their whistles. The deep-laden boats pull in against the coast where the canneries dip their tails into the bay . . . then cannery whistles scream and all over the town men and women scramble into their clothes and come running down to the Row to go to work.  Then shining cars bring the upper classes down: superintendents, accountants, owners who disappear into offices.  Then from the town pour Wops and Chinamen and Polaks, men and women in trousers and rubber coats and oilcloth aprons.  They come running to clean and cut and pack and cook and can the fish.  The whole street rumbles and groans and screams and rattles while the silver river of fish pour in out of the boats and the boats rise higher and higher in the water until they are empty.  The canneries rumble and rattle and squeak until the last fish is cleaned and cut and cooked and canned and then the whistles scream again and the dripping, smelly, tired Wops and Chinamen and Polaks, men and women, straggle out and droop their ways up the hill into the town and Cannery Row becomes itself again—quiet and magical.[22]

After unloading, the fishing boat crew, usually consisting of eleven men, is paid off in shares, following an old-established custom in Dalmatia where one-fourth of the proceeds of the catch are given to the boat owner, another fourth to the net owner, and one-half to the crew. The first share goes to the boat owners, and averages around 40 per cent of the total catch. The remaining 60 per cent is divided into eleven equal shares for all the men in the crew. Generally, the larger the boat, the larger the share to the owners. The crew shares expenses on fuel, equipment, food (largely beef and chicken), and beverages (meant to fortify as well as refresh and therefore includes a wide variety, such as beer, wine, whisky, coke, soda, milk, tea, and coffee). Practically all business transactions are handled by the cooperatives of the boat owners, thus removing this responsibility from the hands of the individual members.

The rapid advances of the South Slav fishermen in San Pedro, the fish capital of the United States, are especially worthy of attention. In 1920 the number of immigrant Yugoslav licensed fishermen was 170, or 11 per cent of the total.[23] By 1946-1947 this had increased to 666, or 14 per cent of the total.[24] These figures do not tell the whole story; in fact, they may be misleading unless accompanied by an explanation. They do not include the second or later generations, which comprise an appreciable number. And although the total of 666 does not appear particularly impressive, it is the highest of any immigrant class, being far ahead of such groups as the Italians, Norwegians, and Swedes, who had, in 1946-1947, 238, 65, and 23 licensed fishermen, respectively, in San Pedro.[25]

That the San Pedro Yugoslavs have prospered is evident on all sides. Much of their earnings, however, has gone to increase and modernize their fleets. Several decades ago Mladineo stated that "a fleet of a hundred modern fishing vessels in San Pedro alone represents an investment of several millions of dollars and is the property of these immigrants."[26] That value has since more than doubled. At one time nets, such as sardine, were small and inexpensive, but today they are 250 to 300 fathoms long and 30 to 35 fathoms deep (1,500 to 1,800 feet long, by 180 to 210 feet wide) and cost approximately $12,000.[27] The same thing is true of boats.

Formerly they cost $2,000 to $3,000, but today they are valued up to $500,000.[28]

The Yugoslavs in San Pedro, as elsewhere in the country, have been successful not only in the catching but also in the canning and marketing of sea food. In order to facilitate and safeguard these varied business enterprises, they have organized their own canneries (e.g., French Sardine, owned and operated by the Bogdanovich family), banks (e.g., Fishermen and Merchants Bank), and insurance companies (e.g., Commercial Fishermen's Inter-Insurance Exchange).

## BUSINESS

The expansion of one enterprise, as has often been demonstrated, gives rise to another. So it was with fishing on the Pacific Coast. The growth of the fishing industry brought in its wake the wholesale type of grocery and meat market, designed to cater primarily to fishing boats. While some of the supplies are still sold to the vessels by Yugoslav retailers, the bulk of this trade is now in the hands of the South Slav wholesale dealers. This trend has not been without benefit to the fishermen, who are thereby enabled to purchase their needs at substantial savings. Selling tons of the foodstuffs, each year, a few of the businessmen have succeeded in amassing small fortunes.

In addition to the occupations of fruit-growers, fishermen, and grocers, the Yugoslavs on the West Coast have been successful in the restaurant business. In a survey made by the Jugoslav Section of America's Making, 235 restaurants were found in San Francisco and 300 in southern California owned by Yugoslavs.[29] These dining establishments serve both foreign and American dishes and cater to Yugoslav and American patrons alike.

Businessmen of many kinds are to be found in the principal South Slav settlements throughout the country. These include hotel owners, storekeepers, coal dealers, and building contractors. Banks, building and loan associations, and real estate firms abound in many areas. Grocery stores and taverns flourish wherever the Yugoslavs are located. In Chicago there are over twenty grocery stores and some fifty taverns owned and operated by Yugoslavs.[30] The businessmen who have arisen are usually the leaders of the South Slav community in which they live.

In Europe an important force in the life of the Yugoslavs was the cooperative. It affected nearly every phase of their existence. In America, on the other hand, cooperatives have not assumed such significance, although there have been several consumer's societies that have cooperated in establishing direct connection between producer and consumer.

## Labor Unions

Any discussion of occupations would be incomplete without mention of labor unions. Although somewhat averse to unions in the early days of immigration, the Yugoslavs today are among the staunchest supporters of labor organizations. This about-face is not difficult to explain. It is the contention of some students of immigrant activities that aliens from backward regions, such as the South Slavs, when once moved by the spirit of unionism are the most dangerous as well as the most determined of unionists. These immigrants, it is maintained, have few obligations, little property, and meager necessities that compel them to surrender to employers.[31] There is perhaps much validity to that argument. A popular but not altogether convincing explanation was offered by Professor Commons, who said:

> Unionism comes to them as a discovery and a revelation. Suddenly to find that men of other races whom they have hated are really brothers, and their enmity has been encouraged for the profit of a common oppressor, is the most profound awakening of which they are capable. Their resentment towards employers who have kept them apart, their devotion to their new-found brothers, are terrible and pathetic. With their emotional temperament, unionism becomes not merely a fight for wages but a religious crusade. It is in the nature of retribution that, after bringing to this country all the industrial races of Europe and Asia in the effort to break down labor organizations, these races should so soon have wiped out race antagonism and, joining together in the most powerful of labor-unions, have wrenched from their employers the greatest advance in wages.[32]

Professor Commons undoubtedly exaggerated the force of the brotherhood of workers. Far more impelling motives to union have been the prospects of higher wages, shorter hours, and improved conditions of work.

Investigations have shown that workers became much more

strongly organized after the advent of Slavic immigration than they had ever been before.  The hours of labor were reduced, wages rose, and the majority of the older, chiefly English-speaking, employees advanced on the scale of occupations.  This significant role of the Slavs in the labor movement is stressed in the following paragraph:

> The foreigners have proven capable of forming labor organizations which are more compact and united than any which ever existed among the various English-speaking nationalities, who first constituted these communities.  It is conceded by men intimate with the situation throughout the coalfields during the last strike, that its universality was more due to the Slav than to any other nationality.  There should have been in all probability a break in the ranks in Schuylkill County had it not been for the firm and uncompromising stand of the Slavs in favor of the strike.  They have been trained to obedience, and when they organize they move with a unanimity that is very seldom seen among the nations who pride themselves on personal liberty and free discussions.[33]

Today, South Slavs, from aviation employees to zinc miners, belong in preponderant numbers to labor unions, including the American Federation of Labor, the Congress of Industrial Organizations, and the United Mine Workers of America.  The fishing industry, embracing fishermen and cannery workers, is almost totally unionized.  The status of the miners, particularly those in the large mines of the East and the Middle West, and workers in the large steel mills, foundries, and automobile plants is not much different.  It is in the smaller plants and mills, stores, and restaurants that the Yugoslav, not unlike other, workers are least organized.

In the writer's survey, which, it must be emphasized, included people from all walks of life, common workers, as well as self-employed professional persons, the number of union members was comparatively high.  Out of 200 Yugoslavs interviewed in Chicago (including 170 manual laborers), 153 stated that they belonged to labor organizations, while 82 out of 100 interviewed (including 85 manual laborers) revealed union membership in Los Angeles.

## A HARD LIFE

Whether union or nonunion, laborer or professional, the immigrant Yugoslavs in general have not attained great wealth.  This is

99

especially true of those who have worked in the mines and factories. The rich are few in number, even though many have their homes paid for and an automobile besides. Being mainly industrial workers, they have undergone considerable suffering during periods of economic contraction. Many of them lost their entire savings and properties during the severe depression of the thirties. Finding any kind of employment in such times was exceedingly difficult, though not always painful as Pribichevich so interestingly points out:

> I began to look for work. When I had tried to get a job in Europe either I could get no appointment or I was treated rudely. Here I was received very politely by bank directors or the heads of law firms. I was helped out of my overcoat, shown a chair, and offered a cigar. Then I would tell my story to an attentive listener. "Right now there is very little I can do for you," the man behind the desk would say apologetically, "but I shall certainly be glad to get in touch with you if anything should come up." Then he would take my address and telephone number and escort me to the door. It was not until I reached the street that I realized I had not got the job. It is almost a pleasure to be turned down in this country.[34]

Some of the Yugoslavs, it is true, have had a struggle in eking out a bare existence, but despite hardships and privation very few of the immigrants have sought charity.[35] Pride would lead some to starve first. By skimping, borrowing, taking in boarders and roomers, living with in-laws or other relatives, and by every other means possible, they managed to keep the wolf from their doors and their names off the relief rolls.

Although endowed with great strength, the immigrants found that a few years in America at backbreaking labor brought unmistakable signs of exhaustion. Marie Orenstein, making a study of the Croats in New York for the Bureau of Social Research of the New York School of Philanthropy, reported:

> Often did I see men with lined, tired faces, bankrupt in health. Especially true was it of those who worked at night, for they could not be thoroughly rested by sleeping during the day. "I am always tired when I go to bed and when I get up," complained one tall, wan man.[36]

That the Yugoslavs have worked hard to earn their living in the United States cannot be denied. Many of them have given their strength and youth to the land of their adoption and now pin their hopes for the future on their progeny.

## Thrift Habits

Although the Yugoslavs have not grown wealthy through their work in factory and mine, they have shown many evidences of thrift. Testimony is found in the many homes owned, in the large number of benefit societies in existence, in the banks and building and loan associations which are wholly or partly owned, managed, and supported by Yugoslavs, and the remittances and other material aid sent to the folks in the old country.

Perhaps not too typical, yet illustrative in some ways of South Slav thrift habits, are the facts revealed in studies made in Pennsylvania. One investigator reported, "In Hazelton I was told in one of the banks that two-thirds of the $5,000,000 of deposits in those three banks were those of 'foreigners.' "[37] Another student, making an investigation of Yugoslav life in the mining communities of Allegheny County, also placed much stress on thrift. One Slovene group called "Grannish" he described as being made up of thrifty people, "many of them having enough to build homes, some by taking in boarders, and some by starting grocery stores or other businesses."[38] In Cloverdale, Sygan, Moon Run, Presto, and Renton they have their own community halls, where meetings, dances, parties, and celebrations of various kinds are held. The younger generation, however, it is pointed out, is in great need of educational and recreational programs, which the parents have not thought worthwhile to provide. "The parents are inclined to think playing and reading stories a waste of time; they do not encourage athletic games because they wear out shoes and clothing; they discourage company in the home by being very careful of the good houses they have built."[39]

The preceding statements could easily be misinterpreted. It must, however, be emphasized that habits and attitudes of Yugoslav parents are very different from those of most Americans. The immigrants are a very practical, matter-of-fact people, and they encourage their children to engage in those activities or pastimes which will directly enhance their material well-being, which, in a sense, can be looked upon as a form of thrift.

101

## BANKS AND SAVINGS

As has already been observed, most of the South Slav immigrants came to the United States with very limited resources, unable to speak the English language, and unfamiliar with American customs and institutions. As a result they generally settled in the poorer sections of cities and found work in industries where conditions were poor, wages low, and hours long. The old-country ways and behavior of the immigrants often made them objects of suspicion and hostility on the part of the older groups in the population. Consequently, in order to gain an elevated status and increased security they turned to their fellow countrymen and to their own little colony. Under such circumstances they became easy prey for exploiters of all kinds, especially the unscrupulous immigrant bankers.

Immigrant banks, though relatively unimportant today, in the earlier decades of the twentieth century flourished in every part of the United States where immigrants from southeastern Europe were gathered in any considerable numbers. These banks arose because there was a definite need for them. The South Slavic, like most immigrant, communities had many needs which could be satisfied only by those who were familiar with the language, thought, customs, and habits of the people. There was money to be sent home, relatives and friends to be communicated with and brought to the United States, and various business affairs to be transacted in America and the old country. Such needs as these gave rise to the new financial institution.

Immigrant banks actually bore little resemblance to regular banking institutions. They were without real capital, had little or no legal responsibility, and for the most part were entirely without legal control. Immigrant bankers, as a rule, were also steamship ticket agents or notaries and usually conducted some other business as well. Consequently, the banks were usually located in groceries, saloons, or other establishments which were natural gathering places for immigrants.

Besides handling the savings of his patrons, the immigrant banker performed many necessary services for them. He wrote their letters, received their mail, and was their general advisor in important affairs. The ability and willingness of the banker to render such services naturally gave him an advantage over regular banking institutions, which would not and could not attend to such matters.

102

In this way immigrant bankers became important factors in the life of the immigrant.

The financial transactions of these bankers were confined mainly to the receiving of deposits and the transmission of money abroad. Deposits were not held as ordinary savings or commercial accounts, but represented, instead, sums of money left with the immigrant bankers merely for temporary safekeeping. They were not subject to check, and, as a rule, no interest was paid on them.[40] Except for an understanding that deposits were subject to demand at any time, no limitation was imposed upon the banker with respect to care or investment of these funds. A common use of deposits was that of direct investment in the proprietor's own business. A reserve fund was seldom maintained by the bank and, in case of failure or defalcation, depositors were left with little or no recourse.[41]

One of the earliest of these banking institutions was established in Pittsburgh in 1866. According to the newspaper *Napredak* (October 13, 1898), it operated under the name of "Croatian Bank," but it served partly as a bank and partly as a travel agency. Its founder was Max Schamberg, an Austrian honorary consul. The two names "Croatian Bank" and "Max Schamberg" appear somewhat confusing. In spite of the German tag, it is highly possible that Schamberg was a Croat or of Croatian descent, for there were Slavs in Austria who gave up their Slavic names and adopted German ones in their place. On the other hand, he could have been an Austrian and used the term "Croatian" in the name of his establishment because he operated in a Croat neighborhood and sought to obtain patronage from the immigrants of that nationality. In any event, whatever the truth of the matter was, Croatians in Pittsburgh did make use of the facilities of the bank.

Quite typical of South Slav immigrant banks was the business done by a Croatian saloonkeeper in Missouri. In this case deposits were received largely as an accommodation which the proprietor extended to his customers. He had a safe in the saloon, and those of his fellow Croatians who knew him well or had cause to trust him, found it convenient, from time to time, to leave small sums with him for safekeeping or for transmission abroad. His chief gain from his informal and friendly arrangement, as he himself asserted, lay in the fact that the accommodation provided served to increase his saloon trade. Accepting only such deposits as were brought in by his customers, he showed no disposition to extend his banking business so that it might become more directly remunerative to himself. He did not solicit deposits nor money for transmission, and did not advertise himself as a banker.[42] In short his banking business was merely subordinate and contributory to his saloon business.[43]

The proprietor had a drygoods store elsewhere in the city but no branch banking offices. His business was not incorporated, and his banking business was under no supervision or control. Beyond his stocks of liquors and drygoods, he had no capital invested and nothing behind his bank as security. He had, however, real estate, stock, and cash, approximately $5,000, with no liabilities, beyond current bills. His business methods and facilities were of the poorest. At one end of his bar was his safe and desk. These constituted his office—and bank. The only record that he had of the amount of deposits on hand was the duplicate of the slips that he issued to each depositor. These were destroyed as the deposits were withdrawn and others were issued upon a renewal of the account. His only records of money orders sold were the stubs in his money-order books. The business received his personal attention.[44]

On the day of the examination by the United States Immigration Commission the proprietor held $1,275 that had been left with him for safekeeping by eleven depositors. He had sometimes held as much as $6,000 of this kind of deposits. These sums he held intact in his checking account against withdrawal, so that they could be obtained in part or whole at any time. Although these deposits were not used for loans or investments, no distinction was made between the proprietor's personal funds and those of his depositors, and he drew upon either indiscriminately in meeting the obligations of his business. He had $500 on hand in his safe on the day of the examination. That amount he claimed to keep available at all times to meet any ordinary demands.[45]

During the first six months of 1909, this saloonkeeper received $3,607.89 for transmission abroad. He sold money orders (postal remittances) of an express company in New York City at a rate barely above cost, except on orders for less than 100 kronen (about $2), upon which he made a fair profit.[46]

The danger connected with banking of this character is obvious. In the long run it spelled disaster for the immigrants, as can very readily be seen by reference to a few outstanding examples.

One of the best known South Slav bankers was Frank Zotti, a Croat. With headquarters in New York and branches in Pittsburgh and Chicago and agencies all over the country, Zotti controlled a large financial empire. Besides the banks, he owned a chain of newspapers and operated a steamship company, the only boat of which was wrecked after being overworked.[47] The whole system came tumbling down in 1908 with unsecured liabilities of over $600,000.[48]

A Slovenian landlord who was in the habit of receiving money for transportation abroad through the mails defrauded his friends by substituting counterfeit money for the good money which they left with him.[49]

A Croatian grocer absconded with several thousand dollars that has been entrusted to him, but later returned and settled with his depositors by giving them notes, on the representation that his father in Europe was a very wealthy man, and that upon his death, he, the banker, would inherit a sum of money sufficient for the payment of these notes.[50]

Not many of these shrewd operators, however, returned from flight to face their depositors once more. Thus, a Croatian banker of Johnstown, Pennsylvania, got away with $75,000, while another of that nationality in Allegheny disappeared with $60,000.[51]

Such frauds perpetrated by these wily private bankers upon their less-wise countrymen caused the immigrants to become more cautious about where and to whom they entrusted their surplus funds. As a result, they sought to invest their savings in stable and dependable securities and institutions, staying clear of all kinds of speculations and wildcat promotions, and patronizing the post office or reputable American banks. Thus, they have been heavy investors in government bonds. In World War I they purchased $30,000,000 of Liberty Bonds,[52] and during World War II they bought $60,000,000 of War Bonds.[53]

In the study made in Chicago and Los Angeles by the author, the immigrants were reluctant to divulge the exact amount of their savings, but were not hesitant at all to explain the character of their investments and places of deposit. Out of 200 Yugoslavs interviewed in Chicago, 138, or 69 per cent, stated that they had savings, while in Los Angeles 91 out of 100 reported sav-

105

ings. Of the 138 depositors and investors in Chicago, 14, or 10.1 per cent, said they had their money invested in Yugoslav institutions, chiefly building and loan associations, 47, or 34 per cent, in American institutions, 74, or 53.7 per cent, in the post office, and 3, or 2.2 per cent, in varied miscellaneous places. It is also interesting to note that 123, or 89.1 per cent, bought war and government savings bonds. In Los Angeles, 29, or 31.8 per cent, out of the 91 showing savings deposited their money in Yugoslav institutions, 36, or 39.6 per cent, in American institutions, and 26, or 28.6 per cent, in the post office. Here the number buying government bonds was even greater than in Chicago—85, or 93.4 per cent. The comparatively large number of depositors in Yugoslav banks in Los Angeles may perhaps be explained by the fact that most of those institutions are closely tied in with the fishing industry, which, it should be re- membered, furnishes the immigrants with means of livelihood.

Since the poll of the writer was taken at a time (1945-1946) that could hardly be called normal, the results may not be typical or representative of the general conditions. Yet they should not be discounted entirely. They may at least be used as evidence of the savings habits of the South Slavs, not to say anything of their support of the government in time of national emergency.

### Aid to the Native Land

The Yugoslavs have frequently made sacrifices and dug deep into their savings in order to aid their relatives and friends in the old country. Like other immigrant groups, they, too, sent back remit- tances with regularity in the earlier days. It was common practice for the males who came to the United States from the 1880's to 1900 to send home as much as 80 per cent of their wages. As living conditions improved, however, this was gradually reduced until it fell to about 20 per cent.[54] Examining this help to the folks back home, one writer commented:

Not only did America absorb countless shiploads of hitherto dissatisfied humanity, but the emigrants sent back a quarter to a half of their wages to relatives in thousands of European com- munities. And this money from America was even more im- portant than the siphoning off of a sizable portion of the popula- tion. Millions of escaped Europeans laboring in American mills, mines and forests not only supported themselves in the United States but helped to feed and clothe their relatives back home.[55]

The Immigration Commission in its investigation of immigrant remittances revealed that $38,700,000 was sent home by the immigrants in the United States through all the banks in Austria in the period from 1892 to 1902, with one-third going to Bohemia, one-third to Galicia, and one-third to Croatia and Hungary.[56] In the same study it was shown that four Croatian banks in 1909 had remitted through them $16,093.94.[57] Although, as is evident, the total amount sent abroad by the immigrants was large, it is interesting to note that individual transmissions were comparatively small. Thus, the average amount of the remittances of the four Croatian banks was $42.24.[58]

War, immigration legislation, and depression acted as serious checks upon remittances. Nevertheless, it is estimated that even after restriction of immigration to the United States, Yugoslavs in this country were sending back from twenty to forty million dollars annually.[59] During the depression years of the thirties most of the remittances were much smaller than formerly, if not stopped completely. As a matter of fact, all remittances were growing steadily smaller since 1919, when the peak of $60,000,000 was reached.[60] Earlier immigrant remittances had averaged $150,000,000 a year.[61] The steady decline of the amount of the remittances is seen in the table below:[62]

TABLE 11

IMMIGRANT REMITTANCES

| Year | Remittances |
|------|-------------|
| 1922 | $400,000,000 |
| 1924 | 285,000,000 |
| 1926 | 253,000,000 |
| 1928 | 217,000,000 |
| 1930 | 195,000,000 |
| 1931 | 173,000,000 |

There are several reasons for the decrease in the amount of money sent to European countries by immigrants in the United States. In the first place, many of the aliens eventually managed to bring their dependents to America, thus eliminating the need for

107

remittances to Europe. Secondly, the depression brought wide-spread unemployment, making it difficult for the immigrants to earn a bare living, let alone send monetary aid to relatives at home. And lastly, the period of prosperity in Europe, following World War I, though of brief duration, improved the material conditions of the population, thereby proportionately reducing the need for help from America.

Although most Americans were indifferent toward the question of immigrant remittances, there were some who expressed vigorous disapproval, asserting that the money taken out of this country was detrimental to the American economy. Jenks and Lauck, carefully analyzing the situation, concluded:

> It can hardly be said that taken by itself the sending back to the old country of the savings of the immigrant is directly an injury to the United States. Speaking broadly, for every dollar sent more than a dollar's worth of productive labor has been expended here. The worker has fully earned his dollar. On the other hand, if that dollar, instead of being invested in his home country, were invested in the United States the benefit would be greater. America would have the productive influence not only of the labor but also of the capital made from the savings.[63]

Assistance to relatives and friends in the old country has not all been in monetary form. Impressive also has been the aid in material goods. Although no reliable figures are available, the value of the commodities has probably corresponded fairly closely to the remittances. According to one source, in just the short period from 1945 to September 30, 1948, Yugoslav immigrants from all over the world contributed $778,000,000 (in money and goods) to the rebuilding of their native land, most of it coming from American Yugoslavs.[64]

Yugoslavs have been especially liberal in supplying the folks in the old country with articles difficult to obtain at home. This has been particularly true during war and the years immediately following, when the economy of the homeland stood at its lowest ebb. Thus, in 1947 Yugoslavs in all parts of the country contributed generously a wide variety of items to be sent abroad. The Yugoslav ship "Radnik" picked up much of it, sailing back in October loaded with over three tons of new and used tools and instruments, scientific books, catalogues, and other publications, all urgently needed for the reconstruction of the mother country.[65]

# 6

# Organizations

ORGANIZATIONS of various kinds are an important part of the pattern of American life. Being a free people, we organize ourselves into small and large groups for a wide variety of purposes: social, religious, political, financial, fraternal, or racial. Some of these organizations are formed to meet a special need, and when the purpose has been achieved the group disbands. Others are more permanent in nature because the needs which bring them into being persist over a longer period. An understanding of the organizational activities in our society is necessary for an appraisal of the forces that motivate our changing pattern of national life.

## SIGNIFICANCE

There is a natural tendency for those who come to America from other lands to form organizations based primarily on similarities of origin, language, or background. In a strange land they feel a special kinship with other immigrants, particularly those from the same country. The desire for companionship and social contacts, the need to solve problems having to do with housing and employment, and the need for help in crises all stimulate the formation of small local groups. Frequently scattered local groups with similar purposes unite to form state and sometimes national organizations. Whatever their purpose or length of existence the chief binding force of these groups is their common origin.

Yugoslav organizations provide us with a view of Yugoslav American life obtainable in no other way. In these groups we see

109

a people struggling to take on a new culture and become self-sufficient in new social and economic situations. The leaders of Yugoslav organizations are frequently prominent persons in the community, and the activities and influence of the organizations often reach far beyond the actual membership.

It has frequently been argued that one of the greatest weaknesses of the Yugoslavs is their inability to work together, but the associations which they have established in the United States seem to invalidate such criticisms. Their achievements are praiseworthy and have been widely recognized. Considering the scattered groups of poor and ignorant immigrants, completely unaccustomed to organization and unacquainted with parliamentary procedure, from which the societies must draw a large part of their membership, one cannot help but conclude that their growth has been phenomenal and their success immeasurable.

## AIMS AND OBJECTIVES

As immigration increased the number of South Slavs in this country, organizations grew in size and number. In time nearly all Yugoslavs in America became members of one or more such societies. Common speech and customs naturally draw immigrants together. At times political aims have caused them to unite. This is true of most Slav immigrants, but more important is the urge to join groups in order to overcome economic insecurity and weakness.[1]*

The economic motivations of union are not difficult to explain. To begin with, the Yugoslavs are predominantly wage earners, and as such are quickly a prey to unemployment during depressions and at times when there is little work due to seasonal lulls. At such times they need the assistance of mutual aid societies. Also, the dangerous character of the work in the mines and foundries which employ so many Slavs is calculated to enhance their appreciation of advantages of mutual aid. The primary reason why Yugoslavs become members of organizations is the financial assistance such associations offer to members. The Yugoslav benevolent fraternal unions often combine the functions of insurance societies and of associations for assisting unemployed and disabled workers.

* Notes to this chapter begin on page 291.

110

Though mutual insurance is the chief purpose of most of the organizations, there are other aims, such as providing recreation and entertainment, promoting study of both Yugoslav and American languages and institutions, encouraging choral, literary, and artistic productions, attending to spiritual needs, stimulating political interest, interpreting America to Yugoslavs here and abroad as well as Yugoslavia to Americans, and providing spiritual and material assistance to relatives, friends, and countrymen in Yugoslavia. The Croatian Fraternal Union, for instance, maintains a sports fund, a relief fund, and an educational fund. Through the sports fund athletic contests of various kinds are promoted among the Slavic youth of the country. From the relief fund many hundreds of thousands of dollars are contributed to victims of floods, earthquake, famine, fire, and similar disasters.[2] The federation maintains a children's home (in Des Plaines, Illinois) for the orphans of its deceased members and children of indigent members. The educational reserve enables talented young Yugoslavs to obtain a formal education at the expense of the society. Slavic organizations similar to the Croatian Fraternal Union devote a large portion of their programs and funds to promote Americanization.

A primary aim of some Yugoslav societies has been to aid their European brethren in their fight for freedom. Their concerted efforts did much to bring about the creation of the Yugoslav state following World War I.[3] Though few, if any, Yugoslavs today regard their communities as colonies of their homeland, they do take pride in the land of their origin and keep in touch with it. Yugoslavia has many contacts with America because there are few villages in Yugoslavia that do not have somebody in America. The United Committee of South-Slavic Americans was founded in 1943 in part to assist the countrymen at home by publicizing in America the facts concerning the internal conditions of Yugoslavia during World War II, particularly the developments in the struggle between the Partisans and the Chetniks.

The South Slavs take pride in their mother tongue, and many groups conduct schools where the children may learn the language of their forefathers. The foreign-language schools are either secular or parochial, and classes are usually held in the afternoon and on Saturday and Sunday mornings. In these classes children learn to read, write, and speak the language of their parents. At times history and folklore are added.

111

Though not as strong as formerly, there are still in existence physical culture groups, such as the Sokol (Falcon) and Orlovi (Eagles) societies. Similar to the German Turnverein, these athletic associations were transplanted to America by the Slavs for the purpose of improving their youth physically, and to build such qualities as courage, devotion to duty, patriotism, and other high moral ideals.

Not infrequently have the original aims of an organization been lost sight of, blurred, and/or subordinated as new ones were added. An excellent illustration of this type of development is seen in the Yugoslav Club of San Pedro, California. A community of social interests was responsible for the establishment of this club. But rapid growth soon led to an expansion of the social aims so as to include political and economic objectives and activities as well. Thus, today, political and economic committees are important organs of the society. It is the function of the political committee to investigate candidates for office, campaigns, and issues, and to explain its findings to the members in order to guide them in making intelligent selections. The economic committee, similarly, studies tax and property problems, harbor facilities and needs, and general civic problems and submits the results of its investigations to the club for discussion and further action. All of this has done much to broaden the scope and activities of the organization and, at the same time, has added to its accomplishments and prestige.

It is thus evident that some societies have social or recreational objectives, others patriotic or nationalistic, striving toward the political independence and the improvement of their nationality in Europe, and still others, by far the greater number, economic, seeking to protect members against loss occasioned by sickness and death. The various organizations play an important role in aiding the immigrant to adjust to the new environment. Some function to protect the uninitiated immigrants in their rights and safeguard them against impostors and other exploiters. In some instances they serve to promote assimilation, especially by encouraging their members to learn English, become citizens, and adopt American ways.

## INCOME

Organizations generally derive their income from four principal sources, namely: dues, sponsored activities, investments, and dona-

112

tions. The bulk of the income of most societies comes from membership dues. These vary from a dollar a year to five or more dollars per month, depending largely upon the nature, purpose, and size of the organization. Various kinds of activities given under the auspices of the societies bring in sizable returns. In this category are included chiefly recreational and educational functions, such as dances, plays, movies, concerts, recitals, card and bunco parties, raffles, bingo games, festivals, picnics, exhibitions, and lectures. Selling books and pamphlets is another device often used to supplement the regular income of the organizations. Investments form a valuable source of income for the large organizations, but are relatively unimportant so far as the small groups are concerned. Surplus funds of the societies are generally invested in securities (private and public), real estate, and commercial and industrial enterprises. Donations, though not as a rule very significant, sometimes help to carry associations through trying times or to boost them over the top in some drive. Such contributions seldom come from wealthy, philanthropic individuals, but rather from generous, sympathetic Slavs who, it seems, are always ready to support a worthy cause by donating whatever few dollars they can spare from their not-too-large paychecks.

## PLAN OF ORGANIZATION

The societies are managed by elected officers, consisting generally of a president, vice-president, financial and recording secretaries, treasurer, sometimes a standard-bearer, and a sergeant-at-arms. In addition, musical organizations have directors; sports associations, coaches and managers; and benefit lodges, visitors of the sick. The societies usually hold monthly meetings at which dues are collected and other affairs discussed and decided. If the local group is a unit of a larger (state, regional, or national) organization, then part of the dues is sent to the home office, while the balance is retained in the local treasury for such expenses as the branch may have.

In cases of federations, reaching across several states or the entire continent, conventions are usually held every two, three, or four years. At these conventions binding decisions are taken as to the use of organizational funds. Here also are elected the supreme officers, including the president, one or more vice-presidents, one or two secretaries, and a treasurer, who together constitute the

113

executive committee, and sometimes, depending on type of organization, three or more auditors, a manager for the association's
printing plant, an editor of its newspaper or magazine, medical and
legal advisors, and, if strongly religious, a spiritual advisor. The
board of directors, and various special committees, such as press,
orphanage, home for children or aged, or whatever may be the
added activity of the association, are also elected at the convention.
The executive committee, the auditors, and the director sometimes
make up what is known as a supreme council. This body convenes
once a year between conventions and makes decisions on current
matters of the organization over which the executive committee
has no jurisdiction.

## MEETING PLACES

To house the diverse activities of the Yugoslavs in various centers, hundreds of buildings have been acquired, some handsome,
well-equipped structures and others merely rented rooms or lofts
over stores in run-down quarters of towns. The general plan of
the buildings and the types of program are everywhere pretty much
the same. As a rule, the community center contains a restaurant,
which is generally filled with smoke and the odor of beer and wine,
but wholly respectable, and used by families for parties, committee
meeting rooms, a gymnasium, sometimes a library, and a spacious
hall for lectures, dances, concerts, and theatrical productions.

The halls are busiest as social and educational centers on Satur-
days and Sundays. In the mornings on these days the young people
come for lessons in the language of their parents. Musical concerts
or plays are usually given on Sunday afternoons, with dancing
following later in the evening. During the week, evenings are devoted to committee meetings, club activities, and physical training
in the gymnasium.

## FRATERNAL BENEFIT SOCIETIES

Nearly every Slavic group has large national fraternal federations, which have branches in every community of any size. In
addition, many communities have their own local clubs and societies. The local groups, known as lodges, branches, assemblies,

circles, brotherhoods, or sisterhoods, form the very foundation of the national organizations. Through them, the individual adult members belong to the parent organization, pay their dues, and participate through direct vote or through delegates in directing their affairs and electing their supreme officers. The children of members, usually up to the ages of sixteen or eighteen years, may also belong to the lodge or to its junior section, generally called a nest, and may benefit from various juvenile insurance features. They, however, are not permitted to participate in elections or in any other administrative activities and decisions until they are old enough to be transferred to the adult division.

Today, Yugoslavs are to be found in every state and territory of the United States; there are some eight hundred urban centers where settlements are sufficiently large to warrant formation of organized bodies. Like other immigrant groups, Yugoslavs maintain numerous fraternal benefit societies. These organizations, for the most part, had their origins in the last decades of the nineteenth century when the immigrant workers, in need of social and economic security, banded together.

The alien learned soon after his arrival that when he got sick there was no household group to take care of him as in Europe. In America he was dependent on the good offices of his companions, who were not as close to him as his family had been. Accordingly, mutual benefit societies were established to provide for him in case of sickness or death.

It is quite natural that men who had come over together, who had the same boyhood memories, who had settled in the same place in the United States, and who had similar needs, should have an organization together. The first associations were formed in San Francisco, New Orleans, New York, Hoboken, and Calumet, Michigan. The first organization on record is the Slavonian Mutual and Benevolent Society, founded in San Francisco in 1857 by the Croats of the area. Its aim was both social and beneficial, bringing into a common brotherhood the South Slav immigrants of the bay region and assisting them in time of illness and distress. The official languages were Croatian and English. In New Orleans, where the South Slavs settled at a relatively early date, the United Slavonian Benevolent Association was formed in 1874. In New York the Austrijansko Dobrotvorno Društvo (Austrian Benevolent Society), later known as the First Croatian Benefit Society, was

115

organized in 1880 by the Dalmatians from Austria. In 1890 the Croats of Hoboken, New Jersey, formed the Slavjansko Dobrotvorno Društvo (Slavonian Benevolent Society). Two years later the Croatians of Benwood and Wheeling, West Virginia, founded the Franje Josipe Društvo (Francis Joseph Society). Then in 1894 followed the establishment of the Hrvatsko Radničko Podupirajuce Društvo Starčević u Allegheny (Croatian Workingmen's Beneficial Society Starčević in Allegheny), which subsequently became Lodge No. 1 of the Croatian Fraternal Union. During the same year the Dalmatians of San Jose, California, formed the Slavonian-American Benevolent Society. The Croatian Fraternal and Beneficial Association Sloga (Harmony) was founded in Pittsburgh in 1905. The earliest benefit lodge of the Serbs was the First Serbian Benevolent Society, formed in San Francisco in 1880. The Slovenes set up their first society in 1882 in Calumet, Michigan, called the Independent Society of St. Joseph. Many of these pioneer organizations still exist, and have some 6,000 sister societies in over 1,000 towns and cities of 39 states (including Alaska) and Canada. When one considers the fact that these fraternal benefit societies were begun by men with limited formal training of any kind, the results are the more remarkable.

At the beginning the societies remained merely small local organizations, but eventually, mainly under the stimuli of tightening insurance laws and hard times, a trend toward federation along national lines developed. An example of this movement in the direction of amalgamation and centralization is seen at work in the creation and growth of the Croatian Fraternal Union. This organization had its beginning when a group of fraternal leaders from lodges in Wheeling, West Virginia, Allegheny City, McKeesport, Etna, Johnstown, and Braddock, Pennsylvania, desiring to create a central capital for the American Croats and encouraged by the combinations of Czechs and Poles into national associations, met in Allegheny City in September, 1894, elected officers from their own number, and took out a charter. The name given to the new federation was the Hrvatsko Društvo u Sjedinjenim Državama Amerike (Croatian Society of the United States of America), but three years later it was changed to Narodna Hrvatska Zajednica (National Croatian Union). Financially, the centralization consisted in having sick benefits administered by the local unit and death benefits emanate from the federation itself. The earliest locals that joined the association, as is evident, were all located near Pittsburgh, but as expansion continued lodges from more distant places signed up, so that in time membership extended across the continent. In 1925 the bonds between the numerous scattered branches were tightened, the administration revamped so as to bring about greater centralization, a merger effected with the Croatian League of Illinois and the St. Joseph Society of Kansas City, and the name of the federation changed to Hrvatska Bratska Zajednica u Americi (Croatian Fraternal Union of America). Thus was created a fraternal giant which today ranks as the twenty-fourth largest fraternal benefit association on the North American continent.

Some years elapsed between the founding of the first federation by the Croats and the last such organization of any permanence. It was not until 1921 that the Hrvatska Katolička Zajednica u Sjedinjenim Državama Amerike (Croatian Catholic Union of the United States of America) was launched in Gary, Indiana. It, too, has enjoyed a vigorous life.

The growth of national federations among the Slovenes and Serbs has paralleled that of the Croats. The Kranjsko-Slovenska Katoliška Jednota v Združenih Državah Ameriških (Grand Carniolian Slovenian Catholic Union of the United States of America), founded in Joliet, Illinois, in 1894, was the first of the Slovene fraternal unions. Then followed in succession the establishment of the Jugoslavanska Katoliška Jednota (South Slavonic Catholic Union)—renamed Ameriška Bratska Zveza (American Fraternal Union) in 1941—in Ely, Minnesota, in 1898; the Slovenska Narodna Potporna Jednota (Slovene National Benefit Society) in Chicago, in 1904; the Zapadna Slovanska Zveza (Western Slavonic Association) in Denver, Colorado, in 1908; the Slovenian Workingmen's Benefit Association in Johnstown, Pennsylvania, also in 1908; the Slovenska Dobrodelna Zveza (Slovenian Mutual Benefit Association) in Cleveland, Ohio, in 1910; the Družba Svete Družine (Holy Family Society of the U.S.A.) in Joliet, Illinois, in 1914; and the Slovenska Ženska Zveza v Ameriki (Slovenian Women's Union of America) in Sheboygan, Wisconsin, in 1926.

The first of the Serbian federations was launched in 1901 in McKeesport, Pennsylvania, under the name of Srpski Pravoslavni Savez Srbobran (Serb Orthodox Federation Serb Sentinel). Others rapidly joined the movement. In 1903 were founded in Chicago

117

the Prvi Srpski Dobrotvorni Savez (First Serbian Beneficial Federation) and the Prvi Crnogorski Savez (First Montenegrin Federation) and in 1906 the Srpski Crnogorski Savez (Serb Montenegrin Federation) in Butte, Montana. Three years later the first three of these joined forces in the Savez Sjedinjenih Srba Sloga (United Serb Federation Harmony) at a meeting held in Cleveland. Harmony, however, proved to be only a name and not a distinguishing characteristic of the new combination. Rivalries, jealousies, and quarrels made any real cooperation impossible. As a result of the dissension a number of the societies withdrew from the federation and subsequently formed new unions, some of the more important of which were the Srpski Savez Sloboda (Serb Federation Freedom) and the Sjedinjeni Savez Srbobran-Sloga (United Federation Serb Sentinel-Harmony). This, in turn, led to the dissolution of the Cleveland federation. Some of the individual lodges in Chicago, Los Angeles, and Cleveland felt the need of a larger organization and so banded together in 1920 at Cleveland to found the Srpski Narodni Savez Jedinstvo (Serbian Beneficial Federation Unity). Finally, in 1929, Srbobran combined with the Sloboda and Srbobran-Sloga groups to create the Srpski Narodni Savez (Serb National Federation) in Pittsburgh. Experience has shown that the formation of these various national federations was a step in the right direction.

The growth of the societies was remarkable. As early as 1893, notes the *Cleveland Plain Dealer* of May 30, 1896, there were delegations from 116 lodges at the convention of the National Slavonic Society held in Cleveland in that year. By the mid-twenties, when the number of immigrants in the country was at an all-time high, the Slovenes had seven national associations consisting of 1,140 local units with more than 124,000 members and assets of over $5,500,000. The Croats had four benefit federations with 580 branches, 84,000 members, and a capital of nearly $4,000,000. Finally, the Serbs had four federations of 269 lodges with 20,000 members and a capital of about $345,000.[4]

The number of national federations was subsequently reduced as further amalgamation became necessary to avert complete dissolution during the depression. In the wake of the mergers of the federations followed additional consolidation through the reduction of the number of adult lodges in each of the associations. This, however, did not mean a decreased adult membership. As a matter of fact, the move was accompanied by a perceptible increase of the older members.

As a result of the many changes and shifts during the past thirty years, today there are eleven national unions with a combined membership of about 350,000 persons. Junior branches include over 100,000 members, the majority of whom are American-born boys and girls. The member lodges of these federations total nearly 3,000. The total insurance in force surpasses $240,000,000 and the assets are about $75,000,000. Approximately $5,000,000 are paid annually in benefits to members and their families. These associations range in size from the huge Croatian Fraternal Union, whose nearly 1,100 branches (including adult and juvenile) have over 100,000 members with nearly $90,000,000 insurance in force, and assets of $25,000,000, to the tiny Holy Family Society, which has only 12 branches with some 1,100 members, $525,000 of insurance in force, and assets totaling $175,000.

During World War II and the years immediately following, large numbers of Yugoslavs joined the International Workers Order, which admitted members of all nationality backgrounds and maintained for each nationality a separate section. In quick order, branches of the society were founded in South Slavic communities across the nation. However, the life of the mushrooming association was cut short by the United States government, which declared it subversive and Communist and ordered its dissolution.

Though not a fraternal benefit lodge but, nevertheless, worthy of mention is an insurance organization that has caught on rapidly and shown unprecedented growth, the Commercial Fisherman's Inter-Insurance Exchange on the West Coast. This maritime insurance association was organized by a group of commercial fishing-boat owners of San Pedro, California, in September, 1943, for the purpose of insuring their rapidly increasing fishing properties. In April, 1944, the company extended its franchise into the state of Washington, and by May, 1946, it began operations also in Oregon. In the short time that the organization has been in existence its assets have risen to over $200,000 and the total insurance in force to over $4,000,000. As the Yugoslavs expand their holdings and interest in the commercial fishing industry on the Pacific Coast, undoubtedly the new company will experience a parallel growth.

Nearly all fraternal benefit societies at first admitted to membership only immigrants of their own nationality, their descendants,

119

and relatives by marriage. More recently, however, such strict rules of membership have been considerably relaxed. As a result, it is no longer unusual to see Croats, Serbs, and Slovenes members of the same society. This new trend has been of tremendous help in breaking down the barriers between the various nationality and minority groups.

The mutual benefit societies have sometimes been accused of hoarding their funds and ignoring the needs of the American-born offspring of the immigrants. This led to the assumption that the organizations would die out with the passing of the aliens. Perhaps in an earlier period of their existence the societies concentrated their attention on the first generation and neglected the later ones. That, however, has not been the practice since at least the 1920's. In the last thirty odd years more and more funds have been expended to promote recreational and educational programs for the children and grandchildren of the immigrants. The result has been a continual growth of the juvenile orders.

The great strides, material and spiritual, made by the many benefit societies and federations must be attributed, at least in part, to the remarkable leadership provided by the officials of these organizations. Their courage, initiative, industry, perseverance, and foresight helped to build bigger, better, and stronger societies. Without such individuals the tremendous gains made in the last generation would have been impossible.

It is not intended to present a directory of the fraternal leaders of the Yugoslav Americans, but it does seem in order to mention some of the more conspicuous ones. For many years one of the outstanding men in the field was John D. Butkovich, former president of the Croatian Fraternal Union. During his long tenure Butkovich did much to erect a strong foundation for the federation. The work of Butkovich has been capably carried forward under his successor, V. I. Mandich. This popular executive has led the association to ever-greater heights, with membership, assets, and amount of insurance in force reaching unprecedented levels. Under his guidance the society joined President Dwight Eisenhower's "People to People" peace and friendship program, in which he was presently invested with the post of chairman of the Nationalities Division Finance Committee. Aiding Mandich in the steady upward climb has been an efficient administrative staff, comprising Joseph Bella, Martin Krasich, John Ovcarich, and Michael Grasha. Among the

Croats of the Midwest well known and respected are the names of Louis C. Samaržija, president of the Croatian Catholic Union, Joseph Saban, vice-president, George Ramuscak, secretary, Steve Cvetetich, treasurer, and Joseph Erdeljac, head of the board of trustees.

The Slovenes too have produced their share of outstanding organizational leaders. Joseph L. Culkar has been a tireless worker in behalf of the Slovene National Benefit Society, which he heads. With the able help of F. A. Vider, Anton Trojar, M. G. Kuhel, Lawrence Gradisek, and Michael Vrhovnik, Culkar has sponsored a sound, constructive program, with the most beneficial results. The Grand Carniolian Catholic Union has been blessed in having such devoted and energetic officials as Anton Grdina, past president and now honorary president, John Germ, active president, and Joseph J. Nemanich, Joseph Zalar, Louis Zeleznikar, and Robert L. Kosmerl, members of the supreme governing board. Other notable fraternalists worthy of mention are John Susnik, John A. Kodrich, and Joško Penko, supreme officers of the Slovenian Mutual Benefit Association; Frank J. Kress, C. J. Rovansek, Frank Tomsich, Barbara Matesha, Louis Champa of the American Fraternal Union; Leo Jurjovec, George J. Miroslavich, Mile Popovich, Anthony Jersin, Michael P. Horvat, and Edward Krasovich of the Western Slavonic Association; Steve Kosar, Nickolas Pavlakovich, Frank J. Wedic, Joseph L. Drasler, and Anton Smrekar, the directors of the Holy Family Society.

The Slovene women have their own organization and their own leaders. Their society is the previously mentioned Slovenian Women's Union. Founded by Marie Prisland, the association is now successfully managed by Josephine Livek, president, and a talented corps of assistants including Frances Globokar, Albina Novak, Josephine Zeleznikar, Mary Otonicar, Katie Triller, and Josephine Sumic.

Like the Croats and Slovenes, the Serbs have also developed a select class of fraternal officials of high caliber. Charles Bojanic, the personable president of the Serb National Federation, has done an admirable job in strengthening and expanding his society. Working along with Bojanic has been a highly dependable group of officers composed of Louis Balta, Dushan Ljubenko, Milan Tomich, Mileta Milovanovich, Dan L. Kovacevich, and Daniel Stepanovich. The growth of Serbian Beneficial Federation Unity has been greatly accelerated by such competent administrators as Steve Zernich, Eli Zegarac, N. J. Vurdelja, Nick Uzelac, and Spiro Andrich.

## CULTURAL AND SOCIAL GROUPS

Though rather uncoordinated and often financially handicapped, organizational cultural and social activities are numerous. Thus, there are something like 125 singing societies, with two federations, one a Serbian and the other a Slovenian. The Croatian singing society Zora (Dawn) is not only the oldest organization of its kind but the model for others. Wherever the Zora performs there is bound to be a large gathering of Yugoslavs. Kolo (circle) dancers are found in nearly all the larger colonies. In addition there are some fifty dramatic groups and as many *tamburica* orchestras.

The *tamburica* claims an ancestry ranging back to early Christian times. It began as a simple one-stringed instrument played by the shepherds, developed as travelers from the East brought word of their lute, and has come into its own as the modern *tamburica*. Like other instruments, *tamburice* are divided into two principal choirs: the *brači* which correspond to the violins, and the *primi* which play an octave higher. The instrument family is completed with various tenor, accompaniment, and bass instruments such as the *cellobrač, bugarija,* and the *berda* (base) which looks like a bass viol but is plucked.

Among the best-known and most widely praised *tamburica* orchestras are the Tamburitzans of Duquesne University, a unique organization of its type, which has performed before large, enthusiastic audiences in many parts of the United States as well as in Yugoslavia. The Duquesne orchestra owes much to its organizer and leader, Matt L. Gouze, who began his work in the 1930's at Minnesota's College of St. Thomas, and who then transferred to St. Edward's University in Texas where he organized the famed American Tamburitza Orchestra before finally moving over to the Pittsburgh institution. Gouze has recruited green musical talent from many Yugoslav communities in the United States and helped it bloom under his capable guidance. Led by such clubs as the Tamburitzans, the musical organizations have not only been instrumental in keeping alive the songs and melodies of the native land among the immigrants but have also been responsible for introducing unfamiliar Slavic folk songs to American audiences.

Also contributing to the variety of American culture are such groups as the Order of Cankar, the Croatian Cultural-Educational Federation, and the Yugoslav Educational Federation. Other cultural organizations include the Yugoslav Federation, the Circle of Serbian Sisters Societies, Croatian Ladies, Yugoslav Ladies, and the Slovene Ladies Federation, all being humanitarian in nature with the exception of the first named. Nearly every large Yugoslav community has a branch of a veterans' organization, such as the American Yugoslav Legion. There are, besides, in the South Slav colonies in the country nearly two hundred national homes which serve as important centers of group activities. Other Yugoslav clubs, including university organizations, also tend strongly toward social, literary, and artistic activities.

The principal religious organizations are the Bishop Baraga Association, the Croatian Franciscan Commissariat, and the Serbian Orthodox Eparchy.

Associations whose aims are primarily political include the Croatian Circle, the Croatian Republican Peasants party, the Jugoslav Socialist Federation, and the South Slavonian Socialist Labor Federation. The last named, particularly, is strongly organized and possesses a capable and enlightened leadership.

In physical culture the names of the Sokol and Orlovi societies stand out. The Sokols have twenty societies in the United States, with a total membership of about 3,000. Fifteen of these are independent societies, while the other five compose the Yugoslav Sokol Federation of Chicago. This federation has two subdivisions, one for the Chicago district and the other for the Pacific Coast.

The physical culture associations enlisted a wide following in the earlier days of immigration, reaching their zenith in the twenties. But in more recent times they have been on the downgrade, which seems to point to either complete dissolution or loss of independent status. One reason for the decline is the injection of politics into organizational activities. But, perhaps, a more important contributing factor to the retrogression is the role of the fraternal federations. These associations have steadily expanded their sports and recreational programs; and thus, with their attractive offers of insurance and recreation, they have been able to lure many of the youth into their fold. Practically all the large national federations now sponsor basketball and baseball teams, which finish each season with a grand national tournament in some large Yugoslav center, giving rise to a community-wide celebration lasting for several weeks.

## ORGANIZATIONS IN WARTIME

During World War I native American feeling against all foreign societies became intense. Their very presence was construed as evidence of nonassimilation, if not outright disloyalty. Nevertheless, the Yugoslavs, who were then largely recent immigrants, took a great deal of personal interest in the developments in their European homeland and in its future. Aside from sending money to the old country, many joined volunteer battalions to fight with the South Slav forces.

A prominent role was played among the Croatian immigrants by the Hrvatski Savez (Croatian Alliance), which had been founded in 1912 under the leadership of Reverend Nikola Gršković, who three years earlier had assumed the important post of editor of *Zajedničar*, the official organ of the National Croatian Union. The organization, originally designed to support the Croatian revolutionary movement in Austria-Hungary, appealed to all the Croats in America to join hands with it in the struggle against the Dual Monarchy. Under the guidance of its dynamic president, Reverend Nikola Gršković, popularly known as Don Niko, and the able assistance of Dr. Ante Biankini and Gabro Rački, its vice-president and secretary, respectively, the society sought to publicize its program by every means possible (using even the pages of the *Zajedničar* for the purpose) and to win adherents for its cause. In a short time, however, Don Niko made a spectacular switch from an ardent advocate of Croatian nationalism to a fervent proponent of the union of the Croats, Serbs, and Slovenes. And so during the period of the war he carried forth the banner of Yugoslav unity.

Simultaneously, the Slovenian Republican Alliance (later expanded and known as the Jugo-Slav Republican Alliance), initially established by the Slovenes in America, had as its primary objective the spread of propaganda in favor of the creation of a Yugoslav federal republic, in which European Slovenes would have full representation and rights, and the erection of national boundaries based on ethnological principles.[5] Led by its chairman, Etbin Kristan, the organization conducted an energetic campaign throughout the country, carrying the fight for Yugoslav rights and recognition to the very floor of the United States Congress. Appearing before the Senate Foreign Relations Committee in 1919, Kristan delivered a forceful speech in behalf of the Yugoslavs, who were at the time engaged in a boundary dispute with the Italians.[6]

Another important organization that was set up during the period of the war was the Jugoslavensko Narodno Vijeće (Yugoslav National Council), which sought to promote the Yugoslav idea in the United States and thus lighten the burdens of the home organizations with similar aims. Several distinguished Yugoslav Americans, including Professor Michael Pupin of Columbia University, the noted Chicago medic and publicist Dr. Ante Biankini, and the aggressive journalist and fraternalist Don Niko Gršković, gave unstintingly of their time and talents in behalf of Yugoslav independence and unity as members of the Jugoslavenski Odbor u Londonu (Yugoslav Committee in London), whose principal function was the promotion of cordial relations between the Allied Powers and the Balkan Slavs. Indeed, during the entire period of the struggle numerous meetings were held in various parts of the country by the South Slavs in order to keep the immigrants and Americans alike informed on the issues and progress of the war.[7]

To be sure, not all the organizations that sprang up during the war years were political and propagandist. Somewhat different in character and purpose was the Society for the Advancement of Slavic Study, which the South Slavs, led by Professor Milosh Trivunac, aided in founding at a meeting in Cleveland on June 15, 1917. This group, made up largely of educators, had as its chief aim the encouragement of the study of Slavic languages, literature, history, art, and culture in the United States as a means of fostering understanding and better relations between the Slavs and Americans.

World War II saw a repetition of the organizations and activities of the earlier struggle, but on a much grander scale. It was not long after the mother country was attacked by Hitler that the American Yugoslavs organized the Yugoslav Relief Committee in New York to aid their beleaguered comrades at home. Millions of dollars in clothing, food, medical supplies, and other necessities were sent to Yugoslavia. After the fighting stopped, the American Association for Reconstruction in Yugoslavia (AARY) was set up and helped to carry on from the point where the relief committee had left off. It, too, was exceedingly successful in its work, shipping to Yugoslavia thousands of tons of badly needed materials.

In April, 1942, the Yugoslavs joined other Slavs in the formation of the American Slav Congress, composed of thirteen national groups and representing through the affiliated organizations, directly or indirectly, the 10,000,000 American Slavs. According to its officials, one of the primary aims of the congress was, "To help win the war as quickly as possible by maintaining and increasing production, promotion of sale of War Bonds, and all other activities necessary to speed up complete destruction of Nazism and Fascism."[8] Unfortunately, this did not bring the desired unity; friction and differences continued even among the smallest branches (e.g., Ukrainians vs. Russians, Slovaks vs. Czechs, and Serbs vs. Croats).

Manifestations of disunity were plentiful among the South Slavs as well as among the members of the large Slavic family. The Union of Slovenian Parishes of America through its support of the Slovenian People's party, a clerical, reactionary, opportunist, and fascist-inclined organization, helped to drive a wedge among the Slovenes. Similarly, the Hrvatski Domobran (Croat Home Defense), a Croat group with headquarters in Pittsburgh and favoring Pavelić's puppet state of Croatia, caused much ill feeling and dissension not only among the Croatians but among all Yugoslavs. Unity was further disrupted by the work of the Serbian National Defense Council of America. Reason gave way to emotion as the members of these and other similar groups became entangled in a vitriolic verbal combat in the fanatic pursuit of their selfish goals. Charges and countercharges were hurled back and forth. "Spy!" "Traitor!" "Assassin!" were among some of the choice invectives which helped to sow seeds of hatred and disunity among all the branches of the Yugoslav family in America.

Fortunately, the disunity engendered by such misguided organizations was at least partially offset by the work of the United Committee of South-Slavic Americans, founded in 1943. The first meeting of the latter was held in the Slovene National Home in Cleveland under the leadership of author Louis Adamic, who was chosen president. The organization formulated a ten-point program of action to unite the South Slavs behind President Roosevelt's win-the-war formula and to aid the Partisan movement in the Balkans. Their support, both spiritual and material, was an important factor in the triumph of the Allies and Partisans over the Axis in Yugoslavia. The committee played an influential role in the sale of government bonds to Yugoslav Americans. With the coming of V-E and V-J days the organization did not promptly close shop but with renewed vigor set to attack the problems of peace. Its main purposes, modified to coincide with the changed conditions, were:

1. To promote the dynamic unity of Americans of South-Slavic descent in order to strengthen the United States and the United Nations in their efforts toward world peace.

2. To encourage Americans of South-Slavic descent to participate fully in all processes to advance political, economic, social and ethnic democracy in the United States of America.

3. To foster in the United States of America an ever greater understanding of the South-Slavic peoples, their history, culture and traditions.[9]

### Organized Life in Selected Communities

To round out the picture let us look in on the organized life of Yugoslavs in representative areas. For this purpose organizations in Michigan, Illinois, and California serve as excellent examples, since they form a good cross section of Yugoslavs in agricultural, mining, industrial, and commercial pursuits—leading occupations of the immigrants.

In the Detroit area are branches of all the Yugoslav national societies. The Serb National Federation has six branches in Michigan. The Serbian Beneficial Federation Unity has one branch in Detroit and one in Wyandotte. Both of these national societies have lodges for junior members. The Croatian Fraternal Union has twenty-six lodges in Michigan, four of the branches being in the Detroit region. Formerly there was also a branch lodge of the Croatian Benevolent Fraternity. The national Croatian Cultural-Educational Federation has a Detroit unit as has the Federation of American Croats. In addition, there are numerous local societies, some of the more important of which are the Croatian-American Ladies Club, Club Zagorje, and Club Jadran. The Slovene National Benefit Society has sixteen branches in Michigan. The Grand Carniolian Slovenian Catholic Union and the American Fraternal Union each have a branch in the Detroit district. The Jugoslav Socialist Federation, also Slovenian, has three branches in the motor city. The Moslem Yugoslavs of Detroit have their own society, called the Moslem Benefit Association of Bosnia.[10]

Second-generation Slovenians belong to two lodges, both of

which are closely connected with the Slovene National Benefit Society. It is the aim of these lodges, the Young Americans and the Wolverines, to spread among members a knowledge of the Slovenian language, culture, and tradition. To aid them in attaining this goal they publish a monthly magazine, half in English, half in Slovenian.

In Detroit are also the Yugoslav Educational Society, whose membership comprises both Serbian and Croatian elements, a dramatic society called Iskra (Spark), the Montenegrin Educational Club, and the Yugoslav American Independent Club. The Montenegrin Educational Club devotes its interest to drama, showing partiality to plays concerning Montenegrin history. The purpose of the Yugoslav American Independent Club is to unite Serbians, Croatians, and Slovenians; but sectional feeling, brought over from Europe, runs high, and to achieve unity or at least a closer relationship is not easy.

Like the Yugoslav American Independent Club, the Yugoslav Central Organization, founded in Detroit in 1932, hoped to unite Croatians, Serbians, and Slovenians. The society also aimed to create better relations between Yugoslav Americans and their neighbors, to encourage American citizenship, and to aid the needy in the city. Its official organ was the *Yugoslav*. The organization no longer exists but out of it arose several Democratic and Republican political clubs, active in local and state politics.

There are a number of fine singing societies which have attracted attention wherever they have performed, in Michigan, Illinois, Ohio, Indiana, and Pennsylvania. In 1923 one of Michigan's well-known Yugoslav music teachers, Thomas Filkovich, organized Slavulj (Nightingale), a Croatian singing society, now directed by his son, John. Eight years later the Serbian singing society Zmaj Jovan Jovanović was started in Flint, Michigan, by Theodore Veljkov, and is now directed by John Crnkovich. Ravanica, the Serbian singing society, named after the famous church in Ćuprija, Serbia, was started in 1931 by Vladimir M. Lugonia, national secretary of the Serbian Singing Federation of America, and first conducted by John Filkovich. Later the group came under the direction of Etheleen P. Adamovich, and grew from a small male choir into a large body of over a hundred mixed voices.[11]

In Chicago the establishment of the numerous and varied societies was a relatively long and difficult process. This is especially

128

well illustrated by the Serbs. The Chicago Serbs, under the leadership of Sava Radaković, Krsto Gopčević, and Petar Bolarin, founded their first benefit lodge in 1899, called Balkan and consisting of eighty members. This was a comparatively large group, since there were no more than eighty-three Serbians in the entire district at the time. A few years later about half the members migrated to Pueblo, Colorado, where they established a society under the same name. After an independent existence of nearly six years, the Chicago unit in 1905 joined the Srbobran federation. At the time of the union Balkan had 183 members and a ladies auxiliary, known as Princess Milena. Upon its founding the auxiliary received as a gift a silk flag from the Montenegrin Princess Milena.[12] Meanwhile, in 1903, the First Serbian Beneficial Federation had come into existence and established its home office in Chicago.

In 1908 Balkan was deeply moved by the annexation of Bosnia and Hercegovina by Austria and, fearing a consequent clash between the Slavs and Austrians, sent a hundred dollars from its treasury to the Red Cross chapters of Serbia and Montenegro. When the Balkan and World wars followed, the Chicago Serbs sent all the material aid possible to their countrymen in Europe, and sixty-five of the Balkan members joined the volunteers to fight against Austria in 1914.

In the meantime, the Balkan society changed its name to King Peter I Karadjordjević, only to abandon it in 1924 in favor of the more alluring title of King Peter I the Great Liberator. In this period of name switching the lodge absorbed three smaller benefit societies: Sveti Jovan (St. John), Sveti Nikola (St. Nicholas), and Srpsko Kolo (Serbian Circle).

Like the Balkan, Lika i Krbava-Sv. Spasitelj (Lika and Krbava Our Savior) also came into being early. It was formed in 1902 by immigrants from the Lika-Krbava district. Following a brief and precarious independent existence, it, too, joined the Srbobran Federation.

After World War I the Serbs of Chicago did not band into new unions for some years. Finally, in 1926, the benefit lodge, Sveti Djuradj (St. George), was established as a branch of the Sloboda federation, with an initial membership of fifty. The following year sixty young people started a junior order. Two years later the organization formally allied itself with the Serb National Federation, and membership increased to over two hundred, with about one hundred and forty children in the juvenile section. Sveti Djuradj helped substantially in the construction of the new church, St. Michael the Archangel.

In June, 1927, the Serbian singing society Sloboda was founded by Bogdan Cuculjević and Djuro Lalić. It began with a membership of thirty-two men and women, and from the beginning produced concerts that won wide acclaim, its programs being heard in Detroit, Gary, and at the Chicago World's Fair. The chorus went forward to many triumphs under the direction of Adam Popović.

A small Serbian benefit lodge, a branch of the federation Jedinstvo, was organized in Chicago in 1933. Known at the beginning as St. Nicholas, the society in 1934, following the assassination of King Alexander of Yugoslavia, changed its name to Gallant King Alexander the First Unifier. During the last months of 1934 the Ličani (immigrants from Lika) collected more than $3,000 among Yugoslavs in the United States and Canada for the purpose of erecting a memorial to the martyred monarch. The memorial, built in the city of Udbine, was unveiled in May, 1938.

Like their kinsmen the Serbians, the Montenegrins of Chicago also early turned their attention to organizational activities. In 1903 the First Montenegrin Federation was founded in Chicago. Two years later the Montenegrins launched their first local society, Ljubav Crnogoraca (Love of Montenegrins). This organization, however, proved to be of short duration. The Balkan wars of 1912-1913 attracted many members to volunteer fighting brigades, while others moved to outlying districts, causing the lodge to break up. The Montenegrins did not have an organization of their own again until 1934, most of them, meanwhile, consequently joining existing Yugoslav societies.

Starting in 1930, when the great economic depression dealt a serious blow to the iron-mining towns of southern Illinois, the Montenegrins, many of them with their families, moved to Chicago once more in the hope of finding employment in the steel mills and foundries there. Obtaining work finally as conditions improved, early in 1934 some fifty Montenegrin families met to discuss the possibilities of setting up a new organization to take care of their requirements of protection and friendship. The result of this meeting was the founding of the society called Njegoš (named after the poet-patriot of Montenegro). Led by Miloš Pejović, Pere Salelić, and Miloslav Tomanović, the organization moved ahead.

From a nucleus of thirty, membership more than tripled during the succeeding five years. Sponsorship by the organization of plays and pageants based on Montenegrin history and folklore as well as other activities calculated to awaken interest in the culture and civilization of Montenegro proved to be popular fare with the Chicago Slavs from the beginning.

The period of World War II saw the peak of organizational expansion and activity in Chicago, as it did, of course, in many other large Yugoslav centers. During the war years not only did the various Serb, Croat, and Slovene federations have branches in Chicago but there was also a multitude of local and regional groups in the city. Among these may be mentioned the Circle of Serbian Sisters, Council of Croatian Women, Croatian Benevolent Fraternity, Serbian Progressive Club Freedom, Croatian-American Yugoslav Club Partisan, Dalmatian-American Club, American Yugoslav Humanitarian Club, and the singing, dramatic society Matija Gubec. With few exceptions, these organizations have remained in existence in the postwar years.

As already noted, one of the largest South Slavic communities on the Pacific Coast is San Pedro, California. Here the center of most activities is the Yugoslav Club. Founded in 1927, the society has a membership of about five hundred. In 1935 it built the Yugoslav Hall, at a cost of $50,000. Since the Yugoslavs enjoy their own recreational programs and like to meet frequently, talk, and sing their folk songs, the society sponsors many entertainment programs and dances during the year. Thus, each December a banquet and dance are held in celebration of the unification of Yugoslavia, and on New Year's Eve a dance is sponsored which is generally attended by over a thousand persons.

The Yugoslav Club, according to official report, is not progressing in proportion to its potentialities because many of the real leaders of the community are not taking active part and the business affairs of the organization are in the hands of a few much overworked part-time administrators. In spite of this unfortunate condition, the future of the group does not appear dark. There has been increased enthusiasm for the proposal to erect an adjoining building to the present club house to provide more adequate recreational facilities for the second and third generation Yugoslavs, with a view of attracting them into the organization and eventually turning the reins over to them.

Among the other noteworthy organizations in the San Pedro area are the Yugoslav American Central Council, a branch of the Federation of American Croatian Ladies, Yugoslav Women's Club, social and cultural groups, Velike Gospe (Assumption), a society of women associated with the Roman Catholic Church, and a lodge of the Croatian Fraternal Union. There is in addition a musical organization, called the Junior Tamburitza Club, which is affiliated with the Yugoslav Club.

## SUBVERSION AND COMMUNISM

Suspicion, distrust, and confusion were cast upon the organizational scene for a time as the United States Attorney General and the Committee on Un-American Activities of the House of Representatives cited society after society as subversive and/or Communist. The assault began shortly after the ending of the war in 1945 and reached its climax in the late forties and early fifties, a period when the cold war between the East and West seemed to be on the verge of breaking out into a hot war and the American authorities frantically sought to eliminate all potential sources of fifth-column activities. During those critical years more than a dozen organizations in which Yugoslavs were members were proclaimed un-American.

One of the first groups to come under attack was the American Slav Congress. In May, 1948, it was pronounced "a Moscow inspired and directed federation of Communist-dominated organizations seeking by methods of propaganda and pressure to subvert the 10,000,000 people in this country of Slavic birth or descent."[13] The Congress promptly replied that this "was part of the general campaign of intimidation of progressive Americans."[14] Since the federation at that very time was aiding in the founding of the Progressive party to support Henry A. Wallace for the presidency, the question was raised, "Was this a punitive, retaliatory measure by the administration, or were the two events purely coincidental?" The government was able to make out a strong case against the Congress, having in its possession information linking a number of the leaders of the association with Communist activities. The evidence presented was damaging enough to start the organization on its way to dissolution.

It was on the International Workers Order that some of the

biggest guns in Washington were trained. This fraternal federation had penetrated into practically every Yugoslav settlement of any size, intrenching itself firmly particularly among the Croats through its auxiliary called the Hrvatsko Potporno Bratstvo Amerike (Croatian Benevolent Fraternity of America) with branches from New York to California and Louisiana to Alaska. The Order was attacked as subversive and Communist and accused of plotting the overthrow of the United States. In its report the House Committee on Un-American Activities described the association as a strong, effective, and closely knitted Communist front "which purports to be a fraternal organization but through its segregated language lodges mobilizes for the revolution in the United States."[15] The government continued its relentless pounding until it succeeded in bringing about the extinction of the federation.

On the heels of the citations against the International Workers Order and the American Slav Congress came charges of subversion and Communism against numerous other organizations. Among the groups included in the rapidly growing list were the American Association for Reconstruction in Yugoslavia, American Serbian Committee for Relief of War Orphans in Yugoslavia, Croatian Benevolent Fraternity, Croatian Fraternal Union, Croatian Educational Club, Serbian-American Fraternal Society, Serbian Vidovdan Council, Slovene National Benefit Society, and the United Committee of South-Slavic Americans.[16]

As the congressional investigations against the internal enemy continued, new evidence was uncovered, showing that several of the organizations were unequivocally anti-Communist and loyal to their adopted country. Included in this category were the Croatian Fraternal Union and the Slovene National Benefit Society. Accordingly, these names were expunged from the subversive list.[17]

## PAST, PRESENT, AND FUTURE

The many Yugoslav organizations throughout the United States are going ahead rapidly today. But it was not always so. The long depression of the 1930's was a dark and difficult period for most of them. During those trying years much doubt was expressed concerning the future of the organizations. Having, however, weathered the storm of the thirties, most of the societies started to climb upward once more. Progress has been especially noteworthy since the end of the war in 1945. There has been an increase in membership among adults and juniors as well. The expansion of the juvenile orders is especially encouraging, for it is upon American-born Yugoslavs primarily that the future of the organizations is dependent.

In good and bad years alike, suggestions have been put forth for the unification of all Slav organizations. The idea is to unite all Slav fraternal organizations into one large federation with sub-federations of Russian, Ukrainian, Polish, Czechoslovak, Yugoslav, and other organizations as the foundation for its structure and an English publication for all membership included in the federations. None of the proposals has yet borne fruit and there seems at the present time but little chance that any will in the immediate foreseeable future.

## ORGANIZATIONS AND THE HOMELAND

The various organizations have affected every phase of Yugoslav life in the United States. That influence is discernible and unquestioned. But what has been the impact of the associations on the Yugoslavs at home? Here, too, though not as abundant and obvious, nevertheless, evidence does exist of the powerful influence of the societies upon conditions in the native land.

Though virtually unnoticed, the multifarious South Slavic organizations have been a significant force in the economic, social, and political developments of the homeland for many years. In war and peace the Yugoslav Americans have demonstrated extraordinary magnanimity toward their less-fortunate relatives and friends in the old country. A good example of this unparalleled generosity is seen in the contributions of the Croatian Fraternal Union. During World War I this benefit federation raised some $15,000 for the orphaned children of Croatia and Serbia and gave a like sum to the Red Cross of Yugoslavia. Again in World War II the association exhibited the same qualities of humanitarianism. Tens of thousands of dollars were given to war victims and half a million dollars was collected for the relief of the homeless and starved victims of the war. Among the more conspicuous efforts of the society in the postwar period has been a donation of $17,000 for medical instruments for an old hospital in Zagreb; an "American textbooks for Yugoslavia" campaign netted 10,000 volumes.

Other Yugoslav societies were just as generous as the Croatian Fraternal Union. This was especially true of the relief organizations which sprang into existence during World War II. They did much in alleviating suffering among the ill, wounded, and starving and in speeding recovery of Yugoslavia by the invaluable assistance they rendered in reconstructing the areas devastated by war. The respect and appreciation of the grateful recipients were demonstrated numerous times and in devious ways. For instance, when Zlatko Balokovic, president of the Yugoslav Relief Committee, visited Yugoslavia in 1947, he was welcomed by enthusiastic crowds everywhere he went, and was honored by decoration with the Order of Brotherhood and Unity. Again, in a letter of February 6, 1947, to Anthony Gerlach, secretary of the American Association for Reconstruction in Yugoslavia, the commercial attaché of the Embassy of the Federal People's Republic of Yugoslavia in Washington, D.C., highly lauded the assistance of the Yugoslav Americans, stating, "The relief work conducted by your organization is well known and much appreciated in my country and the results of your efforts are in evidence throughout Yugoslavia."

The materials shipped into Yugoslavia not only exert an economic but also a social and cultural influence upon the country. American farm implements help in acquainting the peasants with new ways of farming as well as in raising production. Clothing from the United States brings changes from the old outmoded peasant garb to Western dress. Typewriters promote efficiency and learning. Cameras and radios are factors in recreation and education. Books influence the thoughts of the people. In short, every item sent by the Yugoslav American organizations to their kinsmen abroad helps in some way, though small it may be, to modify the life of the South Slavs at home.

In addition to the influence in the economic, social, and cultural spheres, the hand of the American Yugoslavs is seen in the political, albeit the measurement of the effect in the latter is not as easy as in the former. The very structure of the government of Yugoslavia is not without this external influence. Separation from the Habsburgs, establishment of an independent state, and creation of a federal republic were long the dreams of liberal, democratic-minded Yugoslav Americans, and their role in making these ideals realities could hardly be called negligible.

Numerous protest meetings against Austrian and Magyar oppression in Croatia were held in Allegheny County, Pennsylvania, at the end of 1912 and the beginning of 1913 by Croats and Serbs, both of whom had emigrated from Croatia. Croatians and Serbians, as well as Slovenians, joined the Yugoslav Socialist League in 1912, when the Socialist party of the United States began to emphasize the importance of organizing its followers among the different European minority groups.

From the beginning of its existence in 1912 the Croatian Alliance led a crusade against the domination of its Croat homeland by the Austrians and Magyars and sought to aid all who would resist the foreigners. Largely through its efforts, the National Croatian Union sent financial assistance in 1912 to each persecuted Croatian student in Zagreb, to Stjepan Radić, imprisoned member of the Croatian legislature and founder of the Croatian Peasant party, and to several political parties. In the summer of 1913 the Alliance dispatched a young Pittsburgh Croat, Stjepan Dojčić, to Zagreb to assassinate Slavko Cuvaj, the Croat puppet of the Magyars. The aim of Dojčić proved to be poor; he missed Cuvaj and killed a lesser official instead.

After the outbreak of war in 1914 the South Slavs met in frequent congresses throughout the country to devise means to aid their kinsmen at home. At one of the most important of these gatherings, held in Chicago in March, 1915, and attended by nearly 600 delegates representing the varied Croat, Serb, and Slovene organizations, a vigorous resolution was adopted favoring the severance of all ties with Austria-Hungary and sanctioning a plan of union of all South Slav people in a single, independent state. Officials of the numerous organizations, members of the Yugoslav Committee, and many of the eminent social leaders, outstanding among whom were Etbin Kristan, Jože Zavertnik, Dr. F. Potočnjak, Dr. Ante Biankini, and Don Niko Gršković, rendered yeoman service to the cause of unity by publicizing the Yugoslav ideal in America and carrying their case to the American government in Washington. At the same time the Jugo-Slav Republican Alliance carried on an active campaign for a republic, and when the war ended sent representatives to the Paris Peace Conference to see that justice and fair play prevailed in the remaking of the Balkans.

Similarly, during World War II, American Yugoslavs were able once more to make their influence felt, helping to pave the way for a new form of government by demonstrating their partiality for a republic and antagonism toward the monarchy, which they considered nationally prejudiced, autocratic, and anachronistic. Again, in the Tito-Stalin feud they played a part, if only a minor one. As is well known, Yugoslavs at home and abroad have always been a freedom-loving people, ready to make the supreme sacrifice to preserve their independence. They submit to no outside authority without a fight. The American Yugoslavs were not willing to stand idly by while their homeland was being converted into a dependency, even though by another Slav rather than a Teuton. They would aid an independent but not a vassal state. This policy was sharp and clear. It could not be completely ignored.

As has been seen, the influence of Yugoslav Americans has not always been directed into constructive channels, nor has it been successful at all times in accomplishing the desired results. Whether successful or unsuccessful, healthy or unhealthy, there is no doubt that the voice of organized Yugoslav Americans, though not always loud and clear, is formidable and effective, and a force to be reckoned with at all times.

137

# 7

# Voice of a People

As SEEN IN THE PREVIOUS CHAPTER, organizations of various sorts exert a good deal of influence on the life and thought of the Yugo-slav community in America.  Another influence of prime importance derives from the foreign-language press.  The immigrant publications are many, as noted by Louis Adamic in the statement:

> Well-nigh every nationality represented in American immigration has, or has had at some time in the past, more and larger newspapers in the United States than in the old country.  The reasons for this are several; the most important is that events which vitally affect the people's lives transpire in America with greater frequency than back in Italy, Croatia, or Latvia.[1] *

The 1940 federal census revealed that there were 8,354,700 persons in the United States whose mother tongue was a language other than English, and these persons read, or had available to them, about a thousand newspapers and periodicals printed entirely or in part in a foreign language.[2]  In the first six months of 1943, "1,092 such publications were known to exist because they were actually received by the Common Council [Common Council for American Unity, a national organization concerned with minority problems] or Federal Government agencies."[3]

## ROLE OF THE PRESS

Despite the fact that the Slavic population in the United States

* Notes to this chapter begin on page 292.

stems from a predominantly illiterate peasantry, it puts out a large number of periodicals, including newspapers, magazines, pamphlets, almanacs, and the like. It has been said that "there are more newspapers in proportion to the Slavic population in the United States than there are in their homelands."[4] The reasons for the popularity of the foreign-language publications in the United States are capably summarized by Anton Tanasković, editor of *Hrvatski Svijet* (Croatian World), who writes concerning the Croatian press:

1. It is a medium of news about the old neighborhood.
2. It keeps the readers informed on current events taking place in their adopted country.
3. It offers services having to do with assistance and information connected with their (the readers) duties and responsibilities, benefits and privileges, rights and obligations as loyal citizens of the United States.
4. It reports activities taking place in the so-called "colonies" of the larger cities, consequently readers are kept informed about the doings of their fellow-Americans of Croatian birth or descent.[5]

What Tanasković states in regard to the Croatian-language press holds, indeed, also for the Yugoslav as well as the entire foreign-language press in America.

In the old country the immigrants "had used newspapers to make cigarettes, but in America they read them."[6] As Robert E. Park has stated, "The ordinary immigrant newspaper is like a general store in a rural community. It offers to its public a multitude of things. . . . The immigrant reads few journals and fewer books. . . . Almost all that he knows about the larger political, social and industrial life about him he gets indirectly through the medium of his press."[7]

The average American reader usually discards his newspaper after he has read the items of interest to him. The immigrant, on the other hand, holds on to his copy of the foreign-language paper, carrying it with him to be read over and over by his family and neighbors. In many Slav communities "it is still the custom for one man to read aloud in a beer hall so that everybody can hear the news."[8]

It is obvious that Yugoslavs read their own language newspapers more in this country than they did when they were in the old. Tanasković believes that this is because "they, as Americans, have become more news conscious probably because they have more time, a higher standard of living and consequently are more eager to know about events outside of the immediate vicinity in which they live."[9]  In the old country most of the immigrants were peasants, living in isolated villages where life was relatively fixed and settled and where custom and tradition provided for all the exigencies of daily life.  In the United States they went to work in the mines and factories, and thus became a part of the turbulent cosmopolitan life of the industrial cities.

Here, therefore, where there were vast distances and no traditions, where the population was mobile and everything was in process, the aliens were forced to discard their habits and to acquire new ideas.  Whereas life had been rather quiet and humdrum in Europe, in America there was ceaseless activity, something happening all the time, which made news reports a real need.  Moreover, in the United States the immigrants banded together to form numerous organizations, which became the very embodiment of their new needs and their new ideas.  They became members of fraternal orders, singing societies, or physical culture groups, and read papers, because practically every immigrant organization published some kind of paper.

Another reason why immigrants are eager to read their own language publications is that they appreciate the right to read their own language; in their own country many of them were not permitted to use their native tongue.  "Frequently the 'oppressed and independent' peoples of Europe were not allowed to publish journals in their own language."[10]  Those who have had to fight for the right to use their native language in print in the past will naturally take advantage of the privilege.  "In addition to every other reason for the existence of a foreign-language press is its value to the immigrant, in satisfying his mere human desire for expression in his mother tongue."[11]

No serious student of immigration would deny the need of the foreign-language press.  In a new environment the immigrant who needs to make many complex adjustments finds his newspaper an important source of information.  Without periodicals in their own language the immigrants would be seriously handicapped not only in adjusting to the new conditions of America but in their relations with members of their nationality.  By encouraging the immigrants

140

to read, the press has helped to make them more literate, and by printing news about America, it has done much to prepare the aliens for the American way of life. At the same time the foreign-language press enables the immigrants to maintain contacts with their own nationals in various sections of the country. Thus, the Croat in San Francisco reading the *Hrvatski Svijet* knows what his Croatian friends in New York are doing, and the Serb in Gary follows the activities of his countrymen in Pittsburgh through the columns of the *Slobodna Reč* (Free Expression). In writing on the subject of the foreign-language press, Herbert A. Miller very pertinently asked the question, "How many of us who have studied French or German much more than the average immigrant will ever be able to study English would choose a French or German newspaper in preference to an English one?"[12] The answer, of course, is very few, if any. In other words, the immigrants cannot do without their own language periodicals because there is no other way in which they can keep informed on world events and, perhaps more important, on American life and institutions.

It is not surprising, therefore, to find that each Slavic nationality has an extensive press, which includes dailies, weeklies, monthlies, quarterlies, semiannuals, and annuals. A section of the Home Missions Survey of General Foreign Language Literature in the United States completed by the North American Division of the Interchurch World Movement shows that there were in 1920 some 260 publications among the Slavs, a figure slightly higher than that given in N. W. Ayer's *American Newspaper Annual and Directory,* which lists 217 in all. The larger total is perhaps the more nearly correct since Ayer's reference did not at the time include in its files publications which carried no advertising material. The number of journals rose in the twenties, only to fall in the thirties, so that today there are approximately 250 publications of every kind. Even the Lusatian Serbs or Wends (inhabitants of Lusatia, a small area on the upper Spree River northeast of Dresden, Germany), who form a very small minority of the Slavic population of this country, support a periodical.[13]

The foreign-language press in general and the Slavic periodicals in particular serve a need and will continue to do so as long as there are people who find their own vernacular easier than English. To the Slavic immigrant the foreign-language newspaper interprets

America, so that he becomes oriented more rapidly in the new environment,[14] and by giving him news concerning other Slavs in the United States, he does not succumb to the feeling of being alone.

## PUBLISHING PLANTS

In many instances the Yugoslav publication represents the efforts of the individual working against great odds. It has been pointed out that "in many foreign-language editorial offices, scissors are called the first assistant editor."[15] Columns are filled by culling news items from English-language publications and often one person writes all the news, does all the editing, solicits the advertisements, and performs all other miscellaneous tasks that go into the process of publishing.

Few publications are prosperous enough to own their own printing presses, and many consequently send their copy to a commercial printer. The editorial office is often simply one corner of an old loft, for lack of money, and the address is often in a dingy off-the-beaten-path street.

The extreme in newspaper publication is represented by the *Hrvatski Svijet*, a four-page journal published twice a week in New York by the Croatian World Publishing Corporation, as is so well explained in the following paragraph:

Upstairs in a drab building on West Eighteenth Street in New York City is a dingy office with two desks, three chairs, and one ancient typewriter, with keys yellowed like the teeth of an old man. By the window sits a man—owner, publisher, editor, proofreader, advertising manager, and administrator of *Hrvatski Svijet* (Croatian World), a four-page semi-weekly, read by a few thousand Croatian steelworkers, miners, lumberjacks, fishermen, and saloonkeepers scattered over the United States. A few linotypes and presses crowd the gloomy room next to the office; they belong to another man, a job printer who turns out *Hrvatski Svijet* and fifteen other papers. This layout is typical of hundreds of Lilliputian foreign-language newspapers published in this country.[16]

Although not all Yugoslav papers are of the same character as the *Hrvatski Svijet*, many of them face the same technical problems of publishing. Nevertheless, by their skill and ingenuity, the editors have succeeded in surmounting their many difficulties and in getting their papers out to the eagerly awaiting readers.

## CHARACTER OF THE PRESS

The first South Slavic publication in the United States was the *Slavenska Sloga* (Slavonian Harmony), which appeared in San Francisco in 1884.[17] This was a Croatian newspaper, as was also the *Napredak* (Progress), which was launched in Hoboken, New Jersey, in 1891.[18] In the same year the *Amerikanski Slovenec* (American Slovene) made its initial appearance in Chicago. Though it had to be taken finally under the protective wing of the Grand Carniolian Slovenian Catholic Union, the *Slovenec* has managed to stay in business these many years. Other news journals followed in quick succession. *Chicago*, a Croat paper, got underway in 1892; *Glas Naroda* (Voice of the People), a Slovene newssheet, in 1893 in New York; *Danica* (Morning Star), another Croat paper, in 1894 in Pittsburgh; and *Ujedinjeno Sprstvo* (United Serbdom) in 1905 in Chicago. In the wake of the independent organs came the journals of the national benefit associations, whose officers early concluded that their expanding business could best be handled through official newspapers of the organizations. The Croatian Fraternal Union—or more correctly its predecessors, the Croatian Society and National Croatian Union—led the way. After using *Danica* (1894-1896) and *Napredak* (1896-1905), which had been moved from Hoboken to Pittsburgh, as its official organs, it founded the *Zajedničar* (Unifier) in Pittsburgh in 1905. The next year the Slovene National Benefit Society began publication of the *Prosveta* (Enlightenment) in Chicago and the Serb National Federation the *Amerikanski Srbobran* (American Serb Sentinel) in Pittsburgh.

During the course of the three-quarters of a century since 1884, over two hundred publications of various sorts have appeared among the Yugoslav Americans, some lasting for only one issue while others succeeded in flourishing for many years. The Slovenes, for instance, started seventy-five papers in the period from 1884 to 1920, of which only forty-one survived.[19] At the opening of World War II the Yugoslavs had forty-five newspapers in the United States, seven belonging to the Serbs, fifteen to the Slovenes, and twenty-three to the Croats. The publications were largely weeklies, though eight were dailies.[20]   Through merger and suspension of publication, the total has been reduced to nearly a half.  At present there are only twenty-six established Yugoslav newspapers, including six monthlies, twelve weeklies, one semiweekly, two triweeklies, and five dailies, with circulations varying from a low of about 1,000 copies to a high of 100,000.

The leading publication centers are Chicago, Cleveland, Pittsburgh, and New York.  Few periodicals worth mentioning are published outside those cities.  In Chicago the outstanding journals are the *Amerčki Hrvatski Glasnik* (American Croatian Herald), a weekly paper owned by the American-Croatian Publishing Company; *Hrvatski List* (Croatian Gazette), the weekly journal of the Croatian Franciscan Fathers; *Jedinstvo* (Unity), a Serbian paper, and *Jugoslavija*, a Croat sheet, both weeklies put out by the Palandech Publishing House; *Proletarec* (Proletarian), the weekly organ of the Jugoslav Socialist Federation; *Prosveta*, the daily journal of the Slovene National Benefit Society; and *Zarja* (Dawn), monthly publication of the Slovenian's Women's Union.

Cleveland's chief papers include the *Amerikanski Slovenec*, the oldest Slovene paper in America, which is now the weekly organ of the Grand Carniolian Slovenian Catholic Union; *Ameriška Domovina* (American Home), a Slovene Catholic daily put out by the American Home Publishing Company; *Enakopravnost* (Equality), a Slovene daily published by the American Jugoslav Printing and Publishing Company; *Glas Slovenske Dobrodelne Zveze* (Voice of the Slovenian Mutual Benefit Association); *Nova Doba* (New Era), the weekly journal of the American Fraternal Union; and *Radnička Borba* (Workers' Struggle), the Serbian weekly organ of the South Slavonian Socialist Labor Federation.

In Pittsburgh the principal newssheets are the *Amerikanski Srbobran*, the daily mouthpiece of the Serb National Federation; *Narodni Glasnik* (National Herald), a Croat daily formerly published by the Croatian-American section of the International Workers Order but now an independent; *Slobodna Reč*, a Serb paper issued three times a week by the American Serbian Publishing Company; and *Zajedničar*, the weekly publication of the Croatian Fraternal Union and the paper with the largest circulation of all.

The most important newspapers in New York are the *Glas Naroda*, a Slovene triweekly published by the Slovenic Publishing

144

Company; *Hrvatski Svijet,* the Croat semiweekly put out by the Croatian World Publishing Corporation; and *Novi List* (New Gazette), a Yugoslav weekly published by Novi List, Inc. Meriting mention also is the *Naša Nada* (Our Hope), a weekly organ of the Croatian Catholic Union published in Gary, Indiana.

A regular annual feature of most of the newspapers is a type of almanac, dealing with subjects of general interest to the immigrants (songs, poems, short stories, history, description, travel). For the most part, as is evident, the publishers of Yugoslav periodicals are political organizations or interests, or fraternal associations, which themselves are at least partially political, religious, or sociopolitical groups. It is not surprising, therefore, that their activities and interests receive a share of the space.

Though each one has its own peculiarities, most of the newspapers are filled with reports of the activities of the various Yugoslav organizations, news of mutual aid, concerts, dances, picnics, sporting events, and so on. Since the majority of the readers are physical laborers and members of labor organizations, union affairs, wage discussions, and industrial disputes come in for a good deal of discussion. Much space is also devoted to current events in the homeland and in America. As in American papers, there is in the Yugoslav publications news of murder, rape, robbery, fraud, graft, corruption, gang feuds, and catastrophes of all kinds. Robert E. Park, who made a thorough study of the immigrant press, provides a statistical picture of an immigrant paper in his analysis of the *Zajedničar.*

> Thirty-four of its 56 columns are taken up with the affairs of the National Croatian Society. Accounting moneys, 6 1/3 columns. Accounting in regard to members, 7 1/6 columns. Addresses of local societies, 20 columns. Advertisements of books for keeping accounts, 2/3 columns. Total 34 columns.
>
> The other twenty-two columns of the paper discuss the situation of the Croatian workers in the United States in relation to the conflict between capital and labor, and the situation in the home country. There are always letters from the readers. There is some fiction.[21]

A few additional illustrations may perhaps help to make clearer the general character of the papers. Let us first of all take a look at a journal which flourished during the high tide of immigration, in the early years of this century. A good example of one of these early periodicals was the popular and successful *Narodni List* (National Gazette), a Croat daily founded in 1898 by Frank Zotti, a steamship agent and banker. The editorial policy of this paper was violent and personal, many an ambitious Yugoslav intellectual getting a verbal lashing in its columns. Its pages were newsy, sensational, and written in language and concerning matters that an average Yugoslav could easily understand. An admirable description of the paper was provided by Park, who wrote:

> The paper is run on a purely business basis. The editorial department uses a style of its own to attract the uneducated mass of the people, the style being vulgar and personal. Aside from this method of getting circulation, it has a large number of traveling salesmen who solicit subscriptions directly. As to advertising, its rates are of the highest and it carries quite a substantial amount of advertising space.
>
> The significance of the paper lies in its extreme chauvinistic Croatian nationalism and anti-Serbianism, which has always been the camouflage of the pro-Austrian papers and of individuals who did not have the courage to come out openly in favor of Austria.
>
> The circulation of the paper is national. Its readers live all over the Union. They are mostly common laborers, who come from the remote mountainous parts of Bosnia, Croatia, and Dalmatia. They have no education to speak of; most of them have not even been in the normal school.[22]

Many of the contemporary periodicals are similar to the *Narodni List*. But, in any event, it might be helpful to go through the pages of several present-day journals and scrutinize their contents. An examination of two different types of papers, the *Zajedničar*, a fraternal publication, and the *Hrvatski Svijet*, an independent sheet, is very revealing. The *Zajedničar* of August 18, 1948, has on page one a long story on the Croatian Fraternal Union membership campaign; one main article concerned with the United States presidential nominations, and the other with the Eightieth Congress and its work; and a number of shorter stories dealing with farm surpluses, the high cost of living and the worker, and a mine disaster in West Virginia. Page two is filled with editorials on such widely different subjects as death benefits, the ideological struggle between the

East and West, Iraq, and Bosnia. On page three is a three-column feature entitled *Naša Nova Domovina* (Our New Homeland); another four columns are given over to the CFU children's home in Des Plaines, Illinois; and a story on Yugoslav American aid to the native land completes the page. About three-fourths of page four is devoted to the campaign for new members for the CFU, and the rest is taken up with short pieces on Hercegovina and Henry A. Wallace's protest against the Washington "witch-hunt." Skipping over to the English section on page nine, one finds a dozen short articles of particular interest to youth, such as picnics, concerts, and beauty queen contests, together with photographs of three young ladies and a noted concert artist. Page ten contains editorials on the membership drive, the children's home, and the convention of the National Fraternal Congress; a column of veterans' affairs; a story and picture of a Croat wedding; and brief descriptions of various social events. Page eleven is taken up entirely with the campaign for new members, and the final page, twelve, is devoted primarily to sports, supplemented by several pictures from the children's home.

In the *Hrvatski Svijet* of July 29, 1949, page one, the banner headline announces President Truman's signature of the North Atlantic Pact, and the leading two-column story deals with that subject; two relatively long stories discuss the Tito-Cominform rift; another long item pertains to the recall of all foreign citizens from South China, accompanied by a photograph from the area; one column has a collection of brief accounts of happenings around the world; and the rest of the page deals with stories of robberies, accidents, and the like. Page one has a long editorial on Associate Supreme Court Justice Frank Murphy, and another on the British and the atom bomb; a column entitled *Iz Hrvatski Naseobina* (From the Croatian Settlements); obituaries; and letters to the editor. Advertisements, mostly of realtors, travel agents, hotel keepers, and food dealers, and short articles on developments in various parts of Yugoslavia take up page three. Page four, the last, is divided between two short stories, taken from the works of Max Huebler and August Šenoa, and advertisements of a realtor, an optometrist, a musical supply house, and a monument company.

From the beginning the Yugoslav press has been an outlet for political, social, and cultural ideas. Political problems related to

147

Europe were the chief subjects for discussion and comment formerly, but since the 1930's editors have been giving more and more
space to political problems of the American scene.[23]  The American-
born youngsters as well as the more progressive and enlightened
immigrants are interested chiefly in American political life, and the
South Slavic press is taking increasing cognizance of this growing
interest.

This refocusing of the center of attention of the Yugoslav press
is but one part of the process of Americanization which has brought
with it not only modification of content but of format and technique
likewise.  The papers at the beginning were rather dull and unattractive, but now the reading matter is presented in as striking
fashion as in any American journal.  Two-inch headlines, boxes,
pictures, and cartoons are no longer rarities among the Yugoslav
sheets.  Sensationalism is not lacking.  Not even the language has
been beyond this influence, as is so ably demonstrated in the *Fortune* article, which states:

> The editor does strange and wonderful things with words.  In-
> deed, to a newly arrived Yugoslav, many columns of his immi-
> grant paper would have to be translated; they are phrased either
> in a hair-raising version of native grammar or in pidgin English-
> Yugoslav, which might as well be Chinese.  Fairly intelligible
> are coinages such as "koman" (come on), "olrait" (all right), or
> "noser" (no sir).  But they are nothing compared to phrases like
> "ronati za mera" (run for mayor).[24]

Further evidence of the Americanization process is seen in the
English pages of the periodicals.  Of the twenty-six newspapers
previously mentioned three are published entirely in the English
language.  Many more are characterized by their English pages or
sections, designed primarily, of course, to attract American-born
readers as well as to hold Americanized immigrants who have mastered the English language.

In spite of the efforts made by the journals to please the second
generation, the view has been expressed that the American-born
children of immigrants take no real interest in the newspapers published in the language of their parents, with the result that some of
the English sections have been dropped.[25]  Continued indifference
on the part of the youth could very well mean the demise of the
Yugoslav press in America.

As a constructive force in building better citizens, the Slavic press has yet to be fully exploited. Much can be done to mold opinion among the foreign born by cooperation with editors of foreign-language periodicals.

## NEWSPAPER ADVERTISEMENTS

The foreign-language newspapers shed light on the American scene for the immigrant; at the same time the student of immigrant life obtains a great deal of information from the foreign-language press concerning life and thought of the immigrant. Advertisements, which Joseph S. Roucek calls "an Americanizing influence,"[26] are a particularly revealing feature of the South Slavic papers. As Park says, "The advertisements of the priest, the doctor, and the lawyer appear as soon as the immigrant community attains any size."[27] A type of advertisement which is frequently found in Yugoslav journals is the following:

Money remittances to the Old Country are sent by ordinary mail, air mail, and by cable.
For remittances from $10 to $50 the following are the charges: For ordinary mail $1.25; for air mail $1.55; for cable $3.50.
For remittances above $50 the charges are 25 cents more. Special declarations used until now, are no longer necessary.
Immigration: The same laws for immigration are in force as were before the war. If you wish to get any person into this country, write us for information.
Packages: If you need any information about sending packages you may also write to us.[28]

Organizations advertise frequently, and their advertisements give an indication of the kind of activity carried on by them. Meetings, amateur performances for the benefit of churches, lodges, and schools, lectures, services, and goods (American and European) also form a regular part of the advertising columns.

In the days of mass immigration steamship ticket agents and immigrant bankers were important advertisers, but since the quota laws restricting immigration were passed, such advertisers have greatly decreased in Yugoslav newspapers. A classical example of a newspaper that was put out mainly to promote business for a steamship agent and banker is the previously-mentioned *Narodni*

*List,* edited by Frank Zotti. Starting out as a weekly in 1898, this publication became the first Croatian daily in America four years later.[29] At different times Zotti is said to have owned and controlled eight papers. One of these was the *Rail, Sail and American Merchant Marine,* with which he fought the Hamburg-American Line during the first decade of the twentieth century. Among his other papers were the *Gazetta del Banchiere* (Bank Gazette), an Italian sheet, and *Slovenski Narod* (Slovene People), a Slovenian semi-weekly started in opposition to the *Glas Naroda,* the Slovene journal published by Frank L. Dakser, a rival banker in New York. It seems that "all these publications were carried on in the interest of Zotti's bank, and Zotti was known to the immigrants as the 'King of the Croatians.'"[30] In 1908, Zotti's bank failed and 8,000 depositors suffered losses, but in spite of the scandal connected with the failure of the bank, the publication of *Narodni List* continued.[31]

In these early years of the twentieth century, when the number of men far exceeded that of women in the foreign colonies in America, "wife wanted" advertisements were not uncommon in Yugoslav periodicals. Those aliens who had no sweethearts abroad oftentimes tried to obtain mates through the classified columns of their foreign-language papers. Even a more prominent feature at this time was the "help wanted" section, which nearly all journals carried. Factory labor, mine, and steel mill help were in great demand. The advertisements often went into detail about the kind of work offered, living conditions, and pay, as is vividly illustrated in the advertisement from the *Prosveta* below.

### LOADERS
With families or single
### THE RELIANCE COAL AND COKE COMPANY
### GLOMAWR, KY.

The nearest town is Hazard, Ky. Perry Co. This is a drift mine. The upper layer is four feet and four inches high. No slag counted. Work is done with machinery. Steady job. Good workers earn from $80 to $120 in a couple of weeks. The plant is lighted. Cottages with electricity and water are rented for $1.50 per person. School and church. Come in person or write to the RELIANCE COAL AND COKE CO. GLOMAWR, KY. Take the Louisville and Nashville Ry. from Winchester, Ky. or from McRoberts, Ky.[32]

Hard times practically wiped out such advertisements from the pages of the Yugoslav publications, and they failed to reappear in large numbers even after the return of prosperity.

## POLITICS AND THE PRESS

Much unfavorable criticism has been leveled against the Slavic press by native Americans who denounce the publications as radical and organs of aggressive foreign powers. Such condemnation is born of ignorance of the realities and/or malicious thought and design. The critics generally cite the attacks by the periodicals on the capitalist systems and American foreign policy. Thus, they point to an item such as the following taken from the *Radnička Borba*:

> The world is preparing with feverish haste for a third world war and if the workers do not prevent it we shall all go to the devil, because the world today has at its disposal infinite means of destruction which make possible the annihilation of mankind, should they be employed. The workers could easily prevent this war, if they so desired—American workers, Russian workers, all the workers of the world, especially American workers. The workers possess such power, if they only want to use it. This strength they have in industries, wherever they shall organize themselves in Socialist Industrial Unions. When capitalist control over industry vanishes, every war will be impossible, because no present-day war can be waged without modern industries.[33]

These same critics see even more "red" when they read the article below from the *Proletarec*:

> Americans have become so used to seeing their government send relief to other nations that they probably were only mildly interested when President Truman asked a Congressional grant of $150 millions for southern Korea.
> The stated object of this extension of American generosity—at the expense of the American taxpayer—was to establish a bulwark against the further spread of communism in Asia. And if that were all we saw in the matter we'd probably not be using space to write about it.
> However, foreign grants serve an additional purpose. They also prevent, or at least retard, the spread of unemployment in the United States of America.

151

The fact that this business of producing surpluses, in which American capitalism is remarkably proficient and which has never been worked to the limit, is presenting a perplexing problem for any administration that wants to use the power of government to keep the private-profit system functioning in America. For, what use is it to produce surpluses if nobody buys them. Indeed, how can the private enterprisers continue to function at all unless markets are found somehow for what is produced?

It seems to us that our capitalists are in a fix. Their chief worry from here on may be to force people to consume. And while that will be a job that can hardly be done without controls that were lately considered undemocratic, it may be that most Americans are willing to accept a measure of controlled security in exchange for a little freedom.

As for heading foreigners away from communism by supplying them with free "eats," that is a tactic which may yet convince Americans that the best way to get something from the capitalists and their political agents is to threaten with same [sic] radical program. If Truman is willing to pay $150,000,000 in a single installment to keep Koreans from becoming communists, perhaps our lawmakers would pay much more than that to stem a rising Socialist sentiment at home.

Anyway, while American workers are interesting themselves with rewarding "friends" on the political front, those "friends" see the wisdom of taxing workers to keep restless people friendly in other parts of the world.

Perhaps Americans sell their friendship too cheaply. They might get more if they'd threaten to become capitalism's enemies.[34]

However, if those critics would look just a little further, they would see, often in the same publications, attacks on Tito and Yugoslavia and Khrushchev and Russia as well. There simply is not substantial supporting data for the accusations. Though the present writer does not wholly agree with Louis Adamic's conclusions, there is something to be said for his explanation that: "The American hundred-percenters who periodically cried out against the sinister radicalism of the foreign-language press did not know what they were talking about. Most of the Bohunk papers were conservative and stupid, without program. They discussed only the most obvious phases of American life. . . . The Bohunk editors betrayed only the vaguest knowledge of American politics. They wrote nothing likely to put a strain on the brains of their hard-working, tired readers."[35]

The Yugoslav press, like that of the other Slavs, has had a comparatively insignificant number of extreme leftist representatives in its ranks. In recent years there has been only one outright Communist publication among them, the *Organizator*, a semimonthly organ of the Yugoslav section of the Communist party formerly published in Chicago but now defunct. Another paper, the *Radnički Glasnik*, also published in Chicago, has been described by the House Committee on Un-American Activities as "a Croatian daily which the Communist Party admits is under Communist influence."[36] The House Committee put its stamp of disapproval on several other South Slavic publications, including *Enakopravnost, Glas Naroda, Nardoni Glasnik, Proletarec, Slobodna Reč*, and *Zajedničar*.[37]

One of the foremost Socialist publications of the Yugoslavs for over a generation has been the *Radnička Borba*, a Serbian weekly founded in 1910 and published in Cleveland by the South Slavonian Socialist Labor Federation. *Borba* advocates a "democratic socialist state in which the workingmen will be allowed to enjoy the fruits of their labor," but at the same time it opposes Communism of the Tito or Khrushchev variety. On the whole, however, its circulation (slightly over 1,000) and influence have not been very great. Another old publication of the left is the Slovenian *Proletarec*. This weekly journal, founded in 1906 and published in Chicago, is the official organ of the Jugoslav Socialist Federation. A stout defender of the oppressed workingmen everywhere, the *Proletarec* supports a program similar to that of the *Borba*, and like the latter, it too has had little success in reaching a wide audience, especially in recent years.

Although not publishing under either Socialist or labor banners, *Slobodna Reč*, a product of the American-Serbian Publishing Company of Pittsburgh, founded in 1934 and issued three times a week, and *Narodni Glasnik*, a Croatian daily paper dating back to 1907 and also published in Pittsburgh, have frequently been the foci of accusing fingers. Among the criticisms directed against these journals has been one strongly censuring them as voices of Communism for their alleged adherence to the Soviet line at all times. *Radnička Borba* refers to *Slobodna Reč* as a Soviet mouthpiece.[38] Cited by the critics as evidence in the case are the support by the two papers of Henry A. Wallace's Progressive party and their anti-Tito stand in the controversy between the Yugoslav leader and the Soviet-dominated Cominform. Despite these and similar attacks and accusations, *Slobodna Reč* and *Narodni Glasnik* have been immensely popular in Yugoslav communities from coast to coast, principally through their determined opposition to all elements of Fascism and racial and national discrimination in any form or guise.

Two other top-ranking papers that are said to have somewhat socialist editorial policies are *Enakopravnost,* Slovene independent daily of Cleveland, and *Prosveta,* a daily published in Chicago by the Slovene National Benefit Society. Both journals support programs designed to alter, through democratic means, American politics, society, and economy in favor of the common man. They condemn revolution and violence, and abhor dictatorship, Fascist or Communist in form. Liberal and enlightened, they are staunch champions of democracy.

As thus seen, there are left-wing Yugoslav American publications but relatively few which could be called Communist and disloyal. Careful investigation of the conditions reveals that the accusations of radicalism and un-Americanism originate in two highly significant facts. First, as already noted, the Yugoslav publications are not controlled by employers or classes favorable to capital and as a result reflect capitalist interests, but instead they are servants of labor groups and therefore naturally friendly to the cause of the workingmen. And secondly, they profess to see some justice and some injustice on both sides of the East-West controversy. They do not hesitate to show the grey on the side of the West as most English-language papers do. These two factors, misconstrued or twisted, have been responsible for bringing the wrath of reaction and special interest upon the Yugoslav as well as the Slavic press in general.

It does not mean, however, that all the South Slav, or the immigrant, publications are liberal and progressive and that their record is simon-pure, without flaw or blemish. Some of them have been shortsighted and unsound in their policies and practices. This is seen in the fanning of the flames of nationalism and sectionalism by yellow sheets with narrow and selfish interests. It is further evidenced in the support given to Fascists like Francisco Franco in the Spanish Civil War and to the puppet regimes in Yugoslavia during World War II by reactionary, totalitarian, medievalist organs. It is, moreover, attested in the misguided journals which have favored partiality, favoritism, and discrimination in the economic and political phases of life.

In addition to such faults and shortcomings, the Yugoslav press has also suffered from embarrassing entanglements, some reaching back to World War I. These are partly due to the eternal lack of funds which makes the periodicals a likely prey for dishonest promoters, charlatans, and intriguers of all sorts. A case in point is seen in the testimony to a specially-constituted committee of the United States Senate in 1919 presented in the case of Louis N. Hammerling, the head of an agency called the American Association of Foreign-Language Newspapers. Hammerling testified that he had handled over $100,000 in the Republican campaign in 1912.[39] Much of it he used, it was developed, to buy advertising space in foreign-language newspapers, in the hope, no doubt, of influencing editorial opinion. His dealings with German propaganda in this country were on a still larger scale, as he succeeded in obtaining a large portion of the money that was spent by the German and Austrian governments to influence the foreign-language press in the United States. Frank Zotti, editor of *Narodni List*, who probably did more than anyone else to bring the subversive operations of Hammerling's association into public view, testified before the Senate committee that one of Hammerling's agents had asked him to publish in behalf of the Austro-Hungarian government the infamous "Appeal to the American People," which called for stopping, "in the name of humanity," the manufacture and shipment to Europe of munitions of war, but that he had refused.[40] When asked about Hammerling's attempt to control the editorial policies of the foreign-language newspapers, Zotti said:

As I have explained, papers that were not on a stable basis and that needed his help, as I would say, and were afraid to fight him personally, were naturally controlled through him, by always this same threat, "We will withdraw all the patronage"; like, for instance, in the personal-liberty matter. I never spoke to him about it, and never wanted it, although I knew he was getting paid so much per line. I know I saved other publishers, who did not publish that. But then there were others because the easiest way was the best way, and they did not want any trouble

with this man who was giving them $10,000, $20,000, and $30,-
000 a year's advertising; and they took the advertisements and
published them.[41]

This testimony by Zotti, describing how the American Association of Foreign-Language Newspapers exercised control over a
portion of the foreign-language press in the United States, was
substantiated by another South Slav editor, Dushan Popovich, who
had charge of the *Srbobran* (Serb Sentinel), a weekly published in
New York. The *Srbobran* was one of the first papers to join Hammerling's organization, attracted by the advertising money. When
Popovich refused to sign the "Appeal to the American People," he
was promptly punished for insubordination. Questioned by the
Senate committee about his association with Hammerling, Popovich
explained:

He came to me asking if I would take an advertisement for my
paper. I said, "Oh yes; why not?" So that he asked me for the
rates. I told him my rate, I think 25 cents per inch, and he
bought right away advertisements, and I can't say how much,
but he paid me. Every first of the month, in the morning, there
was a bill and a check in the mail, over there, all the time. . . .
He said to me that I can get advertisements from him under
one condition only—if I buy shares in this association; so that I
said to him that I don't want to buy any shares; I have no money
for buying shares. I don't know that man, and to come right
away and ask me to buy a hundred dollars of stock—so that he
says, "You must not pay that. I will give you advertisements,
and every month I will deduct so much, and I will give you the
shares." So that in that way I got the advertisements and they
were paid for, and in the same way I got the shares, too—two
shares.
From the beginning I did not get much [advertising]. I got
about—I don't remember exactly—from $15 to $25 a month, and
gradually it was always more and more, so that I had—up until
he put that appeal before me that I should sign—I had then about
$70 or $80 a month. . . . He sent Mr. Gabriel to me. . . . He came
to my office . . . and said to me, "Mr. Popovich, please sign
that; Mr. Hammerling would like if you would sign it." So that
before I sign something I want to see what I am signing; and I
started to read one line, two lines, and three lines, and then it
was perfectly clear to me what it is. I read a little further, and
so I found that he wants that I should sign an appeal to the

American people that they should stop manufacturing munitions, and stop sending munitions to our allies. As a good Serbian, and a good American citizen, too, I got angry right away, and I said to him, in high words, "Mr. Gabriel, tell to Mr. Hammerling that Mr. Popovich will never sign that."[42]

Popovich not only refused to sign the appeal himself, but warned other editors of foreign-language newspapers not to sign it. As a consequence, Hammerling at first drastically reduced his advertising in the *Srbobran* and then finally stopped it entirely. He hoped in that manner to seriously weaken Popovich's financial status, and thus force him to do his bidding. The scheme, however, failed.

During the war the Central Powers tried in diverse ways to control their subjects in the United States, including even those immigrants who had become American citizens. Austria-Hungary was especially active in issuing warnings to the natives of her revolting dependencies not to take part against her. The grim fate awaiting traitorous Croatians was clearly depicted in an item appearing on May 24, 1916, in the *Narodni List.*

But, Croatian people, although you are absolutely free to give your sympathies and divide your money among whomever you please, you must always bear in mind the following: if you help the enemies of your Croatian country and their lawful authorities, that is a treasonable act, and is terribly punished in every country in the world, including Austria-Hungary. If the Entente should win this war and our Croatian country should be divided among the Italians and Servians, the traitors would then escape punishment; but about such a victory there is no use talking. Everyone knows how little chance the Entente has of such a victory.

Therefore, if the Entente should lose the war, the traitors would be punished. There is no use of thinking that the Central powers (Germany and Austria) will be crushed, and that the Servians and Italians will divide among themselves the Croatian lands.

More straightforward was the admonition in the November 10, 1916, issue of the *Radnička Obrana* (Workers' Sentinel), a Croat journal published in Duluth, Minnesota.

The Imperial Embassy, by high order, notifies all the subjects of the Austro-Hungarian monarchy and the tributary states of

Bosnia and Herzegovina, that in case they are employed in factories where ammunitions and arms are made for the enemies of our country, they are violating Section 327 of the Austrian military law, committing a crime against the defense of their native country, which crime, by the above-mentioned law, is punishable with imprisonment for from ten to twenty years, and under aggravated circumstances by death.

The offenders against this law will be prosecuted after they return to their native country, and will be subjected to the severest penalties of the law.

Another interesting illustration of politics and the press is provided by Reverend Nikola Gršković as editor of *Zajedničar*. During his first years as head of this weekly organ of the National Croatian Union, a time when he was a rabid Croat nationalist, he used its pages to engage in a political campaign against Austria-Hungary and to arouse the spirit of patriotism of the Croatian immigrants to its highest pitch. *Zajedničar* published the most alarming news from Croatia. An open attack was directed against the diplomatic agents of Austria-Hungary in the United States, labeling them as the sworn enemies of the Slavs. When Count Albert Apponyi, a Hungarian politician, visited the United States in March, 1911, *Zajedničar* tried to induce the American authorities to deny him entry into the country. After that plan failed, it sought, in vain, to have him barred from various public meetings. Though Gršković presently shifted his course from extreme Croat patriotism to Yugoslav unity, he continued to use the *Zajedničar* as a political instrument, agitating for the complete freedom of the Croats, Serbs, and Slovenes from Habsburg control and the establishment of one state for all the South Slavs. Thus, it would seem to be obvious that the paper was far more interested in the events abroad and in influencing those events than it was in the developments in the Croat colonies in America.

Following the armistice in 1918 not only the *Zajedničar* but the Yugoslav press in general got into the thick of old-country politics. Conditions in the native land had much to do with the intensity of nationalistic feelings reflected in the press in America. The creation of an independent Yugoslav state brought in its wake many complicated problems of government, particularly concerning proportional representation, and the struggles at home were mirrored in the South Slav publications in this country. Especially intense was the strife between Croats and Serbs. Nationality was strongly played up in the press of these two groups in America.

The head of reaction was not only visible in the struggle in the homeland but also in developments elsewhere. A particularly conspicuous example is found in the Spanish Civil War. In this conflict the *Ameriška Domovina*, a Slovene Catholic daily in Cleveland, came out in full support of Francisco Franco and his Fascist band.

World War II introduced further interesting developments. As an experienced publisher stated, the war "cut deeply through the whole maze of political concepts evolved in previous decades and there is hardly any foreign-language editor whose writing has not been affected by this in one way or another." [43] The Yugoslav press faced a most difficult ideological dilemma. Should it support a free Yugoslavia or the various puppet regimes set up? *Ameriška Domovina* answered with support for the collaborationists of Slovenia, while *Hrvatski List,* a Croat triweekly published at the time in New York but now out of business, declared in favor of Axis-controlled Croatia. A strange case was that of the weekly newspaper, *Zajedničar,* official organ of the large and powerful Croatian Fraternal Union. The English section of this paper promoted Yugoslav freedom and unity, while the Croatian part, on the other hand, attempted to enlist support for Pavelić's puppet regime in Croatia. Serbian nationalism was vigorously supported by *Srbobran,* the publication of the Serb National Federation.

With the few exceptions that joined the quisling press or conducted a campaign of calumny, the great majority of the Yugoslav publications maintained sound, intelligent policies, and cast their lot on the side of a free and united Yugoslav state, fighting with the Allies. The editors of the Yugoslav American press in time gained a favorable position, largely through developments abroad, and could consequently bring some important issues into the open. Nazi cruelty against their European relatives made them determined enemies of the Axis and put them beyond suspicion of fifth-column activities while the gallant resistance of the Yugoslav guerrillas did the same for many of their kinsmen in America.[44] The story of the heroic fight of the Yugoslav patriots against the Axis invaders, carried in detail by many of the Croat, Serb, and Slovene periodicals, helped to offset, at least in part, the divisive propaganda of the extremely nationalistic publications and pave the way to greater unity among the American branches of the South Slav family. The publications also brought to light the Tito-Mihajlović controversy, and clarified, not only for their own readers, but for the American public, the puzzle of Yugoslavia's internal conflict.

That the immigrant press is important in war and peace is seen in the following statement of Yaroslav Chyz:

> In fact, it might be a great help to ultimate unity and the clarification of postwar aims if the English press would pay closer attention to the foreign-language press and get more seriously interested in matters and issues discussed there, which are not so much "stew in the melting pot" as warning grumblings of serious explosions of much concern to America. It would help both ways: the foreign-language press would see situations in the mirror of the English press in more objective perspective. And the English-language writers would learn that Americans of Polish, Croatian, Serbian, Slovak, Czech, Hungarian, and other descents are interested in European issues not so much because Hodza, Matuszewski, Eckhardt, Subotich, or others "stir them up," but often because they better see the possible dangers in the European situation.[45]

With the coming of peace in 1945, Yugoslav editors in America turned their attention to problems of government and reconstruction in their homeland. Excepting the few who would not resign themselves to the abolition of the monarchy and the establishment of a republic, most of them threw their support behind Tito and his party.

The publishers, however, were at no time so absorbed in the affairs of Europe that they forgot about American politics. Up to World War I the periodicals, by and large, supported Republican candidates and policies. But in the years following, they switched to the side of the Democrats, mainly because of their admiration for Woodrow Wilson who had spoken in defense of minorities. Not all editors, of course, joined the Democratic ranks. John R. Palandech (Palandačić), well-known Chicago publisher (*Jugoslavija* and *Jedinstvo*), is a good example of a life-long Republican. He did yeoman service for his party especially in the Harding, Coolidge, and Hoover campaigns.

160

It is claimed that in the elections of 1932 as many as 95 per cent of the foreign-language, including Yugoslav, newspapers were for Franklin D. Roosevelt and the Democratic candidates generally.[46] In the 1936 campaign the South Slavs remained in the Democratic column, with one publication, *Ameriška Domovina*, unashamedly advising its readers to stick to the Democratic party because the Republicans had freed the Negroes who competed with the whites for jobs. Fairly solid support of Democrats by Yugoslavs continued throughout the entire Roosevelt era. Even in his fourth bid for the presidency in 1944, as in his first in 1932, Roosevelt was a favorite of the South Slav press. A survey conducted by *Hrvatski Kalendar*, a Croat almanac, revealed that out of twenty-three periodicals studied, twelve supported Roosevelt, one favored Dewey, two backed other candidates, while the rest were neutral.[47]

In the national elections of 1948 most of the left-wing publications deserted the Democratic ranks and joined the camp of the newly-formed Progressives. *Narodni Glasnik* and *Slobodna Reč* of Pittsburgh, the *Slavic American*, organ of the influential American Slav Congress, and the *Trends and Tides*, a quarterly newsletter in English edited by Louis Adamic, led an intensive campaign among the Slav voters in behalf of Henry A. Wallace and the Progressive party candidates. This shift can perhaps be understood by recalling that these same publications supported the so-called "People's Democracies" of eastern Europe, governments also praised by the Progressives. With such exceptions, the Yugoslav press has remained within the fold of the regular Democratic organization, and it is most likely that as long as the Democratic party tends to favor a free press and the comman man, it will continue to receive the support of the Yugoslav as well as the immigrant press in general.

## PROMINENT JOURNALISTS

When Don Niko Gršković died on March 21, 1949, the Yugoslav American press lost one of its foremost editors. Though living in retirement for some years, his opinions were still respected and he continued to exert considerable influence on the publications of his countrymen.

Don Niko was born in the village of Vrbnik, Croatia, on November 22, 1863.[48] After completing his training for the Roman Catholic priesthood, he accepted a position as a teacher in a convent. But life behind the cloistered walls proved too dull for the effervescent youth, and he soon became embroiled in the Croat struggle for liberation from Hungary. Taking an active part in the resistance movement against Khuen Hedervary, the notorious governor of Croatia, he got into trouble with the authorities, with the result that continued residence in his native land grew increasingly untenable.

Accordingly, in 1901 Don Niko left Croatia and came to Chicago. In the Windy City he not only had the opportunity of making use of his theological training (serving as priest among the Catholic Croats in the city) but he also became associated with the leading Croatians of the day, most notable of whom were Dr. Ante Biankini and Nikola Polić. He presently joined Polić in the publication of the newspaper *Sloboda* (Freedom).

When Polić moved his paper to Cleveland in 1904, Gršković went along. While with *Sloboda,* Don Niko was offered the pastorship of the St. Paul Croatian Catholic Church in Cleveland. Gladly accepting the post, he went on to establish a reputation as one of the most outstanding Croat churchmen in America. With his brilliant sermons he filled the pews to overflowing each Sunday and holy day.

Becoming a member of the National Croatian Union, Gršković climbed up the ladder to the vice-presidency. He worked ceaselessly to bring about the merger of the numerous Croat societies throughout the country and the formation of the Croatian Fraternal Union. With the full cooperation of Josip Marohnić, the president of the organization, he led in the establishment of a juvenile section. But he probably made the most indelible mark upon the society as the editor of its official organ, *Zajedničar,* a position he assumed in 1909 when the publication was transformed from a monthly to a weekly. As chief of *Zajedničar* he not only carried on a running battle with Austria-Hungary, but he also labored industriously to make the journal one of the finest of its kind. When the supreme board of the association attempted to censor him, he fought back with all the powers at his command and emerged triumphant, thus firmly establishing an independent editorial policy for the weekly.

In 1912 Don Niko took over *Hrvatski Svijet* in New York, be-

162

coming its owner, publisher, and editor. For the next twenty-five years his was one of the most powerful voices in Yugoslav American journalism. His stimulating writings—ranging from local social events to international politics—were avidly read by his fellow immigrants throughout the length and breadth of the land. His barbed editorials were classics, required reading for the well-informed Yugoslav Americans. Many people, though disagreeing with the paper's policy, subscribed to *Svijet* because of the brilliant editorial style of its publisher.

At about the same time that he launched his *Svijet* enterprise Grškovic led in the formation of the Croatian Alliance, a patriotic group which aimed at severing the political bonds between Croatia and the Dual Monarchy. During World War I he gave up his priestly vestments (later marrying a Croat schoolteacher, Mandica Atalic) in order to devote more attention to Yugoslav unity. He helped found in Pittsburgh the Yugoslav National Council, whose spokesman he became. He was chosen a member of the Yugoslav Committee, which first had its headquarters in Rome and later in London. Both of these organizations ardently championed a unified Yugoslav state. In keeping with this goal of a union of all the South Slavs he changed the name of his paper to *Jugoslavenski Svijet*—only to return to the original name after the war. As a member of the Yugoslav Committee he called on the then United States Secretary of State, Robert Lansing, in Washington. There is little doubt that the Committee had some influence with the state department in getting official recognition for the new government of Yugoslavia.

Don Niko was disillusioned by the postwar developments in Yugoslavia. He was deeply grieved by the endless strife between the Croats and Serbs. Though he lost some of his former enthusiasm, he remained unyielding with his ideals. Indeed, he continued for the remainder of his active life to give much of his energy to eliminating the sources of friction between the South Slavs in Europe and America, so as to enable them to live in harmony. And in the same fashion he toiled to bring greater understanding among the various branches of the Slav family.

That Grškovic was loved and respected by his fellow Yugoslav Americans is putting it mildly. Louis Adamic called him the dean of the South Slavic editors in America.[49] *Narodni Glasnik* referred to him as the most prominent representative of the Yugoslav immigrants in America and one whose role in the cultural progress of his kinsmen in this country would never be forgotten.[50] Croatian Fraternal Union President V. I. Mandich, writing in the *Zajedničar*, declared that fifty years of diligent labor in behalf of his fellow immigrants in America would always be remembered and that the name of Gršković would remain inscribed in gold letters in the history of the fraternal federation.[51]

When Gršković retired from the *Svijet* and his place was taken by Anton Tanasković, there were some expressions of doubt regarding the caliber of journalism that was to follow. The hard work and resourcefulness of Tanasković, however, soon dispelled the early doubts. Under the new editor, *Svijet* maintained the highest journalistic standards and in consequence continued as one of the topmost publications of the Yugoslavs in America.

Veljko Radojević of San Francisco was also a newspaperman of first rank. Radojević was born in April, 1868, in Herceg Novi in Boka Kotorska, and first began writing in the newspapers of his homeland in 1888. He came to the United States in 1900 and shortly afterward became editor of *Srpska Nezavisnost* (Serbian Independence). From then on he enjoyed a most successful journalistic career, studded with many brilliant accomplishments. He won recognition as one of the most influential and inspiring Serbian American newspapermen during the half century of his active service. Even after his retirement Radojević did not lose any of his earlier love for journals in this country.

Other eminent figures in this early era of Yugoslav American journalism were A. G. Skrivanić, Nikola Polić, Zdravko Valentin Mužina, Josip Marohnić, Frank Zotti, Francis K. Kolander, Špiro Radulović, Dmitar Šaban, Velimir Hajdin, Dushan Popovich, Frank Zemlar, Frank L. Dakser, and Etbin Kristan. The name of Skrivanić stands high on the list of foreign-language newspapermen. He was the founder, editor, and publisher of *Napredak* and *Hrvatska* (Croatia) and the first editor of *Zajedničar*. Polić founded, edited, and published *Chicago*, which he later merged with *Sloboda*. A brilliant and ambitious journalist, Mužina was the founder, editor, and publisher of *Danica* and had far-reaching plans for the establishment of a publishing house which would issue Croatian books regularly, but the project never got off the ground. Marohnić was a

164

versatile and gifted person, being a successful businessman, fraternalist, lexicographer, writer, editor, printer, and publisher. In the field of publications he is best known for his association with *Brico* and *Hrvatski Glasnik*, which he founded, edited, and published. Zotti, New York banker, ship owner, and publisher, used his wealth and his publications to promote his own personal ambitions. He came very close in 1906 to reaching one of his most cherished goals: control of the National Croatian Union. By paying all the expenses of the delegates to the ninth convention of the federation in New York, he succeeded in getting a majority of the votes for supreme president. But his tenure was extremely abbreviated, lasting only from September 24 to October 6, 1906, when he was ousted in a new, free election. Francis Kolander was widely known as a talented editor of *Zajedničar* and one of the early Croat leaders in America.

One of the pioneers of Serbian journalism in the United States was Špiro Radulović, who was associated with various Serb publications in the San Francisco Bay area for many years. Both Dmitar Šaban and Velimir Hajdin are remembered for their pioneer work with *Srbin* (Serb), the official organ of the Srbobran federation and the forerunner of the later *Amerikanski Srbobran*. Šaban, a highly competent immigrant from Montenegro, first attracted attention among the Serbs and Croats of Denver as editor, printer, and publisher of his own paper, called *Srbin*. In 1901 he accepted the invitation of Srbobran to transfer his printery and paper to Pittsburgh and work for the society. Though his career was cut short by death from tuberculosis, Šaban was an important force in the expansion of the fraternal organization in its infancy. Hajdin followed Šaban and tried to maintain the high standards set by his predecessor.

Dushan Popovich was for over a generation an outstanding Serb journalist and businessman. As head of the Dushan Popovich Publishing Company in New York, he was the founder, editor, and publisher of *Srbobran* and *Srpski Dnevnik* (Serbian Daily). Frank Zemlar, a schoolteacher in his native Slovenia, turned to newspaper work after his entry into the United States in the last years of the nineteenth century and eventually became the editor of *Narodni Glas*, a leading Slovene publication in New York. One of the most successful competitors of Zotti in banking and publishing was Frank

Dakser, a Slovene with widespread business interests in New York. Etbin Kristan won wide acclaim as the two-fisted editor of the *Slovenian Review* (later renamed *Jugo-Slav Review*) during World War I, championing the cause of a free and united Yugoslav republic. In later years he served as editor of the Slovenian *Cankarjev Glasnik* (Cankar's Herald), a cultural monthly magazine.

Conspicuous among the distinguished Yugoslav American journalists was also John R. Palandech, one-time president of the Foreign-Language Press Association. Emigrating to the United States in 1887, when only thirteen years of age, Palandech serves as a fine example of success against many odds. After spending several years in northern California, where he won a reputation as an outstanding baseball player, he moved to Chicago. With tremendous energy, industry, and initiative as his assets, he gradually achieved success as an authority on problems relating to immigration in the United States.[52] In one of its leading editorials, a California paper commented:

> John R. Palandech, the Serb, might be described as the "Northcliffe" of the foreign-language newspapers and an immigrant who settled on the land in this country. Palandech came to America with habits of thrift and industry, little else. In his own country those habits could barely keep the wolf from the door. Here he saw they could chase him so far he never could get back, and he acted on this determination and succeeded.[53]

After a long and illustrious career Palandech left his old familiar desk on Chicago's South Clark Street, giving up the operation of the publishing firm to his family.

The list of important Yugoslav American journalists is much too long to be included in its entirety in such a work as this. However, some mention should be made of figures like the late Ivan Mladineo; Vlaho S. Vlahovic, former editor of *Jugoslavenski Glasnik*, *Slavonic Monthly*, and numerous other publications, and now engaged in independent research and writing; Philip Vukelich (Croatian section) and Stephen F. Brkich (English section), editors of *Zajedničar*; Momchilo Sokich (Serbian section) and Milan Karlo (English section), editors of *Srbobran*; Frank Zaitz, editor of *Prosveta*; Anton Šabec, editor of *Glas Slovenske Dobrodelne Zveze*; Stephen J. Dedier, editor of *Slobodna Reč*; Anthony Minerich, editor of *Narodni Glasnik*; Victor J. Valjavec, editor of *Glas Naroda*; Lazar

Petrovich, editor of *Radnička Borba*; Stanley Borić, editor of *Naša Nada;* S. Vrancich, editor of *Američki Hrvatski Glasnik;* Reverend Celestin Raguz, editor of *Hrvatski List;* Vatro J. Grill, editor of *Amerikanski Slovenec*; Anna Krasna, editor of *Novi List*; and Corinne Leskovar, editor of *Zarja.*

## A Rocky Road

Most of the Yugoslav publications have always had a struggle for existence. Of the hundreds of journals started, only a small percentage has survived. The belief has been expressed that in another two decades or so most, if not all, of the foreign-language periodicals will disappear for lack of subscribers.[54] The difficulties of the press, Yugoslav as well as the general immigrant, stem from several vitally important factors.

Many of the publications die because they are neither well conceived nor well conducted. The birth and death statistics of the periodicals are reflections of their immaturity and instability. Financial burdens have pressed heavily upon the press, especially upon the independent organs. To help defray the costs of publication some of the editors resorted to such devices as selling books, pamphlets, phonograph records, sheet music, money orders, steamship tickets, and goods and materials for shipment to Europe. The added income, however, was, in most instances, insufficient to keep the journals afloat. The publications of the several mutual benefit associations, on the other hand, have had a much easier time with their finances, which partially explains why they have survived and remained comparatively strong. Special assessments for the support of the official organs made upon the members of the societies have relieved the publishers of many financial worries. The Croatian Fraternal Union, for example, from the very beginning taxed its members four cents a month for the support of the *Zajedničar,* which made for a revenue of $25,000 annually, providing for better editing and writing.

The Yugoslav as well as the entire foreign-language press suffered the most damaging blow from the restrictive legislation of the twenties. The drastic cut in the number of immigrants meant a similar reduction in the number of potential readers. From this severe stroke the press never recovered. With new immigrants denied admission and the old dying off rapidly or becoming assimi-

167

lated, the editors faced a truly challenging problem. To deal with it, English sections were introduced and programs adopted to teach the second generation the language of their parents. But these efforts were simply not enough to replace the great loss of readers caused by immigration restriction. As Maurice R. Davie says, "Declining immigration and increasing assimilation presage the eventual disappearance of the foreign-language press." [55]

Added disasters followed in the economic depression and World War II, when many periodicals went under. The rapidly declining list of subscribers during the depression caused many a publication to fold up. The war was an especially trying period. As a result of the conflict, steamship lines and foreign banks operating branches in the United States suffered loss of business and consequently ceased to advertise in the foreign-language publications, as did also manufacturers of automobiles, refrigerators, and similar commodities. In return the publications suffered financial losses through the decline of advertising. At the same time, the war stopped the transmission of newspapers and other periodicals from abroad, thereby severing American foreign-language publications from the chief source of European homeland news.[56]

To complicate conditions even more there was talk among the military favoring suspension of some periodicals and the licensing of others. Attorney General Francis Biddle and the Department of Justice, however, would not agree to this, but supported instead a system of general licensing which would enable the government to weed out the undesirable publications while permitting the others to continue.[57] Those officials favoring this latter program of licensing explained that those journals that were not disloyal to the United States were extremely useful in bridging the gap between the government and the aliens, as was so well demonstrated in such instances as alien registration. To legislate against foreign-language periodicals would deprive several million foreign born of all reading matter.[58] Elimination of the press, it was feared, might lead to unrest in some areas; many aliens who were loyal to America but who were not yet able to read or speak English would lose all contact with American policies; and at the same time the government would be deprived of a very useful means of measuring sentiment in places which were heavily populated by aliens.

Nor did the government fail to take note of the agitation of

168

the émigré politicians. Some of the periodicals, such as the *Ameriška Domovina*, carried on campaigns against peoples, parties, and/or regimes. Politicians like Konstantin Fotich, then ambassador to Washington, and Jovan Dučić, a pan-Serb poet and member of the Yugoslav diplomatic corps, tried to use the South Slav, especially the Serbian, press as a means of influencing Yugoslav Americans and the United States government for or against policies or individuals in the old country. In the face of these abuses the Office of War Information asked the entire foreign-language press not to create dissension by arguing about such matters as frontiers or emphasizing divisions among the Allies.

The cessation of hostilities eliminated the problems created by war, but still left many others for the editors of immigrant publications to wrestle with. Some gains were made in the boom period after the war, but not sufficient to remove the many dark shadows that loom along the path of tomorrow.

## RADIO AND TELEVISION PROGRAMS

It is believed that foreign-language radio broadcasts may very well be a factor in the decline of the foreign-language press. Of the nearly 1,000 radio stations in the United States in 1942, over 200 stations broadcast in twenty-six foreign languages to a potential audience of 15,000,000 persons, an estimated 3,000,000 of whom neither spoke nor understood English.[59] It has been pointed out that in the first month after Pearl Harbor these stations put on 6,776 hours of programs in twenty-nine tongues, ranging in time on the air from Italian, Polish, Spanish, Jewish, and German with the most hours, to Armenian, Slovene, and Mesquakie with the least.[60]

As a medium for communicating ideas to Yugoslavs in the United States, radio broadcasts are not yet of great importance. They are neither numerous nor of a high cultural level in comparison to the English-language broadcasts, since most of the listeners, to whom, after all, the advertisers make their appeal, are of backgrounds with lower economic and educational standards.

Yugoslav radio programs usually run from half an hour to an hour, seldom over that. Like the programs of the Poles, Italians, Spaniards, and Jews, those of the South Slavs also devote most of their time to musical items, advertisements, and news reports.

169

Music generally takes up about three-fourths of the time. The pieces played are chiefly of the old-country brand, interspersed occasionally with American songs as an appeal to the American-born listeners. Though records are used most of the time, *tamburica* orchestras and singing societies frequently perform. The commercials, which follow nearly every musical rendition, are usually long and boring, with announcers calling attention to importers' items, neighborhood grocery and meat markets, restaurants, beer parlors, furniture stores, and so on. Squeezed in between the music and advertising are bits of news, dealing largely with politics in the old country and in America. Oftentimes announcements are made calling attention to forthcoming activities (picnics, athletic contests, dances, plays, concerts) sponsored by Yugoslav organizations.

Not many Yugoslavs have as yet demonstrated interest in television programs, due at least in part to the prohibitive costs of this new medium. The few programs that have been introduced emanate from the more important Yugoslav centers, where comparatively large numbers of the immigrants can be reached. Perhaps with the increased growth of television and a reduction of costs more of the immigrants will transfer to the screens.

Much yet remains to be done with Yugoslav radio broadcasts and telecasts in order to make them a major factor of influence in the South Slav communities in America. Until such development, if it comes at all, the press, though on the decline, will undoubtedly continue as one of the most potent influences in the lives of the immigrants.

# 8

# A New Life

ONE OF THE MOST SERIOUS PROBLEMS confronted by the average Yugoslav immigrant was adaptation to the American environment. In Europe he had lived in the country and led a simple peasant existence, while in the United States he settled in the city where life was much more complex. His language, customs, and habits, in fact his entire cultural heritage and experience, were sharply different from the American. In other words, he was a total stranger in the new land. Until the immigrant, therefore, made the necessary adjustments, his life was beset with many difficulties.

## TRIALS OF AN IMMIGRANT

Trouble for the immigrant began immediately upon his arrival. His helplessness made him an easy prey for cheaters and exploiters, who attacked in force as soon as he left the paternal care of Ellis Island. Swooping down upon the unfortunate victim were boarding-house runners, shady employment agents, sellers of shoddy wares, extortionate hack drivers, and expressmen, all of whom aimed at taking away his money. Were the woes of the alien over once he had successfully run this gantlet of sharks, perhaps his lot would not have been such a bad one. But more shocks and jolts were in store for him as is so capably illustrated in the case studies of Edith Abbott, who made a thorough investigation of immigrants in trouble from disembarkation to grave. The following incident shows the misfortunes that befell two Yugoslav young ladies:

Two Croatian girls, Raisa Pavlik, age seventeen, and Maria Pavlik, age nineteen, brought to Immigrants' Protective League office [Chicago] by representatives of Traveller's Aid, from La Salle Street Station where they were found without tickets or money. Maria explained that they were cousins travelling to California from Ellis Island to join John Pavlik, father of Raisa, and that they had lost their tickets to San Francisco. The girls arrived on the Cunard S.S. "Pannonia," from Trieste, second cabin, April 24, [1914]. At Buffalo, where they changed trains, Maria dropped her handbag, which contained their tickets and most of their money. A man picked it up and got away with it before they could make anyone understand what they had lost. The girls had, however, some money in their lunch basket. They said nobody could understand them in Buffalo. They decided to go on to some other large town in the hope of finding a Croatian colony or Croatian interpreter who could send word to their uncle. They said they were walking all around trying to find a Croatian interpreter. Then they spent all their money and got tickets to Chicago and now have not one cent in pocket. They wish to telegraph John Pavlik, the father of Raisa; she has his address in notebook as Oakdale, California. The girls bought their railroad tickets as well as steamship tickets in Fiume for 643 kronen, second-class steamer and third-class railroad. *Later.*—The following night letter sent to John Pavlik, Oakdale, California, P. O. Box 715: "Raisa and Maria Pavlik stranded in Chicago—money and tickets to Oakdale, California, stolen in Buffalo, while changing trains. Wire enough money for tickets and expenses for them to go on. Immigrants' Protective League."

Three days later John Pavlik, of Oakdale, California, telegraphed $150 to the League and the girls were sent at once.[1]*

Much more pathetic was the plight of the maiden who came to America on the promise of marriage only to be disappointed, as was the Croat girl, Nina.

Nina Talpiniuk, Croatian girl, sent by A. K. [Slavic visitor of the Immigrants' Protective League in charge of the Dearborn station in Chicago] in a cab to 1100 Westover Street. She returned in the afternoon to the office. She was crying because she found Jakub Dubiac, man she came to marry, had wedded last week. Girl would not stay with man's sister and wants League to find work her her. Girl had our card from the station

* Notes to this chapter begin on page 293.

172

and came back to us. A. K. asked girl if Jakub sent her ticket. She said he bought her ticket but long time ago. She was kept one week at Ellis Island and telegraphed Jakub. His sister, Mrs. Anastazia Kris, 1100 Westover Street, sent affidavit to Ellis Island; and when this arrived, Nina was released.

Nina was born in Russia and came with her parents to Croatia, where she met Jakub Dubiac and was engaged to him four years ago. Jakub went to America, and two years ago he sent Nina a steamship ticket. Nina was working with a family for six years, and the lady tried to persuade Nina to stay with her and send the passage back. Nina could not decide what to do, because the family was very good to her and she liked them all very much. Finally about a year ago she left but had a hard time to come to this country. First she was detained for a week in Agram, then in Paris, and finally at the port because she did not have a pass from Russia. It took a long time before the important pass from Russia came and the girl could sail. Then in New York she was detained again at Ellis Island. The affidavit was furnished by Jakub's sister, who, to prevent the girl's deportation, promised that Jakub would marry her. At that time Mrs. Kris did not know surely that her brother was ready to marry another girl because he thought Nina did not care for him.

A. K. told girl we will find her place in a few days. [Case closed when Mrs. Kris took Nina into her home and got her a job doing housework.][2]

Another serious problem faced by the immigrant was detention at Ellis Island for illness, as the following case from the records of the Immigrants' Protective League illustrates:

April 25, 1914.—Josef Novak, age 44 years, address 1000 Teal Street [Chicago], in office. He was sent by the Austro-Hungarian consul to our office for B. P. to help in arranging for admission of his wife and four children from Ellis Island. Mr. Novak, a Croatian, is a laborer in the International Plough Works and has been earning $12 a week, but is out of work at present. He saved the money to bring over his wife and four children and has furnished a four-room flat on the installment plan. April 6, when he was expecting his wife and children to arrive, he received a telegram from Ellis Island that youngest child was sick. . . . Soon after this he received also a letter from a Croatian Society in New York explaining that he must deposit $150 for treatment of child Jannina, who is sick, and then the mother and three children can come to Chicago. He had only $30 when the letter came; but now he has borrowed from a Croatian friend the $150, which he wishes the League to send to Ellis Island for him and to bring his wife and other children here. Mr. Novak left money for us to send if we think necessary. . . .

May 2, 1914.—Josef Novak in office with letter from Congressman Henry, saying "that the child Jannina has a fractured leg both bones. She is doing nicely, but it is impossible to say how soon she will be able to travel. . . ."

May 15, 1914.—Reply from Ellis Island containing the following: "Referring to your letter of the 8th instant forwarding money order for $150 from Mr. Josef Novak, I write to inform you that Marya Novak and three children were permitted to land today, to join the husband and father in Chicago. The child Jannina is still detained in the Ellis Island Hospital under treatment for fractured leg."

June 30, 1914.—"Follow up" visit by B. P. B. P. found family living in basement, rear house. The house conditions were bad at Novak's. Man is sick in bed with lung trouble; he attends the Eastern Dispensary, the only time he leaves bed. They do not have any furniture, there are no sheets on beds, other ways all is clean. Mr. Novak is out of work since March, 1914. The only supporter of the family is the fifteen-year-old son, who earns $3 per week at Richards' Box Factory. Oldest daughter (eighteen years) just started work at the Chicago Can Factory on Maxwell Street. She does not know how much she will earn. Mr. Novak received a letter from Congressman Henry that his little daughter . . . must have her foot amputated and father's consent is necessary and his presence. Mr. Novak went to Mr. Henry and told him about his troubles and the situation. Mr. Novak was injured at the International Plough Company, April 18, 1913. He was two months in St. Luke's Hospital, did not work till October, when he got an easier job, worked again until March this year. Since that time he kept going and going to ask for work but did not get any. He has a piece of paper in his hand, he thought it was valuable, but it is a few lines from a manager of one department to a manager of another about a chance of finding work for this man. . . .

July 30, 1914.—Visited the Novaks. Mr. Novak is at home. He stayed in the County Hospital ten days only. The boy does not work because the shop where he worked burned down four weeks ago. The oldest daughter earns $6 per week. . . . Asked Mr. Novak more about his injury. He worked at the International Plough Company as a molder, earning 20 cents per hour, worked 12 hours a day. April 18, 1913, he was injured through the fault of a boy who worked with him, who filled the dipper with the liquid metal to overflowing and spilled it on Mr. Novak's foot. Mr. Novak was two months in St. Luke's Hospital and was getting compensation $6 per week till July, but was not able to work till October, when he got different work, earning $1 less per day—fourth floor, bolts and nuts making. He worked until March, 1914, and lost the job. He could not secure any other work. Now he is sick. He gave his case about the time his family was detained to Mr. James, the brother of Alderman James, whom he asked for help when the child was sick and the family at Ellis Island.[3]

Novak, laid up in bed with tuberculosis, grew progressively worse and died in September, 1914. His family received $14 insurance. The oldest daughter, who had meanwhile quit her job at the can factory and had gone to work for her father's former employer, was discharged by the plough company, who explained that it was too soon after her father's death from tuberculosis and that they employed no one in whose family there was such a sickness for at least two years afterwards. The mother went to work in the stockyards, while the son remained on his old job. Jannina came home after her father's death and was placed in a home for crippled children, where she remained for several years. The family apparently became self-supporting and made no further demands on the charities.[4]

Lest the impression be created that only the earlier immigrants met with difficulties, it should be pointed out that more recent arrivals have had more than their share of troubles. As an interpreter for the United States Immigration and Naturalization Service in Hammond, Indiana, the writer had occasion to witness many interesting cases of immigrants charged with illegal entry. But one of the strangest cases to come to the author's attention is that of Ivan Visić. Visić, a Dalmatian sailor, served for three years during World War II with the United Nations merchant seamen's pool. He hoped this service would aid him in attaining his ambition of building a home in America for his wife and four children, left behind in Yugoslavia. He thought his chance came at last when Congress provided special legislation qualifying members of the merchant seamen's pool as quota immigrants. There was just one hitch: the law stated that such applicants must re-enter this country. Visić, consequently, went to Cuba, filled out the necessary forms, and returned to Miami, Florida, in September, 1948. However, as soon as he set foot on American soil, he was arrested by immigration officials, who claimed to be acting under a new regulation which went into effect on September 1 and which granted the Attorney General of the United States the power to deny admission and deport any person suspected of subversive activities. For the next three months Visić was held on secret charges and denied freedom on bail until a writ of habeas corpus was granted by the federal district judge against the immigration office. According to the immigration authorities the freeing of Visić did not close the case, for they planned to continue the fight, to the United States Supreme Court if necessary.

The experiences of the Visićes, Novaks, Talpiniuks, and Pavliks are undoubtedly extraordinary. There have been, however, many other Yugoslavs who encountered countless obstacles and suffered indescribable hardships in starting a new life in America, but who remained unknown to government officials, immigrant societies, and welfare organizations.

## The Alien and the Law

In nearly every phase of life in the new environment the immigrants began with a strike against them. Distrusted and suspected simply because they were different, the aliens were blamed for most of the crime in the land. Before the law, as elsewhere, they were easy victims of exploitation because of their poverty and ignorance. They suffered from ill usage at the hands of those who should have been officers of justice, from arrests for the sake of fees, from unjust fines, from excessive costs paid in order not to incur greater expenses, and particularly from the foul treatment of the shyster lawyers that they hired. And if they were unable to speak English, which was usually the case, they were really seriously handicapped, for then their fate generally depended upon the interpreters hired by the court. That the court interpreters were disgracefully incompetent was clearly shown by several investigations, especially those conducted by the Massachusetts Commission on Immigration and the Immigrants' Protective League. The type of interpreters employed is admirably illustrated in the

176

following case.[5]  A man regularly used by a Boston court was asked
to translate a paragraph, which in correct form, read:

> Frank Zgodzinoki, sixteen years of age, was arrested for steal-
> ing coal from the N. Y. Central Railroad yard.  During the
> hearing of the case it was learned that the boy was sent by his
> mother to get coal.  The boy was discharged, but the judge
> threatened to send his mother to jail if she taught the boy to steal.

After much struggle, the interpreter came out with the following:

> There was arrested 16 Francis Zgodzinoki for something about
> the mother.  I understand some the mother was arrested in some
> affairs.  Central President, that is New York Central.

Another interpreter brought out this classic result:

> It was arrested about sixteen years ago a man by the name of
> Francisco Zgodzinoki.  The charge was the larceny of the New
> York Central.  He was tried and acquitted.  His mother sent a
> boy.  He was asked the question whether he was going to learn
> the children to steal.

Under such conditions, it should not be surprising that many
aliens were haled into court, falsely accused, and unjustly convicted.

That immigrant and criminal were not synonymous, as had been
believed by many Americans, particularly the Mayflower variety,
was first concretely demonstrated by the United States Immigration
Commission.  In its report of *Immigration and Crime,* the Commission concluded:

> No satisfactory evidence has yet been introduced to show that
> immigration has resulted in an increase in crime disproportionate
> to the increase in adult population.  Such comparable statistics
> of crime and population as it has been possible to obtain indicate
> that immigrants are less prone to commit crime than are native
> Americans.[6]

The National Commission on Law Observance and Enforcement in its report on the incidence of crime among immigrants
disclosed that there was a comparatively low rate of crime among
immigrants of peasant extraction.[7]  The report also made clear that
many charges of crime among immigrants were not supported by
fact.  "Some disorders," stated the report, "have certainly from time

177

to time been chargeable to immigrants, but these have not been so serious or so numerous as to occasion grave concern."[8]   Statistics upon which the National Commission's report was based do not justify association of immigrants with crime increases.   The report elaborated:

> Another reason for the constant repetition of these attacks on the immigrant lies in the ready acceptance of the easy theory that our social difficulties are not to be charged to our own mistakes and failures.   It is easy to shift the responsibilities for what is wrong by charging it upon the nationals of other countries.   It is easier, for example, to charge our crime record against immigrants than against an inefficient and corrupt system of police and an outworn system of criminal justice.
>
> Charging our high crime rates against the foreign born is merely evading the real difficulties of life instead of trying to solve them.   To continue to follow the method of preferring charges against the immigrant is the method of adopting one policy because it is the "easy way"—the line of least resistance—and rejecting another method because it is more difficult.   But an attempt to face squarely the more difficult problems of life is more in line with our American traditions.[9]

Among the new immigrants most arrests by the police used to be on charges of disorderly conduct and drunkenness.   The incidence of more serious offenses was comparatively low.[10]   Peter Roberts, in a study made in 1909 in a section of Pittsburgh, found that 27 per cent of cases of drunkenness and disorderly conduct were charged against immigrants from southeastern Europe.[11]   Out of the thirty-one cases of desertion and nonsupport not one Slav was implicated.[12]   Nicholas Mirkovich, the late Yugoslav American sociologist, found that "cases of Yugoslav immigrants before American courts are in no proportion to their numerical significance in the respective communities."[13]

During the prohibition days, however, there were a good number of bootleggers among the South Slavs.   According to Mirkovich, 80 per cent of male Yugoslavs of working age in Spokane, Washington, were engaged in illegal production and distribution of intoxicating liquors.[14]   In some towns in California, Missouri, Minnesota, and Wisconsin also the ratio was comparatively high.[15]   Mirkovich explains:

178

As for the type of illegal enterprises and activity, there are a few facts to be underlined.  Since the bootleggers had once been immigrant farmers who had produced liquors for domestic consumption in the old country, they were all skilled along the line.  Most of the enterprises were rather small and were operated for the needs of a defined market, based on neighborhood relations.  Facts influencing to some extent the bootlegging activities of the Yugoslavs were their engagement in farming in the Pacific states and Minnesota, and the large number of restaurants and beer parlors owned by them in San Francisco, San Pedro, Sacramento, Oakland, Seattle, Tacoma, Pittsburgh, and other cities.  Very seldom was the violation of prohibition regulations connected with offenses against life, property, and public security.[16]

A Croatian saloonkeeper in Chicago pointed out to the writer that he hadn't known anything but farming in Europe and bartending in America, and explained how he had invested everything he had made in his business.  In that situation he felt that it would have meant ruination for him and his family to have shut shop with the inauguration of prohibition.  He therefore closed the front door and opened the side and back doors, determined to carry on outside the law if he could not do so within its bounds.  Buying "moonshine" from illegal distributors, he often had to carry it home in hot-water bags strapped to his body.  Despite several arrests, he managed to keep his business going and remain solvent during the lean years of prohibition.

It is thus quite evident that Yugoslavs violated the prohibition law unashamed.  Big-time gangsters and racketeers, however, did not flourish at any time in the South Slav communities.  In fact, it was the testimony of a Slovenian immigrant, Gus Korach, supported by that of many other Slovenians in Cleveland including Frank J. Lausche, then city judge and later governor of Ohio, that ended the fraudulent practices of the "cemetery mob" in that city and sent its members behind bars.  Similarly, the detective work of Martin Zarkovich, an East Chicago, Indiana, police officer, was very instrumental in ending the criminal career of the notorious John Dillinger, who terrorized the Midwest with his kill-crazy gang in 1933-1934.

To crime in general, it is plain, the Yugoslavs have contributed only a small percentage.  Their peasant background makes them great respecters of property, and the close-knit character of their colonies retains a social cohesion that serves to keep delinquency and crime to a minimum. The general attitude of the immigrants toward law violation can perhaps be summed up in the statement that what was a crime in Croatia, Serbia, and Slovenia was looked upon as a crime in the United States. That which was regarded as a protest against oppression in the old country had the same status in America. The only exception would be found in a case where the unity of the group was threatened.

An illustration of this is seen in the practice of blood revenge among the Montenegrins in the region of Boka Kotorska. If a Montenegrin in this country heard that his brother had been killed at home, he might very well return and get revenge. But, on the other hand, he might be living in America with a man who had killed a member of his family in Europe and continue on friendly terms with him as long as the two were in this country. If, however, this traditional enemy returned to his native land, he would have to be on guard against possible reprisal from his erstwhile friend. The principle behind this custom is expressed in the Montenegrin proverb, "When you're in strange world, you have to be brothers." As long as the definition of crime in the native land was clear-cut, the immigrant felt that he did not dare commit such an act in America, for then he would be disgraced in the old country and would be disowned by his family. It was a common practice for a South Slav who had committed a crime not to let his family hear from him but to let them think he was dead so that they would make no further attempt to communicate with him.

## CHANGES IN THE IMMIGRANT COMMUNITY

The typical Yugoslav immigrant, as already noted, came to the United States with only a few dollars in his pockets and unfamiliar with the language, customs, and institutions of the Americans. Poverty and ignorance made him the object of suspicion and hostility and an easy victim of exploitation. Therefore, in order to escape from this position of insecurity, the alien joined his countrymen in their homogeneous little colony in a section of an urban center.

These immigrant communities have undoubtedly aided the newcomers in adjusting themselves to the new environment by the establishment of the customs and institutions of the native land, but they have at no time succeeeded in reproducing exactly the cultural pattern of the old country. One of the chief reasons for this is to be found in the fact that these communities have never been wholly isolated and American influences have constantly penetrated into them. Consequently, the American environment has forced changes in both the material and nonmaterial aspects of culture.

Thus, change has occurred in dress, food, home environment, work, language, selection of names, education, religion, and in other phases of life and behavior. The children and grandchildren do not adhere very closely to the old ways but instead take up the the new. As a result the heritage of the groups becomes a strange mixture of old-country and American culture elements. It is neither wholly that of the native land nor that of the United States, but rather partly one and partly the other as each is modified in retention or acceptance. Some of the more significant modifications of the Yugoslav culture pattern will be discussed in the pages that follow.

## SOCIAL LIFE

Many of the first Yugoslav immigrants in the United States, as seen previously, were men without their families or unmarried, and they made their home in boardinghouses near the mills and mines where they were employed. The married men eventually brought their families to this country, and the later immigrants often came with their families or quickly sent for them. The newcomers generally found dwellings in congested, run-down sections, sometimes in cellars or garrets.[17]

Josip Subašić, an early Croat arrival in Millvale, Pennsylvania, gives a glimpse of the conditions of life among the immigrants in the last years of the nineteenth century. In recounting his experiences, he told how he lived in a shack with twenty other aliens and how he and his companions suffered from the torments of the neighborhood children. It appears that these young bullies found it highly amusing to heap ridicule and abuse upon the poor foreigners who did not know how to defend themselves. The immigrants were called "Hunkies" and stoned by the blustering youngsters. Finally Subašić appealed to the police, who put a stop to the attacks by punishing both the guilty children and their parents. Thenceforth the aliens remained unmolested.[18] The experience of Subašić certainly is not unique. Other immigrants undoubtedly

181

underwent similar trials. Their alien language and strange ways made them the natural targets of immature, narrow-minded individuals who could not, or would not, understand them.

Many immigrant families took in boarders in order to make ends meet. The result was overcrowding on an unprecedented scale, a condition which would make present-day tenements appear uninhabited by comparison. It was not unusual to see several beds in the living room and three or four in the bedrooms, with large steamer trunks in the corners.

The South Slavs were among the leading boardinghouse keepers. The investigation of the United States Immigration Commission revealed that out of 617 Croatian households studied, 367 kept a total of 2,344 boarders, or 3.80 boarders per household.[19] Among the Serbians 64 out of 67 families kept a total of 464 boarders, for an average of 6.78 boarders per household.[20] The Slovenians, seemingly more independent, did not adhere as closely to this type of living arrangement. One hundred and seventy-four Slovenian families were studied and only 57 were found to be keeping boarders, a total of 214, or 1.23 boarders per family.[21]

Yugoslav immigrants, being related or coming from the same or neighboring villages, generally lived in homogeneous groups called *društva* (cooperative households), a carry-over no doubt from the *zadruga* in Yugoslavia. In these *društva,* ordinary living expenses were divided equally among the membership. These households were chiefly of two types: (1) those with a male house-boss who was customarily paid for cooking, cleaning, and managing the household; and (2) those without a house-boss, where the work was done cooperatively and the men took turns at various jobs.

The position of the house-boss was frequently that also of banker and general counselor, since he was usually the one best acquainted with the institutions, customs, and language of the Americans. He took care of the boarders' savings, wrote their letters, sent money to Europe for them, and helped them bring relatives and friends to the United States.

If the boss was a married man and devoted his time to a regular occupation outside the home, he was considered as an ordinary member of the *društvo* and had to contribute his share to the household expenses. In that case the boss' wife performed the function of the house-boss, doing the necessary housework. On the first of every month the entire membership met, went over the accounts, and then distributed the cost of food, rent, heat, light, and service equally among the regular members.[22]

Both of these types of *društva* differed from the regular boardinghouse arrangement, where the boarder paid by the month and the husband and wife shared the management problems, with the wife doing the major share of domestic labor. This cooperative life of the immigrants is concisely described in the following passage:

> Under the "boarding-boss" arrangement a married immigrant or his wife, or a single man, constitutes the head of the household, which, in addition to the family of the head, will usually be made up of from two to twenty boarders or lodgers. Each lodger pays the boarding boss a fixt sum, ordinarily from $2 to $3 per month, for lodging, cooking and washing, the food being bought by the boarding-boss and its cost shared equally by the individual members of the group. Another common arrangement is for each member of the household to purchase his own food and have it cooked separately. Under this method of living, which prevails among the greater proportion of the immigrant households, the entire outlay for necessary living expenses of each adult member ranges from $9 to $15 each month.[23]

The ambitious couple in a boardinghouse could always make a slight additional profit by making or buying a keg of beer or a barrel of wine and selling it to the boarders. Since most of the immigrants were financially pressed, they did a great deal of personal borrowing from one another, but it was a point of honor to repay.

These early South Slav colonies at the beginning of the century consisted almost entirely of men, and the *društvo* type of living in a one-sex community undoubtedly encouraged a certain amount of promiscuity. If, however, there were women cooking for the household, they were universally respected as members of the group. Quarreling and feuding among members of different families or different groups were not infrequent, and there was a certain amount of violence. Because of the veritable isolation of the colony from the rest of the community, much of this conflict passed unnoticed, particularly since notifying the police was considered abhorrent. Personal experience with police in Europe engendered suspicions that took many years to overcome in America.

*Društva* and boardinghouses alike flourished in most of the South Slav colonies during the first two decades of the twentieth century,

183

but declined rapidly following the inauguration of immigration restriction. They have not disappeared entirely, but they have lost their former importance in the family life of the immigrants. The writer has found both of these kinds of living arrangements in industrial centers, like East Chicago, Indiana, and in fish towns, like San Pedro, California. Such areas, of course, are exceptions.

For the newcomer, there is no denying, life was hard. The immigrant who came to the United States unattached and who lived in a boardinghouse was able to manage on his wages, but the foreigner who brought his family with him faced a different situation. A report written about the immigrants in Pittsburgh in 1909 states:

> The Slav, as we have seen, has to pay more than the English-speaking man for the same house. The man who earns $37 a month and has to pay $12 has not a large fund on which to raise a family. He belongs to one or two lodges which means an outlay of a dollar to a dollar and a half each month. He must pay fifty cents a month to his church, and he is compelled to send his children to the parochial school at, say, another fifty cents a head, or three for a dollar. He must buy the school books needed by the child; this may amount yearly to from three to four dollars. Is it surprising then, that the children are sent to work at dirty quarters. . . . When the mills are working regularly and the father is able to work each day, the family manages to get along. But when sickness comes or work ceases, then the pinch of hunger is felt.[24]

Only the physically strong could survive in a hard environment of this sort. The infant mortality rate was very high, and in Shenandoah and in Mahanoy City 60 per cent of the deaths were of children under five years of age.[25]

The majority of Yugoslav immigrants, coming from farming communities, found their new occupations in factory and mine somewhat unnatural. They retained, however, their almost instinctive love of land, and many of them, to satisfy the desire to own property, bought a lot as soon as their financial condition enabled them to do so. In a study of the Yugoslavs in Detroit, one investigator stressed the great urge that seems to be in the people to own property.[26] This authority further explained that "many who bought or built their home were able to do so through memberships in the Croatian Building and Loan Association of Detroit."[27] The federal census discloses that in 1940 there were 198,880, or 51.8 per cent of the total, Yugoslavs in the United States who lived in homes that they owned.[28]  In this owner-occupied homes group, a majority (56,360) owned homes valued at $3,000 or $4,000, while a number (5,280) were in the bracket of $7,500 or over.[29]

Family life for the Yugoslav immigrants in America changed considerably from what it had been in the old country.  In Europe the entire family was engaged in farming, with the father as the authority and leader.  In the United States, on the other hand, the family is not united by common occupation, and therefore the interdependence of family members is virtually nonexistent.

Though family solidarity has been somewhat shaken, and social life in general modified, the Yugoslavs have not forgotten nor given up all their old-world traditions or customs.  Holidays, weddings, christenings, and other social events bring celebrations highly reminiscent of Yugoslavia.

A unique social function is a Croat American wedding.  The preliminaries are quite unlike those in Croatia, where the parents arrange the match, but rather are fairly similar to American practices.  However, as is customary among immigrants of many nationalities, all wedding expenses are borne not by the bride but by the groom.  Selecting as many as a dozen bridesmaids and ushers, as well as the usual flower girl and ring bearer, the couple solemnize their nuptial ceremony at a morning mass.  Following the ceremony the newlyweds, together with their families and other relatives and intimate friends, attend, generally at the church hall, a wedding breakfast which in reality is a dinner feast.  The afternoon is usually spent in taking photographs of the wedding party.  And then in the evening, beginning about seven o'clock, comes the biggest event of the day: the wedding reception at the church hall, oftentimes attended by five to six hundred guests.  Food, drink, and music flow freely as the bride and groom are regaled by their well-wishers.  After everyone has had his fill of roasted suckling pig, barbecued lamb, and stuffed cabbage, and a chance to make a few trips to the barroom, a relative or close friend of the couple, acting as master of ceremonies, delivers a short speech, pointing to the pitfalls of matrimony and exhorting everyone present to give (money) liberally to the newlyweds in order to pave the way for an easier and happier life for them.  While the master of ceremonies remains standing in front of the guests, several ushers circulate throughout the room collecting money (gifts, if given at all, are usually taken to the bride and groom themselves at the end of the reception) and passing it on immediately to the speaker, who not only reads the donors' names but also the amounts given, hoping in this manner to stimulate competition among the guests and thus fatten the kitty. A brief respite is followed by the bridal dance in which anyone desiring to dance with the bride must make an additional contribution. Occasionally also during the bridal dance an usher goes around with a lady's shoe soliciting donations for a baby buggy and a crib. The festivities for the couple end at the hall when the groom carries the bride out across the threshold.

Gay, festive, enjoyable is a Croat wedding. But for a truly old-country atmosphere there is nothing to compare with a Serbian Christmas. The Serbs, who are of the Orthodox faith, adhere to the Julian calendar in their religious practices, and therefore observe January 7 as Christmas Day. The celebration, which is enlightening to witness and most delightful to participate in, begins with an elaborate supper on Christmas Eve. After the table is set and the candles are lit, the guests take their places around the table and say prayers. This is followed by a scattering of walnuts to the four corners of the house, symbolizing the appearance of Christ in the four corners of the world. In place of honor on the table stands the *Božićni kolač* (Christmas cake), which is usually decorated with sprigs of the sacred herb, *bosiljak* (sweet basil). The *kolač* rests on top of a plate on which there are fruits, wheat, and coins, symbolic of the products of the earth; in addition, there is a piece of garlic in keeping with an old superstition that this wards off witchcraft—a belief which is not accepted by Serbian Americans but is, nevertheless, adhered to for reasons of sentiment. This plate with its symbols of abundance remains until New Year's Day, when the *kolač* is cut and divided among the family, the fruit given to the children, and the wheat to the chickens and birds, thus indicating to all the expectation of plenty in the coming year.

The supper must conform to the strict rules of the Advent fast, meaning that there can be no meat, animal fat of any kind, eggs, butter, or milk. Consequently, the main dish consists of vegetables, soup and salads, and fish, which are generally floured and fried in olive oil. Among the more popular desserts are homemade noodles sprinkled with nuts and honey and prunes stewed in wine.

Following the conclusion of the meal by prayer, the guests continue to sit around the table, listening to stories and music of the *tamburice* and eating nuts and fruits. The food must remain on the table until breakfast the next morning, so as to insure plenty for the coming year.

The big day, Christmas, begins with an exchange of gifts, which are mostly things to eat, as is customary in the old country. Then comes the morning church service, which is usually attended by all, including the most atheistic persons. Dressed in their Sunday best, the Serbs joyfully greet one another with *Hristos se rodi* (Christ is born), just as Americans say "Merry Christmas."

The Christmas dinner, following the service, is a veritable feast, for the fast has ended and the items forbidden during the fast are again permissible. The dinner is superbly described by an American writer invited to one of these repasts by a Serbian family. She writes:

> Chicken soup with noodles and liver dumplings is followed by chicken *paprikash*, then by ham and the national dish *sarma*, a sort of stuffed cabbage; then comes piggie in all his glory, accompanied by various salads; and finally the excitement of the day, the Christmas cake, *chesnitsa*, the very name of which indicates "respect to our Lord's birthday." *Chesnitsa* is a wonderful achievement in the way of a puff paste. . . . In the old country it is made with the first water drawn from the village well in the morning, and it contains a coin which will bring luck for the year to the fortunate recipient. The cutting of the *chesnitsa* is a rite performed by the head of the house. It must be cut into as many pieces as there are persons present, and one extra for "the poor wayfarer who comes to the door." In America there is no poor wayfarer, so a man who happens to come to the door at the fortunate moment is invited to take his place. The first piece must go to the head of the house . . . the second to the mistress . . . the third to the poor wayfarer; and the fourth to the honored guest . . . and then the rest. With great excitement and breathless suspense we all prod our pieces for the coin, hoping by receiving it to be lucky the whole year through. But, alas, it is the casual guest enacting the poor wayfarer who is the lucky one.[30]

The food and celebrations of the Croats and Slovenes are not unlike those of the Serbs, although their Christmas, since they are Roman Catholic and use the Gregorian calendar, comes on December 25. All three branches of the South Slavic family have retained many of their European social customs and practices, due, in part, to the encouragements of various Yugoslav as well as American organizations and institutions. A Croatian woman explained this situation very well when she said:

> We Croatians never used to dance the old dances in our halls. We were ashamed of them. Then when the International Institute [St. Paul, Minnesota] asked us if we could do some dances that belonged to our own villages, the people said: "What is this? They want our old *Drmes?* Our old dances must be all right!" We were so glad that they were not too old-fashioned. Now we can shout and stamp our feet, and that makes us more happy. We feel young again—just like we did on holidays at home. Now our children dance with us, and we wear our old-country costumes, too.[31]

Apparently, by retention of some of the old-world traits and traditions the Yugoslavs lead happier and fuller lives, thus becoming more responsible and loyal citizens, and what is equally, if not more, important, they add to the diversity and richness of the culture of their adopted homeland.

### POSITION OF WOMEN

Among the social characteristics of the Yugoslav Americans, the most notable concerns the status of women. In Yugoslavia before the establishment of the republic generally, women, especially peasant women, had been regarded as subservient and inferior to men physically, mentally, politically, socially, and in every other way; but in America they have been recognized as equals. Common were such proverbs in Europe as:

> The man is the head, the woman is grass.
> One man is worth more than ten women.
> A man of straw is worth more than a woman of gold.
> Let the dog bark, but let the woman keep silent.
> He who does not beat his wife is no man.
> "What shall I get when I marry?" asks a boy of his father. "For your wife a stick, for your children a switch."
> Twice in his life a man is happy; once when he marries, and once when he buries his wife.

Among the peasants of the older era, women were expected to work and bear children. Motherhood was a woman's primary reason for being, and there was a proverb which said that "a barren woman is of no use in the world." It was quite common formerly to see a man and a woman on the road, the woman bending under a heavy load that she was carrying into the village, while her husband walked alongside entirely unencumbered. Women did most of the heavy work, milking the cow, goat, or sheep, getting food for both family and animals, taking meals to the men in the fields, weaving, mending, baking, laundering, and the like. All this hard work made an old lady out of a young woman.

Some of the unfortunate women were able to escape from the intolerable conditions at home by migrating to America. It was not until about 1904 that women began to appear in South Slav colonies in comparatively large numbers. A common practice was for a young unmarried male to send back to the homeland for a girl, probably one whom he had never seen but who was recommended by his parents. His only way to get her was to pay for her passage. It sometimes happened that the young woman was unwilling to complete the bargain upon arrival. In such an eventuality she was obligated to return the money for the fare. If some other marriage partner acceptable to her could be found, it was customary for him to pay it and in that way settle the problem.

As the number of women in the communities increased, family life took on more stability and permanency. At the same time the shortage of women encouraged marriage outside the group. No general study has been made of the subject, but Professor Clement S. Mihanovich of St. Louis University, a graduate student at the time, conducted an investigation in a fairly representative Yugoslav colony, St. Louis, Missouri. Mihanovich's examination of the marriages in the largest Croatian church in St. Louis from 1904 to 1935 revealed that 43.2 per cent married foreign-born Croats, 25.7 per cent married native-born Croats of foreign parentage, and 30 per cent married native Americans of other groups.[32] This may perhaps be representative of the Yugoslavs throughout the country.

Few of the immigrants permit their wives to work outside the home because this, it is believed, reflects on the ability of the husband. In respect to younger girls, the customs are more varied. In San Pedro, where Dalmatian fishermen predominate, girls work in the canneries, attend dances at the Yugoslav Hall with their families, seldom have dates, and marry young within their own group. In Chicago, on the other hand, Croat, Serb, and Slovene girls work in stores and factories, go out frequently with American boys, and, in general, have more freedom.

## Sex, Sin, and Saloons

Reports of the first investigations into the economic and social life of the Slavic immigrants all make references to the drinking habits of the newcomers. As one writer observed, "Coming from an Elizabethan world, the Slav is as frankly vinous as Falstaff with his 'cup o' sac.' "[33] It was explained, however, that the Slavs, despite their drinking, managed to save something, as shown by their remittances abroad. The Yugoslavs do not believe there is any reason to feel ashamed of their drinking as long as it remains within reasonable bounds and does not produce chronic drunkenness. They drink at weddings, baptisms, birthdays, and other occasions for celebration. The hard work in the steel mills and mines leads many to seek stimulants. Even their heavy drinking is spasmodic, and they are said to lose less time from work on account of intoxication than some of the other immigrant groups.[34]

The writer has seen gallons upon gallons of wine as well as beer and whiskey loaded on Yugoslav fishing boats in San Francisco and San Pedro. He has visited homes where cellars were lined with barrels filled with wine, some of it fifteen to twenty years old. He has been to many *zabave* (entertainments) where wholesale quantities of liquor were consumed. But the number of intoxicated persons seen was, indeed, very small.

In asking a Dalmatian retired steel-mill worker to what he attributed his good health and longevity, the author received the reply: "To this! [pointing to a glass of wine before him]. Wine is the lifeblood of man. Anyone that drinks water is crazy." Another immigrant who died recently had wine sprinkled over her coffin, as requested before death, so that "she could enjoy the good beverage in death as in life." It is not unusual for a Yugoslav, especially a Dalmatian, family to make at home two to three hundred gallons of wine a year. Wine is a favorite drink and is used with most meals.

Heavy drinking was probably more characteristic of the immigrant a generation ago than it is today. Yugoslavs generally were opposed to prohibition, some resorting to distilling and consuming bootleg products. Their feeling on the matter was that such personal habits as drinking were inherent rights of every individual and the government had no right to legislate against them. However, with the increase in Americanization there has been a rise of community sentiment against alcoholic excesses, and there is less drinking at celebrations today than there was in former times.

In the early years of their arrival many immigrants frequented saloons, which were not mere liquor troughs but rather institutions equipped to cater to many of the needs of the foreigners. In the saloon one could not only drown one's sorrows, overcome one's weariness from labor, and meet one's fellows; one could also buy steamship tickets and money orders for friends and relatives in Europe, play poker, eat, dance, enjoy a girl, have one's letters written, subscribe to newspapers, pay one's union, lodge, and club dues, and—if the saloonkeeper was on friendly terms with the local priest, which was not unusual—even one's church dues.[35]

Saloonkeeping, perhaps next to boardinghouse management, offered the Slavic immigrant an escape from the hard work of the coal fields and mills. Roberts, a thorough student of immigrant activities, writing in 1904, stated that the saloons in mining communities were rapidly passing into the hands of Slavic businessmen.[36] English-speaking owners could not compete with the Slav saloonkeepers who spoke the language of their patrons and were generally popular in the community. The ownership of a saloon was at that time one of the easiest and surest ways to prosperity and security. The owner, moreover, was able to gain much influence over his fellow countrymen, as all life outside the plant or mine revolved around the saloon. Being a citizen and knowing the English language—or at least having a command of it above that of the immigrants—he enjoyed a high degree of prestige. The fact that he was usually a jolly fellow who had a glad hand for the humblest working man helped to make him a popular figure in his set. Consequently, he was able to perform a variety of services and favors—for a price, of course—for his compatriots. He acted as an interpreter as well as a political and juridical advisor among the immigrants, whom he served as an intermediary in their dealings with the authorities. If one of the aliens got into trouble with the police, he intervened in his behalf. Frequently he was a banker and a notary public. He also performed numerous functions for a variety of companies, such as recruiting fresh immigrants for the steamship concerns and providing the industrial establishments with new labor forces. His saloon served simultaneously as an

191

employment office, a housing agency, and a meeting hall for church affairs. He permitted unmarried men with no permanent addresses to receive their mail in his place of business. As a rule he had his own orchestra, consisting of an accordion player or two, and he saw to it that his patrons had female company. Sometimes he assumed the task of a matrimonial agent, and wedding festivities were often held in the hall above his saloon.[37]

There is no doubt that the saloon filled an important need in the lives of the immigrants. Much can be said in its favor. Yet it was not without its seamier side. It gave rise to several evils, the most notorious of which were drunkenness, promiscuity, and gambling.

Though the majority of those who frequented the saloons could hardly be classified as drunkards, a small proportion definitely fell into that category. Some of the latter group spent most of their time outside working hours with their feet on the brass rail and their elbows on the bar, imbibing until they emptied their pockets or could no longer stand, when they were retired to a back room of the saloon to "sleep it off," taken home, or simply tossed out, depending on the mood and the temperament of the proprietor. Were the drunkard the only one to suffer from such drinking bouts, it would have been bad enough, but in most cases there were other innocent victims as well. Even if he were an unmarried man, he was likely to have relatives in Europe who, as a consequence of his drinking, failed to get a letter or a remittance. The man with a family not only placed his loved ones in financial straits but brought scorn and disgrace to them. There were saloonkeepers who refused to sell to patrons who showed any signs of intoxication. Others, greedy and selfish, continued to pour the spirits until the victim was completely separated from his cash.

In general, promiscuity was not as widespread nor as serious a problem as inebriety. Nevertheless, it did exist. Single persons and married men away from their wives and families easily fell into the habit of having their carnal desires satisfied in a saloon, where women were plentiful and cheap. Often the habit was not as easily broken after the bachelors married and the already-married men were united with their wives. Some of them continued their extramarital relations in the saloon, with the break-up of families a frequent result. In one of these cases personally known to the writer, the divorced husband married his favorite prostitute and thereafter led a contented and normal married life. The consequence of a husband's illicit sexual intimacies was not always divorce. On occasion it led to similar behavior by the wife, who sought vengeance by engaging in relations with the "star boarder." Of course, not all star boarder cases sprang from the adulterous conduct of husbands. But whatever the cause of the promiscuity, the marriage of such a sinful couple was nothing more than a sham, possessing no real bonds and being held together only by the thin threads of convenience and the fear of the consequences of divorce.

Gambling was an ever-present evil in most saloons. More often than not, it was encouraged by the saloonkeepers, who usually realized sizable "takes" from the games of chance in their drinking emporiums. There always seemed to be men around who were willing to gamble on anything containing the slightest element of risk. This quite naturally played directly into the hands of unscrupulous proprietors, who thought only of their own gain. The commonest form of gambling was card playing. Many a poker game that began on Saturday evening did not break up until the factory whistles summoned the players back to work on Monday morning. And some of the games lasted as long as a week, with the participants losing their earnings and missing time from work. *Boče* (Italian *Bocce*), a game especially popular among the Dalmatians and one that might be called a distant cousin of horseshoes except that it is played with balls, gave the more athletic specimens an opportunity to get rid of their money. Players and spectators alike participated in the betting. Pool, major league baseball cards, and numerous other devices and schemes accorded the patron of the saloon additional means of gambling.

## A NEW LANGUAGE

There is no evidence to show that the Yugoslav immigrant in America learns English faster or slower than any other national. It may be said that the rapidity or slowness with which an immigrant, regardless of his origin, masters the English language depends, among other things, upon the environment in which he settles, the work he does, and the people he associates with both at work and in community activities. Where an immigrant is in contact largely with other immigrants of the same origin and language, his need for learning English is lessened, and so he will continue to use his mother tongue more than English. In other words, the speed with which the alien learns English is contingent on the need he has for the language in everyday life. Adamic says that "the Yugoslav immigrant, as a rule, learns the American language as well as his new environment permits him—in some cases very well indeed."[38] The mother tongue is not forgotten, but rather modified, by the English language, so that the result is a "third language,"[39] a kind of amalgam of Slovene or Serbo-Croat and English.

The modification of the language of the South Slavs in the United States is a development common to all foreign nationals. The average Yugoslav immigrant soon discovers that his limited old-country vocabulary does not meet the expanded needs of the the American environment, which, in contrast to his simple rural background, is industrial and urban—a new world, in fact, composed of conflicting and contradictory culture patterns. Accordingly, he borrows English words and fits them as phonetically as he can into his native Yugoslav. Specific illustrations and further explanation may help to illuminate this point.

When the alien arrives in New York, he rides in a *feribot* (ferry boat) to Ellis Island and back to Manhattan. Here he has a choice of boarding a *teksi* (taxi), an *eleveder* (elevator) or a *subvej* (*subvey*, subway) to take him to the *stacija* (*statsiya*, station), where he gets his *tren* (train) for his destination. While riding, he may buy a *lonč* (*lonch*, lunch), consisting of a *senvič* (*senvich*, sandwich) and perhaps *kek* (cake) or *ajs krim* (*ays krim*, ice cream). Arriving in the new home, the immigrant makes the rounds, visiting his relatives and friends and usually consuming much *viski* (whisky) and *bira* (beer) in the process. After a few days and the celebration is over, he settles down in his status as a *border* (boarder) and soon goes to work in a local *šapa* (*shapa*, shop) as a *leber* (laborer) or, if he had been a sailor at home, as a *riger* (rigger). At first he keeps pretty much to himself, remaining meek and humble, obedient to the every command of his *bas* (boss). However, after drawing a few *pejčeki* (*peycheki*, paychecks), he becomes a little more aggressive and joins a *junija* (*yuniya*, union), becoming a faithful member by paying his *duz* (dues) on time and attending every *miting* (meeting). It is not all work and no play for the new arrival. Occasionally he attends a *besbol* or *futbol gem* (baseball or football game) with the *genga* (gang) or makes a *det* (date) with the best girl friend to attend the *muviz* (movies) or *denc* (dance). The life of a *singel* (single, unmarried man) does not appeal to this family-loving creature, and so, after *roning rand* (running around) for a few years, he decides to marry. With a wife and four or five *kidi* (kids) it is not easy to live *na rendi* (on rent) and therefore the savings are taken out to buy a *lat* (lot) and build a new *hauz* (house), but all that is a big headache for it requires so much *red tep* (red tape), including a *did* (*deed*), *morgić* (*morgich,* mortgage), *tekse* (taxes), and *inšorinc* (*inshorints,* insurance).⁴⁰

The words and phrases used in the foregoing illustration can be divided into several different groups. In the first place, there are those English words, like subway, rigger, union, baseball, movies, ice cream, and red tape, that lack an adequate Yugoslav equivalent. Secondly, there are some words, such as shop, paycheck, boss, rent, deed, and mortgage, that have the foreign equivalents but are unknown to the unenlightened alien. Finally, there are words, as train, cake, beer, dance, dues, and insurance, that are more convenient to use in their English than in their Yugoslav form.

In learning to speak the English language rarely does the immigrant lose his accent without a great deal of effort under the guidance of a competent speech instructor. To the typical South Slav, busy at earning a living and too tired at the end of a long day of hard labor, such instruction is beyond reach. Moreover, having acquired a vocabulary sufficient to make himself understood by his employers, fellow workers, and neighbors, he generally feels that he has attained a level beyond which there is no urgent need to continue. This psychological fact, unfortunately, also holds true among large groups of native-born Americans. Many a person with an American ancestry reaching far into the past, though his accent is American enough, has a vocabulary of a twelve-year-old adolescent, satisfactory for his needs at work and at home. Thus, too much criticism should not be leveled at the apparent lethargy of the immigrant.

### BELICH VERSUS WHITE

As language, so also names of the Yugoslavs are changed in the United States. Many immigrants are sensitive about their names and consequently change them to conform with the American standards. One authority hit at the core of the subject when he wrote:

To some of us the battle over names is not serious at all. It scarcely touches us and we shake off its effects as ducks shed water. For others it is acute. It impinges on their everyday life, and many are unable to extricate themselves either by doing something about it or by viewing it philosophically.[41]

There are many and varied reasons for changes in names. According to Howard F. Barker, who made a special study of the subject, what changes names most is the abrasion of common speech.[42] This process operates in two ways: first, by changing sounds and taking away syllables to fit the ordinary tongue, and secondly, by setting one name against another.[43] Through the abrasion of common speech syllables and letters are removed, tending toward a standard of from five to seven letters and only one or two syllables.[44]

Differences in language and sounds have been responsible for many changes. Thus the Yugoslav names ending in ć (c with a diacritical mark resembling the French acute accent and roughly equivalent in pronunciation to ty in English) are modified to conform with English pronunciation and spelling, and so the diacritical mark is dropped, giving the c the hard sound of a k (as in Adamic) or the sound of an s (as in Gracin), or an h is added to produce the ch sound (as in Kosanovich). Diacritical marks are often dropped for the č (equivalent to ch) and š (equivalent to sh) without the addition of an h, resulting in modified spelling and pronunciation. In like fashion the Slav c (equivalent in pronunciation to the English ts) assumes a k or s sound or is changed to ts (as from Matica to Matitsa). Though not basic, such modifications are frequent, accounting perhaps for most of the minor changes in family names.

Another strong force in the alteration of surnames, according to Barker, is the desire for simplification. The writer explains:

> The city life in which most of our recent immigrants stocks find themselves favors the simple and commonplace moniker over the stranger nationalistic cognomen. Moving from job to job gives a slight fillip to a difficult name, and from city to city a greater one. . . . Certainly few people at present realize how relentless is the force for simplification and that it dictates continuous popularization of the names which already have some advantages in numbers, reputation or fame.[45]

196

Often the modification of names was the work of immigrant officials or payroll clerks in factories or mines who wrote down the names as they sounded to them—the immigrants being unable to spell. In some instances the process of altering names was hastened by the impatience shown by the employers with names that seemed unpronounceable and were difficult to spell. Some changed their names for business purposes, desiring tags which were easy to remember. Others wished to escape the ridicule and embarrassment that their old-country names brought them. Americanization, a desire to show loyalty and devotion to the adopted land, was responsible for some changes. And finally, there is the influence of the second generation, the children often encouraging the parents to make a change.

Basic changes in names among the Yugoslavs are chiefly of two types: dropping the original Slav patronymic altogether and substituting an Anglo-Saxon name, or changing the original name either by translation (e.g., Belich into White) or respelling so as to keep some of the original sound. The latter method has been noted by Adamic in the following examples: Ablak to O'Black, Miklavec or Miklavić to McClautz, Ogrin to O'Green, Črčak into Church, Jakša or Jakšić into Jackson, Oven into Owen, and Stritar into Streeter.[46]

Not only, however, are family names altered but given names as well. Usually the nomens, like the cognomens, are simply translated. Thus, Ivan becomes John, Jura changes to George, and Pavle gives way to Paul. But translations are not always possible, since the Yugoslavs have appellations which are peculiar to them. Such names as Dragutin, Stojan, and Ljubomir do not have English equivalents. Therefore, either the old-country form is retained or a completely new English name is adopted.

Noting this trend of name changing, one observer commented: "In the Pennsylvania mining towns one finds Slavs who call themselves by such names as John Smith or Tim O'Sullivan or Pat Murphy, in an effort to make Americans of themselves."[47]

## EDUCATION

A large portion of the South Slav arrivals in the United States, as already observed, possessed not even the barest fundamentals of education. Federal census figures for 1930 show 32,774, or 15.6 per cent, of the Yugoslav immigrants, ten years old and over, as illiterate.[48]  Although this was a high rate of illiteracy, it was far from being the highest among all immigrant classes.  The Poles, Lithuanians, Albanians, and Syrians had a higher rate than the Yugoslavs, and the Portuguese with a percentage of 34.7 more than doubled the Yugoslav rate.  Of the number of South Slavs who could neither read nor write, the large majority was in the age levels above twenty-five.[49]

Stimulated by the closing gates of immigration, their American-born offspring, as well as their employers who sought to increase efficiency and greater productivity by promotion of English-language studies, the aliens began to attend evening adult-education classes in increasing numbers.  At the outset a large share of the program was borne by the industrialists, but after the transformation of the original aim into the so-called ideal of "Americanization," the entire task was taken over by the public school.  Whatever the underlying motives, it cannot be denied that the scheme was of incalculable value to the unlettered immigrant.

The younger generation of Yugoslavs has had more time to devote to education, and, on the whole, they have taken increased interest in education, if only as a means of elevating their material status.  They were quick to question the intelligence of working in mine or steel mill simply because their fathers went into them.  As one writer pithily states: "Simply because the whole damn bunch of us got into the mills without even thinking twice about it, we got to believing it's the holiest job on earth.  God, people earn money other places too!"[50]

As a result of the new attitudes, many of the younger people have deliberately removed themselves from the close circle in which their relatives live, and have acquired training which qualifies them for office jobs.  Many more, however, have had to leave school in order to go to work and help increase the family income.

Since most children of the immigrants attend public school, it is the public school that has influenced the foreigner and his offspring more than any other single institution.[51]  This important role of the American schools is amplified by Miller, noted student of Slavic American activities:

> As far as the superficial "Americanization" of the second generation is concerned, the knowledge of English, acquaintance with American history and institutions, and training in patriotism, we need look no further than the public school.  Whether

the type and method of education afforded by the public school system is such as to give us the kind of citizens we shall need in the future, is another question, which we must leave to educators to answer. But to all intents and purposes children who enter the schools as Czechs, or Poles, or Slovenes, leave them as American boys and girls.[52]

The influence of the public schools thus reaches the immigrants both through direct and indirect channels. In some instances the indirect contact through the children has been the only source of information for adults concerning American life.

Though not occupying the same status as the public institutions, the parochial schools have, nevertheless, exerted a tremendous influence on the life of Yugoslav Americans. Many immigrants prefer to send their children to full-time parochial schools, which are superintended and controlled by the churches. Statistics on these church-sponsored institutions reveal slight changes during the last generation. J. Poljak, a Yugoslav investigator who appears to have made a very thorough study in 1926, arrived at the figures reproduced in the table below.[53]

TABLE 12

PAROCHIAL SCHOOLS

| Race or People | No. of Schools | No. of Pupils |
|---|---|---|
| Croatian | 14 | 4,400 |
| Slovenian | 15 | 6,638 |
| Serbian | 6 | 276 |
| Mixed | 4 | 656 |
| Total | 39 | 11,970 |

Bjankini, a Croat writer of Chicago, revealed in his investigation of the mid-thirties some thirty-eight full-time parochial schools, with half of them belonging to the Croats and half to the Slovenes.[54] In 1949 Roucek reported the same number of institutions, with an enrollment of 13,000 pupils (8,000 Slovenes and 5,000 Croats).[55] The present writer, making a check in 1950, found figures that corresponded fairly well with those of Poljak, except in enrollment, where the total stood at over 16,000 pupils. Thus, evidence indicates that there has been little change in the number of plants or pupils since the high-tide of immigration.

Nearly all the parochial schools are officially recognized in their respective states. One of the first of these denominational institutions to be established was that in Pueblo, Colorado, in 1895.[56] On April 8, 1945, the Croatian Holy Trinity church and school of Chicago celebrated their thirtieth anniversary.[57] The Serbian Orthodox diocese aside from encouraging attendance at parish schools also conducts a summer camp for boys and girls at the St. Sava Monastery in Libertyville, Illinois. In urging that Serbian children be sent to the camp, one article states:

> Much has been said about our youth, children born here in America, how they are forgetting their national culture and heritage. That they are losing themselves in their environment contributing nothing to the American way of life nor seeking to enrich it with the traditions of their fathers. Much was written and time spent on this problem yet up to now beside this theorizing nothing much was done. Yet the camp idea started from nothing and is succeeding almost unbelievably . . . it has become the first strong spiritual tie between youth and age, the only bridge between Serbian and American ideals.[58]

In Lemont, Illinois, there is a high school for girls, conducted by Slovene Roman Catholics, and a good Yugoslav library, perhaps the best in the United States. The town also has convents and preparatory schools for those who wish to study for the priesthood or sisterhood. Nonreligious schools that offer courses in Yugoslav languages and culture are few; the best is conducted by the Slovene National Home of Cleveland.

The subjects studied in the full-time parochial schools include literature, history, music, mathematics, geography, science, and religion. The English language is used in the classroom, but the national language must be studied as an obligatory part of the curriculum. Instruction is thorough, and is conducted by the Sisters of the Catholic Order of St. Francis.

The significance of the parochial school in the Yugoslav American community is obvious. It not only helps to bind the immigrant colony into a more closely-knit social unit, but also preserves in the American-born offspring the language and cultural traditions of Yugoslavia, thus preventing complete disintegration and holding intact the best of the culture brought from the old country.

## RELIGION

From the earliest times religion seems to have divided the Slavic nationalities, principally because it was around the church that narrow and intense nationalism grew. The divisions of the old country were brought over by the immigrants to their new home. In discussing the subject Miller explains: "The Serbs and Croatians are really one people, but both Serbs and Croats are ardently devoted to their respective churches because it is the church which distinguishes them. Just as a good Serb must be a faithful member of the Orthodox Church, so a Croatian must be of the Roman Catholic."[59]

Each group among the Yugoslavs has many religious subdivisions. A number are outright atheists. Some, through marriage of American-born mates chiefly, have joined the ranks of Protestants. Others, especially in the large colonies such as Chicago and San Pedro, have become adherents of Jehovah's Witnesses, due, they say, to the cloudy teachings, the regimentation, and the extreme materialism of the Roman Catholic Church as contrasted with the appeal of the simple teachings and practices of the new sect. A few, namely Bosnians and Hercegovinians, are Moslems. In the main, however, the Croats and Slovenes are Roman Catholic while the Serbs are Eastern Orthodox. Each possesses a strong tribal consciousness, as a result of which each of the subdivisions of the Yugoslavs leads a more or less independent social and cultural existence.

From the time of their first arrival in the United States, Croatian and Slovenian Roman Catholics were divided under their respective bishops, so that at the present time mixed parishes are few. The Serbian Orthodox Church, on the other hand, was headed until World War I by the Russian bishops in the United States. Following the war, and the revolution in Russia, it became a separate diocese with a bishop for the United States and Canada nominated by the patriarch of the Serbian Orthodox Church in Belgrade, Yugoslavia. The bishop's see is in Libertyville, Illinois.

The Slovene Catholics were the first to organize their religious life in America. Their priests joined the people as pioneers and immigrants, thus helping to pave the way for the establishments of parishes. After worshiping in German and Irish churches for a time, the Slovenes started building their own. The trail blazers

201

were the settlers in Brockway, Minnesota.[60] The predominant element here was Slovene, which as late as 1915 showed sixty-one families in the population enumeration of that year, in comparison to fifteen German, second in the count. The initial step of the Slovenes in Brockway in putting up a church of their own may be said to date from 1869 when the Reverend Joseph Buh, the pastor in Belle Prairie, first visited the town. The congregation was stirred into action, and in February, 1870, began the construction of a frame and log building. The structure was completed the following year and dedicated on April 23, 1871, under the name of the Church of St. Stephen. Father Buh continued to serve the mission church until 1875 when it came under the direction of the Fathers of St. Louis Abbey. Once the ground was broken by the Slovenes in Brockway, those in other communities followed suit. During the next three-quarters of a century the Slovenes founded over sixty churches.

Considering the fact that the Serbians joined the mass immigration movement to the United States somewhat after the Slovenians and Croatians, they really got an early start in the building of their own churches. Credit for laying a strong foundation for the Serb ecclesiastical structure in America must go largely to a small but devoted group of church leaders. One of the most distinguished of these was Archimandrite Sebastijan Dabović. Born in San Francisco on June 9, 1863, Father Dabović took his theological training in Russia. After completing his studies, he was appointed chief of the Serbian Church Mission in America. Returning to the state of his birth, he began his work among the Serbs of Jackson, a small mining town in northern California. In 1894 he prevailed upon the well-paid Serbs working in the local gold mine and their employer to contribute to the building of a church. The edifice, completed before the end of the year and named St. Sava, was the first Serbian church in America.[61] A bitter controversy followed with the Russian bishop who demanded that the church should be chartered as Russian, not Serbian. But in the end a Serbian charter was procured.

When Father Dabović went to Alaska, he again had to contend with the Russians. Nevertheless, in spite of Russian opposition, he succeeded in building a small Serbian church and converting several Eskimo villages to Christianity. Similar conflicts were waged in Galveston, Texas, and Cincinnati, Ohio.

Father Dabović did not remain very long in any one place but was perpetually on the move, preaching the Gospel and rousing the Serbs to build their own churches. He was particularly successful in Chicago, where he organized a parish and built a chapel —on the very spot where the Serbian Church of Resurrection now stands. In Chicago he also started the first Serbian church newspaper, called *Glasnik Srpske Crkvene Misije* (Herald of the Serbian Church Mission). Father Dabović did not confine his missionary activities to North America, but carried on his work in Asia and Europe, until death overtook him in Yugoslavia on November 30, 1940. While he still lived he was decorated for his distinguished services by the king of Serbia, the prince of Montenegro, the tsar of Russia, and the patriarch of Jerusalem.[62]

With a good start given to them by Father Dabović and other outstanding churchmen, the Serbs moved ahead fairly rapidly in the expansion of their religious facilities, though occasionally they encountered numerous stumbling blocks. Some of their churches were built only by great sacrifice and at heavy costs of money and labor. In Chicago, for example, they founded a church in 1904 but did not finish it until 1927. In some communities they still do not have their own churches, and in consequence attend those of the Russians.

The churches of the Serbs are among the most imposing religious edifices in America. Excellent illustrations of awe-inspiring beauty are the Church *Ravanica* in Detroit, Michigan, and the St. Sava Cathedral in Milwaukee, Wisconsin. The former, finished in 1926, is built in pure Byzantine style and is an exact replica of the church of the same name erected in 1381 in Ćuprija, Serbia, by the ruler Lazar. St. Sava Cathedral, built largely of imported Italian marble, also in the classical Byzantine style, and opened for worship in November, 1957, combines the best features of the Orthodox cathedrals of St. Sophia of Constantinople, Gračanica, Studenica, St. Marks, and St. George, of Yugoslavia, with many new elements never used in any other building to make it one of the most magnificent structures of its kind found anywhere.

The Croatians had the earliest ecclesiastical representatives (Ratkay, Konšak, Kundek) in North America, and yet they were the last of the South Slavs to organize their own parishes and erect their own houses of worship. Moreover, they built fewer churches than either the Slovenians or Serbians over the span of years. Perhaps a look into the developments in Allegheny County, Pennsylvania, where the first Croat churches were founded, will help to clarify the situation.

The early Croatian Catholics in America, like their counterparts in Europe, were very devout. The immigrants in Allegheny County tried to attend the Irish and German churches only to meet with disappointment. They felt like outcasts in churches not their own. Discouraged by this condition, some refused to attend mass at all, while others became quite antagonistic toward Catholicism itself. Something had to be done, and done quickly, to preserve and strengthen the faith of the immigrants. A solution to the problem was finally found by Zdravko Valentin Mužina, the noted fraternalist and editor of *Danica*.

Mužina appealed to Bishop Josip Strosmajer, a liberal and intelligent Croat religious leader in Zagreb and a pioneer proponent of the cause of Yugoslav unity. Strosmajer replied by promptly sending to Allegheny City the Reverend Dobroslav Bozić, a priest from Bosnia. Obtaining jurisdiction over all the Croats and Slovenes in the Pittsburgh area from Bishop Ricardo Plehan, Father Bozić celebrated his first mass on Sunday, August 12, 1894, in the chapel below the old St. Paul's Cathedral. Soon afterwards a church committee was formed, headed by Mužina. The committee proceeded to purchase a house on East Ohio Street in Allegheny City and transform it into a church. Named St. Nicholas, the church opened its doors for worship on January 27, 1895.

The acquisition of a church of their own, unfortunately, did not bring peace and quiet to the Allegheny Croats. The harmonious relations which seemed to prevail between Father Bozić and his parishioners during the early months of committee work and church building were more apparent than real. The fact is that there had been a sharp difference from the outset between the pastor and the parishioners over the control of church affairs, with the former maintaining that his authority be unchallenged and the latter insisting that final decision be reserved for a committee of their own choosing. After prolonged argument over the issue Father Bozić departed from the parish in 1898. In his place stepped the Reverend Franjo Glojnarić, a new arrival from Croatia.

Father Glojnarić seemed to be even less tactful than his predecessor in his dealings with his flock. He began his pastorate with a very foolish announcement which evoked the wrath of most of the members of his congregation. In reply to a request by one of the parishioners that he state the salary and conditions he expected to find in Allegheny City, he is said to have stated: "I have come to serve ten thousand Croats, for a yearly salary of 800 dollars, not included [sic] the usual gratifications received for funeral, marriage and christening ceremonies."[63] It did not take the pastor long to learn that his expectations were not going to be fulfilled. When he asked that each parishioner immediately contribute $10 to the church fund, the unanimous decision of the membership was for individual contributions of 10 cents a week. This certainly did not help to cement relations between the two sides. The gulf continued to widen as violent differences of opinion arose over other issues. Matters finally came to a head early in 1900. By that time Father Glojnarić had succeeded in setting up a new parish and building a new church (also named St. Nicholas) in nearby Millvale. He then called upon the congregation in Allegheny City to give up its cramped and inadequate quarters and join him in Millvale. The Croats in Allegheny City rejected the invitation, and began building a new church of their own—finally completed in September, 1901.[64]

For a brief time the Allegheny parish had Irish clergymen assigned to it. But in December, 1900, a new priest from Croatia, the Reverend Bosiljko Bekavac, was appointed in compliance with the wish of the congregation. Father Bekavac was no more successful than his predecessors had been in pouring oil on the troubled waters of the parish. Conflict flared into the open once more as priest, church committee, and parishioners tangled in heated debate. The quarrel became so violent that Bishop Plehan ordered the closing of the church for all services from August 3 to September 4, 1904.[65] During the interim Father Bekavac moved out and the Reverend Dr. Ljudevit Laus took his place. Dr. Laus proved to be more of a diplomat than any of the earlier priests. He was flexible and tactful in his dealings with the church committee and parishioners. He set up a pattern of conduct which most of his successors followed. As a consequence, there was little serious dissension in the Allegheny parish thereafter.

Croats experienced similar difficulties in the neighboring towns of Millvale, Rankin, Braddock, Etna, and McKeesport. In Millvale the church committee, disgusted with a pastor (the Reverend Josip Tusek) who increased the parish debts in the pursuit of selfish

205

interests, obtained a new priest (the Reverend Ilija Gusić) from Bosnia, only to have him rejected by the bishop in Pittsburgh. The contest that followed between the two claimants to the parish had finally to be settled by the courts.[66] The verdict was in favor of the old priest. In Etna the parishioners succeeded in setting up the Croatian Catholic Independent Church. A similar attempt in McKeesport met with failure. There the affairs got so out of hand that priest succeeded priest with regularity two or three times each year. The Croats of Rankin imported as their pastor the intelligent and cultured priest from St. Peter's Church in Zagreb, the Reverend Dr. Mato Matina. But the struggle over finances proved too exhausting for Father Matina, and he left after serving the parish for only several years.

Lest the reader be misled into believing that the experiences of the Croatians in Allegheny County were unique, let it be explained without delay that other centers, Serbian and Slovenian as well as Croatian, ran into similar problems and difficulties. The immigrants brought over their traditions of piety from their homes in Serbia, Slovenia, and Croatia, but after living in America for a time a number of them assumed an attitude of indifference while a few actually drifted toward atheism. This, however, was just one of the serious problems faced by those who would organize the religious life of their fellow nationals. Another handicap was presented by the clergymen. Most of them were definitely not of the highest caliber. In fact, many were thoroughly incompetent and perpetually quarreled with their parishioners, an excellent illustration of which was provided by the Allegheny Croats. Some wandered from church to church and from town to town in a fruitless search for an ideal religious atmosphere. Others, perhaps more easily discouraged, returned to Europe.

In spite of the many hurdles in their path all three South Slavic groups were able to make steady progress. Year after year they continued to establish new parishes and build additional churches until they spanned the continent. Today, there are eighty Roman Catholic churches (forty-six Slovenian and thirty-four Croatian) and thirty-nine Serbian Orthodox.

Both the Roman Catholic and Serbian Orthodox parishioners elect committees, which, under the leadership of their pastors, help in the management of all affairs, including the spending of funds. Each of the three groups has over $5,000,000 invested in its churches and contributes some $500,000 annually toward the upkeep of its churches and parochial schools. The Serbian Orthodox churches are the property of the individual church communities, while the Roman Catholic are the possessions of the dioceses.

In addition to the Orthodox and the Roman Catholic parishes, there are also two Roman Catholic churches of the Greek Rite. The rites of the latter are the same as in the Orthodox Church, the language used is the Old Church Slavonic, instead of the Latin, and, under certain conditions, the priests are allowed to marry. The faith and tenets correspond exactly with the Roman Catholic, and the followers recognize the Pope in Rome as their supreme head.

The holiday which was formerly (until the establishment of the Tito regime) most widely celebrated by Yugoslavs at home and in America was the anniversary of the formation of the Kingdom of Serbs, Croats, and Slovenes on December 1, 1918. The feast of Sts. Cyril and Methodius, who gave the Slavs their religion and written language, is observed on June 7 by Jugoslavs of both the Roman Catholic and Orthodox faiths.

That the church as an institution has played a highly important role in the life of the Yugoslav Americans can hardly be gainsaid. It has not only served the spiritual needs of the people, but has been a cultural and social force as well. Besides providing educational facilities, the church has taken a lead in organizing and sponsoring dramatic and singing societies, parties, games, and dancing, and a variety of athletic teams (e.g., Catholic Youth Organization). Nevertheless, complaints have been registered in many places against the indifference and apathy of numerous Yugoslavs toward matters religious. A Croatian priest of St. Louis writes: "There are some who attend services regularly—the rest are neither cold nor hot. Communism and propaganda confused many of them— so they do not know what they are or what they want."[67]

A Slovenian clergyman blames the lack of interest on poor religious guidance when the immigrants first arrived.[68] Remoteness of church, discrimination, and lack of sense of organization are reasons outlined by a Serbian church official for keeping many at a distance.[69]

There are, however, many Yugoslav churches and parishes which have been able to maintain membership and interest, and others that are experiencing a renascence after a period of stagnation and even decline. This happier side of the picture is seen in the explanation of Father Victor of St. Mary's Church in Joliet, Illinois:

> We priests (there are four of us) can boast of a parish that outdoes all others (14) of Joliet. Doran Hurley, who visited us some five years ago while preparing notes on Croatian parishes in this country, wrote somewhere that not in all his life had he ever witnessed the contact that a given group of priests had with their parishioners as here at St. Mary's. The fact that we average 29 years in age . . . play on C.Y.O. teams . . . etc., might possibly make a difference.[70]

This encouraging state of affairs at St. Mary's may, perhaps, be a beacon, illuminating the path for the less fortunate to reorganization and resurrection. Much, however, will depend on the second generation Yugoslavs. If they choose to remain within their own churches, they may be able to solve their own problems and make their own adjustments, but if they go astray or join American churches, the fate of the Yugoslav church in America is sealed and its days are numbered.

## POLITICS

One of the most revolutionary changes has taken place in the political life of the immigrants. In the old country it had been practically nonexistent, since peasants had little voice in monarchical governments. They were, as seen, like dumb, driven cattle. However, in the United States the situation was drastically altered.

At the beginning of their arrival in America, it is true, the Yugoslavs were negligible as a political force. To begin with, they were unlettered; they were aliens, only a small minority getting citizenship papers; and they were politically inexperienced. Gradually, however, more and more overcame these initial barriers and began participation in American political life, some even joining machines. The members of the political machines served as a source of stimulus for other aliens, exhorting them to become citizens in order to add their votes to the party's total. A lifelike characterization of a local political "boss" is given by Adamic.

> In the early 90's . . . in Cleveland . . . there rose to such a position of leadership in the Slovenian neighborhood along St. Clair Avenue a man whose name in the old country had been Jurij Bostijancich, but who Americanized it to George Boston. A big, rotund but not obese man, with a large, florid, and jovial face and small, close-set eyes, which squinted full of mysterious,

would-be humorous meaning, he was a typical-looking ward heeler. This even in the matter of such details as the plug hat he wore low on his forehead or over to one side and the cigar in the corner of his mouth. As an industrial worker, years before, he had suffered an accident, and now had a wooden leg, which did not detract from his picturesque jauntiness.

Possessing considerable talent for imitation, Mister Boston, as he liked to be called, was out to do in America as Americans did. A citizen of several years' standing, he spoke English; not the best, perhaps, but good enough for his purposes. Except in the matter of pronunciation, it was not much worse than the English of some of his superiors in the party machine.[71]

The immigrant politician was of inestimable aid to his newly-arrived countrymen, many of whom often felt helpless in the strange environment. He urged the immigrants to go to night school and guided them through the steps of naturalization.

With increased Americanization there has been a marked advance in political activity on the part of the South Slavs in America. More of them are now taking an active part in election campaigns, local and national, than ever before, and some of them have risen to responsible positions in government office. John Slavic and Frank J. Lausche served terms as mayors of Cleveland, with the latter now occupying a seat in the United States Senate. John A. Blatnik has represented the eighth congressional district of Minnesota in the United States House of Representatives since 1946. Mike Stepovich, the son of a Yugoslav immigrant who took part in the 1898 Yukon gold rush, was the youngest governor Alaska has ever had, as well as the first native Alaskan and the first Roman Catholic to hold the post. Many others occupy local and state government positions.

During the early years of immigration most of the Yugoslavs supported the Republican party. This was due chiefly to two reasons. In the first place, the aliens felt they were indebted to the Republican factory and mine owners who gave them their jobs. And secondly, the Irish, who were their bitter rivals, were Democrats, thus driving the Slavs into the opposition camp. Gradually, however, coming to the conclusion that the Republicans were not compatible with their own social and economic philosophy and status, the Yugoslavs shifted to the Democratic party. During the years immediately preceding World War I, South Slavic Americans showed keen interest in the emancipation of their fellow country-men abroad, and President Wilson's stand in behalf of self-determination for minorities further swung them into the Democratic fold. The prohibition issue in the 1920's also swayed many, but it was the depression in the 1930's that caused the majority to desert the Republicans and join the ranks of the Democrats. In Illinois, Michigan, Pennsylvania, and New York, Slavs became "prominent participants in the expansion of Democratic strength."[72]

Yugoslav participation in American domestic politics has, on the whole, been wholesome and beneficial and without undue noise or untoward incident. That, however, has not always been characteristic of their participation in foreign politics. As has already been shown, much bad blood has been spilled among the groups over conditions in the native land. Antagonisms reached their height during World War II, following the creation of the fascist puppet state in Croatia and the outbreak of the struggle between Tito and Mihajlović, the leaders of the Partisans and Chetniks, respectively. In the fall of 1941 Croats and Serbs in this country came to blows in some of the industrial centers over the reports that thousands of Serbs in Axis-dominated Croatia were butchered in cold blood. Champions of Tito and Mihajlović continued to brawl during the entire war. Members of the United Committee of South-Slavic Americans, led by Louis Adamic, vigorously pressed Tito's claims, while the cause of Mihajlović was upheld by the men in the Serbian National Defense Council of America.

The divisions did not end with the conclusion of the war and the ascendancy of Tito. Some of the Croats and Slovenes gave their support to the new regime, while others, mainly devout Catholics and the followers of the former Croat leader Vladko Maček, criticized the government for its excesses. The Serbs, too, split on the issue; a number assailed Tito, a Croat, because of their strong feeling against the Croatians in general; others showed sympathy to the new government because its policies were similar to those of the Russians, who are their religious brethren. These remain the prevalent attitudes today throughout the Yugoslav colonies in the United States.

Partly because of their support of the Tito government in Yugoslavia, and partly because of their backing in the United States of candidates such as Henry A. Wallace and the Progressives, and measures that were termed socialist, the South Slavs have been accused of Communist leanings and activities. This misconception had its beginning in the early days of World War II when large numbers of immigrants, in order to share in the rapidly increasing profits, transferred from the Atlantic to the Pacific Coast fisheries. This led men like Congressman John McDowell, a Republican from Wilkinsburg, Pennsylvania, to believe that some of the Yugoslav fishermen were Communists, especially since they were known to be cruising around Alaska. To gather further evidence, McDowell hired a former Yugoslav politician, writer, and linguist, Bogumil Vošnjak, to mingle among the fishermen. In the meantime, the Federal Bureau of Investigation, also watching the Yugoslavs, apparently got suspicious of Vošnjak and took him into custody. The affair was closed with the release of Vošnjak and the dropping of the investigation, with no substantial evidence uncovered.

In conducting their search for Communists on the Pacific Coast, the government sleuths went far astray. The fishermen are among the most loyal citizens of the country, due, in no small part, to their prosperity. What few Yugoslav Communists there are in the United States operate under the very noses of the hunters—in the backyard of Washington. Their nest is in Pittsburgh, the main organizational center for all forms of Yugoslav activities. Spearheading this movement, which, despite the expenditure of much money and effort, has failed to attract more than a nominal minority of adherents, are a few personal messengers of Tito. The chief assignments of these envoys at the present time are to convince the Yugoslav Americans that Tito is not a heretic but remains one of the Communist faithful despite his breach with the Soviet Union, and at the same time to enlist their countrymen's aid in order to bolster the Yugoslav economy.

Perhaps even more detrimental to the peace of mind of South Slavic Americans than the Communists are the émigré politicians, outstanding among whom are ex-ambassador Konstantin Fotich, Miha Krek, former Slovene peasant leader, and Andrija Artuković, former minister in the Pavelić cabinet in Croatia. From their protective perches in the United States these men pour out their propaganda against the new Yugoslavia, keeping alive national rivalries and old hatreds and confusing the immigrants.

Although many of the Yugoslav immigrants continue to support their old homeland materially and spiritually and some have either been duped by clever Communists agents or become victims of émigré propaganda, there is no doubt where the allegiance of the majority lies. They remain loyal to American institutions, principles, and ideals. Experiences of oppression abroad are too deeply rooted in the memories of the aliens for them to become easy prey to schemes which would take away the cherished liberties and opportunities secured in their adopted home.

## ASSIMILATION

Reference has already been made to assimilation, but in view of the importance of the subject, a more complete examination is imperative. It should be noted at the outset that there are some factors that promote and others that oppose assimilation. What some of these are will perhaps become clearer in the pages that follow.

One of the clearest signs of the Americanization of the Yugoslavs is the increasing naturalization. Naturalization before World War I had proceeded at a slow pace. By 1920 only 42,686, or 25.2 per cent, had become American citizens and 28,892 had taken out their first papers, out of a total foreign-born population of 169,437.[73] Out of a population increased to 211,416 in 1930 the number of citizens rose to 97,880, or 46.3 per cent, while the number holding first papers climbed to 29,444.[74] By 1940 many of the older immigrants died and the population decreased to the 1920 level. Though the number making their declarations of intention fell to 16,980, the number obtaining naturalization certificates remained comparatively high, 91,890, or 61.3 per cent of the total.[75] In the decade from 1940 to 1950, 47,711 joined the ranks of citizens, and 16,642 more followed from 1951 through 1957.[76]

Another development that may be cited as evidence of Americanization is the increased cooperation among the several members of the Yugoslav family. It is quite true that not all the old feuds are dead, but much more harmonious relations prevail among the Croats, Serbs, and Slovenes in America today than at any time in the past or is to be found among their countrymen in Europe. This situation has resulted from a variety of factors. Especially helpful have been the Yugoslav organizations, press, and radio. Important also have been the efforts of the second generation, who, being thrown into contact with all sorts of elements in the American environment, have sought to establish friendlier relations among their parents. But most influential have been the institutions, customs, and principles of the United States. For the immigrants these have meant liberty, opportunity, and elevated status, causing many of them to forgive and forget their old-world enemies and grudges.

Some of the Yugoslavs, of course, have been more readily absorbed than others. Generally speaking, this has been true of the Dalmatians and the Slovenians. The relatively easy assimilability of the Dalmatians is explained by the fact that they came to America with traditions of individual initiative in enterprise and trade, and that their migration was not a mass movement but a slow and continual flow of individuals. Added to these forces are the cosmopolitanism and linguistic talents of the people. In favor of the Slovenes, it can be said that they entered the country more "westernized" and with more advantages in the way of education, which accelerated their admission into business and professional occupations. Though there have been differences in the rate of assimilation among the foreign born, the second generation has not exhibited the same tendencies. American-born Croats, Serbs, and Slovenes demonstrate equal facility in adjusting to the American environment.

Thus, for better or worse, the Yugoslavs are gradually being absorbed by the Melting Pot. Some of the immigrants, however, still cling to their own speech and traditions in the home, in the church, and in the parish school. Also, the vernacular press, partly because of self-interest perhaps, exhorts the foreign-born parents to see to it that the younger generation learns the national language.

Aside from their inward urge to preserve old ways, there is also a subtle force from the outside exerted on the Yugoslav community in any given locality, which at least slows down the rate of assimilation. Klein, in his interesting and informative study of McKeesport, Pennsylvania, reported 2,161 Yugoslavs residing in the town and pointed out that few "older American groups who control the cultural and civic institutions invite participation by the 'new Americans.' "[77] He went on to explain:

> One may hear much talk in McKeesport about the failure of the "foreigners" to become Americanized. Yet when one examines the membership lists of American enterprises, one rarely discovers a name suggesting that the McKeesport inhabitants of southeastern European stock have a chance to see more of America than school, mill, shops, and movies! For instance, the Kiwanis, the Lions, the Optimists are said not to have extended

their membership to citizens of foreign stock. There are one or two successful Slavic and Italian businessmen among the Rotarians. According to a social worker formerly in McKeesport, a number of men of various nationalities are members of the American Legion, but these same men do not belong to the fraternal or other groups, predominantly American. Among women's groups there is the same distinction.[78]

The Yugoslavs in McKeesport, few in number in comparison to other groups, are further weakened by being split into separate political factions. One authority believes that "it is this segregation of the various Slavic groups from Americans and from each other that constitutes the greatest obstacle to their assimilation."[79] When the community is large enough, the Yugoslav lives in a miniature world in which he finds his work and recreation, or as Miller phrases it so capably:

> He often works with fellow Slavs. His recreation he finds at the national hall among his own people. He has his own paper. He worships in his own church. He buys at neighborhood stores where his own language is spoken. He deposits his money in his own bank. He invests his savings in real estate sold by a fellow countryman. He is, in fact, submerged in the life of the group. He is often so segregated from American life that it is not until his children grow up that he comes into contact with American people and American institutions, and even then he often feels like a fish out of water.[80]

The younger generation is gradually forcing the immigrants to come into greater contact with American life. Many children of the aliens have grown up and married, moving themselves and their families to other sections of the city or even to another city, away from the Slavic community. Some foreign-born Yugoslavs, successful businessmen and professional people particularly, have long ago thrown off the old ways of life.

Many Yugoslavs, however, loyal Americans in every way, have been working hard to preserve their native cultural pattern. Some of them, for instance, feel that the Americanization of names and language is a sign of retrogression rather than a step forward. There is much logic to their argument that variety enriches and stimulates a culture.

In many cases immigrant parents and their American-born children do not see eye to eye. Often the children look upon their parents as old-fashioned, and do not understand and cannot abide by the old community feeling that surrounded the parents in their old home. The parents' values have been belittled and their loyalties scorned.

The children are determined to drop the mother tongue, and they very soon learn English, while the parents are past the age when it is easy to acquire a new language. One often hears of children refusing to answer in the language of the family. Everything seems to be done for the child independently of the family or the community. The school, the church, the social settlement all emphasize the child's importance. The parents are ignored, left behind and the breach between the new and the old in the family is not spanned as yet by any of the agencies in the community.[81]

The difficulties and differences between immigrant parents and their American children are partly attributable to the fact that the children have no knowledge of the land and culture from which their parents came. The parents, on the other hand, have had little or no schooling, and therefore cannot adequately explain to their sons and daughters the real values of the old country. About the only thing that the immigrants tell their offspring is that they are Croatian, Serbian, or Slovenian, which by itself is meaningless. It is not surprising then that the children cannot respect the rich past of their parents. In fact, they are often ashamed of them. But too often also the children do not comprehend the great sacrifice and labor that was needed to make a home in America.[82] Only when the values, sacrifices, and attitudes of the immigrants are fully understood by the American-born children will the gap between the old and the new be completely bridged.

# 9

# Famous Folk and Plain People

THE HISTORY of Yugoslav immigration is the story of people—all kinds of people: talented and unskilled, rich and poor, renowned and undistinguished. Though the great majority of Yugoslav Americans are relatively unknown, the number rising to eminence compares very favorably with those of other immigrant minority groups, especially those coming from a similar, rural and backward, environment. They, too, have their inventors, writers, statesmen, artists, educators, and professional men. They are undoubtedly behind the representatives of the western and northern European countries. This, however, is not due to lack of native ability, but rather to lack of opportunity—as is partially proven by the attainments of the second generation. Unlike the nationals of western and northern Europe who upon coming here found many of their countrymen occupying positions of power and importance, the South Slavs had no one to extend them a helping hand but rather had to shift for themselves. The struggle to eke out an existence made it exceedingly difficult to train for promotion.

But whether the story deals with famous folk or just plain people, it can be better understood by becoming acquainted with some of the real personalities and their experiences. The human element provides a vital link in the chain of facts and figures. Without that element the data remain cold and meaningless.

One of the most distinguished of the Yugoslav Americans was the late Nikola Tesla, the electrical wizard.[1]* His name will undoubtedly be remembered as long as electricity serves mankind.

* Notes to this chapter begin on page 296.

## The Prodigal Genius

Tesla[2] was born on July 10, 1856, in the village of Smiljan, in the district of Lika, which was at that time a part of the Austrian empire.[3] He was one of the five children of Miljutin Tesla, a priest in the Eastern Orthodox Church, and Djuka Tesla, the daughter of a priest and a member of a prominent Serbian family. Both of the parents were descendants of a long line of inventors, so that an invaluable legacy of distinction and culture was passed on to the boy.

Early in his boyhood Nikola evinced many of the characteristics of an inventive genius. At the age of five he made a blowgun. At seven he made his first "motor," a device driven by June bugs pasted to the spokes of a wheel. At the same time he made his first "transmission" by driving a pulley from the crude motor by means of a thread. When he was twelve he made a vacuum pump and started to build a *perpetuum mobile*.[4]

Nikola attended grammar school in the town of Gospić and then continued his education at the secondary school in Karlovac, from which he graduated in 1873, after only three years of study. The boy's parents wanted him to prepare for a career in the church, but he had a mind of his own. Religion did not have the same fascination for him as did science. Accordingly, instead of entering a seminary as his parents desired, he enrolled in the Polytechnic School in Gratz, Austria, in 1875, with the intention of becoming a professor of mathematics and physics. But while at Gratz he became attracted to electricity, so that he took up a course in electrical engineering. According to most biographies Tesla completed his studies in engineering. But his nephew, Nikola Trbojević, disagrees. He says after two years at Gratz his uncle was expelled from the college and city because he played cards and led an irregular life.[5] Be that as it may, the young scientist next moved to Prague, where he is said to have studied philosophy and languages at the university there, though no official record exists of his enrollment.

In 1880 Tesla moved to Budapest, Hungary, where he began his professional career. He first went to work as a draftsman, but did not find the work entirely satisfying. Fortunately for him, at that time the American telephone interests were installing a system in Budapest. He promptly applied for a position with the new firm and succeeded in getting an appointment as an assistant in the engineering department. While employed in this capacity, he invented a telephone repeater (which he neglected to patent) and conceived the idea of his rotating magnetic field. His work in Budapest attracted a good deal of attention and paved the way for a new job in Paris. In the French capital he became an engineer for the French Edison Company. Although he enjoyed life in France he was not happy in his position, for it did not offer the opportunities he desired for the development of his electrical talents. Consequently, he sought new worlds to conquer. Following a misunderstanding with his employers in regard to the payment of a bonus for an induction motor he had succeeded in putting together, he decided to leave Paris. It was at this time that he seriously turned his attention to the United States, which he believed had a promising field for the fruition of his ideas.

Accordingly, in 1884, at the age of twenty-eight and with only four cents in his pocket, Tesla arrived in New York. Though penniless, he was not friendless—he had the names of many friends in America. And he did not long remain without funds either. The first day he made $20 repairing a dynamo, and the second he went to work for the Edison Company in Orange, New Jersey. There he was able to increase his material wealth as well as to make the personal acquaintance of the Wizard of Menlo Park, Thomas A. Edison. Disagreement between the two giants of the electrical world was common. Their argument concerned largely the respective merits of the systems of direct and alternating currents, with Edison defending the superiority of the former and Tesla the latter. This conflict, together with the limitations of his position, Tesla felt was a serious barrier to the full expansion of his genius. An argument over money provided him with an opportunity to sever his relations with the organization in 1885. Two years later, with the financial assistance of H. K. Brown of Western Union, he established the Tesla Laboratory in New York, where he was able to devote more time to pure research. At about the same time he founded the Tesla Electric Company.

It was in the laboratory in New York that Tesla translated many of his dreams into realities, and within a few years he received recognition as one of the top-ranking scientists of the country. Beginning with a system of arc lighting in 1886, which started a flow of handsome royalties, he proceeded from one successful invention

218

to another.  In 1888 he brought out the Tesla motor and alternating-current power transmission system, then followed with a system of electrical conversion and distribution by oscillatory discharges in 1889, high-frequency generators in 1890, the Tesla coil or transformer in 1891, a system of wireless transmission of information in 1893, and mechanical oscillators and generators of electrical oscillations in 1894-1895.  During the years 1896 through 1898 he carried on researches and made discoveries in radiations, material stream, and emanations.  In 1897 he invented the high-potential magnifying transmitter.  Most of his time from 1897 to 1905 he spent working on a system for the wireless transmission of power.

Of all of Tesla's inventions, the ones that gained him most renown were his alternating-current motors and the Tesla coil or transformer.  This, however, should not lead one to dismiss lightly his other contributions.  It must be remembered that he was the first to conceive a practical method for the utilization of the alternating current, so as to convert electrical into mechanical energy more simply, effectively, and economically than by direct current.  He discovered the principle of the rotary magnetic field which is embodied in the apparatus used in the transmission of power from Niagara Falls, thus opening the modern superpower era in which electricity is transported for hundreds of miles to thousands of factories.  He also invented many new forms of dynamos, transformers, induction coils, condensers, arc and incandescent lamps, the oscillator combining steam engine and dynamo, and many other devices too numerous to mention.  His researches in electrical oscillation were responsible for the creation of a new field of electrical investigation, the full possibilities of which are even now far from being exhausted.

Tesla made an international reputation not only by his many practical inventions but also by the boldness and brilliancy of his ideas, presented before groups and meetings he addressed in various parts of the world and in writings he published. As an illustration, it might be pointed out that long before the atomic bombs burst over Nagasaki and Hiroshima in 1945, Tesla foresaw the possibility of harnessing atomic energy.  These ideas attracted world-wide interest, but at the same time they diverted, to some extent, attention from his many useful contributions.

Tesla was as much a humanitarian as he was a scientist, dedicating his life to the lightening of the burdens of toil of his fellow men and promoting universal peace and welfare alike. He tried desperately to prevent the use of his many inventions for destructive purposes, but when war came, in 1914 and again in 1939, he did everything in his power to aid both his native and adopted lands. Thus, not long after America's entry into World War II, he wrote to his nephew, Sava N. Kosanovich:

> President Roosevelt and Donald Nelson . . . have repeatedly urged the American people, workers and employers, to meet as fully as possible the goals established for the production of war materials. . . . For that reason, my dear brothers and sisters, as the oldest Serb, Yugoslav and American in the U. S., I am addressing this letter to you, asking you to answer the call of President Roosevelt.
>
> The achievements of our brothers in the old country are worthy of the spirit which permeates our folklore . . . the fate of the Serbs, Croats and Slovenes is inseparable.[6]

Though giving his all against a common foe, Tesla was very much disturbed by the periodic bloodletting and sought to draw up a plan for a new and better world. The philosophy behind that scheme is illustrated in a piece he wrote in October, 1942:

> Out of this war, the greatest since the beginning of history, a new world must be born, a world that would justify the sacrifices offered by humanity. This new world must be a world in which there shall be no exploitation of the weak by the strong, of the good by the evil; where there will be no humiliation of the poor by the violence of the rich; where the products of intellect, science and art will serve society for the betterment and beautification of life, and not individuals for the amassing of wealth. This new world shall not be a world of downtrodden and humiliated, but of the free men and free nations, equal in dignity and respect for man.[7]

Tesla uttered no empty phrases here, but in reality was preaching what he himself had already practiced. He had the opportunity to amass millions from his inventions, but personal gain was far from his goal, as is so clearly demonstrated in the incident where he tore up a twelve-million-dollar contract in order to save his friend George Westinghouse from bankruptcy. Because he was pressed for funds during the last years of his life, many of his novel ideas, which might have brought greater prosperity and peace to all mankind, were prevented from materializing—a definite loss to the world.

The great electrician never married. Though he had legions of acquaintances, he was intimate with but few, feeling that a scientist must keep himself free of personal relationships that would be unduly demanding. He died as a relative recluse in a lonely hotel room in New York on January 7, 1943. Thus passed away a phenomenal Yugoslav American who had staggered the world with the brilliance of his achievements and the scope of his imagination.

Tesla was not only widely known and admired the world over while he lived, but he has received recognition for his contributions after death. On the occasion of his eightieth birthday in 1936 many European cities held scientific forums and meetings in his honor. Less than a year after his death, in the fall of 1943, in a belated decision, which helped to clarify the pioneering role of the Serbian American scientific genius in the development of the wireless, the United States Supreme Court declared the Marconi "four tuned circuit" patents invalid on the basis of prior work and anticipation by Nikola Tesla and John Stone, the patents which had established Marconi as the father of radio.[8] On the eve of the world-wide observance of the Tesla Centennial Anniversary in 1956 the International Electrotechnical Commission announced that henceforth the unassigned unit of magnetic flux in the MKS system would be called "Tesla."[9] On May 15, 1957, at a meeting honoring the Tesla Centenary, the Franklin Institute of Philadelphia passed the resolution stating, "Nikola Tesla stands with Benjamin Franklin in electrical achievements which have contributed to the good of all mankind."[10] Also helping to honor and preserve the memory of Tesla are the Tesla Society in Minneapolis, Minnesota, and the Nikola Tesla Museum in Belgrade, Yugoslavia.[11]

## FROM IMMIGRANT TO INVENTOR

Another Serbian immigrant who won universal renown as a brilliant scientist and inventor was Michael Idvorsky Pupin.[12] The Pupin Institute at Columbia University in New York was erected to perpetuate the memory of this talented Yugoslav American. Although unlike the retiring Tesla, to whom money and fame had no meaning, Pupin was an interesting figure, and his life story is an inspiring one.

Michael, or Miša, as he was known in his native land, was born on October 4, 1858, in the village of Idvor, province of Banat, which was then a part of Hungary. He began his formal training in the village school, an experience somewhat uninteresting for a boy with a seemingly insatiable intellectual hunger. The real inspiration in those early years came from his mother and from a village historian, poet, and prophet named Baba Batikin. His mother, a woman who could neither read nor write, convinced him that the greatest power was to be found in learning and knowledge, while Baba, who had participated in some of the campaigns against Napoleon Bonaparte, stimulated the boy's interest in Serbia's past by his recitation of chapters from his own life and that of his country.

From Idvor, Michael went to the school at Pančevo, where he was deeply impressed by the learning of his teachers in natural science, a subject which early attracted his interest. One of his favorite instructors, a Slovenian named Kos, first told him the story of Benjamin Franklin and his experiment with the kite, thereby arousing his curiosity in science as well as in America. Through close observation he discovered that sound spreads faster and better in the earth than in the air. He took an interest in the heavens and learned how to locate the planets Mars and Venus. But science was not his only pursuit in Pančevo. He soon became involved in a nationalist movement of the Serbs against Austria and might have been expelled from school had it not been for the timely intervention of a family friend, a clergyman of the Serbian Orthodox Church. Though saved, he decided to transfer his studies to Prague, after promise of financial assistance from his church.

On the way to Prague two rather amusing and interesting incidents occurred, both of which were to leave deep impressions on Pupin.[13] The first of these happened on the passenger boat he took to begin the trip. Engaging him in conversation, a group of frolicsome theological students stole from his valise the roasted goose his mother had prepared for the trip. It was no joke for a youngster with a ravenous appetite. To him it was a mean trick, and he could not easily dismiss it from his mind. The second episode took place on the train from Budapest to Prague. On this occasion Pupin overslept and found himself in Vienna instead of Prague. Refusing to pay for another fare to his rightful destination, he got into a heated argument with the stationmaster and several other officials. When it appeared that the railroad men were going to beat him, an elderly couple from the United States intervened. The two American tourists offered to take the youth to Prague, where they too were going, and invited him to share their first-class compartment. He accepted without hesitation— he wouldn't even think of rejecting generosity the likes of which he had never seen. The couple treated the boy as they would their own son. They fired his imagination with their stories of Franklin and Lincoln and of America in general, and they advised him to come to America at the earliest opportunity. It was an experience that the youngster could not forget.

Michael's studies in Prague suffered because of his continued nationalist activities. He became a devoted disciple of František Palacky, an outstanding crusader for Czech independence and a great apostle of Pan-Slavism, and plunged deeply into propagandist agitation. His career as a revolutionary, however, was cut short by the sudden death of his father. The youth's first thought upon receiving the sad news from home was to return to Idvor to assume the family responsibilities, but his mother would not hear of it.

Denied the chance to take the place of the head of the family, Michael sought other means to aid his mother. He believed the desirable opportunity arrived one day when he read an advertisement of the Hamburg-American Line offering steerage transportation from Hamburg to New York for twenty-eight florins (about $11.20 in American money). He would go to America and help his family from there. His problem was solved. This experience is most vividly described by Pupin himself.

> I thought of my mellow-hearted American friends . . . and decided on the spot to try my fortune in the land of Franklin and Lincoln as soon as I could save up and otherwise scrape up money enough to carry me from Prague to New York. My books, my watch, my clothes . . . were all sold to make up the sum necessary for traveling expenses. I started out with just one suit of clothes on my back and a few changes of linen, a red Turkish fez which nobody would buy. And why should anybody going to New York bother about warm clothes? Was not New York much farther south than Panchevo, and does not America suggest a hot climate when one thinks of the pictures of naked Indians, so often seen? These thoughts consoled me when I parted with my sheepskin coat. At length, I came to Hamburg ready to embark but with no money to buy a mattress and a

blanket for my bunk in the steerage. Several days later my ship, the "Westphalia," sailed—on the twelfth day of March, 1874.[14]

Arriving after a rough fourteen-day voyage at Castle Garden, the immigrant station in New York, the lone voyager was nearly prevented from entering the country because he had neither money (no more than five cents) nor relatives in America. When, however, he explained that he knew Franklin, Lincoln, and Harriet Beecher Stowe, the immigration inspector was so amused and touched that he allowed the bewildered and much-surprised youth to enter.

Upon setting foot in New York Pupin spent his last five cents for a piece of prune pie, which, however, contained nothing more than seeds. Hungry, but proud and hopeful, he went for a walk. As he strolled through the city a street urchin knocked off his red fez. He got into a fist fight, beat up his assailant, and picked up his fez from the gutter. To his surprise, no one hit him from behind during the bout, and even the policeman in the crowd did not interfere. When it was all over, two of the spectators offered him jobs.

He began working as a driver of a team of mules on a Delaware farm. But the boy, not quite sixteen, was restless and yearned for something more than a life of physical labor. He quit his first job after saving enough to move on. He tried several other farms, in Delaware and Maryland. On one of these, the farmer, a stout Baptist, tried to convert Pupin and forced him to listen to his reading of the Bible every night and all day Sunday. He didn't tolerate that very long. He ran away and returned to New York, where he did various odd jobs, such as painting, wallpapering, and shoveling coal into basements, before he finally obtained work of a more permanent nature in a biscuit factory. Here he had a difficult time in stamping the biscuits fast enough. To his utter surprise and amazement, instead of being discharged, he was made a foreman. This, he was certain, could not happen anywhere but in America. It was an experience he loved to tell about to his friends.

It was at this time that Pupin met a former German scientist named Bilharz. Though he had descended to rather low levels and was perhaps slightly unbalanced, Bilharz exercised an important influence on the young immigrant thirsting for knowledge. In addition to science, he taught Pupin Latin, Greek, history, and literature.  With his intellectual appetite thus whetted, Pupin, who had never forgotten his mother's counsel that knowledge was a prerequisite to success, decided to resume the formal studies that had been interrupted in Prague.  After attending night classes at Cooper Union for a short time, he transferred to Adelphi Academy, where he believed he could make more adequate preparations for entry into Columbia College (now University), his ultimate goal. While at Adelphi he won a ten-mile foot race without any previous training, thus helping to spread his fame in athletic circles.

In 1879 Pupin took his entrance examination at Columbia. Passing with a very high score (he amazed the professors with his faultless recitations of two books of Homer's *Iliad* in Greek and four orations of Cicero in Latin), he received a scholarship and entered the college in September.  His four years as an undergraduate were busy ones, indeed.  He divided his studies between letters and sciences, besides serving as president of the junior class and participating in athletics as a boxer and wrestler.  At about the same time in 1883 he obtained both his Bachelor of Arts degree and his naturalization papers.

It had not been until nearly the end of his fourth year at Columbia that Pupin had decided upon his life's work.  The decision had come with a demonstration by one of his professors of the simple experiment that had led to the discovery of the electromagnetic law of induction by Michael Faraday.  Then and there he had made up his mind to master the subject of physics in order to be able to unravel the secrets of science.

Having compiled a remarkable record as an undergraduate, he had no difficulty in getting assistance for the continuation of his studies on the graduate level.  He applied for and received the John Tyndall Fellowship, becoming the first American holder of the valuable prize.  The fellowship enabled him to study physics and mathematics, first at Cambridge University in England and then at the University of Berlin in Germany.  While studying abroad he came into contact with some of the most brilliant minds of the time, including the famous Hermann von Helmholtz, who was his professor at Berlin.  The experiences were exceedingly stimulating and opened new vistas for the ambitious young scientist.  During his last year at Berlin (1889) Pupin fell in love with and married the sister of one of his classmates, an American named Jackson. With a new bride under one arm and a Doctor of Philosophy degree under the other, he returned to the United States to accept a position as instructor in mathematical physics with his alma mater, beginning in the fall of 1889.

From then on the rise of Pupin in position, fame, and fortune was rapid. In 1892 he was made adjunct professor of mathematics and in 1901 was promoted to full professor of electromechanics, a position he continued to occupy until his retirement in 1931. His interests and activities, however, were not confined to the classroom. He was appointed as the director of the Phoenix Research Laboratories in 1911. Moreover, he championed the cause of the National Research Council, served as a member of the National Advisory Committee for Aeronautics, and during World War I acted as chairman of the Subcommittee on Aircraft Communications, a group which sought to develop a reliable means of communication between aircraft in flight.

Though Pupin was one of Columbia's ablest pedagogues, he is far better known as a scientist and inventor, reaching his highest magnitude in the discovery of electrical principles and devices. He discovered X-ray radiation in 1896, and in the same year invented means for short exposure X-ray photography by the interposition of a fluorescent screen. In 1899 he brought out his high inductance wave conductors, his principal invention. By means of self-inducting coils (called Pupin coils after him) placed at predetermined intervals of the transmitting wire to preserve the vibrations and resonance, he greatly extended the range of long distance telephony, especially over telephone cables.] By 1901 he so perfected his system that he was able to sell his patent to the Bell Telephone Company and German telephone interests, thereby acquiring royalties which made him a rich man. Later on most of the countries of the world adopted his system of telephony, and they continue to use it to this day. In 1917 he presented to the United States government the use of his invention for eliminating static interference with wireless transmission. He also made other valuable inventions in electrical wave propagation, electrical resonance, iron magnetization, and multiplex telegraphy.

Pupin's genius extended to other fields besides science. His literary works, including *Electro-Magnetic Theory* (1895), *From Immigrant to Inventor* (1923), *The New Reformation* (1927), and the *Romance of the Machine* (1930), won prizes throughout the world, the most coveted being the Pulitzer Prize in 1925 for his autobiography *From Immigrant to Inventor*. He was particularly instrumental in bringing about closer relations and cooperation between his native land and the United States. Appointed by Serbia as an honorary consul general in New York, he acted as an agent for that nation during World War I, organizing for relief work a corps of Columbia students who served in Serbia in 1915. After the war he spent many weeks in consultation on matters concerning the Balkans at the peace conference in Paris.

In recognition of his contributions to science and other fields, Pupin was awarded many medals and honors, among them the John Fritz Gold Medal, the Elliot Cresson Medal of Franklin Institute, and the Edison Medal of the American Institute of Electrical Engineers.[15] High compliment was paid to Pupin by President Harding when in a letter to him, dated October 14, 1922, he wrote:

> I take this occasion to record recognition and appreciation of the fact that—by virtue of experiments conducted and directed in your laboratory, you were successful in contributing in an important respect to the development of one of the marvels of our age, the radio telephone.[16]

After a long and productive life, filled with glory and outstanding achievement, the great Serbian American died on March 12, 1935, at the age of seventy-seven, loved and admired not only by men of science but by millions of people who have benefited from his work.

### LAUGHING IN THE JUNGLE

Among the celebrated Yugoslav Americans one of the most colorful and intriguing was the Slovenian immigrant, editor, author, and social philosopher, Louis Adamic.[17] His struggle to gain recognition is a unique chapter in the story of the South Slav immigrants in the United States and deserves special attention.

Adamic, born on March 23, 1899, in the village of Blato, Carniola, then a province of Austria, was the oldest of nine children of relatively well-to-do peasant parents.[18] Beginning his studies at the village school, he transferred at the age of ten to the city school at Ljubljana, where his parents wanted him to begin preparations for the priesthood. The precocious child, however, had other ideas. He had, in fact, already made up his mind to emigrate to America, his interest having been aroused in the country across the sea by the glowing accounts painted by returned immigrants. But a boy of ten could hardly make the long voyage alone, and so there followed four years of study at the gymnasium in Ljubljana, where his political affiliations and nationalist activities brought him into disfavor with the Austrian authorities and ended in brief imprisonment. The events at Ljubljana only served to strengthen his determination to escape to the land of the free. And when finally he was enrolled by his parents at a Jesuit school, he ran away and, after stopping in Blato long enough to pick up his few belongings and borrow money from his father for passage, hastened to Le Havre, France, where he sailed on the "Niagara" bound for America.

The first job in the new land for the fourteen-year-old immigrant was an assistant mailer at $8 a week for the *Narodni Glas*, a Slovenian daily newspaper published in New York. While with the paper, Adamic enrolled in a night school class to learn the English language, which he felt was the first step toward an understanding of American civilization—a vast jungle to him. Night school, however, did not prove to be the answer to his problem. Much more enlightening, he discovered, was extensive reading—books, magazines, newspapers, and even billboards and store signs, in fact, every form of literature available.

*Narodni Glas* suspended publication late in 1916, and Adamic, after having been promoted to assistant editor, was without work. There followed various odd jobs of digging up pavements, loading trucks, and sweeping floors in factories, first in New York and then in Paterson, New Jersey. Several months' taste of industrial life was more than enough for the intellectually-inclined youth. Accordingly, he gave up the work and soon thereafter (February, 1917) he joined the army, which he felt offered the opportunities he sought: to learn, to travel, and to defend democracy against autocracy. His three years of service, during which he rose to the rank of sergeant, proved very eventful and educational, as he met many interesting personalities and saw new and fascinating places in the New World and the Old.

In the years immediately following his discharge from the service, Adamic drifted from job to job (laborer, seaman, stevedore, reporter) and from city to city (New York, Washington, Chicago, St. Louis, Los Angeles), finally anchoring in San Pedro, California, in June, 1923. Early in 1924 he was appointed municipal port

Senator Frank J. Lausche

*Photo courtesy*
*Chase Ltd. Photo,*
*Washington, D. C.*

Congressman John A. Blatnik

Matthew Cvetic

Yugoslav employee
of the large
Inland Steel Co.
plant in
East Chicago, Indiana

*Photo courtesy
Community Relations Dept.,
Inland Steel Co.*

Yugoslav railway car
repairmen at the
General American Trans.
Corp. shop in
East Chicago, Indiana

*Photo courtesy
Joe De Rosa*

Yugoslav coal miners in Windsor Power House Coal Co. mine
in Windsor Heights, Virginia

*Photo courtesy United Mine Workers of America*

Yugoslavs at work
in photographic laboratory
of Ford Motor Co.
in Dearborn, Michigan

*Photo courtesy
Ford Motor Co.*

Repairing net
aboard a purse seiner,
San Pedro, California

*Photo courtesy
Roman Govorchin*

Cannery workers, San Pedro, California

*Photo courtesy Roman Govorchin*

John Germ

Nikola Gršković

Joseph L. Culkar

John R. Palandech

V. I. Mandich

Charles Bojanic

Louis Adamic

Michael I. Pupin

August Korach

Nick Bez

Nikola Tesla

*Photo courtesy The Tesla Society,
Minneapolis, Minn.*

Ivan Meštrović with
his latest masterpiece,
*Socrates Teaching*

Henry Suzzallo

Tania Velia

Frank Yankovic and his polka band

pilots' clerk there, after successfully passing a civil service examination. While at the port he began to write. Starting out slowly, he gradually experienced increasing success after several years of effort. By 1929 his expanding literary interests took him back to New York, where he remained until 1937. In that year he bought a farm in Milford, New Jersey, where he moved with his wife, the former Stella Sanders, whom he had married in 1931.

Adamic's interest in writing began early in his boyhood, as he himself says:

> When I was 12 or 13, in my native country, I wrote something in the Slovenian language which found its way into a juvenile magazine. I suppose I always wanted to write. I scribbled while in the American army; also I recall that I modeled in clay while in the trenches. In the early 1920's while bumming around the country, I began to translate Slovenian, Croatian, and Serbian stories into English; most of these translations appeared in the *Living Age,* then published in Boston.[19]

The first real break for the youth came in the fall of 1927 when Henry L. Mencken accepted his article, "The Yugoslav Speech in America," for publication in *The American Mercury.* Mencken liked the essay so well that he asked for more. Adamic, of course, was more than willing to oblige. Soon, however, he sought bigger game, and the result was his first book, *Dynamite,* an account of labor-management strife in American industry, published in 1931. The next year he followed with *Laughing in the Jungle,* an autobiographical sketch, which won him a Guggenheim Fellowship. This enabled him to return to his native land and study the country and its people firsthand. The material collected in Yugoslavia resulted in the publication in 1934 of his most successful work, a Book-of-the-Month Club selection, *The Native's Return,* a graphic narrative of peasant life and general conditions under the Alexandrian dictatorship. Then in rapid succession followed two novels: *Grandsons* and *Cradle of Life.* After a trip to Guatemala in 1936, he wrote, in 1937, *The House in Antigua.* In 1938 appeared *My America,* a story of the personal experiences of the author—a sort of sequel to *Laughing in the Jungle.*

He then focused his attention on immigrants. With a grant-in-aid from the Rockefeller Foundation, he set out across the country to gather material on the aliens. He published questionnaires in foreign-language newspapers to get the answers to questions about foreign-born minorities in America. Nearly half a million replies came back. Resulting from his labors were three new volumes. The first of these he published in 1940 under the title of *From Many Lands,* consisting of a collection of human-interest stories on America's immigrants. Then in 1942 followed *What's Your Name?,* an intriguing discussion of name changes among the foreign-born. And finally in 1945 came *A Nation of Nations,* a glowing account of the various races and nationalities and their contributions to America. Adamic believed that minorities were part of an all-American problem. "There is no Negro problem, or Italian problem or Jewish problem," he once explained. "It's all part of the American problem. The tragedy of it is that a person who feels prejudice as a member of a minority group too often tries to save his ego by directing his own prejudices at a member of a different minority group."[20]

The most provocative of Adamic's writings have been his *Two-Way Passage, My Native Land,* and *Dinner at the White House,* published in 1941, 1943, and 1946, respectively. The theme of *Two-Way Passage,* that the United States participate directly in the physical and psychological reconstruction of war-torn Europe and that it utilize the services of American immigrants in the tremendous task, stimulated universal interest and discussion, leading to an invitation to dine at the White House early in January, 1942, and discuss the proposal with the Roosevelts and British Prime Minister Winston Churchill. Around this meeting Adamic spun his story of *Dinner at the White House,* containing his impressions of the two wartime leaders, and resulting in a suit for libel by Churchill which was settled out of court in 1947. Even more controversial was *My Native Land,* a penetrating analysis of the Tito-Mihajlović struggle in Yugoslavia together with a journalistic account of the background of that conflict. Champions of the book, including a large number of Yugoslav Americans, proclaimed it a masterpiece, courageous, brilliant, sound, and enlightening, while its enemies denounced it as propaganda of the most rank order, vicious, misleading, and detrimental to South Slav unity.

If the principal literary influence upon Adamic were to be designated, the name of Ivan Cankar, the Slovenian master, would be most fitting. Adamic's style was made all the more rich, smooth, and even because of his reading and translation of the great novelist. It is a direct and simple style without complications or excessive embellishment. Though language was one of his most valuable assets, his artistry reached far beyond it. He excelled particularly in the description of character and conditions, bringing to life people as well as places and events. In his hands common people and everyday happenings were transformed so as to glitter and glow.

After the United States entered World War II Adamic was put to work editing a compilation on war and peace aims of the United Nations, as expressed by the humblest soldiers and workers as well as the highest officials. He was appointed to the War Writers Board, where he helped, among other things, to promote the sale of War Bonds.

For a time (1940-1941) he also served as editor of *Common Ground,* a journal devoted to interracial American culture, and in 1944 he began editing and publishing *Trends and Tides,* a small quarterly newsletter of opinion. Not long afterward he was selected by the J. B. Lippincott Company as editor-in-chief of a new immigrant series. This was the most monumental project of his career: to evaluate America on the basis of her immigrants and diverse racial factors which blended to form the nation—a task for which he was as well fitted as any man in American letters in his time. But hardly was the series begun when the editor met his tragic end amidst mysterious surroundings. On September 4, 1951, he was found dead on his lonely farmhouse in Milford, with a bullet wound in his head and a rifle across his knees. This abruptly ended the brilliant career of one of the best-known as well as one of the most controversial figures among the Yugoslav Americans.

In the later years of his life Adamic had become associated with left-wing political movements. In 1948 he was named vice-chairman of the Progressive Citizens of America, a group which backed Henry A. Wallace in his unsuccessful bid for the presidency. He was one of the most articulate supporters in America of the Tito regime, and in 1949 he made a special trip to Yugoslavia to talk with the head of the government and study the country. After six months he returned with enough material for another book on his homeland. Published posthumously in 1952, under the title of *The Eagle and the Roots,* this volume tells the story of the Yugoslav Communist party; its struggle for existence in the interwar period; its role during the war; its fight to erect a Communist society after the war; and its split with Soviet Communism.

Adamic was a zealous supporter of radical programs, parties, and persons and an outspoken critic of the discrimination, inequality, and injustice that he saw in American life, but at the same time he was deeply attached to the land of his adoption. His love for America is brought out again and again in his writings. This is made clear especially in a statement he made upon his return to the United States in 1933. "Yet, in spite of it all, I was glad to be back. With all her difficulties, faults, and chaos, America, to me, was still America, offering something in life that the Old World did not give. I knew definitely that I belonged here." [21]

The conspicuous achievements of Adamic did not pass without recognition. In 1941 he received the John Anisfield Award and an honorary Doctor of Literature degree from Temple University. During the war he was consultant on immigration to the President's Defense Commission and also served on the executive committee of the United Committee of South-Slavic Americans. As in life, so in death his name will be remembered; it will remain enshrined in the hearts of the many racial and national minorities whose cause he so ardently championed.

## A MODERN MICHELANGELO

One of the best known and one of the most gifted artists living today is the Croatian American sculptor, Ivan Meštrović, now a professor of art at the University of Notre Dame in Indiana. He is one of the more recent immigrants, having arrived in this country only in January, 1947.

Meštrović was born in the village of Vrpolje, Slavonia, on August 15, 1883, the son of a small builder whose home was at Otavice on the Dalmatian plateau overlooking the Adriatic Sea.[22] The parents were very poor, and the village primitive and strictly agricultural. Ivan tended sheep in the rugged hills surrounding his home and passed the time in carving bits of stone and wood. He was fifteen years of age before he had an opportunity to see a town and sixteen before he visited a capital city. As there was no schoolhouse in his village, he got whatever education he could from his father, who taught him to read and write and encouraged him with his carving. The boy's carvings slowly began to attract attention among the townspeople and in the local paper. As a consequence, a group of neighboring monks gave him a commission for a de-

votional carving, offering him a florin for the piece.  But the shrewd
sheepherder held out for three, and eventually got his price.

When Ivan was fifteen, a retired army officer, a certain Captain
Grubišić, started a collection to finance his art education.  Simultaneously, the elder Meštrović took his son to Split, where the youth
was made an apprentice to a marble carver.  Within a year Captain
Grubišić raised enough money to send Ivan to Vienna.  In 1902
the promising student arrived in the Austrian capital, awed and
bewildered.  After finding humble quarters with a Czech family,
he made the rounds of the various art schools and teachers in an
effort to gain acceptance as a pupil, but at first without success.
One pompous master greeted him with the cynical comment: "We
want no Balkan prodigies here." [23]

Finally, however, Ivan managed to get a teacher, first O. König
and then Edmund von Hellmer of the Vienna Academy of Arts.
While studying art, he also continued his general education under
an official of the department of fine arts in the Academy.  After
about a year of the independent study, he was able, with the help
of Hellmer, to enter the great Academy and win, in open competition, a stipend for his lessons.

During his stay in Vienna Meštrović participated in the exhibition of the Secessionists, whose style undoubtedly influenced him.
In 1904, after finishing his work at the Academy, he held a one-man
show in Belgrade and another in Zagreb in 1905.  The following
year he journeyed to London to present his work at the Austrian
exhibition at Earl's Court.  In 1907 he set up a studio in Paris,
where he exhibited at the salons and became intimately acquainted
with the distinguished French sculptors, Auguste Rodin, Emile
Bourdelle, and Aristide Maillol, who taught him a great deal.  But
neither his artist friends in France nor studies of Italian masters in
Italy could in any way alter the proud nationalistic spirit manifesting itself in his work.  In fact, the patriotic sentiment became more
deeply ingrained in his art through his participation in the South
Slavic nationalistic artistic movement, which also included the
sculptors Rosandić and Penić, the painter Rački, and the architect
Plečnik, and which culminated in an exhibition in Zagreb in 1910.
For several years he worked on a huge scheme for a temple at
Kosovo, with a theme of medieval Serbia in the grip of Islam.  The
temple was never built, but the model was shown in Rome at the
Serbian Pavilion of the International Art Exhibition of 1911 and

created a profound impression. It was really this show that made Meštrović a sculptor of international renown.

After living in Paris for four years, he moved to Rome, staying there for another three years in order to study the sculpture of the great Michelangelo and the style of the archaic Greeks.[24] From Italy the sculptor went to England, where he held exhibitions and received the praise of prominent critics. Also during his stay with the British he was commissioned to do portrait busts of such eminent personages as Sir Thomas Beecham and Lady Cunard. During a part of World War I he stayed in Geneva and at Cannes. With stone difficult to get because of the conflict, he turned increasingly to wood sculpture, in which he became very proficient.

When the war was over Meštrović returned to his homeland, to the new state of Yugoslavia, which he had helped to found. He took up his permanent residence in Zagreb, where in 1922 he was appointed the rector of the Academy of Fine Arts. Many commissions and honors were awarded to him in the years that followed. However, experiences in World War II convinced the aging artist that Europe was no longer for him. As a consequence, he came to the United States in 1947 and joined the art faculty at Syracuse University in New York. In 1955 he left Syracuse to accept a similar position at the University of Notre Dame.

Teaching assignments in America have not been so pressing for Meštrović as to cause a slackening in his creations or exhibitions. In 1947 he had a highly successful one-man show at the Metropolitan Museum of Art in New York, where he exhibited, among other masterpieces, a Pieta figure weighing more than five tons and the symbolic figures of "Job" and "Despair." Since 1947 he has had one-man exhibitions in Pittsfield, Massachusetts; Colgate University; Syracuse University; Buffalo, New York; Dayton, Ohio; Washington, D.C.; Toronto, Ottawa, and Montreal, Canada; Notre Dame University; Rosewell Museum, New Mexico; Museum of Fine Arts in Houston, Texas; American Academy of Arts and Letters; and many other places.[25]

Like his ideal, the sixteenth-century Italian Renaissance genius, Michelangelo, Meštrović is a very versatile artist. He is a carver as well as a modeler. Though wood is his favorite medium, he carves marble, stone, and granite, and also casts with exceptional skill. In addition to his sculpture he practices engraving, painting, and lithography. Being one of the foremost chroniclers of the Slav spirit, he imbues his art with an intense patriotism and religious fervor. His subjects are generally religious themes, mythological figures, and others representative of Slav folklore. He has also made some fine busts, catching the psychological importance of his sitters. He has created greatly impressive figures of women, long-limbed, rapt in dream, glowing in soul, full of health, and intensely human.

At one time or another Meštrović has tried nearly every type of sculpture, from portrait busts to huge architectural schemes. But no matter what the form or the subject of his art, he leaves upon it the mark of virile intelligence and a far-reaching imagination. All his sculpture is characterized by a marvelous flow of rhythmic line, large plastic masses carved with a degree of vehemence, the decorative pattern always in harmony with the inherent quality of the material. He always seems to strike the correct balance between the static and the dynamic. In his best works there is a balance of realism, formal design, and content that makes him one of the most distinctive sculptors of the twentieth century. During his long and active career he has varied his style a good deal. At times, as in "Virgin and Child," he shows Byzantine feeling; at others he is at once dramatic and realistic, as in "The Indian"; and on still other occasions he demonstrates a vein of tenderness, as in "The Artist's Mother in Prayer."

Most art commentators divide the work of Meštrović into three classes. In the first category are placed his so-called "heroic" sculptures, which were designed to illustrate South Slavic history or legend or were created under the stimulus of the wars of his native land. Examples of this class include "Bishop Gregory of Nin," "Widows," and "Maiden of Kosovo." The second group encompasses his studies in form "in which his strong originality in composition is pre-eminent particularly in female figures."[26] "Girl with a Guitar" is an illustration of this style. Finally, in the third class are put his exquisite and rhythmic reliefs which are carved in wood or in a similar technique in stone, with two simple planes of relief. An example of this last group is his "Christ and the Woman of Samaria."

Galleries, institutes, academies, universities, museums, churches, and other types of depositories throughout the world house the many masterpieces of this modern South Slavic Michelangelo. His art can be seen in Zagreb, Split, and Dubrovnik, Yugoslavia; Rome;

Paris; London; Edinburgh; New York City, Rochester, Syracuse, Buffalo, and Ithaca, New York; Detroit, Michigan; and Chicago, Illinois. Besides the works already mentioned, others of importance include "Rodin," "Portrait of a Lady," "Chapel of Our Lady of the Angels," "The Well of Life," "The Temple of Kosovo," "The Račić Mortuary Chapel," and the two Indian equestrian statues in Grant Park, Chicago. Of the last the *Chicago Tribune* once said:

> Another of Chicago's treasures which art lovers are glad to travel thousands of miles to see is the Ivan Mestrovic pair of equestrian Indians which face each other across the broad expanse of the Congress Street concourse. Guests of the old Auditorium Hotel used to ask for window seats on the Michigan Avenue side of the dining room so that they might feast their eyes as well as their palates. These statues, lean of limb, on saddleless horses, are so placed that strollers on the avenue see them against a background of the sky itself.[27]

Of the many talents and achievements of Meštrović, little seems to be known or said about his writings. This can, of course, easily be understood. His art has completely overshadowed everything else. Yet a word on his publications should be in order. Besides writing a variety of articles and brief monographs, he is the author of longer works, including *Dennoch will ich hoffen* and *The Life of Christ*.

Meštrović holds membership in numerous organizations and has been the recipient of many awards and honors. He is a member, among others, of the American Academy of Arts and Letters, the National Institute of Arts and Sciences in Belgium, Scotland, Austria, Germany, Rumania, Czechoslovakia, and Yugoslavia. More than half a dozen universities have bestowed honorary degrees upon him, including Wesleyan (Ph.D.) and Columbia (D. Lit.). The French recognized his genius through the Legion of Honor. Medals were presented to him by the American Academy of Arts and Letters and Assumption College, Windsor, Ontario.

## BARON OF THE BRINE

The biography of Nick Bez (Nikola Bezmalinović), wealthy Dalmatian fisherman of Seattle, Washington, reads like a narrative from the pen of Horatio Alger, but is a true-to-life rags-to-riches story. Until 1945 he remained relatively unknown east of the

Rockies. In that year, however, he was photographed rowing a boat as the then President Harry S. Truman was fishing for salmon in Puget Sound, and suddenly he was shoved into the national limelight. He became the subject of much speculation and inquiry. Who was Nick Bez?

Though this fabulous fisherman is a man of national repute and one of the most eminent Yugoslav immigrants in America today, only the barest details of his life are available. He was born on August 25, 1895, on the Dalmatian island of Brač, one of the larger Adriatic isles situated southwest of the town of Split on the mainland.[28] As a mere boy he became acquainted with fishing, sailing, the hardships, and the adventures on the Adriatic. Like many other Dalmatians brought up on the sea, Nick learned about greater opportunities across the Atlantic, and so he early left his home and emigrated to the United States. Though he was fortunate enough to have his passage paid for him by his father, he arrived virtually penniless and friendless in New York in 1910. He was a mere boy in a strange new land. As he explained to this writer, "I had no relatives, friends or acquaintances in the United States so I was on my own." He made his way to the West Coast, where he knew there were other South Slavs, many of them engaged in the fisheries.

Not knowing any other life or trade but that of the sea, Nick Bez started his career in the new land by borrowing a rowboat and fishing for smelts on the Pacific. For an ordinary lad of fifteen to break into the fishing business would have been virtually impossible. But Nick seemed to have something that most of those around him lacked. He was strong, courageous, resourceful, and, above everything else, determined to succeed. After six years of hard work, dogged persistence, and extraordinary thrift, he became the owner of a big salmon boat, a purse seiner.

Possession of his own equipment, however, did not mean the end of the struggle for survival but, instead, the beginning of a new phase of that fight, an exciting though a somewhat unpleasant experience. As a boat owner he became involved in a contest, with no holds barred, for control of the lucrative Alaskan salmon industry. Big Nick (who is 6 feet 2 inches in height and weighs 225 pounds) led the purse seiners against the beach seiners (who use horses to drag flat nets up on the shore). The conflict was long, drawn-out, and bloody, but ultimately he succeeded in completely crushing the opposition.

Thenceforth Bez had comparatively smooth sailing. He expanded his holdings by buying one boat after another. In 1931 he branched out into the airlines business with the purchase of Alaska Southern Airways, which he later sold to Pan American at a large profit. He bounced back into competition, however, with the West Coast Airlines in 1946. Also in this same year he began canning fish on board a large converted freighter belonging to the United States (something he had been doing on his own ships on a limited scale for a number of years), supported by the government in Washington and financed by the Reconstruction Finance Corporation. The avowed purpose of this undertaking was to prove that American fishermen could replace the Japanese, who, in the years preceding World War II, caught and processed 66 per cent of the world's tuna in their floating canneries and virtually monopolized the multimillion-a-year catch of the Bering Sea's huge king crabs. The experiment ended in 1948, deemed a complete success, and Bez returned to the use of his own floating canneries.

Today Nick Bez is one of the wealthiest and most influential of the Yugoslav Americans. He owns or controls a string of fishing boats, four of the biggest salmon canneries in the Pacific Northwest, two gold mines, and an airline. He is married (to the former Magdalene Doratich, an American-born Yugoslav) and has two grown boys. He is a member of the Transportation Council of the United States Department of Commerce, the National Democratic Club, and many other organizations.

Because of his generous contributions to the Democratic party and his friendship with high government officials, Bez has been accused of using his political connections to the detriment of small fishermen.[29] This hurts the big fellow. He confesses that processors, including himself, "cotch too damn many feesh" to maintain an adequate supply. He favors a stabilization of the industry by developing new grounds and methods.

## GANGBUSTER

Unlike the individuals thus far described, August Korach is neither influential nor nationally famous. Yet he is a hero in his own right. He has been responsible for driving scores of racketeers out of Cleveland and the entire state of Ohio and for the institution of reforms by both state and federal agencies.[30]

The background of this gangbuster is very similar to that of thousands of other Yugoslav immigrants. Gus, as he is called by his friends, was born in 1896 in the Slovenian village of Vače—the only son of a widowed mother so poor that she raised him only with the greatest difficulties. At the age of thirteen he went to work as a cowherd. Three years later his mother inherited $300 from a relative who had gone to the United States. She gave a part of it to her son and sent him with her blessing to the land whence the money had come.[31]

Upon his arrival in America Gus went to an aunt in Marianna, Pennsylvania, where he got a job in the coal mines. Several years of the underground work were more than enough, and he quit, leaving Pennsylvania and roaming around the country for a while. In his travels he visited Cleveland and liked it so well that he decided to settle in the large Slovenian colony in the city.

With America's entry into the war in 1917, Gus quit his job and enlisted in the army. Though he was shipped to France, he did not get into action, as he froze his feet while on guard duty and was confined to a hospital. While in the service, he obtained his citizenship papers.

Discharged in 1919, Gus returned to Cleveland and went to work for White Motors. The job was steady, at least until the depression, and he was able to save some money. He got married, bought a small home, and began raising a family—a son and a daughter. He was contented. He asked for nothing more out of life than a chance to earn a living and to lead a peaceful life. Had he had his wish, Gus would probably have remained just another unknown immigrant. However, so it was not to be, and that because of the rackets that infested Cleveland in the 1930's.

Gus' city was filled with all sorts of shrewd operators, gangsters, and other characters from the underworld. Among the most successful was the "cemetery mob," so called because it sold cemetery lots through a complicated arrangement involving legitimate savings and loan associations and the unauthorized use of well-known and reputable names. Thousands of immigrants were swindled out of their life savings by these racketeers, who preferred to operate in the alien communities, relying on the thrift and ignorance of the foreigners. The mobsters might have succeeded in their plan and escaped with their loot had not Gus fallen a victim to their treacherous scheme.

Taken to the extent of $2,000—a vast sum for a man with only a wage-earner's income and a family to support—Gus determined to do something about the swindle. First of all he demanded his money back, only to be humiliated by the gangsters. That was in the summer of 1936. Next he discussed the case with lawyers, but received no satisfaction. He then sought help from the city officials. However, the administrators, many of them being on the racketeers' payroll, balked at any investigation. With the refusal of aid by the city fathers, Gus seemed stumped—momentarily. To make matters worse, he was discouraged by his fellow victims, who told him that he didn't stand a chance in face of the great odds against him. At the same time the swindlers spread a general warning to all "meddlers."

But at this very critical juncture, Gus decided upon a new approach. He took his problem to the *Cleveland Press* and discussed it with the paper's Clayton Fritchey. The journalist was not only interested but quite sympathetic and, after receiving the assurance of full support by the publication, went to work on the case with Gus. The two men went from home to home to visit the victims of the swindle and to enlist their support. They had little success, however, until they got Frank J. Lausche (American-born son of Slovenian immigrant parents and then a judge in Cleveland) to persuade the frightened men to tell the truth and stick to it regardless of the threats of the racketeers.

The publicity that followed in the *Press* in 1937 brought on three grand-jury investigations resulting in the arrest, indictment, conviction, and long-term imprisonment of many of the racketeers and the forcing of many others out of town. Several police officers, including a captain who had taken a $125,000 bribe, were exposed, tried, and jailed; others resigned; the police department was then reorganized from top to bottom. The back of the Cleveland racketeers was thus broken.[32]

For its part in the case the *Press* was awarded the Pulitzer Prize in 1937. Gus, on the other hand, though not successful in recovering his money, had the satisfaction of having smashed a racket and having helped his neighbors. He did not try to act the part of a hero; as a matter of fact, he was not fully aware of the real import of his accomplishment, as his friend Fritchey tersely points out:

The general public is unaware of him, even in Cleveland; in

fact, Gus' own idea of the dent he has made in his own community is extremely sketchy. He asks and expects no credit for the achievement.[33]

Today, some twenty-five years after the swindle, Gus lives (with his wife, his children all being married) in Euclid, a small suburb of Cleveland, in virtual obscurity. He is still trying to dispose of the cemetery lots (to ease his life in its twilight years), but he has not been able to find any takers yet.

### POLITICAL PRODIGY

The accomplishments of the Yugoslav immigrants are noteworthy. But important also are the achievements of the descendants of the aliens. It is true that most of the American-born sons and daughters did not have to begin the climb up the ladder of success from the very lowest rung as did their parents. They had a head start—if only through birth in the land of opportunity. That should not, however, detract from their high attainments, for many of them, too, had to struggle against seemingly insurmountable barriers to reach the top. An excellent illustration of an uphill battle to success is found in the career of the nationally-known Slovene American statesman Frank J. Lausche, the popular United States Senator and the five-time governor of Ohio. His life is typical of the fight of many second-generation Yugoslav Americans to win recognition.[34]

Lausche was born in Cleveland, Ohio, on November 14, 1895, the son of Louis and Frances Lausche, who emigrated from Slovenia in 1885 and settled in Cleveland.[35] His father worked in a steel mill to take care of his ten boys and girls. In 1908 the elder Lausche died and Frank and his older brother had to help their mother in providing for the large family by working part time. When four years later the older brother died, Frank was forced to leave high school to assume the burdens of the head of the household. He got a job lighting street lamps for which he was paid $2 a week. He did not, however, neglect his education; he completed his high school course in the evening. After graduation he acted as interpreter when called upon in different courts, where he was able to observe at first hand cases of law, a subject which began to interest him more and more.

In those days, however, law was not Lausche's primary interest.

241

From early boyhood he had been attracted to baseball. He demonstrated exceptional skill as a third baseman on the sandlot teams, and in 1916 he grasped the opportunity to play with a semiprofessional team in Cleveland. From there he went on to teams in Lawrence, Massachusetts, and Duluth, Minnesota. His baseball earnings he used to help send two brothers and a sister through college and to pay his own way through the Central Institute in Cleveland in 1915-1916. A batting slump ended his ballplaying career with Duluth just before the United States entered World War I. Lausche joined the army in 1918, and after attending an officers training school at Camp Gordon, Georgia, he was commissioned a second lieutenant. But before the young officer could get into action the war was over. Upon returning to civilian life, he was offered a position on the Atlanta team in the Southern Association, which was only a step from the major leagues. Though tempted, he decided against a baseball career, because he felt it lacked the security he sought.

Instead of baseball, Lausche selected the more promising field of law for a lifetime career. He attended the John Marshall School of Law in Cleveland and, after his graduation in 1920, was admitted to the Ohio bar. In the same year he began practice with a prominent local firm, which included among others, Cyrus W. Locher, the late United States Senator, who helped Lausche to become one of Cleveland's best trial lawyers and encouraged him to enter politics. Lausche then joined the Democratic party, and in 1922 he ran for the state assembly, only to be defeated. Undiscouraged by his first failure, he tried two years later to get a seat in the state senate, but once more bowed down in defeat. In 1928 he forgot about politics long enough to take a bride, Jane Sheal of Cleveland.

Not until 1932, when he was appointed to fill a vacancy on Cleveland's municipal bench, did Lausche enter public office. The next year he was elected to the same post from among ten candidates, and in 1937 he was elected judge on the county court of common pleas, where he won much acclaim but also made some enemies. He accepted the labor cases that other judges were apparently afraid to try because of the antagonism which decisions in such cases were likely to arouse among the voters. He gained widespread attention as well as many enemies among union workers for his handling of the Crosby Restaurant case in which he granted an injunction against picketing by the Hotel and Restaurant Employees' International Alliance, an affiliate of the American Federation of Labor, which sought to force the restaurant employees to join the union. Though his decision was at first upheld by the United States Supreme Court, it was later reversed.

Lausche's work as a judge was not confined to making decisions on the bench. In the fall of 1940 he took the initiative in closing three large gambling houses in a suburban section of Cleveland, where, after failing to get the cooperation of the county officials, he sent a special police squad which surprised the gamblers at their trade. Such action won him considerable public attention, and he was asked to run for mayor of Cleveland in 1941. Resigning his position in the court, he accepted and polled 60 per cent of the votes.

Lausche promised the electorate such improvements as better sanitation and transportation, lower taxes, and city beautification. But with the entry of the United States into the war a month after he took office, the mayor found that he had more vital tasks to perform. He was confronted with numerous problems in organizing Cleveland for an efficient contribution to the war effort. More than half the city's population of nearly a million were foreign-born or offspring of immigrants, who were representative of many different nationalities and were divided in their loyalties. Most of the people were employed in industry at low wages, and strikes were frequent. Moreover, there were racial problems caused by discrimination against Negroes, setting the stage for riots.

Working for the good of all the people and not for any special group, Lausche achieved extraordinary success in his efforts. He organized committees to mediate in labor and racial controversies, to improve transportation facilities, and to look after the health of the workers. He increased the number of playgrounds and enlarged the police force in an effort to combat juvenile delinquency. His success in fighting the black market won him the plaudits of the Office of Price Administration.

In 1943 Lausche was re-elected by the largest majority in any mayoralty election in Cleveland when he polled 71 per cent of the total vote. The victory was achieved under the most unfavorable conditions. Being out of favor with the Democratic county chairman, he organized his own campaign and announced at the beginning that none of those campaigning for him could expect any reward. Immediately before the election he risked his chances of winning by further antagonizing the American Federation of Labor through his veto of a pay increase for building-trade-craft municipal employees. Though he lost the support of the AF of L, Lausche received the backing of the CIO and other diverse groups. His support of a Negro candidate for judge brought colored people to his side. Other votes came from big business, the bar association, and Republicans.

The record Lausche established as a vote-getter attracted the attention of national Democratic leaders, who saw his value to the party as governor of Ohio. Accordingly, he was nominated for that high office in 1944. Again he waged his own campaign, independent of party help. The campaign was conducted by his friends at a cost of $25,000, one-tenth the amount spent by the Republican candidate. When the campaign committee began to run out of money for stamps, a news story brought in contributions. During the time he campaigned he would not accept his salary as mayor. His wide popularity swept him into office by a majority of over 100,000 votes, this at a time when President Roosevelt lost Ohio to his Republican opponent, Thomas E. Dewey. Lausche's election as governor represented a victory over tradition. It was the first time in the history of Ohio that a Roman Catholic and a son of immigrants had been elected to the governor's office.

In the 1946 elections Lausche's personal popularity could not deflect the Republican tide that inundated Ohio. Though running far ahead of Democratic candidates in the state, he lost the gubernatorial race to his Republican opponent, Thomas J. Herbert, by a narrow plurality of 38,000 votes. However, he came back strong in 1948 and again in 1950 to win by substantial majorities. In 1952 and 1954 he was elected to unprecedented fourth and fifth terms.

One of Lausche's first acts as governor was the announcement that key men in the state government would be retained regardless of party affiliation. Among those kept in their positions, in compliance with the policy, was a Republican in the important office of director of finance. Lausche opposed a bill to raise the governor's salary, and at the same time vetoed an act which would have made pay increases for state employees retroactive because "it smacked of pork." From the outset he attacked gangsters, racketeers, and crooks. He closed gambling clubs, removed public officials for failure to halt gambling, and repeatedly asked the legislature for greater powers to preserve law and order. His entire

244

administration was based more or less on principles he outlined when he first took office in January, 1945: "First, law and order. Second, economy. Third, equality of treatment among conflicting economic groups. Fourth, the development of unity between city and rural interests." [36]

After completing his fifth term as governor, Lausche ran for the United States Senate in 1956 and defeated the Republican incumbent, George Bender. In the Senate he has exhibited the same qualities of sincerity, frankness, aggressiveness, and ingenuity that had been his trademarks in public office in Ohio. He is a member of the Foreign Relations and Foreign Commerce committees. [37]

## A REPRESENTATIVE OF THE PEOPLE

Another prominent figure in the national political arena is John A. Blatnik, United States Congressman from Minnesota. His story, too, is one of a steady uphill fight to attain success. [38]

John was born on August 17, 1911, in Chisholm, Minnesota. He was the oldest of the three children of Janez and Margaret Blatnik, immigrants from Slovenia. The home of the Blatniks was a weather-beaten, scrawny old house that belonged to the mining company for whom the father worked. Conditions were primitive. A coal stove provided the only heat in the freezing temperature. Water had to be fetched from a distant pump. Boarders, mostly lonely, unwed Slovenians, were kept to help make ends meet.

The future Congressman early showed that he had inherited his parents' eagerness for knowledge. He zealously plunged into his lessons at school. Poring over books and burning the midnight oil were not without reward. He graduated from Chisholm High School in 1929 as an honor student.

John had climbed the hill, but the mountain was still ahead. He looked forward to college. Then suddenly came a crash, bang! The stock market collapsed, factories and mines closed, and millions of men were thrown out of work. It was a terrible blow to the ambitious plans of the youth. He knew that he would have to forget about higher learning—at least for a time—and look for work. But the only jobs available were low-paying country-school teaching positions. Nevertheless, even such jobs meant some income and John eagerly grabbed one. His earnings, though small, enabled him to help his family, who found themselves in financial difficulties, and also to set something aside for college.

After two years of teaching the three R's to farmers' children, John was off to work his way through Winona State Teachers College in southeastern Minnesota. College for him was not a round of fraternities, dances, and football games. Nor did it mean simply grinding academic studies. It meant also working long hours in restaurants, sleeping in cheap rooms, and living precariously from hand to mouth. He proved himself more than equal to the task, and graduated in 1935 with the highest scholastic honors in his class.

For two years after graduation from college, Blatnik served as educational advisor in the Civilian Conservation Corps camps in northern Minnesota, giving up the position in 1937 to become chemistry instructor in the high school in his home town. No sooner did he unpack his bags than opportunity knocked again, and in a short time he was on his way to Duluth to become assistant to the St. Louis County Superintendent of Schools.

In Duluth he not only attended to his academic duties but also became active in the local junior chamber of commerce, which at the time was vitally concerned with the Mesabi range iron ore problems. Interest in ore soon led to politics. He became a close associate of Richard Kelly, who was elected state senator in 1938. When Kelly died suddenly in 1939, Blatnik was persuaded to fill the unexpired term. Well liked by fellow senators and constituents alike, he was returned to his seat in 1940 and again in 1942 by an overwhelming majority of votes.

Between sessions of the state senate the budding statesman, eager to learn more about political office, took graduate courses in public administration at the universities of Chicago and Minnesota. But his academic and political careers were both interrupted by the war. Although exempt from military service by virtue of his public office, he volunteered and served in the army three years, 1942-1945. Much of the time he spent behind the lines with the Yugoslav Partisans in Croatia and Slovenia. His job was to keep in radio contact with the Allied Headquarters in Italy, sending out reports of enemy movements, rescuing American airmen who bailed out behind enemy lines, and evacuating wounded Partisans as well as working with them on military operations. For his conspicuous achievements he was awarded three battle stars, the Bronze Star Medal with the Oak Leaf Cluster, and the Air Medal. He was discharged from the Army Air Corps as a paratrooper captain.[39]

Returning home, the war hero was endorsed for Congress by

the Democratic-Farmer-Labor party. In one of the hardest-fought campaigns in the country, he defeated by a sizable plurality the Republican incumbent of fourteen years, William Pittenger. In view of the fact that only three Republicans in the entire nation were unseated by Democrats in the fall elections of 1946, the victory of the young Slovene American was all the more remarkable.

Congressman Blatnik has won the respect of his colleagues at the nation's capital and the hearty support of his nearly three hundred thousand constituents in Minnesota's eighth district, and he has been returned regularly to his post in Washington since his great triumph in 1946. During his entire tenure he has kept a sharp eye on the country's resources and their use. He has demonstrated steadfast loyalty especially to the little people—miners, small businessmen, and farmers struggling under their mortgages. All progressive labor bills as well as most reform measures have received his hearty support. On the other hand, he has been an irreconcilable foe of any type of legislation cleverly drawn up to hamstring and hog-tie organized labor or designed to curtail the rights of the common people.[40] Thus, during the debates on the Mundt-Nixon Bill he joined with other liberal-minded legislators in Congress to block the measure which he believed threatened the constitutional rights of every American. He opposed Senator Joseph McCarthy and his methods of ferreting out Communists. He has consistently championed civil rights for all Americans. As a member of the Government Operations and Public Works committees, he has sought to eliminate red tape and bring greater efficiency into the national government and at the same time he has promoted a variety of public works projects, including cross-country superhighways and housing for low-income families.

Though burdened with work at the capital, Congressman Blatnik has maintained close contact with the people he represents. Indeed, he insists that his greatest pleasure is to go back home and meet the Yugoslavs, Poles, Finns, Swedes, Norwegians, Irish, and Italians who put him into office.

In 1955 the busy legislator married Gisela Hager and began raising a family. He has one son.

## Spy for the FBI

When Matt Cvetic, a second-generation Slovene from Pittsburgh, appeared before the United States House Committee on Un-American Activities in February and March, 1950, to tell his story of posing as a Communist for the Federal Bureau of Investigation, there was unfolded before the American public a real-life drama that for thrills, excitement, and suspense has had few equals. In fact, the tale of Cvetic was so stirring and engrossing that Hollywood promptly got out its cameras and ground out the film "I Was a Communist for the FBI," narrating the undercover experiences of this courageous Slovene.

For nine agonizing years Cvetic mingled with the Communists, serving as secretary of the American-Slovene Communist Bureau, heading the Communist party finance committee for western Pennsylvania, aiding the party's organizational, educational, and nationality committees, and performing many similar tasks, in order to be able to report on their subversive activities to the FBI. The exact nature of his work necessarily remaining a secret, he was considered a traitor by his friends and family and treated with contempt and disdain. His mother died without learning the truth. But he continued his double life until he had ferreted out the Communist leaders from their snug quarters in the nation's most important industrial center.

Matt Cvetic is one of the twelve children of Slovenian immigrants who came to this country at the end of the nineteenth century from Vinica, Slovenia.[41] Born on March 4, 1909, in Pittsburgh, he attended St. Mary elementary school and Curry Business College in that city and St. Vincent College in Latrobe. After beginning work with a farm supply company, he went from one job to another, working for a furniture company, selling radios, aiding the United States Department of Justice in the preparation of a crime survey, and so on. He married and had twin sons. But the union was of short duration, ending in separation by the court.[42]

Rejected for service in the United States Army Intelligence in 1939, Cvetic got a job with the United States Employment Service in Pittsburgh. It was there that he was visited in April, 1941, by two agents of the FBI, who explained to him that because of his position and background he had an excellent opportunity to perform an invaluable service for his country by joining the Communist party and obtaining information concerning the activities of subversives who were infiltrating American war plants. Though he was not to receive any pay until he became a card-carrying member of the Communist party, he agreed to the proposal.

It took a lot of hard work and clever acting on the part of Cvetic to break into the ranks of the Communists. After demonstrating clear-cut Soviet sympathies, such as buying the *Daily Worker* and other Communist literature and speaking out against War Bonds and the "capitalist war," he was asked to attend Communist and party-front meetings. This hurdle out of the way, he proceeded to schools of Marxist indoctrination. Much more maneuvering and anxious waiting followed before he was finally admitted into the party—twenty-two months after being approached by the FBI.

Had it not been for the $65 that he earned each week as an interviewer with the United States Employment Service, Cvetic would have found it difficult to live on the initial weekly salary of $15 he received from the FBI. To be sure, his FBI pay was gradually increased until it reached a peak of $85 per week, but not even that was adequate to provide for his many expenditures (such as contributions to the Communist party fund and to various front organizations, and the purchase of radical literature). For this reason, as well as not to arouse the suspicions of the Communist comrades with whom he worked, it was necessary for him to keep an outside job at all times. After being ejected from the USES for his "Communist affiliations," Cvetic served for a short time as secretary of the Yugoslav Relief Committee in Pittsburgh and later went to work as an insurance agent.

During his first years in the Communist party Cvetic was placed in a number of important positions. One of these was membership in the executive committee of the party's Tom Paine Professional Branch in Pittsburgh, encompassing in its fold Communists in scientific, legal, medical, governmental, social, health, and welfare fields. The principal duties of this unit were to prepare the agenda for the meetings of the Professional Branch and its various clubs, to organize educational discussions, and to assign such jobs as collecting dues and selling and distributing the *Daily Worker* and other party literature. Later on he was made a member of the Organizational, Educational, and Financial committees. Another assignment was on the Nationality Commission of western Pennsylvania. To aid them in their work among the Slav nationals, the Communists saw to it that Cvetic became a member of the Slovene Council, a political-action group. From these posts then he worked with the Communists, generally a small highly-trained minority, in carrying on their propaganda and conspiracies. He helped to make the Pittsburgh Civil Rights Congress a Communist mouthpiece. He aided in the infiltration of numerous innocent and unsuspecting organizations. The Labor Youth League, the youth arm of the Communist International in the United States, came into existence through his assistance. He obtained statistical data on the Pittsburgh industries, which, after alterations by the FBI, were passed on to the Communist headquarters. All of these activities, of course, were reported in detail to the local office of the FBI. During the entire time Cvetic was checked and rechecked by his Communist partners, who were constantly on the lookout for espionage by the FBI. But he played his part well, so well that he fooled his associates as well as kinsmen and friends.

After some four years of "good" service Cvetic apparently lost some of his usefulness to the Communist party, and he began his descent down the ladder, being compelled to give up important positions to more influential and useful men. By that time, however, he was tiring of his dual role and sought to obtain his freedom as an undercover informant. The decision, as it happened, was not easy to carry out, since the FBI refused to reveal the facts to the public; and so several more years of anxious waiting followed. The opportune time seemed to have arrived in 1949 when the increasingly nervous and impatient agent was summoned to New York to testify in the trial of the eleven Communist leaders charged with conspiracy against the United States government. But, after the collection of a mountain of evidence and endless rehearsals, his testimony, he was told, was not needed for conviction, and he had to continue with his FBI duties. Finally, through the intervention of a local anti-Communist organization in Pittsburgh, he was subpoenaed to appear before the House Committee on Un-American Activities in Washington in February and March, 1950. His testimony before the government committee, made public, helped to get him back in the good graces of his friends and relatives and at the same time paved the way for the conviction of Communist leaders in Pittsburgh. As a matter of record, it might be pointed out that Cvetic soon thereafter obtained his release from the FBI and went to work as a special investigator for the United States Bureau of Immigration and Naturalization Service, where he could pursue a less exciting but a more normal life.

Since he gave up his cloak-and-dagger activities Cvetic has

stumped the country making speeches before various groups to arouse the people against the Red menace. He has also written a book entitled *Escape to Nowhere,* revealing the story behind his long struggle against Communism.

## POLKA KING

A very interesting figure among the prominent second-generation Yugoslav Americans is Frank Yankovic, son of Slovenian immigrants. He is recognized as a master of the polka in America, holding the title of "America's Polka King," which was bestowed upon him by polka fans at the First Annual Polka Festival in Milwaukee.[43]

Frank was born on July 28, 1915, in Davis, West Virginia. Six months later the Yankovics moved to Cleveland, which became their permanent home. It was here that the boy went to school and grew up.

Frank's music lessons began when he was old enough to sit on his mother's knee and listen to her rollicking tunes which she brought over from Slovenia. Getting his first accordion (a small and inexpensive version) when he was nine years old, he mastered the instrument without a single formal lesson. It was not until he was sixteen that he received his first piano accordion, a gift from his parents. After taking only six lessons, he formed his own three-piece orchestra, made up of friends of Slovenian descent.[44]

He began to play for neighborhood gatherings, for lodge dances, for receptions, and for other affairs where music was in demand. From the very outset he concentrated on polkas, completely ignoring the brassy jazz of the era.

In these early stages of his career the monetary rewards of his music were meager, and Frank had to turn to other pursuits to make a living. His father was only a small businessman (owner of a hardware store) and could not help him. Accordingly, he went to a trade school and learned patternmaking. After working in a foundry for a while, he got a job on a bakery truck and also helped his father in the store. In 1940 he married June Erworthe, who had studied voice and violin and had sung with his orchestra. A year later, with the help of his father, he opened his own place—a modest cafe in the Collinwood district of Cleveland. With June waiting on tables and Frank playing the accordion, business boomed.

In the meantime Frank did not neglect his music. He and his orchestra continued to play polkas for a variety of social functions. Gradually his style of music caught on with the audiences in Cleveland, and presently he began making recordings to satisfy the local demand for his gay, lively renditions. His rhythms became so popular that two radio stations in Cleveland featured him on their programs.

This happy state of affairs was suddenly interrupted in 1943 when Frank was drafted into the United States Army. He was sent to the European theater of war in time to participate in the Normandy invasion and the Battle of the Bulge. While in combat his fingers were seriously frostbitten. He recovered, fortunately, and was subsequently transferred to the Special Services Unit to play with a band, getting discharged finally in December, 1945.

Returning to his Cleveland cafe, Frank got a band together again and resumed playing polkas. In 1947 he recorded a polka arrangement of an old hillbilly tune and called it "Just Because." The song was an overnight sensation. Over a million records were sold. This was the first time in the history of recording that a polka tune had so captivated the record fans throughout the nation. With that song Frank's reputation was made. He followed the first success with another folk tune called "Blue Skirt Waltz," which also went over the million mark in record sales. Then in quick order came "Three Yanks Polka," "Cafe Polka," "Clairene Waltz," "Rendezvous Waltz," "Bye, Bye, Baby Polka," and a long list of others. Through his recordings he revolutionized the polka. Before he was aware of what was happening, he was famous.

He couldn't remain in his cafe any longer. He was in too great demand on the outside. In 1948 Frank Yankovic and his Yanks— as his band is called—traveled 70,000 miles filling engagements on the expanding polka circuit. His was the first polka orchestra to undertake a "one-nighter tour" coast to coast. Since 1948 the personable polka maestro has traveled an average of 80,000 miles a year, playing in hundreds of cities, towns, theaters, ballrooms, clubs, hotels, and theater restaurants, from the Village Barn in New York City to the celebrated Mocambo in Hollywood. He has not only appeared on nation-wide television programs, including those of Lawrence Welk, Arthur Godfrey, Faye Emerson, Patti Page, and Kate Smith, but he has also had his own shows.[45] At the present time he has his own weekly show over WGN-TV in Chicago.

His many travels and numerous engagements have not interrupted Frank's recordings. Among his latest hits are "Chop Susy Polka," "Frankie Polka," "Happy Polka," "Ya Ya Wonder Bar," and "Enie Clinie Cha Cha." Besides making many of his own arrangements, he writes some of the tunes for his records and orchestra. His latest achievements are the compositions of Slovenian polkas and waltzes, the more popular of which are "Jutranja Zarja Valcek" (Twilight Waltz), "Slovenski Valcek" (Slovenian Waltz), "Rožica Polka" (Daisy Polka), "Bod Moja, Bod Moja Polka" (Be Mine, Be Mine Polka), and "Veseli Prijatelji Polka" (Jolly Fellows Polka).

Frank's success has not been without benefit to some of his friends also. Pete Sokach, Eddie Habat, John Vadnal, John Pecon, Lou Trebar, Henry Broze, and Chester Budney, who, like Frank, grew up with an accordion in their hands and Slovenian folk tunes filtering through their heads, have hopped on the polka band wagon.[46] Eddie Blatnick, known in the Chicago area as "Your Polka Pal," is another of Frank's friends (a fan and a business associate, too) who has made good with polka tunes. Eddie is a well-known disc jockey who features polka recordings on his popular radio programs in Chicago. But he is more than a "run-of-the-mill dee-jay" who merely turns over platters and shouts "Great!" twenty-five times a minute. He is a promising composer, having already turned out such hits as "Polka Pal Polka," "Chicagoland Twirl," and "Wondering Waltz." Another Chicagoan who has been able to capitalize on the increasing popularity of polka rhythms is Eddie Korosa, who is known to his many fans as "America's Prince of Polkas." The fact is that many musicians have caught the polka fever from him and have admired and imitated him.

Music is not Frank's only love. He is a very devoted family man. He maintains a sumptuous home for his loved ones in South Euclid, a suburb of Cleveland. His wife, June, in addition to taking care of her household chores and eight children (five boys and three girls), helps the maestro with his fan mail, publicity, and the numerous details of his bookings. Frank's heavy schedule and widespread appearances, unfortunately, keep him away from South Euclid much of the time. It is unusual, indeed, for him to spend even one month out of each twelve with his family. Whenever possible he flies home between engagements—though he may be able to remain for only a few hours.

## Plain People

The individuals who by natural talent, initiative, drive, and ambition attained fame and, in some cases, fortune have been well publicized and are widely known. But what of those immigrants who are not in *Who's Who?* How have the plain people fared? Their story, too, must be told.

Little is heard of men who by their hard work and perseverance managed to obtain a formal education and rise to a position of leadership in their communities. Such a person is the Reverend Pius J. Petrić, who came to the United States as a youth of twenty. Using earnings from his jobs in the steel mills of Joliet, Illinois, Father Petrić succeeded in completing his training for the priesthood. He was ordained and placed in St. Cyril's parish in New York, where he soon became an admired leader of his flock.

Even less is heard of men like Jack Rokov, who first entered the country in the prewar era when immigration was at high tide. Having had nothing more than brief schooling at the hands of a parish priest in his native village in Dalmatia, Jack could do no better than get a job as a laborer in a factory. A restless youth, he drifted from one factory to another with no obvious improvement in status. He soon tired of his lonely life without a mate and hurriedly made a trip to his homeland to marry a woman who would know his ways and understand him, perhaps better than an *Amerikanka.* Coming back to the United States with his newly-acquired wife, Jack went back to the factory and settled down to raising a family. Conditions in the mill became increasingly repulsive as he grew older, so that he switched to fishing. At present, Jack, the father of a son and two daughters and the grandfather of three boys and two girls, is one of the many fishermen in San Pedro, California. Unheralded and struggling for a living, Jack is a good example of the average Yugoslav immigrant in America.

Passing unnoticed, too, are immigrants such as Roman Orovich, who came here with the post-World War I avalanche. Roman, not yet out of his teens when he arrived in the country, found employment in the industries of northern Indiana, shifting from one monotonous, backbreaking job to another until he finally worked his way up to the position of a laboratory technician in one of the numerous metallurgical plants in the area. Preoccupied with his work, Roman had little time for anything else, except to attend evening classes long enough to prepare him for naturalization. During the war he worked from ten to eighteen hours a day, seldom missing any time at all. Too much work and too little play helped to keep him a bachelor, with the result that he has lived as a boarder with one relative after another. Yet, few immigrants have been happier with the life they have found in America than Roman.

The struggles, the achievements, and the contributions of the ordinary Yugoslav immigrants are depicted in the following story of a Dalmatian American widow. Her experiences, though unpublicized and unknown, are typical of many immigrants.

Teta Mary was just another young Yugoslav wife who came to the United States with her daughter, Celia, to join a husband who had preceded her. When she arrived in East Chicago, Indiana, in August, 1922, she was *Teta Marija*. *Marija* was soon Americanized into "Mary," but *Teta* (aunt) remained a permanent tag.

Like thousands of other southeastern Europeans who rushed to America in the immediate postwar years before rigid immigration restriction, Teta Mary believed that she had come to the True Land of Promise. She would no longer need to worry about the dreadful *bura* (north wind) destroying the few crops which were so vital for existence, or about getting a place on one of the fishing boats so as to provide a change in the monotonous vegetable diet. Now that she was in America with her Ivan again, surely her troubles were over.

The little family first occupied a three-room concrete-block apartment lacking plumbing and adequate electricity. After a boy (Marion) was born a year later and the number of men boarders increased to three, larger quarters were desperately needed. A timely promotion and a raise to fifty cents an hour enabled Ivan to move his family to a four-room flat, but the combined discomforts of a leaky roof, flimsy walls, and a disagreeable landlady soon became unbearable. A bank loan, the assistance of relatives, and Ivan's backbreaking labor made possible a new house in the Calumet district, called "Siberia," which was populated primarily by Slavic peoples. Here a third child, christened Isaac, was born.

Soon the family became comfortably rooted in the activities of the community. Every Sunday and holy day the family attended the Croatian Holy Trinity Church. Ivan had joined the Dalmatian Benevolent Society and the Croatian Fraternal Union shortly after his arrival in East Chicago. These organizations held frequent

255

*zabave* and *večerinke* (entertainments and suppers) at which mountains of *pečene janjetine* (barbecued lamb) and barrels of *hladne pive* (cold beer) were consumed to the tunes of the *tamburica* orchestra. Teta and Ivan happily joined in the songs and gay talk.

Gradually life became a little easier. Ivan had secured a better job, the mortgage had been paid off much more quickly than at first thought possible, and Ivan was even thinking of building a bigger house for his family. But in August, 1929, tragedy struck. While at work, Ivan fell from a scaffold to his death.

Stunned for weeks by the shock, Teta Mary finally responded to the anxious care of friends and relatives, and started to make plans for the support of her three children, the oldest of whom was not yet ten. Financial aid given by the benefit societies to which Ivan had belonged barely covered funeral expenses. Teta's greatest assistance came through the workingmen's compensation law, which entitled her to $5,000, to be paid over a five-year period.

In order to supplement this small income, Teta decided to take up tailoring and dressmaking. After a three-month course at the Forrest Academy of Needlecraft in Chicago, Teta Mary opened shop in the enclosed back porch of her home, where she put her old sewing machine and a chest of drawers filled with patterns and an assortment of needles and thread.

Through the years that followed, Teta worked tirelessly. In 1937 Celia graduated from Washington High School and went to work in a tin mill. This assistance enabled Teta Mary to send money and merchandise regularly to her aged mother and other relatives in Iž Mali.

When her two boys were almost through high school, Hitler's armies began to march across Europe. After graduation, the boys entered college, working to pay for their education. In March, 1943, however, Teta Mary's apprehensions were realized, for both were called to the service. Marion eventually earned second lieutenant's bars and the Bronze Star; while Isaac, who became a sergeant, won the Purple Heart.

The war finally ended and the boys returned, to Teta Mary's great joy. Isaac resumed his engineering course and upon graduation in 1950 accepted a good position in Kansas City. Marion, after a few years of college, joined Celia's husband, a grocer, in an expanding business. Both boys married their high school sweethearts.

Teta Mary's life has not been an easy one; the realities of life in America had not the faintest resemblance to the rosy paradise she had envisioned. But her heart swells with pride at the thought of her three children, now grown up and rearing families of their own. Teta Mary is content.

# 10

# Contributions to America

F ROM THE EARLIEST TIMES in American history the immigrants have been victims of many attacks instigated by the older elements of the population. This hostility of the "natives" toward the "foreigners" became deeply rooted in American thought and practices. That one's status was not determined by his origin or time of immigration was clearly brought out by St. John de Crèvecoeur in his *Letters from an American Farmer,* previously mentioned. "When then," Crèvecoeur asked, "is the American, this new man?" He proceeded to explain: "He is either an European, or the descendant of an European. . . . I could point out to you a family whose grandfather was an Englishman, whose wife was Dutch, whose son married a French woman, and whose present four sons have now four wives of different nations. . . . *He* is an American, who leaving behind him all his ancient prejudices and manners, receives new ones from the mode of life he has embraced, the new government he obeys, and the new rank he holds. He becomes an American by being received in the broad lap of our great *Alma Mater.* Here individuals of all nations are melted into a new race of men."

## IMMIGRANTS AND AMERICAN CIVILIZATION

Unfortunately, not even today do all the people in the country agree with this enlightened eighteenth-century writer. There are still two widely conflicting schools of thought on the subject, one upheld by the old immigrants—which, for the want of a better name, may be called the "Mayflower" point of view—and the other

258

championed by the new immigrants—which may similarly be called the "Steerage" view. The first holds that the United States is an Anglo-Saxon country with a White-Protestant-Anglo-Saxon civilization which is struggling to preserve itself against infiltration and adulteration by other civilizations brought here by Negroes and aliens. The second maintains that the pattern of America is not essentially Anglo-Saxon with haphazard additions of unrelated patches. The pattern is, indeed, all of one piece: it is a blend of cultures from many lands.[1]*

The United States has from its infancy been a nation of immigrants (a nation of nations as Walt Whitman called it), and their contributions have, to a great extent, been responsible for the development of American civilization. The interplay and interstimulation of the diverse ethnic and national groups have made the history and shaped the destiny of the United States.

Though some immigrants have perhaps been more influential than others, no one single nationality has directed the course of American development to the exclusion of all the others. All immigrant groups have made some contributions, profoundly influencing the material, institutional, and cultural aspects of American life. The immigrant's part in America's making was stressed by a former United States Secretary of the Interior, Franklin K. Lane, when he said:

> America is a land of but one people, gathered from many countries. . . . Whatever the lure that brought us, each has his gift. Irish lad and Scot, Englishmen and Dutch, Italian, Greek, and French, Spaniard, Slav, Teuton, Norse, Negro—all have come bearing gifts and have laid them on the altar of America.[2]

The alien has been an important factor in the material development of the country. In the mill and in the mine, on the railway and on the skyscraper, on the farm and in the orchard, he has strained his muscles and carried the heavy burdens. The foreigners have done a large part of America's work. They have made steel, machines, automobiles, and clothes; they have mined coal, iron, and copper; they have built railroads, tunnels, highways, and office buildings; they have grown cabbage, wheat, apples, and oranges. The high standard of living in America is attributable, in some measure, to the productive genius of the foreigners on the farms.

* Notes to this chapter begin on page 297.

Immigrants from countries where land was scarce developed methods unknown to Americans who have been accustomed to great stretches of land. As Edward A. Ross has said:

Certain of the South Europeans who are upon the soil have something to show American farmers facing the problems of intensive agriculture. Italians are teaching their neighbors how to extract three crops a year from a soil already nourishing orchard or vineyard. The Portuguese raise vegetables in the walnut groves, grow currants between the rows of trees in the orchard, and beans between the currant rows. . . . From the slopes looking out on the Adriatic the Dalmatian brings a horticultural cunning which the American fruit-grower should be eager to acquire.[3]

Considerable credit must be given to the immigrants for the strong impetus they gave to idealism. The foreigners came to the United States not only because of economic opportunities, but also because of dislike for religious intolerance, militarism, injustice, and tyranny. Inspired by these ideals, they labored diligently until American thought and practice were perceptibly elevated. Thus, when liberalism was crushed in Germany by the autocratic sovereigns, thousands of revolutionary idealists took refuge in the United States and brought with them the important quality of democratic leadership. Seeing liberty strangled at home, they were all the more solicitous to nourish it in America. In a similar fashion, the Protestant Croats and Slovenes, who were denied the right to worship God as they pleased by their Roman Catholic rulers, migrated to Georgia and helped to promote the ideal of toleration. There is no denying that immigrants have done much to make and keep America democratic. This fact was noted by Frederick Jackson Turner in his masterpiece on the frontier, wherein he stated: "He who would take stock of American democracy must not forget the accumulation of human purposes and ideals which immigration has added to the American populace."[4]

The American language has been immeasurably enriched by the impact of the immigrants. A German dialect used since colonial days in Pennsylvania is still in use and has modified both the vocabulary and pronunciation of English in the area. Likewise, the common speech of lower Louisiana reflects a French influence. Texans have borrowed words from the Mexicans. In Minnesota and the neighboring states Swedish terms and idioms have been incorporated into the language of the people. The Italian word *spaghetti* is now as American as apple pie. Several words have been brought into the language by the Yugoslavs: (1) *argosy*, meaning a cargo of exotic goods, is a corruption of Ragusa (Dubrovnik), the great trading port of Dalmatia during the Middle Ages; (2) *cravat*, which is the French word for Croat (*Hrvat* in Croatian), has an interesting origin: Croatian soldiers who entered French military service in the seventeenth century wore bright-colored neckpieces and this name was eventually transferred to them; (3) *maraschino* was originally the name of a liqueur manufactured from Dalmatian cherries, or *maraške*.

It is not easy to assess or evaluate all the gifts of the immigrants. Many of their contributions are so intangible as to be incapable of measurement or even visible demonstration. How can one, for instance, accurately measure the influence of the moral codes or the domestic virtues of an immigrant group upon American society? Obviously, there is no infallible method. Be that as it may, the writer on immigration should at least enumerate and classify the alien gifts, even though he may not always be able to define or measure them correctly. The way was pointed out by a leading authority on the subject, who wrote:

> As we see the immigrant struggling to gain an economic foothold in the world, his first step toward citizenship, his cultural gifts are not alway easy to discern. He has helped to clear the land, till the soil, tend the herds, shepherd the flocks, cut the timber, work in the mines, fish the waters, build the roads, man the ships, labor in mills and factories. But he has done more— much more. Wherever he works he carries with him the traditions, the folkways, the wisdom based upon the race experience of his homeland. These are his heritage; they are the roots which feed his growth in American soil. Upon these and the manna he receives in the new land he builds his spiritual life.[5]

From the above passage it is evident that the contributions of the immigrants can be roughly divided into two categories: one consisting of labor and the other of tradition and folkways. Some mention has already been made of the endowments of the Yugoslavs in both of these areas, but the subject is of such great importance that it needs expansion and elaboration. It will then be seen more clearly what they have done for American industry, agriculture, science, invention, education, literature, arts, politics, sports, and national defense and security. The purpose of this chapter is not to repeat—or even summarize—that which has already been said—though repetition cannot be entirely avoided—but to bring into sharp focus the principal contributions of the South Slavs.

## INDUSTRY

Thousands of South Slavs have for many years devoted their talents and energies to the two great basic industries of America: mining and the manufacture of steel. But miners and laborers cannot, as a rule achieve fame or fortune; their names are seldom seen in the headlines of newspapers. Nevertheless, their work during the past fifty years or more has helped to transform the United States into the richest nation on earth. Along with other immigrants the Yugoslavs came to America at the very time when industry was in great need of labor in order to expand. As Adamic explained:

Immigration was a large factor in the upbuilding of America. The immigrant flood during the last seven or eight decades, and especially from about 1890 to 1914, included large numbers of my countrymen—"Bohunks," or "Hunkies": Slavs from the Balkans and from eastern and central Europe—whose contribution as workers to the current material greatness and power of the United States, albeit not generally recognized, is immense.[6]

Croatians, Slavonians, Slovenians, Bosnians, Hercegovinians, Montenegrins, and Serbians were drawn into the toughest jobs of the large and expanding heavy industries. They had been inured through centuries to sparse living and endless hardship. They were young, big, brawny, and, though mostly peasants, they were able rapidly to pick up American production methods. They formed a valuable addition to American manpower in mining, steel and iron, and construction. Together with the Czechs, Lithuanians, and Poles, they became known as the best steelworkers in the country.

Most of the Yugoslav workers have remained in comparative obscurity, though some have invented various devices now used in the industries. But there are others who have won renown in other sectors of American enterprise. One of the pioneers in the oil industry in Texas was Captain Anthony F. Lucas (Lučić), a native of Yugoslavia. He was the first to strike oil in Texas and subsequently played a large role in the development of the industry.  A. Dilić, a tunnel builder, has the reputation of a big boss who gets big jobs done fast.  A noted industrial engineer is George Perazich, a Slovene who was formerly with the United Nations Relief and Rehabilitation Administration.  John Jager is a Slovene architect, builder, and engineer in Minneapolis.  Well-known in Chicago industrial circles is Hugo Tomich, a Croat metal manufacturer.  An important industrialist in Arizona and Michigan is Peter Ruppe, a Slovene mining operator.

Among the Pacific Coast shipbuilders the names of John Rados and Joe Martinac, both Croats, loom large.  Joe Jurich, a Dalmatian, has been for many years an official of the CIO Fishermen's Union, with authority over both the Atlantic and Pacific coasts. Marcus Nalley (Marko Narancić), an immigrant from Croatia who worked his way up from a steel-mill laborer in Pittsburgh to a wealthy industrialist in Tacoma, Washington, is the owner of a fish cannery in Tacoma that is reputed to be one of the finest in the country as well as of a well-known food-processing firm whose brands are sold in groceries and supermarkets throughout the nation.  Martin Bogdanovich, John Zuanich, and Nick Bez, all Dalmatians, have been instrumental in making the American fisheries one of the most efficient and productive enterprises in the world. A prominent figure on the East Coast is Samuel Zorovich.  This Dalmatian, who came to the United States in 1923 practically penniless, today owns a fleet of 200 taxicabs in New York and a cement company in Miami, Florida—enterprises which gross over $10,000,-000 annually.

### AGRICULTURE

Though a relatively small number of Yugoslavs turned to farming in the United States, many of the early immigrants settled in the midwestern states, and became pioneers in plowing the prairies into productive farm lands.  Overcoming seemingly insurmountable barriers, some of them made a success of farms that had long before been abandoned.  They readily adapted themselves to the new environment and techniques.  Then, too, they were not only fortified by their experiences on their meager holdings in the old country, but they were strong, industrious, and bent upon success.  With few exceptions, such as those who went into dairying, the Yugoslavs took up general farming.  Becoming fairly rooted to their lands, they raised American and European products, thus contributing to the enrichment and stabilization of American agriculture. Many of the splendid farms in the Midwest, especially in Michigan, Ohio, Wisconsin, and Minnesota, owe a debt to the hard-working Slavs.

Others of the early arrivals staked their claims in California. There, instead of raising corn, wheat, barley, or oats as in the Midwest, they engaged in the production of fruits and vegetables. Led by such outstanding pioneers as Mark Rabasa and Steve Mitrovich, they built an agricultural paradise in beautiful Pajaro Valley, raising figs, apples, prunes, apricots, grapes, and raisins that became universally known and demanded. In this way the Yugoslavs gave impetus to an industry that was to become one of the richest and most important on the Pacific Coast.

The important achievements of Reverend Francis Jager in apiculture are well known. Father Jager, a Slovene, served for many years as chief of the Bee Culture Division of the Minnesota Experiment Station at the University of Minnesota farm and helped to revolutionize the honey industry through his discoveries.

## SCIENCE

In the field of science the Yugoslavs have made conspicuous contributions. The two most important figures here are Michael Pupin and Nikola Tesla, fully described in the previous chapter.

Pupin achieved renown as an inventor in long-distance telephony and wireless telegraphy.

Some seven hundred inventions are formally listed under Tesla's name, but he probably made many more discoveries which are not registered. His biographer, John J. O'Neill, describes Tesla's achievements thus:

> Tesla was an inventor but he was much more than a producer of new devices: he was a discoverer of new principles, opening many new empires of knowledge which even today have been only partly explored. In a single mighty burst of invention he created the world of power today; he brought into being our electrical power era, the rockbottom foundation, on which the industrial system of the entire world is builded; he gave us our mass-production system, for without his motors and currents it could not exist; he created the race of robots, the electrical mechanical men that are replacing human labor; he gave us every essential of modern radio; he invented the radar forty years before its use in World War II; he gave us our modern neon and

264

other forms of gaseous-tube lighting; he gave us our fluorescent lighting; he gave us the high-frequency currents which are performing their electronic wonders throughout the industrial and medical world; he gave us remote control by wireless; he helped give us World War II, much against his will—for the misuse of his superpower system and his robot controls in industry made it possible for politicians to have available a tremendous surplus of power, production facilities, labor and materials, with which to indulge in the most frightful, devastating war that the maniacal mind could conceive. And these discoveries are merely the inventions made by the master mind of Tesla which have thus far been utilized—scores of others still remain unused.[7]

Another writer puts it cogently when he states that, "Today nearly everything electrical bears his [Tesla's] touch."[8]

In addition to their extraordinary accomplishments in electricity, Yugoslavs have also made noteworthy contributions to other branches of science. Professor Emil Weise, formerly at Zagreb University but now on the faculty of Loyola University in Chicago, is a recognized authority on pathology and bacteriology. Dr. Milislav Demerec is a geneticist at the Cold Spring Harbor, Long Island, research center of the Carnegie Institution. Matthew M. Braidech is a specialist in industrial water supply and water pollution problems. Nikola Trbojević (also known as Nikola Terbo), a nephew and student of Nikola Tesla, is an inventor in the automobile industry, with many patents under his name. Dr. Stevan Durović gained universal attention and admiration for his development of krebiozen, a cancer drug. Among the outstanding meteorologists in the employ of the United States government is George Cvijanovich. Dr. Victor Vecki, a San Francisco physician, was for many years a leading authority on venereal diseases. Prominent in Chicago medical circles a generation ago was Dr. Ante Biankini, a Croat who was perhaps as well known for his activities as a publicist and leader of South Slavic movements in America as for his cures.

## EDUCATION

Yugoslav contributions to American education began with the early missionaries, especially with churchmen like Bishop Baraga and Father Pirec. These South Slav pioneers in the Midwest, it should be remembered, were teachers as well as preachers. They established both schools and churches, and taught crafts, reading, writing, and arithmetic along with the Golden Rule and the Sermon on the Mount.

In more recent times, one of the most eminent educators in America was Dr. Henry Suzzallo, the son of Peter Zucalo, an immigrant from Dalmatia.[9] Suzzallo received his education in the schools of his native city, San Jose, California, and at Stanford and Columbia universities. After two years as assistant professor of education at Stanford he moved to Columbia University in 1909, where he served as adjunct professor of elementary education for several years before being elevated to the position of professor of philosophy of education at the teachers' college there. In 1915 he was elected president of the University of Washington, which he developed into one of the outstanding institutions of learning in the West. During his administration the student enrollment increased from less than 2,000 to nearly 7,000 and the faculty from about 200 to over 300. Acting on the belief that education should, before all else, train students to think, the president devoted himself to raising the entrance requirements of the university and to expanding and enriching its curriculum. In his capacity as a member of the state boards of education and vocational education, he aided immensely in building a more effective public education system. He instituted in the state schools courses in forestry and fish culture, on which the state's two most important industries were based. During the war he was made chairman of the State Council of National Defense and later head of the National Metal Trades Board which concerned itself with labor adjustments in the munitions factories. In 1918 President Wilson appointed him as one of ten arbiters to sit in controversies under the War Board and later he was made an advisor to the War Labor Policy Board. In 1926 he was dismissed as president of the university, the result of a controversy with Governor Roland H. Hartley, who subjected the entire state educational system to rigid political control.

Upon leaving Washington Suzzallo was elected chairman of the board of trustees of the Carnegie Foundation for the Advancement of Teaching. About this time the Carnegie Endowment for International Peace decided to send abroad an able interpreter of American education and selected Suzzallo as its representative. As a consequence, he spent most of 1928 lecturing in some of the leading universities in Europe, including Belgrade and Zagreb in Yugoslavia. Shortly after his return to the United States, he was made special director of the National Advisory Committee on Education, a group of fifty-two educators appointed by President Hoover to recommend a policy for governmental participation in educational activities. In 1930, upon the retirement of Henry S. Pritchett, he succeeded to the presidency of the Carnegie Foundation for the Advancement of Teaching, a position he occupied until his death in September, 1933.

Perhaps less known is Dr. Paul R. Radosavljevich, a Serb American who was for many years a member of the faculty and chairman of the Experimental Education Department at New York University. He made a reputation not only as a fine teacher but also as a stimulating author, writing numerous articles and books in Serbo-Croatian, Russian, German, and English. Well regarded by scholars are especially his *Experimental Psychology, Experimental Pedagogy, History of Experimental Psychology,* and *New Movements in Education.* His most significant literary contribution is perhaps his two-volume work, *Who Are the Slavs?*, which is one of the most comprehensive studies of the Slavs and their culture.

Another prominent educator and writer is Dinko F. Tomašić, a Croat formerly at the University of Zagreb and now associate professor of sociology at Indiana University. He is considered an authority on the sociology of Yugoslavia and southeastern Europe. He has contributed many articles to magazines and learned journals, in Europe and in America. In 1948 he published his interesting monograph, *Personality and Culture in East European Politics,* showing how closely intertwined are politics and social structures. His other publications include *The Impact of Russian Culture on Soviet Communism* and *National Communism and Soviet Strategy.*

A Yugoslav American who has steadily gained stature in the educational world is Wayne S. Vucinich. After receiving his Doctor of Philosophy degree at the University of California, he served as Eastern European specialist with the Coordinator of Information and the Office of Strategic Services during the war. Since 1947 he has been professor of history at Stanford University. In addition to contributing many splendid articles to scholarly periodicals, Professor Vucinich has written a book called *Serbia Between East and West.* Also showing considerable promise are Alex N. Dragnich, Michael B. Petrovich, and Charles Jelavich. Dragnich, a member of the political science department at Vanderbilt University, is the author of *Tito's Promised Land: Yugoslavia* and numerous shorter works. Petrovich, an associate professor of history at the University of Wisconsin, has been a regular contributor to learned journals since his student days and has published a monograph entitled *The Emergence of Russian Panslavism.* Professor Jelavich of the history staff at the University of California in Berkeley has written, in addition to numerous articles, the very fine study, *Tsarist Russia and Balkan Nationalism.*

Other important figures in education are Professor Francis R. Preveden of the University of Chicago, University of De Paul, and University of Minnesota, a noted philologist, historian, and author (*A History of the Croatian People*); John Zvetina, professor of history of law at Loyola University in Chicago; Dr. Hugo Bren, until recently professor of theology at the Slovene Theological Seminary in Lemont, Illinois; Dr. Christopher Spalatin and Dr. Joseph Gorsic of the Slavic Institute at Marquette University; Dr. Stoyan A. Bayitch, professor of international law at the University of Miami, Florida; Dr. Clement S. Mihanovich, chairman of the department of sociology at St. Louis University; Alexander Vucinich, associate professor of sociology and anthropology at San Jose State College, California; Ante Kadić, assistant professor of Serbo-Croatian language and literature at Indiana University; Traian Stoianovich, assistant professor of history at Rutgers University; and Gojko Ruzičić, associate professor of Serbo-Croatian language and literature at Columbia University. Meriting mention also is the late Dr. Nicholas Mirkovich, who was cut short in his brilliant career by a German shell in 1944.

The above names do not by any means exhaust the list of Yugoslav American educators. There are hundreds of men and women in the elementary grades, high schools, and colleges who are giving their wholehearted attention and devotion to the education of American youth.

## LITERATURE

As in education so in literature, the earliest contributions were those of the missionaries. Here the name of Bishop Baraga is most important. While working among the Indians in the Midwest, he found time to write *The History, Character, Life and Manners of the North American Indians* in German, a prayer book in the Chippewa language, a life of Jesus, also in Chippewa, and a sermon book (*Gawikwemasinsigan*), which included the epistles and gospels of all the Sundays and holy days of the year, as well as a brief Bible history of the Old Testament and instructive extracts from the four Gospels, the Acts of the Apostles, and the Epistles.

Until his death in 1951 the most famous Yugoslav in American letters was Louis Adamic, from whose works the present writer has copiously quoted in this volume. Adamic's biography has been fully given in the previous chapter.

Next to Adamic, the best known Yugoslav writer in the United States is Stoyan Pribichevich, son of the famous Serbian liberal statesman, Svetozar. He obtained a sound education in Belgrade, receiving from the university there a doctoral degree in political science and a bachelor degree in law. After graduation he settled down to the practice of law. But this comparatively sedate life was suddenly interrupted in 1932 when the young attorney became involved in university students' riots and in printing pamphlets against the dictatorial government of King Alexander and was, as a consequence, forced to flee from his homeland. He went to Paris and joined his father, also a political exile, helping him to write a book on Yugoslavia (*La Dictature du roi Alexandre: contribution à l'etude de la démocratie*).

After two years in France, Pribichevich came to New York to visit a relative. So impressed by what he found in this country that he decided to live here permanently, he went back to Europe in order to be able to return to America as an immigrant. Coming back at the end of 1935, in the midst of the economic depression, he experienced difficulty in getting suitable work, being thus compelled to do physical labor, including toil in a factory. Finally, however, after several years of this precarious existence, he received an invitation to become a member of the editorial staff of *Time* and *Fortune* magazines. Since that time he has gained wide acclaim as a sincere and intelligent correspondent and author. With his clear, readable, and dispassionate writing, he has done much to elucidate the history, politics, and society of the Balkans for his many readers. In addition to numerous articles, he has written longer works, the best-known of which is his *World Without End*, a classic on southeastern Europe.

Bogumil Vošnjak, a Slovenian political émigré, is a distinguished statesman and author. He was a member of the Yugoslav Committee in London during the period from 1915 to 1919, and played an active role in the creation of Yugoslavia. He represented the

Slovenes at the Corfu Conference in 1917 and helped draft the famous Corfu Declaration. In 1919 he was secretary general of the Yugoslav peace delegation in Paris and a member of the Yugoslav constitutional assembly in 1920. After serving in various official capacities for the new Yugoslav government, he was elected to the *Skupština,* where he remained during the years 1931 to 1935. In World War II he joined the forces of Mihajlović. He became a member of the Slovene National Committee in 1945, but as Tito and his supporters gained supremacy throughout the country, he fled his native land and made his way to the United States. Although he has been busily occupied these many years with politics, Vošnjak has also had the time to write numerous books on a variety of subjects. This prolific writer has produced thirty books dealing with the history of the South Slavs, among which are included *Yugoslav Nationalism, Political and Social Conditions in the Slovene Lands, Bulwark against Germany,* and *Dying Empire.* Since his arrival in America he has written several informative articles on Yugoslav history.

Another recent immigrant whose name should be added to the list of Yugoslav American authors is P. D. Ostović, a Croat who helped in erecting the South Slav state in 1918 from his post as secretary of the Yugoslav Committee. He worked long and diligently in his homeland in an effort to reduce the frictions among the conflicting national and religious groups and to bring about greater unity among them all. In the United States he has played an important role in the clarification of Yugoslav developments. His fascinating book, *The Truth About Yugoslavia,* contains an illuminating account of Yugoslav history and politics, which does much to set the record straight on some of the most controversial issues in the evolution of the South Slav state.

A leading Serbian American who is noted as an economist, author, editor, and publisher is Vaso Trivanovich. He is a descendant of a family that distinguished itself in the struggle of the South Slavs against Austria-Hungary and in the creation of an independent Yugoslav state. He came to the United States as a student in 1919 and liked it so well in this country that he remained permanently. After obtaining degrees from the universities of Maryland and Columbia, he became a government economist. From 1927 to 1939 he was chief of the Department of International Relations of the National Industrial Conference Board. During the war he served as head of the Yugoslav Short-Wave Department of the Columbia Broadcasting System and as Economic Intelligence Officer and Property Control Specialist of the Foreign Economic Administration. Trivanovich is remembered as the editor and publisher of the magazine *Yugoslavia*. He is the author of *Rationalization of German Industry* and *The Economic Development of Germany under National Socialism*.

Also famous as an economist and author is Jozo Tomašević. Before coming to the United States he was with the National Bank of Yugoslavia in Belgrade. In this country he has held a number of high positions, including those of assistant economist for the Food Research Institute at Stanford University, senior analyst for the Foreign Economic Administration, and economist with the United Nations Relief and Rehabilitation Administration. He was formerly the editor of *Ekonomist*, a monthly review published in Zagreb. Among his more important books are his *Die Staatsschulden Jugoslaviens* (Yugoslavia's Public Debts), *Financijska Politika Jugoslavije* (The Fiscal Policy of Yugoslavia), *Novac i Kredit* (Money and Credit), and *International Agreements on Conservation of Marine Resources*. One of his more recent works is *Peasants, Politics, and Economic Change in Yugoslavia*.

Vlaho S. Vlahovic, a Dalmatian, was editor and publisher of the *Slavonic Monthly* until its demise after World War II. This magazine was the only all-Slav publication in the English language that promoted the ideal of a better understanding of the American and European Slavs. This ideal also formed a basis of his *Two Hundred Fifty Million and One Slavs*. Ivan Zorman, M. Sojat, the Reverend Alexander Urankar, and Vinko Ujčić have produced some fine poetry. Francis A. Bogadek, Dr. F. J. Kern, Josip Marohnić, and George Schubert are known as compilers of dictionaries. Ivan Mladineo, author of *Narodni Adresar* (National Directory), and coauthor with B. Angelinović of *Jugoslaveni u Ujedinjenim Državama Amerike* (The Yugoslavs in the United States of America), J. Poljak, who wrote *Almanak i Statistika Južnih Slavena u Sjedinjenim Državama Sjeverne Amerike* (Almanac and Statistics of the South Slavs in the United States of North America), Luka M. Pejović, author of *Prikazi Naših Iseljenika* (Stories of our Immigrants), Jože Zavertnik, author of *Ameriški Slovenci* (American Slovenes), and numerous journalists have contributed immensely to the knowledge of the American Yugoslavs and their history.

## The Arts

In the plastic arts the Yugoslavs have a representative who is a celebrated genius. This is the master sculptor Ivan Meštrović, who has won universal renown through his originality, imagination, and technique, as is fully described in the preceding chapter. In discussing Meštrović a French critic stated: "He is great because he pursues a higher reality showing through appearances and makes of every work at once an affirmation of the present, and appeal to the future and an aspiration toward the divine." [10]

Not as well known as Meštrović, but nevertheless a great artist in his own right is Maximilian "Makso" Vanka, a gifted Croat American painter. Born in Zagreb in 1890 of fairly well-to-do parents, Makso was educated at the Zagreb Real Gymnasium and University. He studied painting at the Royal Academy of Beaux Arts in Belgium, from which he graduated with first prize and gold medal. Subsequently he worked in Paris, London, Amsterdam, and various cities in Italy. After the establishment of the new Yugoslav state he aided in the founding of the Academy of Arts in Zagreb, where he held the position of professor of painting and design for a number of years. Being hailed by critics as the leading painter in Yugoslavia, he was decorated in 1926 with the Order of Saint Sava by the Yugoslav government. At about the same time he was honored with the *Médailles d'Or* and the *Palme Académique* at the Paris International Exhibition.

In 1934 Vanka left his native Yugoslavia and came to this country with his American-born wife and small daughter. Presently he took up his abode in Bucks County, Pennsylvania, where he still lives with his wife in an old stone house tucked away on a side road near Rushland and decorated with his own deft touch, largely fresco paintings (his favorite medium of expression). From his home studio have come streams of pastels, oil pastels, wash water colors, water colors, and oils on canvas and on panels.

Makso has a deep feeling for his fellow Yugoslavs in America and has tried to help them in every way possible. When the pastor of the St. Nicholas Croatian Church in Millvale, Pennsylvania, sought ways to beautify his old yellow brick building, Vanka responded with an effort that was truly reminiscent of a Michelangelo. He left the outside untouched, but he transformed the interior to the extent that it took on the appearance of an Old World cathedral. The arched ceiling of the church he crowded with saints and apostles. Behind the altar and in the apse he placed a 36-foot Madonna and Child in Croatian dress. In one of the many murals decorating the walls he depicted miners and workers with their priest offering the great Madonna and Child their church, which one of them holds in his hands. In a second he showed a Croatian family bowing in prayer in a pastoral setting. In a third he portrayed sorrowing women weeping at the bier of a son killed in battle. Still another mural focused attention on mothers and wives mourning beside sons killed in the mines. Throughout all of these frescoes Croatian dress and embroideries were featured and the faces shown were those of Croatian peasants. As Makso himself explained his main purpose was to show the humanity in divinity and the divinity in humanity—divine justice, human injustice.

Vanka has not only shown his masterpieces in leading art centers in the United States, but he has also exhibited in most of the capitals of Europe. He is represented in the National Art Museum of Budapest, Hungary, Municipal Art Museum of Stuttgart, Germany, the Prince Paul Museum of Belgrade, and the Strosmajer Gallery of Zagreb, Yugoslavia.

Also occupying a high rank among the Yugoslav American artists is Yuca Salamunić. This talented sculptor has executed figures of some of the leading personalities in America, including the late President Franklin D. Roosevelt. His portrait statues are extremely lifelike, the principal characteristics of the sitters being clearly depicted. There is vitality and realism in all of his works.

Among the younger artists one of the most gifted is Savo Radulovich. A native of Montenegro, Radulovich came as a youngster to the United States, living in St. Louis until he moved to New York after World War II. During the war he served with General Mark Clark's Fifth Army headquarters staff in Italy and had an opportunity to visit Yugoslavia, a journey which inspired his fine drawing "Partisans, Yugoslavia." After the war a number of his pictures appeared in *Life* magazine and other publications. He holds the Fogg, St. Louis, and Kansas art museums' prizes. He once explained to a newspaper correspondent, "An ingenious American art is emerging from the talents of many different national backgrounds fusing together. It is my ambition to make some small contribution in enriching the art." [11]

The paintings of Borislav Bogdanovich have also drawn the

highest praise from critics. One of these described his works as "realistic, masculine and constructed with maximum solidity in slabs of bright color." The same critic then went on to add, "He knows how to associate strong hues without their doing violence to each other. His work is the act of sturdy surrender to the arguments of plain visual facts." [12]   Another expert stated, "Paintings by Borislav Bogdanovich bring to bear upon still life and occasional outdoor themes the clear, direct feeling for primary and simple color typical of folk art. . . . [The paintings] are large in form, solid, and in organization not unlike the early work of Cezanne." [13]

Other noteworthy figures in the world of art are Harvey Gregory Perushek, Raymond Prohaska, Tanasko Milovich, and Vuk Vucinich, most of whom have had their works on exhibit in art centers in New York, Chicago, and Los Angeles.

In music, too, the Yugoslavs boast of many distinguished representatives. Artur Rodzinski, a Pole born in Split, Dalmatia, was one of the leading conductors in the United States until his death in 1958. The late Louis Svecenski was a member of the famous Kneisel Quartet, a pioneer organization in presenting chamber music in America. Death ended the promising career of Tomislav Milostic, who received widespread praise as an opera and concert singer during his short lifetime. Among those carving a niche for themselves in the opera hall of fame have been J. Naval-Pogačnik, Tino Patiera, J. Marion Vlahović, and M. Nikolić, long-time singers with the Chicago Opera Company, and Teodor Lovich (Paško Alujević) and Mate Čulić-Dragun, noted performers with the San Francisco Opera Company.

One of the greatest opera stars at the turn of the century was Milka Ternina, who sang Wagnerian roles for many years with the Metropolitan Opera Company in New York. A most worthy successor to Ternina has been Zinka Milanov, also a star of the Metropolitan. She made her debut in Yugoslavia when she was nineteen years old and could sing only in Croatian. After Bruno Walter discovered her in Vienna, she came to New York in 1937. Making her debut with the Metropolitan in *Il Trovatore,* she scored an instant hit, and became the first choice for roles in *Aida, La Forza del Destino,* and *Norma.* She still remains one of the brightest stars in the opera firmament.

A rising young star is Mija Novich (Bosiljka Mijanovich), a dramatic soprano from Chicago. Besides appearing in practically every large city in the United States and Canada, Mija has toured England, Europe, and South America, giving performances in *Aida, Tosca,* and other celebrated operas. Critics have been lavish in bestowing praise upon this Serb American nightingale.

Marjorie Radovan and Anton Subelj have also won recognition as outstanding singers. Zlatko Balokovic is a violin virtuoso, a concert and recording artist whose music is admired by Yugoslavs and Americans alike. The name of Alexander Savine Djimić is high on the list of America's finest composers. Frank Yankovic, who has already been discussed in some detail, enjoys the title of "polka king."

Highly skilled dancers and actors represent the Yugoslavs on stage and screen. One of the world's leading ballerinas is Mia Slavenska. Before taking up her residence in this country after World War II, this *danseuse étoile* from Zagreb attracted universal attention and praise as the star of the Ballet Russe de Monte Carlo, in leading roles in the large cities of Europe and North and South America, and as the outstanding performer in the prize-winning French film *Ballerina.* In the United States she has been very successful in taking the art of the ballet to the small town with her remarkable Ballet Variante. She holds an Olympic award, and is an accomplished pianist and choreographer, having composed her first ballet at the age of fourteen for the Zagreb Opera House. Like Slavenska, Tashimara has been a top-ranking Croat American dancer, captivating theater-goers with her brilliant performances.

A number of Yugoslavs have achieved distinction in moving pictures, on the stage, and on television. For over a generation one of the better-known names in Hollywood has been that of Slavko Vorkapic, a Yugoslav-born film director and editor. Becoming interested in movies while an art student in Paris, Vorkapic set aside his books and hastened to America's film capital, arriving there in 1920. In Hollywood he became known as one of the foremost exponents of a film art that attempts to exploit the motion picture as a distinct and separate medium with unique potentialities of its own, and drew attention to his work by his imaginative use of film techniques. His name is most closely linked with montage— the technique of superimposing one picture upon another, which he did more than anyone else to develop—and the use of special effects. Vorkapic has been associated as codirector with some of the finest cinema productions. During World War II he produced

275

the *This Is America* series for the United States Office of War Information. Other eminent Yugoslav American personalities behind the Hollywood cameras are Michael Lah, the distinguished cartoon animator, and Paul Zastupnevich, a leading dress and costume designer.

Just as impressive have been the Yugoslav Americans appearing before the cameras and lights. Their names have glittered on theater marquees from the earliest days of movie making. Laura La Plante (Turk) was one of the great stars of the silent films. The career of John Miljan, who has had roles in some of Hollywood's best pictures, has extended from the silents through the talkies and on into color, cinemascope, and cinerama, with no evidence that the end is yet in sight. Among the later entrants on the Hollywood movie scene the best kown is Karl Malden (Mladen Sekulovich), a former steelworker from Gary, Indiana. A natural, polished actor, Malden has marched from triumph to triumph not only in the Hollywood studios but on the New York stage as well. George Zorich has been dancing his way to movie and stage success. After starring in football with the University of Southern California Trojans and the Detroit Lions professional team, Bill Radovich has become one of the big tough men on the screen. Guy Mitchell, a singer, is known to many moving picture, television, and radio fans. A recognized stage actress in England, Marta Mitrovich is rapidly winning the plaudits of American audiences as an accomplished performer on the screen, television, and radio. Another newcomer in the American entertainment world is Tania Velia, the Yugoslav Marilyn Monroe, who in a few years moved from singing engagements in New York night clubs to a Hollywood studio. A promising stage and television actor is John Vivyan (Ivan Vukojan), who has impressed New York critics with the way he has carried out all his assignments. At present Vivyan is giving most of his time to a television serial which is telecast nationally each week. Gene Rayburn is another of the Yugoslavs moving up the ladder of success as a television and radio artist. One of the most skilled artists in his field is Bob O'Bradovich (Obradović), the chief make-up man for the National Broadcasting Company television studios in New York.

The many Yugoslav singing societies and dramatic clubs, which also serve to enrich the arts of America, have been described in an earlier chapter.

## POLITICS AND GOVERNMENT

Yugoslav participation in American political life is of fairly recent date, the principal reason being late naturalization. As a consequence, the number of distinguished persons in politics and government is not so large as in some of the other fields mentioned. This does not mean that the South Slavs are without political representatives.

The career of Frank J. Lausche, former Ohio governor and now United States Senator, has been fully outlined. Raymond Moley, one-time advisor of President Franklin D. Roosevelt and a keen observer and analyst of the political scene, said of Lausche after his strong comeback in 1948:

In sheer popularity Lausche ranks exceedingly high. He would be hard to beat for any office. . . . Moreover, it is not at all unlikely that Lausche, if reelected governor, will be a natural choice for a place on the national ticket in 1952. He is a Catholic and would have some difficulty in getting the nomination for President. But there would be strong political advantages in his running as a candidate for Vice President.[14]

Others already mentioned are John A. Blatnik, Minnesota representative in Congress since 1946; Mike Stepovich, ex-governor of Alaska; Matt Cvetic, former undercover agent for the FBI; and Vaso Trivanovich and Jozo Tomašević, economists in the United States government service. Anne Erste is a Federal Reserve agent. Donald R. Perry (Dragoslav Perišić) is an ex-assistant commissioner of the United States Immigration and Naturalization Service. Colonel Emil Antonovich is a construction engineer in the United States Army Quartermaster Corps.

## SPORTS

Possessing many fine physical attributes, the Yugoslavs have made good athletes. Many of them have excelled in football, baseball, boxing, swimming and diving, running, walking marathons, and other athletic activities. The sports pages of newspapers and periodicals are filled with Yugoslav names.

A headline halfback of the war years was Frank Sinkwich, former All-American at the University of Georgia, where some of the records he set still stand. Sinkwich, who came to this country from Yugoslavia as a boy, became one of the greatest players in the country in the early 1940's. The Associated Press annual poll named him the outstanding athlete of 1942.[15] After graduation he starred for several years with professional teams before shifting to coaching.

During the early 1950's among the nation's best football players honorably mentioned were Tom Yewcic, the All-American backfield ace for the 1952 national champion Michigan State College eleven; Rudy Bukich and George Bozanich, whose great work as halfbacks made the University of Southern California a serious challenger for national honors; and John Siskowic, one of the leading scorers in the nation as a halfback for Wooster College in Ohio. More recently, Ralph Jelic and Ivan Toncic of the University of Pittsburgh, and Joe Plevel and Jon Mirilovich of the University of Miami have helped to boost their teams to top rating. In the professional ranks first-rate players include Charles Drazenovich, former Pennsylvania State College star quarterback now doing chores for the Washington Redskins, George Tarasovich, erstwhile Louisiana State University great presently a rugged line backer for the Pittsburgh Steelers, and John Martinkovic and Steve Ruzich, stalwarts of the Green Bay Packers. Among America's football coaches Mike Pecarovich occupies a high rank. He has developed many strong teams for Loyola University in Los Angeles, Gonzaga, and the now-defunct New York Yankees. Nick Skorich has done well as a player and a coach with the Philadelphia Eagles. Joe Kuharich, former coach of the Washington Redskins and now head coach at Notre Dame University, won the reputation of being one of the most successful young coaches in the country by his ability to produce consistent winners at the University of San Francisco. Earlier he had played guard for the University of Notre Dame and the Chicago Cardinals. In 1955 he was named professional coach of the year. Eddie Erdelatz (Erdeljac) is another top-flight football coach. He deserted the professional ranks in 1950 to take over a winless and dispirited Navy team and within a few years converted it into one of the most powerful football machines in the country. He left the Navy after the 1958 season and, following the organization of the new American Football League, accepted the position as head coach of the Oakland team.

The Yugoslavs have contributed many outstanding performers to major league baseball. Mike Kreevich, who played for many years with the Chicago White Sox, was the first South Slav to break into the big leagues. Joe Kuhel served as manager of the Washing-ton Senators for several years after a successful career as a first baseman for the team. Other former players well known to major league fans are Emil Verban (Chicago Cubs), George Metkovich (Pittsburgh Pirates), Andy Seminick (Philadelphia Phillies), Walter Judnic (Cleveland Indians), and Johnny Pesky (Boston Red Sox). Playing in the majors at the present time are Walt Dropo, the hard-hitting first baseman of the Baltimore Orioles, who was voted the "rookie of the year" at the beginning of his career; Bob Cerv, out-fielder for the New York Yankees; Steve Bilko, first baseman for the Los Angeles Angels; and Andy Pafko, veteran outfielder for the Milwaukee Braves.

Basketball has produced few stars of the caliber of George Mikan, who in 1951 was voted by a select committee of sport writers and radio announcers as the greatest player of the game ("Mr. Basketball") in the first half of the twentieth century. This honor was the climax of a brilliant athletic career. Mikan first at-tracted attention on the high school court. In college he carried De Paul University of Chicago to new heights as its All-American ace in the early 1940's. Following his graduation, the giant center joined the Minneapolis Lakers and proceeded to pile up records, most of which still remain intact. His prowess enabled the Lakers to dominate the professional field for nearly a decade.

Another Yugoslav American to attain distinction on the basket-ball court is Peter "Press" Maravich. Like many another Yugoslav youth, Maravich gained some of his earliest experience in the leagues and tournaments sponsored by the South Slavic national benefit federations. Later he went on to star with the David-Elkins College team in West Virginia, and after graduation turned to coaching. At the present time he is the head coach of the Clem-son College Tigers in South Carolina.

Hockey, which for many years was considered as a monopoly of Canadian-born players, is not without Yugoslav representatives. Mike Karakas of Chicago was the first non-Canadian goalie in the history of the game. Marty Pavelich starred for the Detroit Red Wings. The late Joe Cattarinich (Katarinić) of New Orleans, pop-ularly known as "Silent Joe," was the owner of the Canadiens team until his death.

Martin Stanovich, Tony Barkovich, and Milan Marusic are top-ranking golfers, participating in many of the big tournaments throughout the country. A big name in speed-car racing circles until his tragic death in 1955 was Bill Vukovich, a former Fresno grape picker who rose to the top of his dangerous occupation by winning two consecutive 500-mile Indianapolis Speedway races before meeting his end in his overturned, burning racer while bidding for his third victory. In boxing, Fritzie Zivic and Gus Lesnevich have stood out. Zivic, who comes from a Croat family with several exceptional boxers, won the world's welterweight championship in 1940. Lesnevich was for several years a serious light-heavyweight contender. For over twenty-five years Fred Bozic received featured billing in wrestling, and then after his retirement exposed the frauds of the grunt and groan game. Frank Benkovic is one of the leading bowlers in the country. Pete Radenkovic, a former Olympic goalie for Yugoslavia, is an outstanding soccer player. The list of names in the different sports could be expanded *ad infinitum,* but there is neither the need nor space for that.

## NATIONAL DEFENSE

Especially significant have been the Yugoslav wartime contributions. At the outset of each of the two World Wars they organized and collected their resources to help both their native and adopted countries. In World War I they set up numerous aid organizations and sent contributions to their kinsmen abroad, in addition to purchasing some $30,000,000 of United States Liberty Bonds. About 20,000 South Slavs responded to President Wilson's call to arms, making an enviable record in the service.[16] Captain Louis Cukela of the United States Marines was the only man in the war to win two Congressional Medals of Honor. Two other Yugoslavs, Jake Alex Mandusich and Jacob Mestrovich, were also decorated with Congressional Medals.

During World War II the Yugoslavs again put forth their best efforts to bring victory to the Allies and aid to their devastated homeland. To the colors of the United States rallied approximately 50,000 Yugoslavs. Many of the immigrant families had four to seven boys and girls in the service. For example, Joe Govorchin of Chicago had four in the armed forces and one in a war plant, while Matt Babich of Detroit had six in the service and four in essential war jobs.

A proportionately high number of Yugoslav Americans distinguished themselves in service. The first gold-star mother of the war was Jennie Dobnikar, a Slovene of Cleveland whose son died in action aboard the destroyer "Kearny." Peter Tomich, who lost his life at Pearl Harbor by remaining at his post in the engineering plant of the U.S.S. "Utah" until all fireroom personnel had left, was awarded the Congressional Medal of Honor posthumously. Lieutenant Mitchell Page (Milan Pejić) of the United States Marines, who killed 110 of the attacking Japanese on Guadalcanal, also received the Congressional Medal. Lieutenant Commander Milton Pavlic, an immigrant from Slovenia and a graduate of the United States Military Academy at Annapolis, destroyed three enemy ships and thirty-two planes before giving his life for his adopted country on the U.S.S. "South Dakota." A new destroyer was named U.S.S. "Pavlic" after him, and he was posthumously awarded the Congressional Medal. The same decoration, for exceptional heroism in France, was given to Lieutenant John J. Tominac. Captain George S. Wuchinich, attached to the Office of Strategic Services, received the Distinguished Service Cross for his superb work in connection with secret military operations in the Balkans. Sergeant George W. Mirich, the "one-man-army" of the Attu campaign, was also a recipient of the Distinguished Service Cross for cleaning out single-handed with machine guns and grenades seven Japanese pillboxes defending a strategic pass. Lieutenant J. Luksich, commander of a P-51 Mustang, shot down five German planes in a single afternoon, earlier having destroyed fifteen of the enemy planes.

On the home front most of the Yugoslavs worked in basic war industries, and oftentimes put in fourteen, sixteen, and even eighteen hours a day. They helped build ships, planes, tanks, guns, and ammunition, breaking many production records to speed the supplies to the war fronts. Many stories are told of their expeditiousness and efficiency. One of these relates the experiences of a crew composed mainly of Yugoslavs immigrants who relined a blast furnace at the Youngstown Sheet and Tube plant at Indiana Harbor, Indiana, in the incredible time of twenty-eight days, shattering the previous record by a full thirty-two hours. Shortly after Hitler's attack upon their homeland the South Slavs organized the Yugoslav Relief Committee in New York to aid their kinsmen with money and materials. In 1943 they established the United Committee of South-Slavic Americans, whose declared purpose was to aid the war efforts of the United States and its allies. The United

Committee was largely responsible for the $60,000,000 of War Bonds purchased by Yugoslav Americans.[17] Prominent Yugoslavs appeared at bond rallies in all sections of the country and urged the purchase of War Bonds and Stamps.

Yugoslav American writers and press kept the foreign-language readers informed of the progress of the war and of the internal conditions in Yugoslavia. The Tito-Mihajlović struggle, which was little understood in the United States, was publicized and clarified by such prominent writers as Adamic and Pribichevich. They did much to bring the true facts before the English readers.

Thus, there is no doubt that the Yugoslavs have, in the vast majority, shown themselves to be good American citizens. In time of war they have demonstrated their loyalty by working and fighting for their adopted country. In time of peace they are industrious and talented contributors to the general welfare and progress of the United States. As a group, through hard work, they have prospered in their American home, but many thousands of immigrants, now too old for employment in industry, find their physical strength gone and little personal savings to show for it. Their youth and power are in the steel girders of bridges and skyscrapers and in the rails that span the continent.

# Notes to Chapters 1–10

## CHAPTER 1

1. Throughout this work the Library of Congress system of transliteration for Serbo-Croatian words is generally used. Several modifications are made, especially in connection with names and other words already in common use. On the whole, consistency and uniformity are sacrificed in favor of clarity and convenience. Thus, "Yugoslavia" is used instead of "Jugoslavija," "Bosnia" instead of "Bosna," "Partisans" instead of "Partizane," but "Stevan" and "Stjepan" instead of "Stephen" and "Ivan" instead of "John." Names of Yugoslavs in America are slightly modified, in keeping with English spelling and usage.

2. Throughout this volume the term "South Slav" will be used to designate only those Slavic people who occupy the territories within the bounds of present-day Yugoslavia. Thus, embraced within this usage will be the three basic nationalities of the Croats, Serbs, and Slovenes and the various regional groups such as the Dalmatians, Istrians, Carniolians, Bosnians, Hercegovinians, Montenegrins, and the like. Not included are the Macedonians, who are non-Slavs in origin.

3. United States Immigration Commission, *Reports of the Immigration Commission,* Vol. I, *Abstracts of the Reports of the Immigration Commission,* Sixty-First Congress, Third Session, Senate Document No. 747 (Washington: Government Printing Office, 1911), pp. 60-65. Hereafter cited as U.S. Immigration Commission, *Abstracts.*

4. "In an American Factory," *Within Our Gates,* ed. by Mary B. McLellan and Albert V. De Bonis (New York: Harper and Brothers, 1940), p. 110. Quoted by permission.

5. Branko Lazarevitch, "The Present Outlook for Immigration from Jugo-Slavia," *Proceedings of the National Conference of Social Work,* 48th Annual Session (Chicago: University of Chicago Press, 1921), p. 460.

6. *On New Shores* (New York: The Century Company, 1925), p. 5.

7. J. M. Trunk, *Amerika in Amerikanci* (Celovec: J. M. Trunk, 1912), p. 390.

8. Kate H. Claghorn, "Slaves, Magyars and Some Others in the New Immigration," *Charities,* XIII (December 3, 1904), 203.

9. Exactly how many of the three million immigrants who entered the United States were South Slavs it is impossible to say, since the United States government did not begin to keep records of immigrants according to races or peoples until 1899.

10. Oscar Jaszi, *The Dissolution of the Habsburg Monarchy* (Chicago: University of Chicago Press, 1929), p. 238.

11. June N. Miljevic, "The Jugoslav People in Michigan," *Michigan History Magazine,* XXV (Autumn, 1941), 359.

12. Emily Greene Balch, *Our Slavic Fellow Citizens* (New York: Charities Publication Committee, 1910), p. 238. Hereafter cited as Balch, *Slavic Citizens.*

13. United States Immigration Commission, *Reports of the Immigration*

283

*Commission,* Vol. IV, *Emigration Conditions in Europe,* Sixty-First Congress, Third Session, Senate Document No. 748 (Washington: Government Printing Office, 1911), p. 361. Hereafter cited as U.S. Immigration Commission, *Emigration Conditions.*

14. *Ibid.,* p. 362.  15. *Ibid.,* p. 363.  16. *Ibid.,* p. 365.  17. *Ibid.*
18. *Ibid.,* p. 367.  19. *Ibid.,* p. 370.

20. Stjepan Radić, *Politički Katekizam* (Cleveland: Hrvatski Savez, 1913), p. 144.

21. Milan Marjanović, *Jugoslavija* (New York: Jugoslavenska Biblioteka, 1916), p. 29.

22. U.S. Immigration Commission, *Emigration Conditions,* p. 56.

23. *Immigration and Labor: the Economic Aspects of European Immigration to the United States* (New York: G. P. Putnam's Sons, 1912), p. 4. Hereafter cited as Hourwich, *Immigration and Labor.*

24. "The Land of Promise," *Harpers Magazine,* CLXIII (October, 1931), 618-619. Hereafter cited as Adamic, "Land of Promise." Quoted by permission.

25. U.S. Immigration Commission, *Emigration Conditions,* p. 57.

26. *Ibid.*  27. *Ibid.,* p. 56.  28. *Ibid.*, p. 60.  29. *Ibid.,* p. 61.  30. *Ibid.*

31. Balch, *Slavic Citizens,* p. 237.

32. U.S. Immigration Commission, *Emigration Conditions,* p. 61.

33. Alois B. Koukol, "The Slav's a Man for A' That," *Charities and the Commons,* XXI (January 2, 1909), 590.

34. The author, without exaggeration, has interviewed hundreds of Yugoslavs in many parts of the country, but, unfortunately, he obtained a written record only in Chicago and Los Angeles, where he spent considerable time. He does not, of course, accept these data as conclusive proof that all the immigrants were drawn to America by anticipation of adventure, but they are, nevertheless, a good indication of the real importance of this motive.

35. "Land of Promise," p. 619.  Quoted by permission.

36. U.S. Immigration Commission, *Emigration Conditions,* p. 369.

37. United States House of Representatives, *House Executive Documents,* Vol. XXIV, *Consular Reports on Emigration and Immigration,* Forty-ninth Congress, Second Session, House Document No. 157 (Washington: Government Printing Office, 1887), p. 47.

38. Kenneth L. Roberts, *Why Europe Leaves Home* (Indianapolis: Bobbs-Merrill Company, 1922), pp. 3-4. Quoted by permission.

39. Balch, *Slavic Citizens,* p. 54.

## CHAPTER 2

1. Jurica Bjankini, "Yugoslavs in the United States: Their Contributions to American Culture and Civilization," *First All-Slavic Singing Festival Given by the United Slavic Choral Societies* (Chicago: National Printing and Publishing Co., 1934), p. 95. Hereafter cited as Bjankini, "Yugoslavs in U.S."

2. Francis J. Brown and Joseph S. Roucek (eds.), *One America, The History, Contributions and Present Problems of our Racial and National Minorities* (rev. ed.; New York: Prentice-Hall, Inc., 1945), p. 158. Hereafter cited as Brown and Roucek, *One America.*

3. Francis L. Hawks, *History of North Carolina* (Fayetteville, North Carolina: E. J. Hale and Son, 1859), pp. 225-226.

4. William Edward Fitch, *The First Founders in America* (New York: The New York Society of the Order of the Founders and Patriots of America, 1913), pp. 24-25.

5. Bjankini, "Yugoslavs in U.S.," p. 95.

6. Zephyrin Engelhardt, *The Missions and Missionaries of California,* Vol. I, *Lower California* (2nd ed.; Santa Barbara: Mission Santa Barbara, 1929), p. 282.

7. Joseph S. Roucek, "The Yugoslav Immigrants in America," *The American Journal of Sociology,* XL (March, 1945), 603. Hereafter cited as Roucek, "Yugoslav Immigrants."

8. *The Jugoslavs in the United States of America* (New York: Jugoslav Section of America's Making, Inc., 1921), p. 14.

9. P. Chrysostomus Verwyst, *Life and Labors of Rt. Rev. Frederic Baraga, First Bishop of Marquette, Michigan* (Milwaukee: H. M. Wiltzius and Co., 1900), pp. 74-85; and Joseph Gregorich, *The Apostle of the Chippewas, the Life Story of the Most Rev. Frederic Baraga, D. D., the First Bishop of Marquette* (Chicago: The Bishop Baraga Association, 1932), p. 13.

10. Janes Ziegler (trans.), *Bratovshina S. Leopolda, k pomozhi misijonarjam, to je poslanin osnanovavzam Kirshanske Katolshske vere v Ameriki; ali popis kako se Kershanska vera v Ameriki rashirja* (Ljubljana: 1833), p. 17. Bonaparte Collection, Newberry Library, Chicago.

11. Letter dated October 4, 1834. Original in Archives of Notre Dame University, South Bend, Indiana.

12. Verwyst, *op. cit.,* pp. 370-371.

13. Joseph Gregorich, "Contributions of the Slovenes to the Chippewa and Ottawa Indian Missions," *Michigan History Magazine,* XXV (Spring, 1941), 184.

14. Sister Grace McDonald, "Father Francis Pierz, Missionary," *Minnesota History,* X (June, 1929), 107.

15. J. B. Tennelly, "Father Pierz, Missionary and Colonizer," *Acta et Dicta,* VII (October, 1935), 104.

16. United States House of Representatives, *Indian Office Reports, 1846, House Executive Documents,* Twenty-ninth Congress, Second Session, House Document No. 4 (Washington: Ritchie and Heiss, 1846), p. 262.

17. Verwyst, *op. cit.,* p. 385.      18. *Ibid.*

19. Grace Lee Nute, "Father Skolla's Report on his Indian Missions," *Acta et Dicta,* VII (October, 1936), 218.

20. Hugh MacCall, *The History of Georgia,* I (Savannah: Seymour and Williams, 1811), 50; and Charles C. Jones, *The Dead Towns of Georgia* (Savannah: Morning News Steam Printing House, 1878), p. 11.

21. Allen D. Candler (comp.), *The Colonial Records for the State of Georgia,* I (Atlanta: Allen D. Candler, 1904), 77, 187.

22. *Ibid.,* XXV, 180-181.   23. *Ibid.,* III, 428-430.   24. See p. 27.

25. Ivan Mladineo (ed.), *Narodni Adresar, Hrvata-Slovenaca-Srba* (New York: Ivan Mladineo, 1937), pp. xxi, xxii. Hereafter cited as Mladineo, *Narodni Adresar.*

26. Balch, *Slavic Citizens,* p. 233.

27. *Jugoslavs in the United States,* p. 14; and Louis Adamic, *A Nation of Nations* (New York: Harper and Brothers, 1945), p. 239.

28. Adamic, *A Nation of Nations,* p. 239.

29. Jože Zavertnik, *Ameriški Slovenci, Pregled Splošne Zgodovine Združenih Držav Slovenskega Naseljevanja in Naselbin in Slovenske Narodne Podporne Jednote* (Chicago: Slovenska Narodna Podporna Jednota, 1925), p. 250. Hereafter cited as Zavertnik, *Ameriški Slovenci.*

30. *Ibid.,* p. 253.

31. Stjepan Gaži, *Croatian Immigration to Allegheny County, 1882-1914* (Pittsburgh: Croatian Fraternal Union of America, 1956), 24-28, 42-43.

## CHAPTER 3

1. Balch, *Slavic Citizens*, p. 4.

2. United States Department of Labor: Bureau of Immigration, *Annual Report of the Commissioner General of Immigration, 1930* (Washington: Government Printing Office, 1930), p. 202. Hereafter cited as Bureau of Immigration, *Annual Report*.

3. Maurice R. Davie, *World Immigration* (New York: The Macmillan Co., 1939), p. 120.

4. *Ibid.*

5. U.S. Immigration Commission, *Emigration Conditions*, pp. 371-372. There seems to be some discrepancy between the figures given by the Commission for South Slav immigration. Here the total for the years 1899 to 1910 is given as 401,300, but in data elsewhere (reproduced in Table 1) the total for the same period is 464,630. It may be, perhaps, that the Bulgarians are excluded in the first figure, although that is not indicated.

6. Balch, *Slavic Citizens*, p. 179.

7. *Ibid.*, p. 153.

8. U.S. Immigration Commission, *Emigration Conditions*, p. 373.

9. *Ibid.*, p. 375. Since the Immigration Bureau did not separate the Serbians and Montenegrins from the Bulgarians, it is, therefore, necessary to include the latter group in the tables throughout.

10. United States Department of Labor: Bureau of Labor Statistics, "A Century of Immigration," *Monthly Labor Review*, XVIII (January 1924), 2.

11. *Ibid.*, pp. 2-3. 12. *Ibid.*, p. 3. 13. *Ibid.* 14. *Ibid.* 15. *Ibid.*

16. Bureau of Immigration, *Annual Report, 1926*, pp. 182-183.

17. *Ibid.*

18. United States Department of Justice: Immigration and Naturalization Service, *Annual Report of the Immigration and Naturalization Service, 1947* (Washington: Government Printing Office, 1947), p. 55. Hereafter cited as Immigration and Naturalization Service, *Annual Report*.

19. Bureau of Immigration, *Annual Report, 1926*, pp. 182-183.

20. Arthur E. Cook and John J. Hagerthy, *Immigration Laws of the United States Compiled and Explained* (Chicago: Callaghan and Co., 1929), *passim*.

21. United States Department of Justice: Immigration and Naturalization Service, *Immigration and Nationality Laws and Regulations as of March 1, 1944* (Washington: Government Printing Office, 1944), p. 49.

22. Immigration and Naturalization Service, *Annual Report, 1958*, p. 96.

23. Mimeographed material furnished the author by the United States Department of Justice: Immigration and Naturalization Service, Office for Research and Education.

24. Bureau of Immigration, *Annual Report, 1913*, p. 46.

25. Bureau of Immigration, *Annual Report, 1921*, p. 34.

26. U.S. Immigration Commission, *Emigration Conditions*, p. 377.

27. Immigration and Naturalization Service, *Annual Report, 1947*, p. 81.

28. Chamber of Labor for Croatia and Slavonia, *Quarterly Review of Yugoslav Migration* (January-March, 1929), quoted in United States Department of Labor: Bureau of Labor Statistics, "Effects of Restrictive Legislation Upon Immigrants from Yugoslavia," *Monthly Labor Review*, XXIX (July, 1929), 235.

29. United States Department of Commerce: Bureau of the Census, *Fifteenth Census of the United States: 1930, Population*, Vol. II, *General Report Statistics by Subject* (Washington: Government Printing Office, 1933, pp. 406-

407. Hereafter cited as *Fifteenth Census, General Report Statistics by Subject.*

30. *Ibid.*

31. United States Department of Commerce: Bureau of the Census, *Sixteenth Census of the United States: 1940, Population, Nativity and Parentage of the White Population, Country of Origin of the Foreign Stock* (Washington: Government Printing Office, 1943), p. 81. Hereafter cited as *Sixteenth Census, Country of Origin of the Foreign Stock.*

32. U.S. Immigration Commission, *Emigration Conditions*, p. 376.

33. *Ibid.*, p. 380.

34. *Intelligence and Immigration* (Baltimore: The Williams and Wilkins Co., 1926), p. 17.

35. U.S. Immigration Commission, *Emigration Conditions*, pp. 378-382.

36. Severin K. Turosienski, *Education in Yugoslavia*, United States Office of Education Bulletin 1939, No. 6 (Washington: Government Printing Office, 1939), p. 11.

37. Bureau of Immigration, *Annual Report, 1913*, pp. 46-47, 64-66; and *Annual Report, 1921*, pp. 34-35, 67-69.

38. Jeremiah W. Jenks and W. Jett Lauck, *The Immigration Problem: A Study of American Immigration Conditions and Needs* (6th ed. rev.; New York: Funk and Wagnalls, 1926), p. 37. Hereafter cited as Jenks and Lauck, *Immigration Problem.*

39. Bureau of Immigration, *Annual Report, 1930*, pp. 212-216.

40. *Ibid.*

41. Mimeographed tables of Immigration and Naturalization Service.

42. *Ibid.* 43. *Ibid.*

44. United States Department of Commerce: Bureau of the Census, *Statistical Abstract of the United States, 1951* (Washington: Government Printing Office, 1951), p. 97; hereafter cited as Bureau of the Census, *Statistical Abstract;* and Immigration and Naturalization Service, *Annual Report, 1958*, p. 46. The Immigration and Naturalization Service stopped keeping records of immigrants and emigrants according to race or nationality after 1952. This obviously makes it impossible to separate the various Yugoslav nationals after that date.

45. Bureau of the Census, *Statistical Abstract, 1958*, p. 96.

46. It is true that the Yugoslav immigrants today are not the same as those of yesteryear. Yet there are some newcomers who demonstrate all of the daring, love of adventure, and initiative of the earliest trail blazers. An example of the twentieth-century pilgrims are the three Zorovich brothers, Jakov, Kristo, and Gaudenzio, and their families, who in the spring of 1954 gambled with their lives in a sixty-foot sailboat on their long and perilous journey from the Adriatic to Miami, Florida.

CHAPTER 4

1. *Sixteenth Census, Country of Origin of the Foreign Stock*, pp. 9-10.

2. *Ibid.*

3. United States Department of Commerce: Bureau of the Census, *Sixteenth Census of the United States: 1940, Population*, Vol. II, *Characteristics of the Population* (Washington: Government Printing Office, 1943), p. 42. Hereafter cited as *Sixteenth Census, Characteristics of the Population.*

4. United States Department of Commerce: Bureau of the Census, *Sixteenth Census of the United States: 1940, Population, Nativity and Parentage of the White Population, Mother Tongue, By Nativity, Parentage, Country of*

*Origin, and Age* (Washington: Government Printing Office, 1943), p. 7. Hereafter cited as *Sixteenth Census, Mother Tongue.* 5. *Ibid.*

6. "Iseljenistvo," *Narodna Enciklopedija, Srpsko-Hrvatsko-Slovenačka,* II (Zagreb: Bibliografski Zavod, 1925), 51.

7. "Yugoslavs in U.S.," p. 97.

8. *Narodni Adresar,* pp. 909-911; and *The Jugoslavs* (New York: Jugoslav Center of Propaganda, 1921), p. 12. Adamic and Roucek also hold that the Croatian group is the largest, with the Slovenians second and the Serbians last.

9. United States Senate, *Miscellaneous, Senate Documents,* Seventieth Congress, Second Session, Senate Document No. 259 (Washington: Government Printing Office, 1930), p. 5.

10. *Hrvati u Americi* (Madrid: Osoba i Duh, 1953), p. 120.

11. *Sixteenth Census, Country of Origin of the Foreign Stock,* p. 11.

12. *Ibid.,* pp. 4, 11. 13. *Ibid.,* p. 4. 14. *Ibid.,* pp. 4, 11.

15. *Ibid.* 16. *Ibid.* 17. *Ibid.,* pp. 19-27.

18. *Sixteenth Census, Mother Tongue,* p. 11.

19. *Ibid.* 20. *Ibid.,* pp. 11-13.

21. *Sixteenth Census, Country of Origin of the Foreign Stock,* pp. 52-71.

22. *Sixteenth Census, Mother Tongue,* p. 27.

23. *Ibid.,* pp. 27-29. The census does not show any Croatians in California. There is no doubt, however, that many of them live in that state. Croatians from Dalmatia are to be found all along the coast from San Francisco to San Diego as well as in many of the cities and towns in the interior. The failure of the census to include them may perhaps be explained by the fact that Yugoslavs in California generally refer to themselves as "Slavonians" (another form of Slavs), and it may very well be that the census enumerators, unaware of this practice, grouped most of them under the classification of "Slovenians."

24. *Ibid.,* pp. 26-32. 25. *Ibid.,* pp. 33-35.

26. *Sixteenth Census, Country of Origin of the Foreign Stock,* pp. 14-17.

27. *Ibid.,* pp. 19-25. 28. *Ibid.,* pp. 25-41. 29. *Ibid.,* pp. 52-71.

30. *Sixteenth Census, Mother Tongue,* pp. 26-32.

31. *Narodni Adresar,* p. 909.

32. Francis J. Brown and Joseph S. Roucek (eds.), *Our Racial and National Minorities, Their History, Contributions, and Present Problems* (New York: Prentice-Hall, Inc., 1937), p. 248. Quoted by permission. Hereafter cited as Brown and Roucek, *Our Racial and National Minorities.*

33. "Jugo-Slavs in the United States," *Literary Digest,* LXI (June 7, 1919), 43.

34. Gaži, *op. cit.,* pp. 24, 43.

35. Marie S. Orenstein, "The Servo-Croats of Manhattan," *The Survey,* XXIX (December 7, 1912), 279.

36. Lois Rankin, "Detroit Nationality Groups," *Michigan History Magazine,* XXIII (Spring, 1939), 163-164.

37. *Ibid.,* p. 164.

38. Eleanor E. Ledbetter, *The Jugoslavs of Cleveland, with a Brief Sketch of Their Historical and Political Backgrounds* (Cleveland: The Mayor's Advisory War Committee, 1918), pp. 11-14.

39. *Sixteenth Census, Mother Tongue,* p. 33.

40. Luka M. Pejović, *Prikazi Naših Iseljenika* (Chicago: Luka M. Pejović, 1939), p. 20.

41. "Yugoslavs in the United States, a National Directory of Yugoslav Organizations, Institutions, and Business, Professional and Social Leaders," *Interpreter Releases,* XV (January 6, 1938), 2.

42. Billyana Niland, "Yugoslavs in San Pedro, California: Economic and Social Factors," *Sociology and Social Research*, XXVI (September-October, 1941), 37. Hereafter cited as Niland, "Yugoslavs in San Pedro."

CHAPTER 5

1. U.S. Immigration Commission, *Emigration Conditions*, p. 27.
2. *Ibid.*, p. 28.
3. *Jugoslavs in the United States*, p. 21.
4. U. S. Immigration Commission, *Abstracts*, I, 330-333.
5. *Narodni Adresar*, pp. 898-908.
6. *Immigration and Labor*, p. 19.
7. *Op. cit.*, pp. 112-113. Quoted by permission.
8. *Jugoslavs in the United States*, p. 19.
9. *Ibid.*
10. Frank Julian Warne, *The Slav Invasion and the Mine Workers: a Study in Immigration* (Philadelphia: J. B. Lippincott Co., 1904), *passim*.
11. John R. Commons, "Slavs in the Bituminous Mines of Illinois," *Charities*, XIII (December 3, 1904), 227.
12. Edward A. Ross, *The Old World in the New: the Significance of the Past and Present Immigration to the American People* (New York: The Century Co., 1914), p. 124. Hereafter cited as Ross, *The Old World in the New*.
13. "Wage Earners of Pittsburgh," *Charities and the Commons*, XXI (March 6, 1909), 1055. Commons made his study in 1908.
14. *Jugoslavs in the United States*, p. 19.
15. *Ibid.*, p. 20.
16. *Immigration Problem*, p. 101.
17. *The Valley of the Moon* (New York: Grosset and Dunlap, 1913), p. 363.
18. *Jugoslavs in the United States*, p. 27. 19. *Ibid.*, p. 28.
20. "River's End," *Woman's Home Companion*, LXVII (August, 1940), 53. Quoted by permission.
21. The many perils of the sea are symbolized in a single word used by the fishermen looking for work. They don't ask for a job but for a "chance." Nearly everything in the fishing industry is predicated on chance: the chance that you will come back with a pay load; the chance that you will come back with the equipment (a lost net may mean the loss of many thousands of dollars); the chance that you will come back uninjured; the chance that you *will come back*. The risks in fishing are so great that in California, for example, of over 200 marine insurance companies, not more than half a dozen will insure boats or crews.
22. *Cannery Row* (New York: The Viking Press, 1945), pp. 1-2. Quoted by permission.
23. Edwin F. Bamford, *Studies in Sociology*, Sociological Monograph No. 18, *Social Aspects of the Fishing Industry at Los Angeles Harbor*, V (Los Angeles: Southern California Sociological Society, University of Southern California, 1921), 1.
24. State of California, Department of Natural Resources, Division of Fish and Game: Bureau of Marine Fisheries, *The Commercial Fish Catch of California for the Years 1945 and 1946*, Fish Bulletin No. 67 (n.p. : California State Printing Office, 1947), p. 35.

25. *Ibid.*
26. *Narodni Adresar,* p. xviii.
27. *San Pedro News-Pilot,* July 27, 1946, p. 1.
28. "Ill Wind of the Western Seas," *Script,* XXX (November, 1947), 59.
29. *Jugoslavs in the United States,* p. 27.
30. Data based on author's personal investigation.
31. Hourwich, *Immigration and Labor,* p. 33.
32. *Races and Immigrants in America* (New York: The Macmillan Co., 1920), pp. 154-155.
33. Hourwich, *Immigration and Labor,* p. 456.
34. *Op. cit.,* pp. 110-111. Quoted by permission.
35. U. S. Immigration Commission, *Abstracts,* II, 89-157.
36. *Op. cit.,* p. 279.
37. Balch, *Slavic Citizens,* p. 305.
38. Philip Klein *et al., A Social Study of Pittsburgh: Community Problems and Social Services of Allegheny County* (New York: Columbia University Press, 1938), p. 74. Hereafter cited as Klein, *Social Study of Pittsburgh.*
39. *Ibid.,* p. 77.
40. Although the bankers paid the depositors no interest at all, they themselves often realized a handsome profit by reinvestment. A Croatian banker in Chicago, for example, drew 2 per cent on $14,000 left by 220 depositors. Prior to the panic of 1907 he generally had from $70,000 to $90,000 of such funds available, and the aggregate handled during a year easily reached $500,000. United States Immigration Commission, *Immigrant Banks,* Sixty-first Congress, Second Session, Vol. 63, Senate Document No. 381 (Washington: Government Printing Office, 1911), p. 51.
41. *Ibid.,* p. 11.
42. Not all of these self-styled bankers were as modest as the man from Missouri. One Croatian saloonkeeper prominently displayed in his window the sign *Narodna Banka* (national bank). When questioned about it, he explained that he wanted to convey the fact that he was a correspondent of the Croatian National Bank. *Ibid.,* p. 40.
43. *Ibid.,* p. 93. 44. *Ibid.,* p. 100. 45. *Ibid.* 46. *Ibid.*
47. The steamship agents were in a very competitive business, and to stay in it they had to be clever and resourceful. In order to solicit trade they often circulated guide books for prospective passengers. These guides are quite revealing, as the following passage illustrates: "Preeminently the plan of voyage must be prepaid well in advance, the indispensable ship ticket must be purchased, and a person who shall safely guide must be provided for— one who shall wait at the railway and ship depots, who can afford protection against extortion of vicious beguilers, and who points out the way, lest the countryman, especially he who does not speak English, expose himself to the danger of losing his passage, because all the tickets for the ship just about to sail have been purchased by others, so that he is compelled to tarry for weeks and squander the bit of money saved for his sustenance or to fall into the hands of unconscientious swindlers, cheaters, and thieves who will rob him of everything before he gets on board ship. And especially do I recommend to my esteemed countrymen to turn to me for ship tickets for the reason that I take under my supervision, upon arrival here in New York, the passengers of those of my countrymen who come on tickets which have been bought of me. My man will wait for him at the depot here and will conduct him to my office. In order to find one another I shall send to each of my honorable countrymen a green button, with inscription, which he is to put in the buttonhole of his coat in a visible place when he arrives, and from which he will be easily recog-

nized by my representative, or directed by the policeman upon request. My representative will take with him the original letter written to me by my honored countryman who wishes to travel, and will show the same. It can be positively recognized from this as to who my genuine representative is. There are many fake agents and fraudulent guides, also, who by using my name, take charge of, cheat, and injure the passenger, but they have no letter to identify them." *Ibid.*, pp. 144-145.

48. *Ibid.*, p. 31.  49. *Ibid.*, p. 121.  50. *Ibid.*, p. 122.  51. *Ibid.*, p. 113.

52. Lazarevitch, *op. cit.*, p. 461.

53. Adamic, *A Nation of Nations*, p. 247.

54. Balch, *Slavic Citizens*, p. 304.

55. Louis Adamic, *Two Way Passage* (New York: Harper and Brothers, 1941), p. 51.  Quoted by permission.

56. U. S. Immigration Commission, *Immigrant Banks*, p. 80.

57. *Ibid.*, p. 85.  58. *Ibid.*

59. Adamic, *Two Way Passage*, p. 53.

60. "The Decrease of Immigrant Remittances," *Interpreter Releases*, IX (August 3, 1932), 164.

61. *The Review of Economic Statistics*, I (Cambridge: Harvard Economic Society, 1919), 230-232.

62. "Immigrant Remittances," *Interpreter Releases*, IX, 164.

63. *Immigration Problem*, p. 16.

64. *Narodni Glasnik* (Pittsburgh), January 6, 1943, p. 3.

65. *AARY News*, October 30, 1947 (Mimeographed sheet prepared by the American Association for Reconstruction in Yugoslavia, New York).

## CHAPTER 6

1. Kenneth D. Miller, *Peasant Pioneers: an Interpretation of the Slavic Peoples in the United States* (New York: Council of Women for Home Missions and Missionary Education Movement, 1925), p. 92.  Hereafter cited as Miller, *Peasant Pioneers*.

2. *Zajedničar* (Pittsburgh), August 18, 1949, p. 12.

3. *Jugo-Slav Review*, III (July 15, 1919), 1-2.

4. Borivoe B. Mirkovitch, "Les Yougoslaves aux Etats-Unis," *Les Annales Politiques et Littéraires*, LXXXVI (November 7, 1925), 498.

5. *Slovenian Review*, I (October 15, 1917), 4.

6. United States Senate, *Senate Documents*, Vol. X, *Treaty of Peace with Germany: Hearings before the Committee on Foreign Relations, United States Senate*, Sixty-sixth Congress, First Session, Document No. 106 (Washington: Government Printing Office, 1919), pp. 1091-1093.

7. *Chicago Tribune*, March 11, 1915, p. 1.

8. George Pirinsky, *Slavic Americans in the Fight for Victory and Peace* (New York: American Slavic Congress, 1946), pp. 6, 11.

9. United Committee of South-Slavic Americans, *The Bulletin*, IV (September, 1946), 3.

10. Rankin, *op. cit.*, p. 168.

11. Miljevic, *op. cit.*, pp. 361, 363.

12. Pejović, *op. cit.*, p. 23.

13. United States House of Representatives Committee on Un-American Activities, *Guide to Subversive Organizations and Publications*, Eighty-second Congress, First Session, House Document No. 137 (Washington: Government

Printing Office, 1951), p. 25. Hereafter cited as Committee on Un-American Activities, *Guide.*

14. *The Slavic American,* II (Fall, 1948), 11-13, 39ff.

15. Committee on Un-American Activities, *Guide,* p. 66.

16. *Ibid., passim.* 17. *Ibid.,* Appendix, p. 11.


CHAPTER 7

1. *My America, 1929-1938* (New York: Harper and Brothers, 1938), p. 238. Quoted by permission.

2. Yaroslav J. Chyz, "Number, Distribution and Circulation of the Foreign-Language Press in the United States," *Interpreter Releases,* XX (October 13, 1945), 290.

3. *Ibid.*

4. Miller, *Peasant Pioneers,* p. 98.

5. Letter dated February 22, 1946, to author.

6. Miller, *Peasant Pioneers,* p. 98.

7. *The Immigrant Press and its Control* (New York: Harper and Brothers, 1922), p. 84. Hereafter cited as Park, *Immigrant Press.*

8. "The Foreign-Language Press," *Fortune,* XXII (November, 1940), 90.

9. Letter to author.

10. Park, *Immigrant Press,* p. 9.

11. *Ibid.,* p. 11.

12. "The Oppression Paychosis and the Immigrant," *Annals of the American Academy of Political and Social Science,* XCIII (January, 1921), 143.

13. Miller, *Peasant Pioneers,* p. 99.

14. "Foreign-Language Press," *Fortune,* XXII, 91.

15. Adamic, *My America,* p. 240.

16. "Foreign-Language Press," *Fortune,* XXII, p. 90. Actually the circulation of *Hrvatski Svijet* was at the time 17,300.

17. Bjankini, "Yugoslavs in U. S.," p. 98.

18. *Ibid.*

19. Park, *Immigrant Press,* p. 313.

20. Roucek, "Yugoslav Immigrants," p. 608.

21. *Immigrant Press,* p. 273. 22. *Ibid.,* p. 342.

23. Although during these recent years the balance has generally been tipped in favor of American developments over European, such has not always been the case. There have been times, during the war and the reconstruction period immediately following, when European events held the center of the stage. With the increasing stabilization of conditions abroad, however, the trend is shifting once more.

24. "Foreign-Language Press," *Fortune,* XXII, 91.

25. *Ibid.,* p. 104.

26. Brown and Roucek, *One America,* p. 371.

27. *Immigrant Press,* p. 121.

28. *Amerikanski Slovenec,* February 5, 1946, p. 4.

29. Park, *Immigrant Press,* p. 121.

30. *Ibid.* 31. *Ibid.* 32. *Ibid.,* p. 132.

33. June 30, 1949, p. 1. 34. June 22, 1949, p. 6.

35. *Laughing in the Jungle: the Autobiography of an Immigrant in America* (New York: Harper and Brothers, 1932), p. 108.

36. Committee on Un-American Activities, *Guide,* p. 148.

37. *Ibid., passim.* 38. June 30, 1949, p. 2.

39. United States Senate, *Brewing and Liquor Interest and German and Bolshevik Propaganda*, Sixty-sixth Congress, First Session, Vol. I, Senate Document No. 62 (Washington: Government Printing Office, 1919), p. 640.

40. *Ibid.* 41. *Ibid.*, p. 644. 42. *Ibid.*, pp. 621-622.

43. Yaroslav J. Chyz, "The War and the Foreign-Language Press," *Common Ground*, III (Spring, 1943), 4.

44. Brown and Roucek, *One America*, p. 378.

45. "The War and the Foreign-Language Press," *Common Ground*, III, 7-8.

46. "Certain Issues of Special Interest to the Foreign-Born Voter in the Presidential Campaign Just Ended," *Interpreter Releases*, IX (November 9, 1932), 271.

47. *Hrvatski Kalendar*, 1945, p. 265.

48. Much valuable information on Don Niko was furnished the author by his widow, Mandica Gršković.

49. *My America*, p. 244.

50. March 24, 1949, p. 1. 51. March 30, 1949, p. 1.

52. *San Francisco Chronicle*, July 16, 1925, p. 17.

53. *Ibid.*

54. "Foreign-Language Press," *Fortune*, XXII, 104.

55. *Op. cit.*, p. 489.

56. Chyz, "The War and Foreign-Language Press," *Common Ground*, III, 4.

57. "What to Do with Foreign Press Puzzles Officials," *Advertising Age*, XIII (April 20, 1942), 25.

58. "Foreign-Language Press," *Fortune*, XXII, 104.

59. *Time*, XL (July 13, 1942), 64.

60. Brown and Roucek, *One America*, p. 384.

## CHAPTER 8

1. *Immigration: Select Documents and Case Records* (Chicago: University of Chicago Press, 1924), pp. 604-605.

2. *Ibid.*, pp. 722-723. 3. *Ibid.*, pp. 789-793. 4. *Ibid.*, pp. 793-797.

5. Davie, *op. cit.*, p. 474. The writer himself, having frequently served in the capacity and observed others, can bear witness to the incompetency of many of the interpreters.

6. U. S. Immigration Commission, *Abstracts*, II, 163.

7. National Commission on Law Observance and Enforcement, *Report on Crime and the Foreign Born* (Washington: Government Printing Office, 1931), p. 168.

8. *Ibid.*, p. 415. 9. *Ibid.*, p. 416.

10. U. S. Immigration Commission, *Abstracts*, II, 163-211.

11. "The New Pittsburghers: Slavs and Kindred Immigrants in Pittsburgh," *Charities and the Commons*, XXI (January 2, 1909), 544. Hereafter cited as Roberts, "The New Pittsburghers."

12. *Ibid.*, p. 545.

13. "Yugoslavs and Criminality," *Sociology and Social Research*, XXV (September-October, 1940), 29.

14. *Ibid.*, p. 30. 15. *Ibid.* 16. *Ibid.*, pp. 30-31.

17. Roberts, "The New Pittsburghers," p. 540.

18. Dobroslav Sorić, *Spomen Knjiga Zlatnog Jubileja Rimokatoličke Crkve Sv. Nikola* (Pittsburgh: Dobroslav Sorić, 1944), p. 7.

19. U. S. Immigration Commission, *Abstracts*, I, 425.

20. *Ibid.* 21. *Ibid.*

22. Orenstein, *op. cit.*, pp. 279-280.

23. Jenks and Lauck, *Immigration Problem*, p. 141.

24. Roberts, "The New Pittsburghers," p. 546.

25. Peter Roberts, "The Sclavs in Anthracite Coal Communities," *Charities*, XIII (December 3, 1904), 220. Hereafter cited as Roberts, "The Sclavs in Anthracite Coal Communities," *Charities*.

26. Rankin, *op. cit.*, XXIII, 169.

27. *Ibid.*

28. *Sixteenth Census, Country of Origin of the Foreign Stock*, p. 99.

29. *Ibid.*

30. Eleanor E. Ledbetter, "My Serbian Christmas," *The Survey*, XLIX (December, 1922), 308-309.

31. Alice L. Sickels, *Around the World in St. Paul* (Minneapolis: University of Minnesota Press, 1945), p. 195.

32. "Americanization of the Croats in St. Louis, Mo., during the Past Thirty Years" (M. A. Thesis, St. Louis University, 1936), pp. 42-43.

33. Edward A. Ross, "The Slavs in America," *The Century Magazine*, LXXXVIII (August, 1914), 591.

34. *Ibid.*

35. Adamic, *Laughing in the Jungle*, p. 107.

36. "The Sclavs in Anthracite Coal Communities," *Charities*, XII, 219.

37. Adamic, *Laughing in the Jungle*, p. 107; and Gaži, *op. cit.*, pp. 41-42.

38. Louis Adamic, "The Yugoslav Speech in America," *The American Mercury*, XII (November, 1927), 319.

39. *Ibid.*

40. There are many amusing anecdotes concerning the Yugoslav and his language difficulties in America. One of the more popular ones relates the experience of a newly-arrived Croat sent to buy a colander. Entering a small neighborhood store, he was greeted smilingly by the proprietor and asked what he wanted. Not knowing the English name of the article, the much-embarrassed immigrant thought for a moment and then stammeringly replied, "Give me macaroni stop, water go." He got what he wanted.

41. Louis Adamic, *What's Your Name?* (New York: Harper and Brothers, 1942), p. 18.

42. "Surnames in the United States," *The American Mercury*, XXVI (June, 1932), 227.

43. *Ibid.* 44. *Ibid.*, p. 228. 45. *Ibid.*

46. *What's Your Name?*, p. 47.

47. Balch, *Slavic Citizens*, p. 412. The Americanization of Yugoslav names has not been without its lighter side. Among the twice-told tales is that of one Vlković, who in rapid succession changed his name to Wilkins and then to Williams. Asked by the judge to explain the second alteration, the alien answered, "When someone asks me what my name was before I changed it to Williams, I can truthfully say it was Wilkins."

48. *Fifteenth Census, General Report Statistics by Subject*, p. 1315.

49. *Ibid.* Unfortunately, the 1940 census does not refine the figures for illiteracy so as to differentiate between peoples or foreign nationals, but gives them instead according to major races: White, Negro, Japanese, and Chinese.

50. Gabro Karabin, "Honorable Escape," *Scribner's Magazine*, CLL (December, 1937), 40.

51. *Peasant Pioneers*, p. 134.

52. *Ibid.*, pp. 134-135.

53. *Almanak i Statistika Južnih Slavena u Sjedinjenim Državama Sjeverne Amerike* (Chicago: Jugoslav Dictionary and Almanac Publishing Co., 1926), p. 199.

54. "Yugoslavs in U. S.," p. 97.

55. Robert J. Kerner (ed.), *Yugoslavia*, The United Nations Series (Berkeley: University of California Press, 1949), p. 143.

56. Marija Pomagaj Župnija, *Spominska Knjiga, 1895-1945* (Pueblo: Marija Pomagaj Župnija, 1945), n.p.

57. *30th Anniversary* (Chicago: Holy Trinity Croatian Church and School, 1945), n.p.

58. Rev. Milan Brkich, "A Record Success of the Children's Camp at Libertyville," *The Serbian Orthodox Herald*, I (August, 1945), 5-6.

59. *Peasant Pioneers*, p. 35.

60. Brown and Roucek, *One America*, p. 161.

61. Archimandrite Georgije Kodzić, "Prva Srpska Crkva u Americi," *Spomenica Pedesetovo Dišnjice od Osnivanja Prvog Srpkog Saveza Srpskog Pravoslavnog Saveza Srbobrana, 1901-1951*, ed. by Nikola J. Vurdela and Sava N. Vujinović (Pittsburgh: Srpski Narodni Savez, 1951), p. 68. Hereafter cited as *Spomenica Srpskog Narodnog Saveza.*

62. Bishop Nikolai, "Father Sebastian Dabovich," *Spomenica Srpskog Narodnog Saveza*, pp. 193-197.

63. Gaži, *op. cit.*, p. 35.

64. *Ibid.*, pp. 35-36. 65. *Ibid.*, p. 36.

66. Reverend Bosiljko Bekavac, "Povijest Hrvastske Župe u Millvale, Pa.," *Hrvatski List i Danica Koledar, 1930* (New York: Hrvatski List i Danica, 1930), p. 216.

67. Letter of Rev. Teofil Pehar, St. Joseph's Croatian Church, St. Louis, Missouri, December 18, 1946, to author.

68. Letter of Rev. Victor Tomc, St. Mary's Slovenian Church, Cleveland, Ohio, January 24, 1946, to author.

69. Letter of Rev. Miodrag Mijatovich, Serbian Orthodox Church Ravanica, Detroit, Michigan, December 17, 1945, to author.

70. Letter dated February 7, 1946, to author.

71. "The Old Alien by the Kitchen Window," *The Saturday Evening Post*, CCXIII (July 6, 1940), 45.

72. Brown and Roucek, *Our Racial and National Minorities*, p. 656.

73. *Fifteenth Census, General Report Statistics by Subject*, p. 407.

74. *Ibid.*, p. 406.

75. *Sixteenth Census, Country of Origin of the Foreign Stock*, p. 81.

76. Immigration and Naturalization Service, *Annual Report, 1958*, p. 78.

77. *Social Study of Pittsburgh*, p. 258.

78. *Ibid.*

79. Miller, *Peasant Pioneers*, p. 106.

80. *Ibid.*, pp. 105-106.

81. Mary E. McDowell, "The Struggle in the Family Life," *Charities*, XIII (December 3, 1904), 197.

82. Emilian Glocar, *A Man from the Balkans*, trans. Fern Long (Philadelphia: Dorrance and Co., 1942), p. 32.

## CHAPTER 9

1. John J. O'Neill, *Prodigal Genius: The Life of Nikola Tesla* (New York: Ives Washburn, Inc., 1944).

2. The original name of the family seems to have been "Draganić." Nikola Trbojevich, "Life of Nikola Tesla," *Spomenica Srpskog Narodnog Saveza*, p. 170.

3. Slavko Bokšan, *Nikola Tesla und sein Werk* (Vienna: 1932).

4. Trbojevich, *op. cit.*, p. 170.

5. *Ibid.*, p. 172.

6. Quoted by Pauline Klopacka, "Nikola Tesla," *"The Slavic American*, I (Winter, 1947), 4.

7. *Ibid.*

8. Leland I. Anderson, "Nikola Tesla—Last of the Pioneers?" *Journal of Engineering Education*, XLIX (June, 1959), 969.

9. *Ibid.*, 967.   10. *Ibid.*, 968.

11. In 1956 the Nikola Tesla Museum in Belgrade, undoubtedly spurred on by the Tesla Centenary celebrations throughout the world, published in English the anniversary volume entitled *Nikola Tesla, 1856-1943; Lectures— Patents—Articles.* Within the pages of this work are included five of the most important lectures delivered by Tesla in America and Europe, complete facsimile drawings and specifications of his major patents, and twenty-five articles on science and philosophy written by him between 1891 and 1917.

12. Michael Pupin, *From Immigrant to Inventor* (new ed.; New York: Charles Scribner's Sons, 1938).

13. Nikola Trbojevich, "Life of Michael Pupin," *Spomenica Srpskog Narodnog Saveza*, p. 176.

14. *From Immigrant to Inventor*, p. 35.

15. Milos Vujnovich, "Michael Pupin," *The Slavic American*, II (Fall, 1948), 27.

16. Pupin, *op. cit.*, p. 386.

17. Carey McWilliams, *Louis Adamic and Shadow America* (Los Angeles: Arthur Whipple, 1935).

18. Adamic, *Laughing in the Jungle, passim.*

19. Stanley J. Kunitz and Howard Haycraft (eds.), *Twentieth Century Authors: a Biographical Dictionary of Modern Literature* (New York: H. W. Wilson Company, 1942), p. 5.

20. *San Pedro News-Pilot*, September 4, 1951, p. 2.

21. Louis Adamic, "An Immigrant's America, *"The American Magazine,* CXVI (December, 1933), 84.

22. Maxine Block, *Current Biography: Who's Who and Why* (New York: H. W. Wilson Company, 1940), p. 575.   Hereafter cited as Block, *Current Biography.*

23. *Ibid.*

24. *The New Standard Encyclopedia of Art: Architecture, Sculpture, Painting, Decorative Arts* (New York: Garden City Publishing Company, 1939), p. 231.

25. Dorothy B. Gilbert (ed.), *Who's Who in American Art* (New York: R. R. Bowker Company, 1956), p. 323.

26. Block, *Current Biography*, p. 576.

27. *Chicago Sunday Tribune, Grafic Magazine*, July 10, 1949, p. 5.

28. *Time*, XLVIII (November 4, 1946), 92; and Letter of Nick Bez, Seattle, Washington, October 13, 1959, to author.

29. *Time*, XLVIII, 94.

30. Clayton Fritchey, "Cleveland's Humble Hercules," *Common Ground,*
III (Spring, 1941), 20-24.
31. Adamic, *A Nation of Nations,* p. 243.
32. *Ibid.,* p. 245.
33. *Op. cit.,* p. 20.
34. *The National Cyclopaedia of American Biography, G* (New York:
James T. White and Company, 1946), 525-526.
35. *Current Biography: Who's Who and Why* (New York: H. W. Wilson
and Company, 1947), pp. 327-329.
36. *Newsweek,* XXV (January 8, 1945), 88.
37. *Official Congressional Directory,* Eighty-sixth Congress, First Session
(Washington: Government Printing Office, 1959), p. 123. Hereafter cited as
*Congressional Directory.*
38. Edward Falkowski, "John A. Blatnik, Mesabi Congressman," *The
Slavic American,* I (Summer, 1948), 14-15, 22, *et seq.*
39. *Congressional Directory,* p. 79.
40. Falkowski, *op. cit.,* I, 28.
41. Letter of Matthew Cvetic, Hollywood, California, September 9, 1959,
to author.
42. Matt Cvetic and Pete Martin, "I Posed as a Communist for the FBI,"
*Saturday Evening Post,* CCXXIII (July 15, 22, 29, 1950), 17, 34, 30, *et seq.*
43. *The Frank Yankovic Story.* An advertising brochure without name
of author, place of publication, publisher, or pagination.
44. *The American Weekly,* July 31, 1949, p. 20.
45. Letter of Frank Yankovic, South Euclid, Ohio, August 25, 1959, to
author.
46. *American Weekly,* July 31, 1949, p. 20.


CHAPTER 10

1. Adamic, *A Nation of Nations,* p. 6.
2. Allen H. Eaton, *Immigrant Gifts to American Life: Some Experiments
in Appreciation of the Contributions of our Foreign-Born Citizens to American
Culture* (New York: Russell Sage Foundation, 1932), p. 28.
3. *The Old World in the New,* pp. 202-203.
4. *The Frontier in American History* (New York: Henry Holt and Company, 1920), p. 264.
5. Eaton, *op. cit.,* pp. 28-29.
6. *Laughing in the Jungle,* p. ix.
7. *Op. cit.,* pp. 4-5.
8. Adamic, *A Nation of Nations,* p. 24.
9. *National Cyclopaedia,* XXIV, 39.
10. Block, *Current Biography,* p. 575.
11. *Narodni Glasnik,* January 7, 1949, p. 3.
12. "Yugoslav-American Artists Recently in the News," *Yugoslav Review,*
I (May, 1952), 9.
13. *Ibid.*
14. *Newsweek,* XXXIV (July 11, 1949), 72.
15. *Time,* XL (December 28, 1942), 59.
16. Lazarevitch, *op. cit.,* p. 461.
17. Adamic, *A Nation of Nations,* p. 247.

# Appendix I

## HISTORICAL BACKGROUND

THE TERMS *Yugoslavia* (land of the South Slavs) and *Yugoslaveni* (South Slavs) are comparatively recent creations, although both the country and people date from ancient times. During the early historical period that section of the Balkan Peninsula now occupied by the Yugoslavs formed a part of the so-called Illyrian state. In his monumental history Herodotus makes frequent allusions to Illyria and its inhabitants.[1]* The Illyrian kingdom, established in the second and third centuries B.C., extended along the eastern shore of the Adriatic from Rijeka (Fiume) to Drač (Durazzo) and inland as far as the Danube and the Serbian rivers Timok and Vardar, territory subsequently occupied by Serbia, Montenegro, Dalmatia, Bosnia, Hercegovina, Croatia, Slavonia, and Albania.[2]

Illyria did not long remain intact. In 229 B.C. the Greeks and Romans carved out a sizable portion of the country for themselves. Slavs from Galicia began to invade the unfortunate kingdom in the fifth century A.D. Thus in the course of time the ethnical character of the Illyrians was considerably modified.[3]

The primordial home of the Slavs, according to reliable modern scholarship, was the region northeast of the Carpathian Mountains, in the upper basins of the Western Bug, Pripet, and the Dniester rivers—what is now northeastern Poland and northwestern Russia.[4] There they long lived as a simple agricultural people, organized along tribal lines and worshiping pagan deities. However, when the Roman Empire in the West fell apart and the German barbarians poured across the borders, the Slavs, too, were stimulated to leave their homeland and to settle in the rich dominions of the Caesars.[5] Thus in the sixth and seventh centuries

* Notes to this chapter begin on page 311.

298

they moved west, south, and southwest, following in the footsteps of the Teutonic tribes. Before the end of the seventh century the Slavs were in possession of most of central and southeastern Europe. But as a result of these migrations and settlements and the subsequent incursions of Asiatic tribes, the Slavic family was divided into three distinct branches: (1) the Eastern Slavs or the Russians, later subdivided into Great Russians, Little Russians or Ukrainians, and the White Russians or Belo-Russians; (2) the Western Slavs, comprising the Poles, Slovaks, and Czechs; and (3) the Southern Slavs, composed of Slovenes, Croats, Serbs, and Bulgars.

The first of the South Slavs to make their appearance in the Balkans were the Croats and Serbs, who were reported along the coast of Salona in 536 and at Drač in 548. The Slovenes followed somewhat later. Pushing all resistance before them, the South Slavs inundated nearly all of the Balkan Peninsula by the end of the seventh century and drowned out the remnants of most of the nationalities that had been there before them.[6]

## SLOVENIA

After leaving their original home in northeastern Europe, the Slovenes in 627 joined in the formation of a Czech-Slovene empire (West Slavic Kingdom) under Samo. This union was of short duration, for the empire rapidly crumbled after the death of Samo in 658. The Slovenes subsequently moved westward, most of them settling in the area they now occupy (then a part of the Frankish empire) in the first half of the eighth century. Coming under the influence of the German clergy in their new home, they presently adopted Christianity. But life was hard, filled with danger and tragic experiences. Concentrated in the northernmost provinces of the Balkans—Carniola, Styria, and Carinthia—they were subject to the constant pressure of the Franks, Magyars, and Germans. Their very survival is nothing short of phenomenal, or to use the words of a renowned writer on Balkan affairs: "That this tiny people, numbering a little over a million, could maintain itself through eleven centuries under such conditions, is one of the miracles of southeastern Europe." [7]

For several centuries after their arrival in the Balkans the Slovenes remained under the sovereignty of the Franks, namely the dukes of Bavaria and Friuli. Following the dissolution of the Frankish empire, they broke away from the Franks and sought to lead an independent existence. In 952 they were instrumental in the creation of the Duchy of Carantania, which embraced most of the Slovenes and in a sense may be called a "Slovenia." Had they been unmolested in Carantania, they might have been able to establish a stable and prosperous state. But they were not. They became a prize which was fought over by the Magyars, Czechs, and Germans.[8] After much strife the unfortunate Slovenes in 1278 fell under the direct control of the Austrian Habsburgs, where they remained until the end of World War I, with the exception of the period 1809-1813, when they formed a part of the Napoleonic kingdom of Illyria.

Under the Habsburgs the Slovenes were subjected to feudal bondage and Germanization.[9] The free Slovenian peasants were forced into serfdom by German nobles and clergymen, leading to numerous peasant uprisings. The small Slavic minority seemed to be forgotten by its German overlord. For centuries there were no Slovenian schools or books, and it appeared as if the Slovenes would lose their national identity. However, so it was not to be, for in spite of all obstacles they managed to survive.

## CROATIA

The earliest Croats in the Balkans settled on the shores of the Adriatic and established their own community in the district directly north of Zadar (Zara). At that time they were organized and ruled as tribes by *župani*, or tribal chieftains.[10] But like their kinsmen, the Slovenes, the Croats, too, were absorbed into the Frankish empire. In the Frankish realm they came into contact with a more advanced civilization, which led to a modification of their culture, including the abandonment of paganism in favor of Christianity.

When the Frankish empire weakened and finally collapsed after the death of the brilliant ruler Charlemagne in 814, Slavs in all sections of the kingdom revolted. After much warring the Croats finally freed themselves from the Franks in the second half of the ninth century, only to fall prey to Byzantine conquest in 877. Byzantine control was speedily ended by a successful insurrection in 910, and an independent Croat state was promptly established. The first Croatian king was Tomislav, who, during his reign from 910 to 928, greatly reduced the earlier tribal anarchy and began the centralization of authority. To insure a stable government and discourage foreign invasion a strong army and navy were organized and maintained. The possession of a fleet also meant that the Croats were in a position to challenge the Italians on the sea, and thus there began an endless Slav-Latin conflict over the Adriatic.[11]

In the second half of the eleventh century the Croats occupied as their homeland the coast of Dalmatia and about half of modern

Yugoslavia. Their ruler at this time was King Petar Krešimir IV (1058-1074). Under this highly individualistic and despotic monarch Croatia rose again to great heights of political power.[12] Following his death, however, the kingdom quickly broke up. The throne fell vacant, and some of the Croat nobles called in King Ladislas I of Hungary, whose sister had been married to a member of the Croat ruling family. Ladislas placed the crown on the head of his nephew Almos. After an abbreviated reign of two years, Almos was succeeded by Petar Svačić, the last Croat national king. Petar's career, too, was cut short when he fell in battle in 1097. There followed a tragic period of anarchy and strife, which was ended only when King Koloman of Hungary defeated the Croats and compelled them to accept him as their sovereign in 1102. Shortly afterward a pact was drawn up whereby the Croat nobility promised to recognize Hungarian rule in exchange for protection and perpetuation of their rights.

The union with Hungary lasted four hundred years, but Croatia gradually became a vassal of Turkey. By 1526 Slavonia (the territory between the Drava and Sava rivers) and a part of Croatia were subjugated by the Turks, while the Habsburgs retained the rest. During this period the South Slav element in Croatia increased with the immigration of the Serbs who fled northward from the Turks. In 1687 both Croatia and Slavonia came under Hungarian control, remaining in that subordinate position to the end of World War I. Starting in 1868, both regions were granted a degree of autonomy. To facilitate administration of the provinces, however, Slavonia and Croatia were combined into a single unit in 1881.[13]

Nationalism made itself manifest early among the Slavs. To suppress this sentiment the Hungarian diet passed several laws, starting in 1830. As a consequence Magyar-Croat relations became strained and a series of serious disturbances followed.[14] This not only served to intensify the hatred between the two peoples but also aided the growth of national consciousness among the Slavs. A movement was soon initiated which aimed at the eventual union of all South Slavs.

Becoming alarmed at the growing menace of the Slavs, the Hungarian government suspended the Croatian constitution in April, 1912, and appointed Slavko Cuvaj, a Croat puppet, as dictator. Unsuccessful attempts were made to murder Cuvaj and Baron Ivan Škrlec, who became *ban* in November, 1913, upon the abolition of the dictatorship. The assassination of the Austrian archduke in 1914 was the final of a series of violent actions on the part of the radical Slavs.

301

## SERBIA

Among the South Slavs the Serbs were the last to form a state.[15] Little is known about the early Serbs, except that they lived for a time in Galicia, near the source of the Dniester, and then, after crossing the Danube in the sixth century, gradually moved into the northwestern section of the Balkan Peninsula.[16] Like the Croats and Slovenes but for a much longer time, the Serbs were organized under tribal chieftains, *župani*. Formally under Byzantine rule, in practice they were almost fully independent.

Between the eighth and twelfth centuries the bulk of the Serbs were under the nominal sovereignty of either Greeks or Bulgars, who introduced them to the Orthodox faith and culture. As the foreigners sought to tighten their grip, the Serbs united under a *Veliki Župan,* or Grand Chieftain, to counteract this external control by increased centralization in government.[17] The *Veliki Župan* of Raška, Stevan Nemanja, made considerable progress in uniting the various clans and provinces under his rule in the latter part of the twelfth century, so as to earn for himself the title of "Founder of the Serbian Kingdom." With the Byzantine empire on the downgrade, Stevan was able to conquer lands to the south and thus lay the foundation for the future Serb kingdom. He made the Orthodox Church supreme and persecuted the Bogumili, who were forced into Bosnia.

Though this unity of the twelfth century was not always maintained the Serb state continued to grow under the succeeding Nemanjić rulers. During the reign of Stevan Nemanja II (1196-1223), St. Sava, the brother of the sovereign, received recognition by the patriarch as archbishop of all Serbia and as head of an autocephalous church, with its seat at Užice (later moved to Peć). Important territorial gains were made by Stevan Uroš II (1282-1321), who captured Usküb (Skoplje) in 1282 and gradually pushed into Macedonia, along the Adriatic, and in the north toward the Danube and Sava rivers. Stevan Uroš III (1321-1331) continued the expansion by the seizure of Prilep, Veles, Prošenik, and Ištip, following his crushing defeat of the Bulgars at Velebužde in 1330. These annexations gave the Serbs control of most of the Vardar Valley.

Serbia reached the zenith of its power and influence during the reign of Stevan Dušan. From his accession to the throne in 1331 to his death in 1355 he was the most feared and the most respected ruler in the Balkans. His one big ambition from the very beginning was to place the crown of Constantinople on his own head. The early years of his reign he spent in the conquest of Macedonia, Albania, Thessaly, and Epirus. By the time that he had completed these conquests he was powerful enough to proclaim himself "Tsar of the Serbs, Greeks, Bulgars, and Albanians." From 1349 to 1354 he was engaged in the compilation of the famous *Zakonik,* the first Serbian code of laws. With the stage fully set Stevan Dušan made ready for his great campaign against Constantinople in 1355. But en route to the city he suddenly died, and with him perished his scheme for the consolidation of the Balkans.[18]

Following the death of the mighty Dušan, the Serbian empire rapidly disintegrated and broke up into petty, mutually jealous principalities, thus paving the way for foreign conquest. After some years of intermittent fighting, the Turks in the fourteenth century overwhelmed the Bulgars and Serbs, inflicting a disastrous defeat upon their combined forces in 1389 at the historic Battle of Kosovo. Between 1389 and 1459 the Serbs paid tribute to the sultans, but had their own government, headed by the *despot.* The first such *despot,* Lazar II of the Hrebeljanović family, was succeeded in 1427 by his nephew George Branković, who worked for an alliance of Serbs, Bosnians, and Hungarians. However in 1437 the Turks attacked Serbia, and George had to take refuge in Hungary. Undismayed, he shortly afterwards organized an expedition against the Ottomans and, with the aid of a Hungarian leader, defeated the sultan's army at Kunovice in 1444. As a consequence the Turks relinquished the territory they had previously conquered, only, however, to reoccupy it fifteen years later.

During the subsequent period of nearly three hundred and fifty years Serbia was a Turkish state. But the national consciousness was never extinguished. It was kept alive with *pesme,* or folksongs, traditionally recited to the accompaniment of the one-stringed *gusle.* The *pesme* preserved the memory of famous Serbs and the struggles against the Turks, the legendary Marko Kraljević and the *hajduci,* guerrilla warriors who continued to fight the Turks from their mountain hide-outs. By the end of the eighteenth century many of the Serb leaders began to come into contact with foreign lands and ideas through trade. As a consequence, insurrections became more rife.[19] Successful uprisings in 1804, led by George Petrović (Kara George), and in 1817 brought recognition of autonomy in the Treaty of Adrianople in 1829. It was not until 1878 and the Treaty of Berlin that Serbia gained full independence, and not until 1882 that she was proclaimed a kingdom. Nevertheless, the country was not completely unrestricted in its actions, inasmuch as in 1881 she contracted with Austria-Hungary a ten-year alliance, pledging herself to make no political treaties without first getting the Viennese government's consent and to allow on her soil no political or religious agitation against the Dual Monarchy.

In 1885 King Milan, hoping to recoup his rapidly decreasing popularity by foreign conquest, led his kingdom into a war against Bulgaria. But the Bulgars proved too strong for the ill-prepared and badly-led Serbs, and only the timely intervention of Austria-Hungary saved Milan from total defeat. Although by the Treaty of Bucharest, which ended the hostilities in March, 1886, the *status quo ante bellum* was restored, Serbia's prestige suffered greatly.

Following a palace revolution in Belgrade in 1903 when the Austrophobe Karadjordjević family supplanted the Austrophile Obrenović dynasty, Serbia in 1905 attempted to sign with Bulgaria an agreement, which, it was hoped, would lead to a political alliance and common action in the Balkans. But Austria-Hungary, having her own plans and ambitions in the peninsula, intervened, vetoed Serbia's ratification of the agreement, and began a tariff war against her erstwhile ally.

Relations between Serbia and the Dual Monarchy continued to deteriorate. When in 1908 the Habsburgs annexed the provinces of Bosnia and Hercegovina, in violation of the provisions of the Treaty of Berlin, radicals in Serbia clamored for war. A year later, however, Serbia, acting on the advice of Russia with whom she had reached a *rapprochement* following the accession to the throne of the pro-Russian Peter I in 1903, recognized the annexation as a *fait accompli*. During the Balkan wars in 1912-1913 Austria-Hungary assumed a most hostile attitude toward the Serbs. First, she forced them to give up a number of coastal towns which they had captured from the Turks. Then, in order to prevent them from gaining an outlet to the sea, she obtained the approval of the Great Powers for the creation of an autonomous Albanian state. Finally, when the Serbs obtained new spoils as a result of the war against Bulgaria in 1913, the Habsburgs decided that their Slavic adversary must be crushed. Because of the protests of Italy and Germany, however, the decision was postponed—for a year.

## MONTENEGRO

Crnagora, or Montenegro (Black Mountain) as it was named by the Italians and as it is called by non-Slavs, was originally the province of Zeta, and formed a part of the Serbian state until the collapse of Serbia in 1389 at Kosovo.[20] Constant attacks by the Turks in the years that followed finally extinguished the independence of Zeta in 1499. The Ottomans, however, were never able to subjugate completely the belligerent Montenegrins who found refuge in the inaccessible mountain strongholds. After three centuries of incessant warfare the sultan recognized their independence in 1799.[21]

Notable internal progress followed in the nineteenth century under the guidance of a series of capable leaders. Petar Petrović Njegoš, the great poet-ruler (1830-1851), founded new schools, brought in printing presses, and published the ballads in which the history of the country is recorded. Upon his accession in 1851 Danilo II dropped the old title of *vladika* and proclaimed himself prince, but his reforms proved unacceptable to the nobility and led to his assassination in 1860. His successor, Nicholas, did much to modernize the state and to elevate it to an important position among the lesser powers of Europe during his long reign from 1860 to 1918. He started many new schools and made education compulsory. He reorganized the army. In 1905 he granted his subjects a constitution which provided for an assembly elected by universal suffrage. For increased prestige he assumed the title of king in 1910. Despite the liberal reforms Nicholas ruled as an absolute monarch until he was deposed in November, 1918, and Montenegro joined the new state of Yugoslavia.[22]

## DALMATIA

Dalmatia, populated chiefly by Croats, changed overlords many times.[23] Until the twelfth century it remained a part of the independent state of Croatia, falling at that time together with its parent under Hungarian control. In the fifteenth century some of its coast towns and islands were seized by the Venetians, while the interior was taken over by the Turks. After three centuries of strife Venice, by 1718, succeeded, with the aid of Austria, Poland, and Russia, in gathering under its wing all coastal Dalmatia, excluding the independent republic of Dubrovnik (Ragusa).[24] In 1797 Napoleon Bonaparte, concluding a successful campaign against the Habsburgs in northern Italy, handed over Dalmatia to the Austrians to compensate them for losses in other areas. But in 1805, after the Austrians had once more risen against the French general and had been defeated, the province was transferred to the puppet kingdom of Italy. Four years later Napoleon incorporated Dalmatia into his short-lived Illyrian Provinces. The Congress of Vienna in 1814 placed the hapless Dalmatians, including the Ragusans, under the Habsburgs, where they remained until 1918.

## BOSNIA AND HERCEGOVINA

The early history of the regions known as Bosnia and Hercegovina is extremely obscure.[25] It is believed that Slavic tribes occupied these provinces about the same time that they settled in

305

other Balkan lands, and for hundreds of years led a primitive existence in their mountain abode.

With the establishment of the Croat kingdom in the tenth century Bosnia became a part of that monarchy and remained under its sovereignty for some two hundred years. Then in the middle of the twelfth century Bosnia was conquered by the Magyars, but because of the character of the country complete control could not be maintained. Under the guidance of such leaders as *Ban* Kulin (1180-1204) the Bosnians enjoyed virtual independence. Bosnia's sister province Hercegovina, then known as Hum or Hom, was a part of Serbia until 1325, when it was conquered by the Bosnian ruler.

Led by *Ban* Kotromanić (1322-1353) the Bosnians finally overthrew Hungarian sovereignty and, in a series of wars with Hungary, Croatia, Venice, and Serbia, laid the foundation for an independent kingdom. The little state reached the high tide of its development during the reign of *Ban* Stevan Tvrtko I (1353-1391), who proclaimed himself king about 1377, and considerably expanded Bosnian possessions by defeating Raška, Croatia, and Dalmatia. After the death of Tvrtko the kingdom was divided by the endless feuds of the nobility. This undoubtedly hastened the Turkish conquest of the country in 1463.

Under the Turks a large number of the nobility, especially the Bogumili landlords, adopted the Moslem faith, and thereby retained their lands, but the more devout Christians fled northwards into Hungary, westwards into Dalmatia, or southwards into the hills of Montenegro. Surrendering themselves completely to the Turks, the converted Bogumili landlords were granted many special privileges, with the result that they lost nearly all sense of unity with the other South Slavs. The Christian peasants, on the other hand, were bitter and discontented because of their virtual enslavement.

Nevertheless, both peasant and landlord of Bosnia and Hercegovina remained under Ottoman rule for some four hundred years.[26] During that time they have practically no history apart from the Turkish empire. The oppression of the sultan led to numerous revolts. One of the more serious of these, occurring in 1875 and causing the Serbo-Turkish and Russo-Turkish wars of 1876-1878, ended in the occupation of Bosnia and Hercegovina by Austria-Hungary. In 1908 occupation turned into annexation.

## South Slav Unity

Although the South Slavs had dreamed of union for centuries, it was not until the revolutionary year of 1848 that the idea of such unity began to assume concrete form.[27]   It was in that year that Serbia helped Croatia rebel against Hungary, though the effort was in vain.   Serbia, aside from little Montenegro, was for many years the only free Balkan state, but the Treaty of Berlin in 1878 made Serbia helpless politically, and the idea of a Yugoslavia seemed doomed.   Bosnia and Hercegovina were at this time Turkish provinces under Austrian control; Croatia was ruled by Hungary; and Dalmatia acknowledged Austria's sovereignty.

Despite the unpromising outlook the South Slavs continued to hold on to the idea of Yugoslavia, encouraged and led by members of the intelligentsia like Bishop Josip Strosmajer.   Especially active in the cause of unity were the South Slavs in Austria-Hungary. About 1878 the Croats and the Serbs in the Dual Monarchy established the Croatian Progressive party and the Independent Serb party.   The Serbo-Croat Coalition was organized in 1905.   With the blossoming of these organizations, Austria-Hungary, fearful of the consequences, began to cast about for means to suppress the mounting South Slav vigor.   She found her answer in the Sarajevo tragedy, and promptly declared war on Serbia.   But the Slavic idea was not to be crushed so easily, for Serbia turned to Russia for protection and received not only the support of that country but eventually of all of its allies.   Military resistance on the part of the South Slavs was not effectively possible, but many of their leaders escaped to Italy, France, and England, where they continued to propagandize in behalf of the South Slavic cause.

In the spring of 1915 the Yugoslav Committtee was formed in Rome (later transferred to London), led by Ante Trumbić, dynamic statesman from Dalmatia.   South Slavs in Dalmatia, Istria, Trieste, Bosnia, Carniola, and Hungary as well as those in North and South America received representation on the Committee.   Members of the Committee in the United States sought to coordinate the efforts of the American South Slavs in the promotion of the Yugoslav idea. In South America the Yugoslavs, chiefly Croats from Chile, formed a central organization at Antofagasta known as the National Defense, which contributed valuable financial aid.

On July 20, 1917, the representatives of the Serbian government and the leaders of the Serbo-Croatian Coalition met at Corfu.   The result of this historic meeting was the "Declaration of Yugoslav Independence" and the formulation of the "Great Charter of Liberties."   On October 1, 1918, Bulgaria having surrendered, the South Slav and Czech deputies of the Austrian diet declared that they themselves would decide their future state allegiance.   A few days later the National Council of the Slovenes, Croats, and Serbs, constituted at Ljubljana in August, 1918, was moved to Zagreb, and the South Slavs repudiated the Habsburg emperor's plan for federalization. Local committees in Dalmatia and Bosnia, expressing allegiance to the Council in Zagreb only, began to disarm troops coming back from the crumbling Balkan fronts. A Croat regiment took control of Rijeka on October 23, and five days later the National Council accepted the authority turned over to it by the military. On October 24 Croatia's independence from Hungary was declared by the Council and on October 29 followed the proclamation of independence of the remaining South Slavic subjects of the Habsburgs. The next month a resolution was passed at Zagreb uniting the former Austrian-controlled South Slav provinces with Montenegro and Serbia, and, on December 1, the delegates representing the Council invited Prince Alexander to act as regent and to proclaim the union.

## YUGOSLAVIA, A NEW NATION

Out of the variety of political regions a new nation was created: the Kingdom of Serbs, Croats, and Slovenes. In this new state were the formerly independent kingdoms of Serbia and Montenegro; the provinces of Bosnia and Hercegovina, formerly annexed territories of the Austro-Hungarian empire; Dalmatia, portions of Styria, Carniola, and part of Carinthia; Croatia-Slavonia, once a Hungarian province; portions of Baranja, Bačka, and the Banat of Temešvar, which had been a part of Hungary proper.[28]

The union of the provinces having been proclaimed, the first Yugoslav cabinet was formed in January, 1919. The Serbian politician Stojan Protić became premier, the Slovene clerical leader Father Anton Korošec, vice-premier, and the Dalmatian spokesman Trumbić, foreign minister.[29] From the beginning there was disagreement between federalist and centralist factions. The Croats, as well as a large fraction of the Slovene liberals, favored a system of federalism, while the Serbs led by Nikola Pašić, who replaced Protić as premier, and the Serbian Radical party desired a unitary and centralized state. Many Serbs, including the ambitious Alexander, looked upon Yugoslavia as an expansion of Serbia, and therefore wanted to dominate the entire administration.

The new constitution of June 28, 1921, particularly article 95, provided for a reorganization of the country into several regions, the boundaries of which would be determined in accordance with geographic, economic, and social conditions. In 1922 thirty-three such regions were formed by decree.

The constitution was centralist in character, the Croat Peasant party, led by Stjepan Radić, having capitulated to Pašić and his Serb followers. After refusing to participate in the government for several years, Radić entered the cabinet in 1925. Nevertheless, the bitter strife between Serb and Croat continued to hamper the efforts of the regime. Quarrels between Serbian and Croatian deputies in the legislative chamber at Belgrade were frequent, resulting eventually, in June, 1928, in the assassination of Radić and several of his friends.

This violent action led King Alexander to dissolve parliament early in 1929. Supported by the army, Alexander also suspended the constitution and proclaimed himself dictator. He changed the name of the state to Yugoslavia, in the hope, no doubt, of eliminating some of the dissension and opposition. For a time he personally appointed the ministers and all local officials, and exercised a rigorous press censorship, suppressing all dissent. The dictatorship was nominally ended in 1931 with the promulgation of a constitution, but the new instrument more than safeguarded the absolute powers of the sovereign, giving him control of the army and civil service as well as over the *Skupština*. During the next three years the ministry was all Serbian, with the Croats getting no representation at all.[30]

In 1934 the autocratic Alexander was assassinated at Marseilles, and his eleven-year-old son succeeded to the throne as Peter II. A regency was set up under Prince Paul, first cousin of the dead king. Under the regency the Alexandrian *diktatura* continued, though less stern in outlook, and not so relentless in carrying out policies.

### THE FEDERAL PEOPLE'S REPUBLIC OF YUGOSLAVIA

After pursuing an increasingly pro-Axis policy under Paul, especially after the outbreak of World War II in 1939, Yugoslavia finally openly joined the dictators by signing the Axis Tri-Partite Pact on March 25, 1941. This was more than the good people of Yugoslavia would tolerate, and so the opposition, led by a small group of military officers, two days later overthrew the regency and proclaimed Peter sovereign. The new government, however, was short-lived. The Nazis attacked the country on April 6, 1941, and within twelve days succeeded in conquering the country and forcing Peter and his government to flee into exile to London. Yugoslavia was subsequently divided into German, Italian, and Bulgarian occupation zones, and puppet regimes were established in Croatia and Serbia.[31]

Resistance to the Axis occupation forces soon passed into the hands of two groups of underground fighters, the Chetniks under the Serb General Draža Mihajlović, who supported the monarchy, and the Partisans under the Moscow-trained Croat Marshal Tito (Josip Broz), who demanded a new deal for all the Yugoslavs. To Mihajlović and his group, resistance represented a continuation of the anti-Axis struggle by the Yugoslav government, and the general himself became a member of the royal government-in-exile. Tito and his supporters, on the other hand, considered resistance an opportunity to fight the invaders as well as to launch a revolution against the prewar political, economic, and social order in Yugoslavia. As a result of the conflicting philosophies and aims, the Chetniks and Partisans were presently not only fighting against the Axis but also against each other, with the Tito men ultimately emerging triumphant.

In November, 1942, Tito established the National Committee of Liberation and the following year directed it to act as a provisional government, thus repudiating the Yugoslav London government. In the general elections of November 11, 1945, Tito's party scored an overwhelming victory. Convening on November 29, the new assembly abolished the monarchy and set up the Federal People's Republic of Yugoslavia. Tito became premier and won British and American recognition for his government on December 22. On January 31, 1946, a new constitution, patterned after that of the Soviets, was adopted.

With the organization of the administration and the creation of a strong central government, the new regime turned its attention to the problems of reconstruction. It early moved to stamp out the black market, stabilize the currency, restore communication and transportation, and increase industrial and mining production. On April 28, 1947, the parliament unanimously adopted a five-year plan calling for an expenditure of $5,566,000,000 for the industrialization and electrification of the country and the drainage of farm land. Simultaneously the nationalization of industry was undertaken, the process being completed by 1948.

During the first few years that he was in power Tito cooperated with the Soviet Union and the so-called people's democracies of eastern Europe, joining with them in the establishment of the Communist Information Bureau, popularly known as the Cominform. However, the honeymoon was hardly begun when Moscow assailed the Yugoslav leader as a traitor and expelled his state from the organization. The West, long engaged in a cold war with the Soviets, naturally welcomed a break in the Communist front and therefore responded favorably. American and British aid was promptly extended to the hard-pressed Yugoslavs.

310

Though Yugoslavia remained a Communist state after 1948, a number of subsequent developments confirmed the independent status of the Titoist regime. The process of land collectivization, which the Kremlin had sought to accelerate, was slowed down in order to pacify the rebellious peasantry. The Russo-like constitution of 1946 was amended in 1953 and new organs of government quite unlike those of the Soviet Union set up.

Following the death of Stalin in March, 1953, the new Soviet leaders sought to mend the rupture with Belgrade. Exchanges of visits between the heads of the two governments helped to ease some of the old tensions, but did not bring about complete reconciliation. A few threads remained to bind Yugoslavia to the West.

# NOTES TO APPENDIX I

1. *History*, trans. George Rawlinson, I (Everyman's edition; New York: E. P. Dutton and Company, 1927).

2. Milan Prelog, *Pregled Povijesti Južnih Slavena: Srba, Hrvata i Slovenaca*, 2 vols. (Sarajevo: B. Buchwald, 1922-1926).

3. Ferdinand Schevill, *The History of the Balkan Peninsula, from the Earliest Times to the Present Day* (New York: Harcourt, Brace and Company, 1922).

4. Samuel Hazzard Cross, *Slavic Civilization Through the Ages* (Cambridge: Harvard University Press, 1948), pp. 1-26; Leonid I. Strakhovsky (ed.), *A Handbook of Slavic Studies* (Cambridge: Harvard University Press, 1949), pp. 1-17; and Vlaho S. Vlahovic, *Two Hundred Fifty Million and One Slavs* (New York: Slav Publications, Inc., 1945). The best original sources on the subject are *Polnoe Sobranie Russkikh Letopisei*, which has been translated into English by the late Professor S. H. Cross (*The Russian Primary Chronicle*, Harvard University Press, 1930), and Lubor Niederle, *Slovanské Starožitnosti* (Prague: 1926).

5. Edward Gibbon, *Decline and Fall of the Roman Empire*, ed. J. B. Bury, 7 vols. (New York: The Macmillan Company, 1900-1902).

6. Anton Melik, *Zgodovina Srbov, Hrvatov i Slovencev*, 2 vols. (Ljubljana: Tiskovna Zadruga, 1919-1920); and Paul R. Radosavljevich, *Who Are the Slavs?*, 2 vols. (Boston: Richard G. Badger, 1919).

7. Stoyan Pribichevich, *World Without End: The Saga of Southeastern Europe* (New York: Reynal and Hitchcock, 1939), p. 33.

8. Franc Kos, *Gradivo za Zgodovino Slovencev v Srednjem Veku*, 4 vols. (Ljubljana: 1906-1928); and Louis Adamic, *My Native Land* (New York: Harper and Brothers, 1943).

9. Dragotin Lončar, *The Slovenes: a Social History, from the Earliest Times to 1910*, trans. A. J. Klancar (Cleveland: American-Jugoslav Printing and Publishing Company, 1939).

10. Vekoslav A. Klaić, *Povjest Hrvata od Najstarijih Vremena do Svršetka XIX Stoljeća*, 3 vols. (Zagreb: L. Hartman, 1899-1911).

11. Ferdo Šišić, *Hrvatska Povjest od Najstarijih Dana do Potkraj 1918,* 3 vols. (Zagreb: 1925).

12. John Buchan (ed.), *Yugoslavia,* The Nations of Today series (Boston: Houghton, Mifflin Company, 1923).

13. Josip Horvat, *Politička Povijest Hrvatske* (Zagreb: 1936).

14. R. W. Seton-Watson, *Racial Problems in Hungary* (London: Constable and Company, 1908); and R. W. Seton-Watson, *The Southern Slav Question in the Habsburg Monarchy* (London: Constable and Company, 1911).

15. Rebecca West, *Black Lamb and Grey Falcon, a Journey Through Yugoslavia* (one volume edition; New York: The Viking Press, 1943).

16. Konstantin J. Jireček, *Istorija Srba,* 4 vols. (Belgrade: 1923).

17. Harold W. V. Temperley, *History of Serbia* (London: G. Bell and Sons, 1919).

18. Neville Forbes, Arnold J. Toynbee, D. Mitrany, and D. G. Hogarth, *The Balkans: a History of Bulgaria, Serbia, Greece, Rumania, and Turkey* (Oxford: The Clarendon Press, 1915).

19. R. W. Seton-Watson, *The Rise of Nationality in the Balkans* (London: Constable and Company, 1917).

20. Francis Stevenson, *A History of Montenegro* (London: Jarrold and Sons, 1912).

21. G. M. Towle, *A Brief History of Montenegro* (Boston: J. R. Osgood and Company, 1897).

22. Nikola Djonović, *Crna Gora pre i posle Ujedinjenja* (Belgrade: Biblioteka Politika, 1939).

23. Lujo Vojnović, *Histoire de Dalmatie,* 2 vols. (Paris: Librairie Hachette, 1934).

24. Luigi Villari, *The Republic of Ragusa, an Episode of the Turkish Conquest* (London: J. M. Dent and Company, 1904).

25. Ljubomir Kosier, *La Bosnie et l'Herzegovine,* 3 vols. (Zagreb: 1927-1938).

26. Vladimir Ćorović, *Istorija Bosne* (Belgrade: 1940).

27. Robert J. Kerner (ed.), *Yugoslavia,* The United Nations series (Berkeley: University of California Press, 1949).

28. Charles A. Beard and George Radin, *The Balkan Pivot: Yugoslavia* (New York: The Macmillan Company, 1929).

29. Henry Baerlein, *The Birth of Yugoslavia,* 2 vols. (London: L. Parsons, 1920).

30. Hugh Seton-Watson, *Eastern Europe Between the Wars, 1918-1941* (2d. ed.; Cambridge: Cambridge University Press, 1946).

31. Joseph S. Roucek *et al., Central Eastern Europe, Crucible of World Wars* (New York: Prentice-Hall, 1946).

# Appendix II

## STATISTICAL SURVEY

TABLE 13

POPULATION OF AUSTRIA CLASSIFIED BY RACE OR PEOPLE, 1910

| Race or People | Number | Per Cent |
|---|---|---|
| Germans | 9,500,600 | 33.2 |
| Czechoslovaks | 6,373,564 | 22.3 |
| Poles | 4,300,273 | 15.1 |
| Ruthenians | 3,474,663 | 12.2 |
| *Serbo-Croatians and Slovenes* | 2,036,038 | 7.1 |
| Jews | 1,313,687 | 4.6 |
| Italians | 765,177 | 2.7 |
| Magyars | 10,797 | — |
| Rumanians | 274,804 | 1.0 |
| All Others | 522,331 | 1.8 |
| Total | 28,571,934 | 100.0 |

*Source*: I. Ferenczi and W. F. Willcox, *International Migrations*, II, 391.

TABLE 14

DISTRIBUTION OF THE POPULATION OF AUSTRIA BY LANGUAGE, 1900

| Province | German | Italian-Latinish | Rumanian | Magyar | Bohemian Moravian Slovak | Polish | Ruthenian | Slovenian | Serbo-Croatian |
|---|---|---|---|---|---|---|---|---|---|
| Lower Austria | 95.0 | | | | 4.7 | | | | |
| Upper Austria | 99.4 | | | | | | | | |
| Salzburg | 99.5 | | | | | | | | |
| Styria | 68.7 | | | | | | | 31.1 | |
| Carinthia | 74.8 | | | | | | | 25.1 | |
| Carniola | 5.6 | | | | | | | 94.2 | |
| Trieste and district | 5.9 | 77.4 | | | | | | 16.3 | |
| Goritzia Gradisca | 1.6 | 36.0 | | | | | | 62.4 | |
| Istria | 2.1 | 40.5 | | | | | | 14.2 | 42.6 |
| Tyrol | 55.5 | 44.3 | | | | | | | |
| Vorarlburg | 94.7 | 5.0 | | | | | | | |
| Bohemia | 37.3 | | | | 62.7 | | | | |
| Moravia | 27.9 | | | | 71.4 | | | | |
| Silesia | 44.7 | | | | 22.0 | 33.2 | | | |
| Galicia | 2.9 | | | | | 54.8 | 42.2 | | |
| Bukovina | 22.0 | | 31.7 | 1.3 | | 3.7 | 41.1 | | |
| Dalmatia | | 2.6 | | | | | | | 96.7 |
| All Austria | 35.8 | 2.8 | .9 | .3 | 23.2 | 16.6 | 13.2 | 4.7 | 2.8 |

Source: U. S. Immigration Commission, *Emigration Conditions in Europe*, p. 371.

## TABLE 15

CIVIL POPULATION OF HUNGARY, BY LANGUAGE, 1900

| Language | Kingdom of Hungary, including Croatia-Slavonia | | Hungary Proper, excluding Croatia-Slavonia | |
|---|---|---|---|---|
| | Number | Per Cent | Number | Per Cent |
| Magyar | 8,679,014 | 45.4 | 8,588,834 | 51.4 |
| Rumanian | 2,785,265 | 14.6 | 2,784,726 | 16.7 |
| German | 2,114,423 | 11.0 | 1,980,423 | 11.8 |
| Slovak | 2,008,744 | 10.5 | 1,991,402 | 11.9 |
| *Croatian* | *1,670,905* | *8.7* | *188,552* | *1.1* |
| *Serbian* | *1,042,022* | *5.5* | *434,641* | *2.6* |
| Ruthenian | 427,825 | 2.2 | 423,159 | 2.5 |
| Other | 394,142 | 2.1 | 329,837 | 2.0 |
| Total | 19,122,340 | 100.0 | 16,721,574 | 100.0 |

*Source*: U. S. Immigration Commission, *Emigration Conditions In Europe*, p. 372.

## TABLE 16

DISTRIBUTION OF SERBO-CROATIANS IN 1900

| | |
|---|---|
| Croatia and Slavonia | 2,102,000 |
| Dalmatia | 565,000 |
| Bosnia and Herzegovina (estimated) | 1,550,000 |
| Serbia | 2,299,000 |
| Montenegro (estimated) | 250,000 |
| Elsewhere (estimated) | 1,434,000 |
| Total (estimated) | 8,200,000 |

*Source*: U. S. Immigration Commission, *Dictionary of Races or People*, p. 47.

315

## TABLE 17

### POPULATION OF YUGOSLAVIA, BY MOTHER TONGUE, 1921

| Province | Serbs and Croatians | Slovenians | Czechoslovaks | Ruthenians, Little Russians | Poles | Russians | Magyars | Germans | Albanians | Turks | Rumanians | Italians | French | English | Others, unclassified and unidentified |
|---|---|---|---|---|---|---|---|---|---|---|---|---|---|---|---|
| Kingdom of Yugoslavia | 8,911,509 | 1,019,997 | 115,532 | 25,615 | 14,764 | 20,568 | 467,658 | 505,790 | 439,657 | 150,322 | 231,068 | 12,553 | 1,163 | 453 | 68,262 |
| Serbia | 3,339,369 | 3,625 | 2,801 | 35 | 286 | 4,176 | 2,532 | 5,969 | 420,473 | 149,210 | 159,549 | 503 | 717 | 231 | 44,002 |
| Montenegro | 181,989 | 55 | 40 | 3 | 3 | 54 | 17 | 33 | 16,838 | 108 | 6 | 39 | 3 | 1 | 38 |
| Bosnia and Hercegovina | 1,826,657 | 4,682 | 6,377 | 8,146 | 10,705 | 2,636 | 2,577 | 16,471 | 626 | 231 | 1,334 | 1,762 | 39 | 14 | 8,183 |
| Dalmatia | 611,323 | 1,048 | 363 |  | 71 | 712 | 68 | 1,068 | 204 | 43 | 77 | 4,706 | 15 | 35 | 699 |
| Croatia, Slavonia, Medumurje, Krk, and Kastav | 2,437,858 | 23,260 | 54,344 | 349 | 3,077 | 5,923 | 71,928 | 124,156 | 652 | 300 | 541 | 4,659 | 200 | 114 | 6,527 |
| Slovenia and Prekomurje | 11,898 | 980,222 | 2,941 | 35 | 338 | 1,630 | 14,429 | 41,514 | 103 | 237 | 31 | 701 | 125 | 38 | 677 |
| Banat, Bačka, and Baranja | 502,415 | 7,105 | 48,666 | 11,047 | 284 | 5,437 | 376,107 | 316,579 | 761 | 193 | 69,530 | 183 | 64 | 20 | 8,136 |

*Source:* Kraljevina Jugoslavija, *Definitivni Rezultati Popisa Stanovništva, 1921*, p. 3.

## TABLE 18

### POPULATION OF YUGOSLAVIA, BY RELIGION, 1921

| Province | Orthodox | Roman Catholic | Greek Catholic | Evangelical | Moslem | Israelite | Other | Without Faith and Unclassified | Total |
|---|---|---|---|---|---|---|---|---|---|
| Yugoslavia, Kingdom of | 5,593,057 | 4,708,657 | 40,338 | 229,517 | 1,345,271 | 64,746 | 1,944 | 1,381 | 11,984,911 |
| Serbia | 3,351,574 | 37,720 | 1,025 | 2,749 | 728,476 | 11,814 | 21 | 99 | 4,133,478 |
| Montenegro | 167,499 | 8,319 | 32 | 55 | 23,300 | 20 | 1 | 1 | 199,227 |
| Bosnia and Hercegovina | 829,360 | 444,309 | 9,308 | 6,627 | 588,173 | 12,031 | 538 | 94 | 1,890,440 |
| Dalmatia | 106,132 | 513,268 | 37 | 64 | 478 | 314 | 128 | 11 | 620,432 |
| Croatia, Slavonia, Medumurje, Krk, and Kastav | 658,769 | 1,992,519 | 16,226 | 47,990 | 2,537 | 20,562 | 1,096 | 189 | 2,739,888 |
| Slovenia and Prekomurje | 6,611 | 1,018,771 | 531 | 27,282 | 649 | 936 | 17 | 122 | 1,054,919 |
| Banat, Bačka, and Baranja | 473,112 | 693,751 | 13,179 | 144,750 | 1,658 | 19,069 | 143 | 865 | 1,346,527 |

*Source:* Kraljevina Jugoslavija, *Definitivni Rezultati Popisa Stanovništva, 1921,* p. 2.

## TABLE 19

REASONS FOR SLOVENIAN EMIGRATION

| Year | To Earn More | Because of Debts | Fear of Military Service | Other Reasons |
|---|---|---|---|---|
| 1893 | 374 | 12 | 1 | 31 |
| 1894 | 143 | 11 | — | 56 |
| 1895 | 891 | 86 | 2 | 350 |
| 1896 | 1,979 | 23 | 1 | 896 |
| 1897 | 713 | 24 | — | 381 |
| 1898 | 1,292 | 58 | — | 341 |
| 1899 | 2,766 | 51 | 2 | 512 |
| 1900 | 2,466 | 50 | 2 | 339 |
| 1901 | 1,920 | 32 | 6 | 237 |
| 1902 | 4,513 | 63 | 9 | 534 |
| 1903 | 6,067 | 52 | 1 | 392 |
| 1904 | 2,443 | 23 | 3 | 414 |
| Total | 25,567 | 485 | 27 | 4,483 |

*Source:* J. M. Trunk, *Amerika in Amerikanci,* p. 393.

## TABLE 20

AVERAGE DAILY WAGE (WITH SUBSISTENCE) OF FARM LABORERS IN AUSTRIA IN 1897, BY PROVINCE (IN CENTS)

| Province | On Small Farms | | | | On Large Farms | | | | Net Loss or Gain per 1000 Population by Migration 1891-1900 |
|---|---|---|---|---|---|---|---|---|---|
| | Winter | | Summer | | Winter | | Summer | | |
| | Men | Women | Men | Women | Men | Women | Men | Women | |
| Upper Austria | .19 | .14 | .27 | .21 | .24 | .16 | .35 | .23 | −2.80 |
| Lower Austria | .17 | .14 | .26 | .21 | .31 | .16 | .36 | .26 | 6.97 |
| Salzburg | .23 | .14 | .30 | .20 | | | | | 5.64 |
| Styria | .14 | .12 | .22 | .17 | .23 | .17 | .29 | .21 | − .44 |
| Carinthia | .16 | .10 | .22 | .15 | | | | | −4.32 |
| Carniola | .17 | .12 | .24 | .16 | .28 | .16 | .41 | .24 | −6.51 |
| Tyrol | .25 | .13 | .31 | .18 | | | | | .25 |
| Voralberg | .37 | .24 | .50 | .36 | | | | | 4.43 |
| Goritzia and Gradisca | .21 | .15 | .26 | .19 | .22 | .17 | .30 | .23 | −3.68 |
| Istria | | | | | | | | .33 | −2.38 |
| Dalmatia | .20 | .16 | .30 | .16 | | | | | −2.37 |
| Bohemia | .21 | .14 | .32 | .19 | .18 | .13 | .25 | .17 | −2.08 |
| Moravia | .14 | .11 | .23 | .16 | .19 | .15 | .26 | .18 | −3.32 |
| Silesia | .18 | .12 | .28 | .15 | | .16 | .35 | .18 | − .09 |
| Galicia | .13 | .10 | .23 | .16 | .11 | .08 | .20 | .15 | −4.58 |
| Bukovina | .12 | .10 | .21 | .16 | .12 | .10 | .16 | .13 | −2.11 |

*Source:* U. S. Immigration Commission, *Emigration Conditions in Europe,* p. 363.

## TABLE 21

Total immigration to the United States of races or peoples specified, and per cent of such immigration which originated in Austria-Hungary, fiscal years, 1899 to 1910, inclusive

| Race or People | Total Number of Immigrants | From Austria-Hungary | |
|---|---|---|---|
| | | Number | Per Cent |
| Bohemian and Moravian | 100,189 | 98,469 | 98.3 |
| Bulgarian, Servian, and Montenegrin | 97,391 | 39,099 | 40.1 |
| Croatian and Slovenian | 335,543 | 331,154 | 98.7 |
| Dalmatian, Bosnian, and Herzegovinian | 31,696 | 31,047 | 98.0 |
| German | 754,375 | 265,366 | 35.2 |
| Hebrew | 1,074,442 | 180,802 | 16.8 |
| Italian, North | 372,668 | 19,410 | 5.2 |
| Magyar | 337,351 | 333,429 | 98.8 |
| Polish | 949,064 | 432,809 | 45.6 |
| Roumanian | 82,704 | 76,775 | 92.8 |
| Ruthenian | 147,375 | 144,710 | 98.2 |
| Slovak | 377,527 | 374,624 | 99.2 |

*Source*: U. S. Immigration Commission, *Emigration Conditions in Europe.* p. 375.

## TABLE 22

Immigration to the United States of the races or peoples which predominated in the immigration from Austria-Hungary, fiscal years, 1899 to 1910, inclusive, by sex

| Race or People | Total Number of Immigrants | Number | | Per Cent | |
|---|---|---|---|---|---|
| | | Male | Female | Male | Female |
| Bohemian and Moravian | 100,189 | 57,111 | 43,078 | 57.0 | 43.0 |
| Bulgarian, Servian, and Montenegrin | 97,391 | 93,200 | 4,191 | 95.7 | 4.3 |
| Croatian and Slovenian | 335,543 | 284,866 | 50,677 | 84.9 | 15.1 |
| Dalmatian, Bosnian, and Herzegovinian | 31,696 | 29,252 | 2,444 | 92.3 | 7.7 |
| German | 754,375 | 448,054 | 306,321 | 59.4 | 40.6 |
| Hebrew | 1,074,442 | 607,822 | 466,620 | 56.6 | 43.4 |
| Italian, North | 372,668 | 291,877 | 80,791 | 78.3 | 21.7 |
| Magyar | 338,151 | 244,221 | 93,930 | 72.2 | 27.8 |
| Polish | 949,064 | 659,267 | 289,797 | 69.5 | 30.5 |
| Roumanian | 82,704 | 75,238 | 7,466 | 91.0 | 9.0 |
| Ruthenian (Russniak) | 147,375 | 109,614 | 37,761 | 74.4 | 25.6 |
| Slovak | 377,527 | 266,262 | 111,265 | 70.5 | 29.5 |

*Source*: U. S. Immigration Commission, *Emigration Conditions in Europe,* p. 376.

## TABLE 23

Number and per cent of immigrants admitted to the United States who were 14 years of age or over and who could neither read nor write, during the fiscal years 1899 to 1910, by races or peoples predominating in immigration from Austria-Hungary

| Race or People | Number 14 years of Age or Over Admitted | Unable to Read or Write | |
|---|---|---|---|
| | | Number | Per Cent |
| Bohemian and Moravian | 79,721 | 1,322 | 1.7 |
| Bulgarian, Servian, and Montenegrin | 95,596 | 39,903 | 41.7 |
| Croatian and Slovenian | 320,977 | 115,785 | 36.1 |
| Dalmatian, Bosnian, and Herzegovinian | 30,861 | 12,653 | 41.0 |
| German | 625,793 | 32,236 | 5.2 |
| Hebrew | 806,786 | 209,507 | 26.0 |
| Magyar | 307,082 | 35,004 | 11.4 |
| Polish | 861,303 | 304,675 | 35.4 |
| Roumanian | 80,839 | 28,266 | 35.0 |
| Ruthenian (Russniak) | 140,775 | 75,165 | 53.4 |
| Slovak | 342,583 | 82,216 | 24.0 |

Source: U. S. Immigration Commission, *Emigration Conditions in Europe*, p. 380.

## TABLE 24

OCCUPATIONS OF EUROPEAN IMMIGRANTS (INCLUDING SYRIAN) TO THE UNITED STATES, BY RACE OR PEOPLE, IN THE FISCAL YEARS 1899 TO 1909, INCLUSIVE

| Race or People | Professional | Skilled | Farm Laborers | Farmers | Common Laborers | Servants | No Occupation | Miscellaneous | Total |
|---|---|---|---|---|---|---|---|---|---|
| Armenian | 370 | 5,971 | 3,080 | 377 | 2,481 | 1,588 | 6,385 | 738 | 20,990 |
| Bohemian and Moravian | 748 | 22,601 | 8,247 | 1,580 | 7,341 | 13,695 | 36,505 | 1,010 | 91,727 |
| Bulgarian, Servian and Montenegrin | 107 | 2,608 | 36,746 | 2,782 | 34,755 | 683 | 4,291 | 289 | 82,261 |
| Dalmatian, Bosnian, and Herzegovinian | 31 | 2,523 | 7,178 | 569 | 12,837 | 668 | 2,799 | 180 | 26,785 |
| Dutch and Flemish | 1,768 | 13,111 | 7,139 | 3,106 | 10,579 | 3,558 | 32,543 | 2,842 | 74,646 |
| English | 20,041 | 105,707 | 4,902 | 4,954 | 24,928 | 27,851 | 137,662 | 29,071 | 355,116 |
| Finnish | 314 | 6,380 | 5,604 | 1,520 | 68,243 | 27,581 | 25,982 | 414 | 136,038 |
| French | 5,903 | 20,829 | 5,372 | 1,680 | 8,942 | 10,331 | 35,525 | 6,094 | 94,676 |
| German | 14,550 | 125,594 | 72,733 | 12,021 | 84,531 | 78,803 | 266,819 | 27,944 | 682,995 |
| Greek | 594 | 13,632 | 33,253 | 2,092 | 104,472 | 3,892 | 15,935 | 3,957 | 177,827 |
| Hebrew | 6,836 | 362,936 | 9,633 | 908 | 66,311 | 61,611 | 445,728 | 36,219 | 990,182 |
| Irish | 4,264 | 41,486 | 15,717 | 6,047 | 106,497 | 161,844 | 57,033 | 8,454 | 401,342 |
| Italian, North | 3,006 | 56,854 | 51,349 | 5,656 | 128,579 | 21,465 | 69,170 | 5,809 | 341,888 |
| Italian, South | 5,586 | 199,024 | 420,262 | 12,290 | 587,540 | 76,440 | 400,546 | 17,572 | 1,719,260 |
| Lithuanian | 148 | 8,243 | 29,918 | 355 | 64,174 | 19,819 | 29,596 | 291 | 152,544 |
| Magyar | 1,281 | 20,966 | 102,456 | 1,586 | 82,501 | 29,558 | 70,236 | 1,465 | 310,049 |
| Polish | 1,193 | 41,541 | 162,372 | 2,549 | 320,061 | 111,100 | 180,148 | 1,752 | 820,716 |
| Portuguese | 192 | 3,076 | 3,023 | 400 | 22,363 | 12,869 | 21,921 | 1,396 | 65,240 |
| Roumanian | 139 | 1,852 | 38,285 | 217 | 20,411 | 1,617 | 5,723 | 261 | 68,505 |

TABLE 24 (Continued)

Number

| Race or People | Profes- sional | Skilled | Farm Laborers | Farmers | Common Laborers | Servants | No Oc- cupation | Miscel- laneous | Total |
|---|---|---|---|---|---|---|---|---|---|
| Russian | 843 | 5,348 | 20,323 | 862 | 24,803 | 2,273 | 10,965 | 863 | 66,280 |
| Ruthenian | 97 | 2,095 | 38,633 | 322 | 44,336 | 18,046 | 15,858 | 81 | 119,468 |
| Scandinavian | 5,076 | 86,921 | 30,060 | 11,009 | 158,967 | 131,760 | 102,878 | 7,598 | 534,269 |
| Scotch | 4,219 | 42,589 | 2,235 | 1,484 | 6,353 | 9,125 | 38,935 | 7,290 | 112,230 |
| Slovak | 184 | 12,088 | 85,419 | 1,899 | 124,201 | 39,417 | 81,463 | 440 | 345,111 |
| Spanish | 1,504 | 15,000 | 2,483 | 837 | 6,695 | 1,808 | 11,531 | 5,356 | 45,214 |
| Syrian | 396 | 7,360 | 9,756 | 1,762 | 6,797 | 3,548 | 17,731 | 3,242 | 50,592 |
| Turkish | 117 | 822 | 3,510 | 619 | 4,878 | 154 | 1,056 | 515 | 11,671 |
| Welsh | 585 | 6,517 | 440 | 332 | 1,277 | 1,426 | 7,115 | 816 | 18,508 |
| Croatian and Slovenian | 228 | 13,952 | 80,167 | 4,290 | 146,278 | 17,558 | 32,825 | 683 | 295,981 |
| Others | 2 | 48 | | 41 | 434 | 5 | 383 | 10 | 923 |
| Total | 80,322 | 1,247,674 | 1,290,295 | 84,146 | 2,282,565 | 890,093 | 2,165,287 | 172,652 | 8,213,034 |

Source: U.S. Immigration Commission, Emigration Conditions in Europe, p. 27.

322

## TABLE 25

Occupations of European immigrants (including Syrian) to the United States, by race or people, in the fiscal years 1899 to 1909, inclusive

| Race or People | Professional | Skilled | Farm Laborers | Farmers | Common Laborers | Servants | No Occupation | Miscellaneous | Total |
|---|---|---|---|---|---|---|---|---|---|
| | | | | Per Cent | | | | | |
| Armenian | 1.8 | 28.4 | 14.7 | 1.8 | 11.8 | 7.6 | 30.4 | 3.5 | 100.0 |
| Bohemian and Moravian | .8 | 24.6 | 9.0 | 1.7 | 8.0 | 14.9 | 39.8 | 1.1 | 100.0 |
| Bulgarian, Servian, and Montenegrin | .1 | 3.2 | 44.7 | 3.4 | 42.2 | .8 | 5.2 | .4 | 100.0 |
| Croatian and Slovenian | .1 | 4.7 | 27.1 | 1.4 | 49.4 | 5.9 | 11.1 | .2 | 100.0 |
| Dalmatian, Bosnian, and Herzegovinian | .1 | 9.4 | 26.8 | 2.1 | 47.9 | 2.5 | 10.4 | .7 | 100.0 |
| Dutch and Flemish | 2.4 | 17.6 | 9.6 | 4.2 | 14.2 | 4.8 | 43.6 | 3.8 | 100.0 |
| English | 5.6 | 29.8 | 1.4 | 1.4 | 7.0 | 7.8 | 38.8 | 8.2 | 100.0 |
| Finnish | .2 | 4.7 | 4.1 | 1.1 | 50.2 | 20.3 | 19.1 | .3 | 100.0 |
| French | 6.2 | 22.0 | 5.7 | 1.8 | 9.4 | 10.9 | 37.5 | 6.4 | 100.0 |
| German | 2.1 | 18.4 | 10.6 | 1.8 | 12.4 | 11.5 | 39.1 | 4.1 | 100.0 |
| Greek | .3 | 7.7 | 18.7 | 1.2 | 58.7 | 2.2 | 9.0 | 2.2 | 100.0 |
| Hebrew | .7 | 36.7 | 1.0 | .1 | 6.7 | 6.2 | 45.0 | 3.7 | 100.0 |
| Irish | 1.1 | 10.3 | 3.9 | 1.5 | 26.5 | 40.3 | 14.2 | 2.1 | 100.0 |
| Italian, North | .9 | 16.6 | 15.0 | 1.7 | 37.6 | 6.3 | 20.2 | 1.7 | 100.0 |
| Italian, South | .3 | 11.6 | 24.4 | .7 | 34.2 | 4.4 | 23.3 | 1.0 | 100.0 |
| Lithuanian | .1 | 5.4 | 19.6 | .2 | 42.1 | 13.0 | 19.4 | .2 | 100.0 |
| Magyar | .4 | 6.8 | 33.0 | .5 | 26.6 | 9.5 | 22.7 | .5 | 100.0 |
| Polish | .1 | 5.1 | 19.8 | .3 | 39.0 | 13.5 | 22.0 | .2 | 100.0 |
| Portuguese | .3 | 4.7 | 4.6 | .6 | 34.3 | 19.7 | 33.6 | 2.1 | 100.0 |
| Roumanian | .2 | 2.7 | 55.9 | .3 | 29.8 | 2.4 | 8.4 | .4 | 100.0 |
| Russian | 1.3 | 8.1 | 30.7 | 1.3 | 37.4 | 3.4 | 16.5 | 1.3 | 100.0 |
| Ruthenian | .1 | 1.8 | 32.3 | .3 | 37.1 | 15.1 | 13.3 | .1 | 100.0 |
| Scandinavian | 1.0 | 16.3 | 5.6 | 2.1 | 29.8 | 24.7 | 19.3 | 1.4 | 100.0 |
| Scotch | 3.8 | 37.9 | 2.0 | 1.3 | 5.7 | 8.1 | 34.7 | 6.5 | 100.0 |
| Slovak | .1 | 3.5 | 24.8 | .6 | 36.0 | 11.4 | 23.6 | .1 | 100.0 |
| Spanish | 3.3 | 33.2 | 5.5 | 1.9 | 14.8 | 4.0 | 25.5 | 11.8 | 100.0 |
| Syrian | .8 | 14.5 | 19.3 | 3.5 | 13.4 | 7.0 | 35.0 | 6.4 | 100.0 |
| Turkish | 1.0 | 7.0 | 30.1 | 5.3 | 41.8 | 1.3 | 9.0 | 4.4 | 100.0 |
| Welsh | 3.2 | 35.2 | 2.4 | 1.8 | 6.9 | 7.7 | 38.4 | 4.4 | 100.0 |
| Other | .2 | 5.2 | | 4.4 | 47.0 | .5 | 41.5 | 1.1 | 100.0 |
| Total | 1.0 | 15.2 | 15.7 | 1.0 | 27.8 | 10.8 | 26.4 | 2.1 | 100.0 |

Source: U. S. Immigration Commission, *Emigration Conditions in Europe,* p. 28.

TABLE 26

YUGOSLAV NATIONAL MUTUAL BENEFIT FEDERATIONS

| Society | Date Founded | No. of Lodges | | No. of Members | | Assets | | Insurance in Force | | Principal Investments* |
|---|---|---|---|---|---|---|---|---|---|---|
| | | Adult | Juvenile | Adult | Juvenile | Adult | Juvenile | Adult | Juvenile | |
| American Fraternal Union | 1898 | 157 | 157 | 17,134 | 11,931 | $ 6,794,932 | | $12,687,761 | $ 7,167,257 | (a) |
| Croatian Catholic Union | 1921 | 91 | 81 | 7,863 | 4,093 | 2,377,054 | | 9,250,638 | | (b), (a), (d) |
| Croatian Fraternal Union | 1894 | 58 | 485 | 71,908 | 36,129 | 23,268,597 | 1,660,798 | 62,363,812 | 23,458,500 | (c), (a), (b), (d) |
| Grand Carniolian Slovenian Catholic Union | 1894 | 172 | | 30,486 | 15,162 | 10,423,147 | 1,180,599 | 25,317,706 | 11,862,167 | (c), (a), (d) |
| Holy Family Society | 1914 | 12 | | 1,064 | | 178,129 | | 525,800 | | (a), (b), (c), (d) |
| Serbian Beneficial Federation Unity | 1920 | 25 | 15 | 1,390 | 422 | 456,586 | | 1,250,000 | | (a), (c), (b) |
| Serb National Federation | 1901 | 176 | 146 | 16,120 | 7,629 | 4,822,296 | 301,032 | 13,300,794 | 3,932,108 | (a), (b), (c), (d) |
| Slovenian Mutual Benefit Association | 1910 | 56 | | 12,300 | 8,774 | 4,656,573 | | 14,533,997 | | (a), (d) |
| Slovene National Benefit Society | 1904 | 548 | | 48,272 | 21,543 | 18,005,257 | 1,510,245 | 52,195,405 | | (a), (c), (d) |
| Slovenian Women's Union | 1926 | 94 | | 10,128 | 2,712 | 387,812 | | 1,353,100 | | (a) |
| Western Slavonic Association | 1908 | 48 | 10 | 4,680 | 6,056 | 1,234,488 | 217,319 | 3,441,359 | 1,806,292 | (a), (d) |

*Source:* Reconstructed from data compiled by the author in 1957.
*(a) Government bonds; (b) Industrial stock; (c) Public utilities; (d) Real estate.

# TABLE 27

## DISTRIBUTION OF FRATERNAL BENEFICIAL ORGANIZATIONS OF NATIONALITY GROUPS BY STATES

| State | Armenian | Carpatho-Russian | Croatian | Czech | Danish | Finnish | French | German | Greek | Hungarian | Italian | Jewish | Lithuanian | Norwegian | Polish | Portuguese | Rumanian | Russian | Serbian | Slovak | Slovene | Spanish | Swedish | Ukrainian | Wendish | IWO |
|---|---|---|---|---|---|---|---|---|---|---|---|---|---|---|---|---|---|---|---|---|---|---|---|---|---|---|
| Alabama | – | – | 1 | – | – | – | – | 2 | – | – | 1-1 | 1 | – | – | – | – | – | – | – | 1 | – | – | – | – | – | – |
| Arizona | – | – | 1 | – | – | – | – | 1 | – | – | – | – | – | – | 2 | – | – | – | – | – | 1 | 1-1 | – | – | – | – |
| Arkansas | 1 | – | – | – | – | – | – | 1 | – | – | – | – | – | – | 1 | – | – | – | – | – | – | 1 | – | – | – | – |
| California | 1 | – | 2 | 1 | 1 | – | – | 5 | – | 1-1 | 1-1 | 2 | – | 1 | 1 | 3-3 | – | – | – | 1 | 1-2 | 1 | 1 | 1 | – | 1 |
| Colorado | – | – | 1 | 1 | 1 | – | 1 | 3 | – | – | – | 2-5 | 2 | – | 4 | – | – | – | – | 1 | 1-4 | – | – | – | – | – |
| Connecticut | – | – | – | – | – | – | – | 2 | – | – | – | 1 | – | 1 | 3 | – | – | – | – | 1-5 | – | – | 1 | 1 | – | 1 |
| Delaware | – | – | – | – | – | – | – | 1 | – | 2-2 | – | 2 | – | – | 2 | – | – | – | – | – | – | – | – | – | – | 1 |
| Dist. of Col. | – | – | – | – | – | – | – | 4 | – | 1-1 | – | 1 | – | – | – | – | – | – | – | – | – | – | – | – | – | – |
| Florida | – | – | 1-2 | – | 1 | – | – | 2 | – | 1-1 | – | 2 | – | 1 | 1 | – | – | – | – | – | – | – | 1 | – | – | – |
| Georgia | – | – | – | – | – | – | – | – | – | 1 | – | 1 | – | – | – | – | – | – | – | – | – | – | – | – | – | – |
| Idaho | – | – | – | – | – | – | – | 1 | – | – | – | – | – | – | – | – | – | – | – | – | – | – | – | – | – | 1 |
| Illinois | – | 1 | 1 | 3-5 | 1 | – | 1-3 | 7-11 | – | 4 | 2-2 | 7 | 1-3 | 1-2 | 5-10 | – | 1 | 1-1 | 1 | 3-9 | 3-4 | – | 2-4 | 2 | – | – |
| Indiana | – | 1 | 1 | 2 | 1 | – | 1 | 5 | – | 4 | 1 | 2 | 1 | 1 | 7 | – | 1 | – | 1 | 7 | 3 | – | 2 | 1 | – | – |
| Iowa | – | – | 1 | 1-3 | – | – | – | 4 | – | – | – | 1 | – | – | – | – | – | – | – | – | – | – | 1 | – | – | 1 |
| Kansas | – | – | 1 | 3 | – | – | – | 3 | – | – | – | 1 | – | – | – | – | – | – | – | – | – | – | – | – | – | – |
| Kentucky | – | – | 1 | – | – | – | – | 1 | – | – | – | 1 | – | – | 3 | – | – | – | – | 1 | 3 | – | – | – | – | 1 |
| Louisiana | – | – | – | – | – | – | 2 | 2 | – | – | – | 2 | – | – | – | – | – | – | – | – | – | – | – | – | – | – |
| Maine | – | – | – | – | – | – | – | 4 | – | – | – | 3 | – | – | – | – | – | – | – | – | – | – | 2 | – | – | 1 |
| Maryland | – | – | 1 | 3 | – | – | – | 4 | – | – | – | 1 | – | 1 | 5 | – | – | – | – | 3 | – | – | – | – | – | – |
| Massachusetts | 1 | 1 | 1 | – | – | – | 1-3 | 1-5 | 1 | 5 | 1-1 | 5 | 2 | 1 | 5 | – | – | 1 | 1 | – | 1 | – | 1 | 1 | – | 1 |
| Michigan | – | – | 1 | 1-4 | 1-2 | – | 1 | 4-5 | – | 1 | – | 5 | 1-3 | 2-3 | 1-6 | – | 1 | – | – | 5 | 3 | – | 2 | 1 | – | 1 |
| Minnesota | – | – | – | 3 | 2 | – | – | 5 | – | – | – | 3 | 2 | 1 | 3 | – | – | 1 | 1 | 4 | 3 | – | 1-2 | – | – | 1 |
| Mississippi | – | – | 1 | 1 | – | – | – | 5 | – | – | – | 5 | – | – | 1-6 | – | – | – | – | 1 | 1-4 | – | 3 | – | – | – |
| Missouri | – | – | 1-1 | 5 | 1-1 | – | – | 2 | – | – | – | 1-4 | – | 1 | 4 | – | 1 | – | 1 | 4 | 2 | – | 1 | – | – | 1 |
| Montana | – | – | 2 | – | – | – | – | 1-4 | – | – | – | – | – | – | – | – | – | – | – | 1 | 3 | – | – | – | – | – |
| Nebraska | – | – | 1 | – | 2 | – | 1-2 | 1 | 1 | 1 | – | 1 | 3 | 2-1 | 1-2 | – | – | – | – | – | 2 | – | 2 | – | – | – |
| Nevada | – | – | – | – | – | – | – | – | – | – | – | – | – | – | – | – | – | – | – | – | – | – | – | – | – | – |
| N. Hampshire | – | 1-3 | 1-1 | – | – | – | – | 5 | – | 5 | 1-9 | 6 | – | – | 1-11 | – | – | – | – | – | 2 | – | 1 | 1 | – | – |
| New Jersey | – | – | – | – | 1 | – | 1 | 1 | 1-1 | 1-5 | 1-1 | 6-7 | 2-3 | 1 | 4-8 | – | 1-1 | 2-2 | 1-2 | 3-8 | 3 | 1-1 | 1 | 1-3 | – | 1 |
| New Mexico | – | 1 | 1-1 | – | – | 1-1 | – | 4-8 | – | – | – | 1 | – | – | – | – | – | – | – | – | – | 1-1 | 2 | – | – | – |
| New York | 1-1 | 1-3 | – | – | – | – | – | 2 | – | – | – | 2 | – | 2 | – | – | – | – | – | – | 3 | 1-1 | 1 | 1 | – | (1) |
| N. Carolina | – | – | – | – | – | – | – | 4 | – | – | – | – | – | – | – | – | – | – | – | – | – | – | – | – | – | – |
| N. Dakota | – | – | – | 2 | – | – | – | – | – | – | – | – | – | 2 | – | – | – | – | – | – | – | – | 1 | – | – | 1 |

# TABLE 27 (Continued)

| State | Armenian | Carpatho-Russian | Croatian | Czech | Danish | Finnish | French | German | Greek | Hungarian | Italian | Jewish | Lithuanian | Norwegian | Polish | Portuguese | Rumanian | Russian | Serbian | Slovak | Slovene | Spanish | Swedish | Ukranian | Wendish | IWO |
|---|---|---|---|---|---|---|---|---|---|---|---|---|---|---|---|---|---|---|---|---|---|---|---|---|---|---|
| Ohio | — | 1–3 | 2 | 2–6 | 1 | — | — | 1–5 | — | 2–5 | 1 | 5 | 3 | — | 3–7 | — | 1–1 | — | 1–2 | 3–10 | 1–4 | — | 1 | 3 | — | — |
| Oklahoma | — | — | — | 1 | 1 | — | — | 1 | — | — | — | — | — | — | — | — | — | — | — | — | — | — | — | — | — | — |
| Oregon | — | 6–6 | 2 | 1 | 1 | — | — | 4 | — | 2–5 | 1–1 | 1–1 | 1–3 | 1 | 1–1 | — | — | — | 1–1 | 7–10 | 2 | — | 2–1 | 3–4 | — | — |
| Pennsylvania | — | — | 1–2 | 2 | 1 | — | 2–3 | 1–5 | — | — | 1–1 | 1–5 | — | 1 | 6–10 | — | — | — | — | 1 | 3 | 1 | 1 | 1 | 1–1 | 1 |
| Rhode Island | — | — | — | — | — | — | — | 2 | — | — | — | 3 | — | 1 | 2 | — | — | — | — | — | — | — | — | — | — | 1 |
| S. Carolina | — | — | — | 2 | — | — | — | — | — | — | — | — | — | — | — | — | — | — | — | — | — | — | — | — | — | — |
| S. Dakota | — | — | 1 | — | — | — | — | 3 | — | — | — | 2 | — | 1 | — | — | — | — | — | — | — | — | — | — | — | — |
| Tennessee | — | — | 1 | — | — | — | — | 1 | — | — | — | 3 | — | — | 2 | — | — | — | — | — | 3 | 1 | 1 | — | — | — |
| Texas | — | — | 1 | 3–4 | — | — | — | 2–5 | — | 2 | — | 1 | — | — | — | — | — | — | — | — | — | — | — | — | — | — |
| Utah | — | — | — | — | — | — | — | 1 | — | — | — | — | — | — | — | — | — | — | — | 1 | — | — | — | — | — | — |
| Vermont | — | — | — | — | — | — | — | — | — | — | — | 2 | — | — | 1 | — | — | — | 1 | 1 | — | — | — | — | — | 1 |
| Virginia | — | — | 2 | 1 | — | — | 1 | 3 | — | 4 | — | 1 | — | 1 | 1 | — | — | — | — | 1 | 3 | — | 1 | — | — | — |
| Washington | — | 3 | 1 | — | — | — | — | 3 | — | 4 | — | 2 | — | — | 2 | — | 1 | — | — | 3 | 3 | — | — | — | — | 1 |
| W. Virginia | — | — | 1 | 2 | 1–2 | — | — | 2 | — | 1 | — | 4 | — | — | 3 | — | — | — | — | 2 | 3 | — | 3 | — | — | 1 |
| Wisconsin | — | — | 1 | — | — | — | — | 2–3 | — | — | — | 2 | — | 1–2 | 2–5 | — | — | — | — | 1 | 2 | 1 | 1–2 | — | — | — |
| Wyoming | — | — | — | — | — | — | — | 1 | — | — | — | — | — | — | — | — | — | — | — | — | 3 | — | — | — | — | — |
| Canada | — | — | 1 | — | — | — | 8–5 | 2 | — | — | — | 7 | 1 | 1 | — | — | — | — | 3 | 2 | 1 | 1 | 1 | 2 | — | — |
| Total (Organizations) | 1 | 9 | 4 | 10 | 2 | 1 | 7 | 23 | 1 | 8 | 7 | 8 | 5 | 3 | 22 | 3 | 2 | 3 | 3 | 18 | 6 | 2 | 4 | 5 | 1 | — |
| (in States) | 3 | 8 | 29 | 25 | 13 | 1 | 9 | 43 | 1 | 18 | 8 | 38 | 10 | 9 | 31 | 1 | 7 | 5 | 8 | 22 | 23 | 8 | 26 | 14 | 1 | 17 |

Source: *Interpreter Releases*, XI (August 30, 1944), 275-276.

## TABLE 28

NUMBER OF FRATERNAL ORGANIZATIONS, THEIR BRANCHES, MEMBERSHIP
AND ASSETS, BY NATIONALITY GROUPS

(Figures in parentheses indicate the number of organizations or
branches for which data were available)

| Nationality Group | Number of Organizations | Branches | Members | Assets |
|---|---|---|---|---|
| Armenian | 1 | (1) 119 | (1) 5,000 | (1)$ 86,003 |
| Carpatho-Russian | 9 | (8) 2,605 | (9) 94,471 | (8) 19,258,757 |
| *Croatian* | *4* | *(3) 730* | *(4) 112,402* | *(2) 14,384,477* |
| Czech | 10 | (9) 1,601 | (10) 161,402 | (10) 32,212,533 |
| Danish | 2 | (2) 248 | (2) 12,632 | (2) 3,845,798 |
| Finnish | 1 | | (1) 1,149 | |
| French[1] | 4 | (4) 667 | (4) 106,913 | (4) 12,489,119 |
| German | 23 | (18) 5,350 | (22) 524,037 | (22) 106,289,141 |
| Greek | 1 | | (1) 1,411 | |
| Hungarian | 8 | (6) 1,107 | (8) 131,204 | (7) 15,068,790 |
| Italian | 7 | (6) 561 | (4) 54,501 | (5) 1,456,716 |
| Jewish | 8 | (7) 1,749 | (8) 175,886 | (7) 16,008,593 |
| Lithuanian | 5 | (5) 912 | (5) 38,860 | (4) 4,309,108 |
| Norwegian | 3 | (3) 448 | (3) 25,383 | (3) 4,983,085 |
| Polish | 22 | (20) 6,231 | (21) 696,708 | (18) 86,348,847 |
| Portuguese | 3 | (3) 394 | (3) 29,061 | (3) 4,981,638 |
| Russian | 3 | (2) 81 | (3) 21,248 | (2) 632,124 |
| Rumanian | 2 | (1) 80 | (2) 8,549 | (1) 946,043 |
| *Serbian* | *3* | *(2) 341* | *(3) 26,148* | *(2) 2,765,492* |
| Slovak | 18 | (16) 4,022 | (18) 344,210 | (15) 54,868,049 |
| *Slovene* | *6* | *(6) 1,197* | *(6) 158,564* | *(5) 22,316,366* |
| Spanish | 2 | (1) 278 | (2) 16,913 | (1) 1,080,246 |
| Swedish | 4 | (4) 451 | (4) 49,788 | (4) 3,497,242 |
| Ukrainian | 5 | (4) 1,111 | (5) 85,590 | (4) 12,122,086 |
| Wendish | 1 | (1) 7 | (1) 1,520 | (1) 299,021 |
| I. W. O.[2] | | (14) 1,700 | | (14) 2,839,381 |
| Total | 155 | (146) 31,990 | (150) 2,883,550 | (145)$423,088,655 |

*Source: Interpreter Releases*, XI, 277.

1. Three French organizations with 1,479 branches, 156,219 members, and $29,650,772 of assets have their headquarters and more than two-thirds of their membership in Canada. They are not included in this table.

2. The nationality sections of the International Workers Order are included as separate organizations in each group and in figures of membership. Branches and assets are added at the end.

## TABLE 29

DISTRIBUTION OF KNOWN FRATERNAL PUBLICATIONS BY NATIONALITY GROUPS AND FREQUENCY AND WHETHER THEY ARE OWNED BY THE ORGANIZATION OR ONLY USED BY THEM

| Nationality | Daily | | Semi-weekly | | Weekly | | Semi-monthly | | Monthly | | Bi-monthly and quarterly | | Total | | Grand Total |
|---|---|---|---|---|---|---|---|---|---|---|---|---|---|---|---|
| | O | U | O | U | O | U | O | U | O | U | O | U | O | U | |
| Armenian | — | — | — | — | — | — | — | — | 1 | — | — | — | 1 | — | 1 |
| Carpatho-Russian | — | — | 1 | 1 | 3 | — | — | — | 3 | — | 1 | — | 8 | 1 | 9 |
| *Croatian* | — | *1* | — | *1* | 2 | 2 | 1 | — | — | — | — | — | 2 | 2 | *4* |
| Czech | — | — | — | 1 | — | — | — | — | 6 | — | — | — | 7 | 3 | 10 |
| Danish | — | — | — | — | — | 1 | — | — | 1 | — | — | — | 1 | — | 1 |
| Greek | — | — | — | — | — | — | — | — | — | — | — | — | — | 1 | 1 |
| Finnish | — | 1 | — | — | — | — | — | — | — | — | — | — | — | 1 | 1 |
| French | — | — | — | — | — | — | — | — | 2 | — | — | — | 2 | — | 2 |
| German° | — | — | — | — | 2 | — | — | — | 9 | — | 0 | 1 | 11 | 1 | 12 |
| Hungarian | — | 1 | — | — | 1 | — | — | — | 4 | — | — | — | 5 | 1 | 6 |
| Italian | — | — | — | — | 1 | 1 | — | — | 4 | — | 1 | — | 6 | 1 | 7 |
| Jewish | — | — | — | — | — | — | — | — | 8 | — | 1 | — | 9 | — | 9 |
| Lithuanian | — | — | — | — | 3 | — | 1 | — | 2 | — | — | — | 6 | — | 6 |
| Norwegian | — | — | — | — | — | — | — | — | 3 | — | — | — | 3 | — | 3 |
| Polish | — | 1 | — | — | 13 | 4 | — | — | 2 | — | — | — | 15 | 5 | 20 |
| Portuguese | — | — | — | — | — | — | — | — | 2 | — | — | — | 2 | — | 2 |
| Rumanian | — | — | 1 | — | — | 1 | — | — | — | — | — | — | 1 | 1 | 2 |
| Russian | — | 1 | — | — | — | 1 | — | — | 1 | — | — | — | 1 | 2 | 3 |
| *Serbian* | *1* | — | — | *1* | — | *1* | — | — | — | — | — | — | *1* | 2 | 3 |
| Slovak | — | 2 | — | — | 7 | — | 5 | — | 3 | — | — | — | 15 | 2 | 17 |
| *Slovene* | *1* | — | 2 | — | 3 | — | — | — | *1* | — | — | — | 7 | — | 7 |
| Spanish | — | — | — | — | — | 1 | — | — | 1 | — | — | — | 1 | 1 | 2 |
| Swedish | — | — | — | — | — | — | — | — | 4 | — | — | — | 4 | — | 4 |
| Ukrainian | 1 | 1 | 1 | — | 2 | — | — | — | — | — | — | — | 4 | 1 | 5 |
| Wendish | — | — | — | — | — | 1 | — | — | — | — | — | — | — | 1 | 1 |
| Total | 3 | 8 | 5 | 4 | 37 | 13 | 7 | 0 | 57 | 0 | 3 | 1 | 112 | 26 | 138 |

Source: *Interpreter Releases*, XI, 278.
°This is a quarterly.

## TABLE 30

CIRCULATION OF THE FOREIGN LANGUAGE PRESS IN THE UNITED STATES (FIGURES IN PARENTHESES SHOW NUMBER OF PUBLICATIONS THE CIRCULATION OF WHICH IS NOT KNOWN)

| Language | Dailies | | Semiweeklies and Weeklies | | Others | | Total | |
|---|---|---|---|---|---|---|---|---|
| | No. | Circ. | No. | Circ. | No. | Circ. | No. | Circ. |
| Albanian | 2 | — | 1 | 400 | (1) | | 1 (1) | 400 |
| Arabic | 1 (1) | 7,500 | 1 (5) | 3,500 | (3) | | 3 (8) | 11,000 |
| Armenian | 1 (1) | 3,754 | 7 (2) | 14,906 | 1 (5) | 1,140 | 9 (8) | 19,800 |
| Bulgarian | | — | 1 (3) | 8,500 | | | 1 (3) | 8,500 |
| Carpatho-Russian | | | 2 (3) | 70,000 | (7) | | 2 (10) | 70,000 |
| Chinese | 7 (4) | 67,874 | (1) | | | | 7 (5) | 67,874 |
| *Croatian* | | | 6 (2) | 85,594 | (4) | | 6 (6) | 85,594 |
| Czech | 5 | 141,384 | 26 (1) | 381,752 | 2 (27) | 21,980 | 33 (28) | 545,116 |
| Danish | | | 5 (6) | 23,393 | 3 (4) | 17,100 | 8 (10) | 40,493 |
| Dutch | | | 7 | 36,335 | (8) | | 7 (8) | 36,335 |
| Esperanto | | | 1 | 500 | (1) | | 1 (1) | 500 |
| Estonian | | | 1 | 500 | (1) | 500 | 1 (1) | 500 |
| Finnish | 5 | 31,877 | 8 (2) | 52,749 | 2 (6) | 1,618 | 15 (8) | 86,244 |
| Flemish | | | 1 | 8,200 | | | 1 | 8,200 |
| French | 3 (1) | 14,298 | 15 (5) | 69,754 | 5 (14) | 57,605 | 23 (20) | 141,657 |
| German | 6 (3) | 134,611 | 39 (14) | 354,354 | 7 (82) | 53,688 | 52 (99) | 542,653 |
| Greek | 2 | 28,632 | 5 (4) | 34,496 | 2 (17) | 5,300 | 9 (21) | 68,428 |
| Hebrew | | | 1 | 23,000 | (13) | | 1 (13) | 23,000 |
| Hungarian | 3 | 75,092 | 20 (17) | 235,714 | (17) | | 23 (34) | 310,806 |
| Italian | 3 (2) | 98,757 | 35 (33) | 357,570 | 4 (40) | 66,556 | 42 (75) | 522,883 |
| Japanese | | | 2 (1) | 1,210 | | | 2 (1) | 1,210 |
| Korean | | | 1 (1) | — | | | 1 (1) | — |
| Ladino | | | 1 (1) | 16,890 | (2) | | (3) | 16,890 |
| Latvian | | | (1) | — | | | — | — |

TABLE 30 (Continued)

| Language | Dailies | | Semiweeklies and Weeklies | | Others | | Total | |
|---|---|---|---|---|---|---|---|---|
| Lithuanian | 4 | 120,742 | 7 (6) | 113,785 | (10) | | 11 (16) | 234,527 |
| Norwegian | | | 9 (7) | 72,021 | 9 (12) | 28,684 | 18 (19) | 100,705 |
| Polish | 9 | 253,812 | 35 (18) | 647,290 | (16) | | 44 (34) | 901,102 |
| Portuguese | 1 | 10,500 | 4 (2) | 21,679 | (10) | | 5 (12) | 32,179 |
| Rumanian | | | 1 (3) | 8,500 | (1) | | 1 (4) | 8,500 |
| Russian | 5 | 87,971 | 1 | 27,545 | (13) | | 6 (13) | 115,516 |
| *Serbian* | 1 (1) | 8,975 | 1 (2) | 17,894 | | | 2 (3) | 26,869 |
| Slovak | 2 | 42,684 | 8 (8) | 182,171 | 1 (13) | 6,200 | 11 (21) | 231,055 |
| *Slovene* | 4 | 57,530 | 5 | 62,354 | 1 (2) | 7,800 | 10 (2) | 127,684 |
| Spanish | 8 (2) | 71,801 | 32 (28) | 79,774 | 4 (68) | 49,995 | 44 (98) | 201,570 |
| Swedish | | | 10 (11) | 138,137 | 5 (21) | 25,650 | 15 (32) | 163,787 |
| Ukrainian | 2 | 27,500 | 3 (2) | 19,200 | (7) | | 5 (9) | 46,700 |
| Welsh | | | | | (2) | | (2) | |
| Wendish | | | 1 | 2,730 | | | 1 | 2,730 |
| Yiddish | 8 | 388,769 | 6 (5) | 141,084 | 2 (29) | 40,500 | 16 (34) | 570,353 |
| | | | | | | | | |
| Total Circulation | 81 | 1,674,063 | 307 | 3,312,981 | 49 | 384,316 | 437 | 5,371,360 |
| Circulation not known | 15 | | 191 | | 449 | | 655 | |

Source: *Interpreter Releases*, XX (October 13, 1943), 297.

## TABLE 31

THE FOREIGN-LANGUAGE PRESS IN AMERICA AND ITS STAND ON THE U.S. PRESIDENTIAL CANDIDATES IN 1944

| Language | Periodicals | Number Studied | For Roosevelt | For Dewey | For Other Candidates | Neutral |
|---|---|---|---|---|---|---|
| Arabian | 11 | 10 | 1 | 1 | | 8 |
| Armenian | 17 | 8 | 4 | 1 | | 3 |
| Bulgarian | 4 | 4 | 1 | | 1 | 2 |
| Czech | 61 | 24 | 19 | 1 | | 4 |
| Danish | 15 | 7 | 3 | | | 4 |
| Finnish | 23 | 14 | 5 | 6 | | 3 |
| French | 43 | 19 | 4 | 10 | | 5 |
| Greek | 30 | 9 | 3 | 3 | | 3 |
| Dutch | 16 | 5 | | 1 | | 4 |
| *Croatian* | *12* | *10* | *6* | *1* | *1* | 2 |
| Japanese | 4 | 4 | | | | 4 |
| Chinese | 12 | 8 | 2 | 1 | | 5 |
| Lithuanian | 27 | 16 | 7 | 2 | | 7 |
| Hungarian | 57 | 43 | 25 | 7 | 1 | 10 |
| German | 151 | 50 | 4 | 5 | | 41 |
| Norwegian | 34 | 9 | 4 | 1 | | 4 |
| Polish | 78 | 45 | 16 | 16 | | 13 |
| Portuguese | 17 | 7 | 4 | 1 | | 2 |
| Rumanian | 5 | 3 | 3 | | | |
| Russian | 31 | 12 | 2 | 1 | | 9 |
| Slovak | 29 | 15 | 6 | 5 | | 4 |
| *Slovenian* | *12* | *10* | *5* | | *1* | 4 |
| *Serbian* | *3* | *3* | *1* | | | 2 |
| Spanish | 142 | 38 | 10 | 1 | | 27 |
| Swedish | 47 | 18 | 1 | 6 | 1 | 10 |
| Italian | 117 | 65 | 14 | 21 | | 30 |
| Ukrainian | 14 | 7 | 2 | 1 | | 4 |
| Jewish | 50 | 13 | 9 | | | 4 |

*Source:* Hrvatski Kalendar, 1945, p. 265.

331

## TABLE 32

NUMBER OF PERSONS ARRESTED BY POLICE, OR ARRAIGNED IN CITY MAGISTRATES' COURTS, PER 10,000 OF SAME POPULATION CLASS, BY NATIVITY AND COLOR, AND BY COUNTRY OF BIRTH, FOR CITIES HAVING MORE THAN 500,000 INHABITANTS IN 1930

| Nativity and Country of Birth | Arraigned Magistrates' Courts New York (1929) | Number of Persons per 10,000 of same population class arrested by police | | | | | | | | |
|---|---|---|---|---|---|---|---|---|---|---|
| | | Chicago (1929) | Philadelphia (1930) | Detroit (1930) | Los Angeles (1929-30) | St. Louis (1930) | Baltimore (1930) | Boston (1930) | San Francisco (1929-30) | Milwaukee (1930) |
| Total | 559 | 642 | 826 | 130 | 410 | 1,315 | 687 | 1,198 | 992 | 725 |
| Native White | ( 616) | ( 555) | 952 | ( 96) | 388 | ( 973) | 734 | 1,322 | 945 | 776 |
| Negro | | (3,975) | | ( 923) | | (5,259) | | | | |
| Foreign Born | 454 | 385 | 377 | 97 | 488 | 631 | 330 | 937 | 1,098 | 565 |
| Austria | 474 | 166 | 280 | 129 | 674 | 1,045 | 324 | 847 | 737 | 899 |
| Canada | 195 | 42 | 108 | 64 | 216 | 895 | 137 | 778 | 755 | 630 |
| Czechoslovakia | N.D. | 141 | N.D. | 9 | N.D. | 114 | 108 | | N.D. | 114 |
| England, Scotland, Wales | 188 | 67 | 158 | 81 | 210 | 359 | 204 | 503 | 616 | 410 |
| France | 185 | 232 | 106 | 98 | 210 | 206 | 241 | 768 | 498 | 183 |
| Germany | 203 | 152 | 212 | 41 | 198 | 253 | 101 | 447 | 380 | 327 |
| Greece | 3,152 | 1,532 | 1,152 | 358 | 664 | 1,235 | 1,359 | 1,660 | 1,239 | 1,456 |
| Hungary | N.D. | 129 | Inc. with Austria | 66 | N.D. | 282 | 20 | N.D. | N.D. | Inc. with Austria |

332

TABLE 32 (Continued)

Number of Persons per 10,000 of same population class arrested by police

| Nativity and Country of Birth | Arraigned Magistrates' Courts New York (1929) | Chicago (1929) | Philadelphia (1930) | Detroit (1930) | Los Angeles (1929-30) | St. Louis (1930) | Baltimore (1930) | Boston (1930) | San Francisco (1929-30) | Milwaukee (1930) |
|---|---|---|---|---|---|---|---|---|---|---|
| Ireland | 194 | 200 | 360 | 196 | 620 | 722 | 259 | 129 | 848 | 1,382 |
| Italy | 542 | 801 | 425 | 93 | 338 | 1,452 | 626 | 893 | 728 | 704 |
| *Yugoslavia* | N.D. | 467 | 102 | 55 | N.D. | 792 | 148 | N.D. | N.D. | 544 |
| Lithuania | N.D. | 1,157 | 842 | 115 | N.D. | N.D. | 248 | 164 | N.D. | 1,225 |
| Poland | 309 | 513 | 961 | 112 | 237 | 1,172 | 512 | 247 | 226 | 431 |
| Russia | 590 | 174 | 309 | 72 | 368 | 678 | 216 | 775 | 953 | 992 |
| Scandinavian Countries | 307 | 305 | 678 | 131 | 431 | 739 | 1,517 | 1,170 | 1,280 | 1,170 |
| China | 2,036 | 983 | 1,143 | 29 | 555 | 1,101 | 2,618 | 5,013 | 6,306 | 625 |
| Japan | 552 | N.D. | 584 | 191 | 210 | 612 | 1,250 | 769 | 191 | Doubt-ful |
| Mexico | All figures open to question or left out entirely | | | | | | | | | |
| All Other | 464 | 940 | 402 | 154 | 635 | 683 | 1,346 | 1,233 | 113 | 1,247 |

*Source:* National Commission, *Report on Crime and the Foreign Born*, p. 100.

333

## TABLE 33

### YUGOSLAV SETTLEMENTS, BY STATES

| State | Number of Communities |
|---|---|
| Alabama | 3 |
| Alaska | 3 |
| Arizona | 7 |
| Arkansas | 5 |
| California | 59 |
| Colorado | 31 |
| Connecticut | 4 |
| District of Columbia | 2 |
| Florida | 2 |
| Georgia | 8 |
| Idaho | 3 |
| Illinois | 100 |
| Indiana | 17 |
| Iowa | 21 |
| Kansas | 22 |
| Kentucky | 3 |
| Louisiana | 8 |
| Maryland | 4 |
| Michigan | 45 |
| Minnesota | 48 |
| Mississippi | 3 |
| Missouri | 10 |
| Montana | 15 |
| Nebraska | 5 |
| Nevada | 4 |
| New Jersey | 29 |
| New Mexico | 6 |
| New York | 22 |
| Ohio | 83 |
| Oklahoma | 3 |
| Oregon | 3 |
| Pennsylvania | 265 |
| South Dakota | 2 |
| Texas | 8 |
| Utah | 18 |
| Virginia | 1 |
| Washington | 21 |
| West Virginia | 40 |
| Wisconsin | 29 |
| Wyoming | 15 |

*Source:* Ivan Mladineo, *Narodni Adresar*, p. 911.

## TABLE 34

FOREIGN-BORN WHITE AND NATIVE WHITE OF FOREIGN OR MIXED PARENTAGE, BY MOTHER TONGUE

| | Foreign-Born White | | | |
|---|---|---|---|---|
| | Number | | | |
| Mother Tongue | 1940 | 1930 | 1920 | 1910 |
| Total | 11,109,620 | 13,983,405 | 13,712,754 | 13,345,545 |
| **Northwestern Europe:** | | | | |
| English | 2,506,420 | 3,097,021 | 3,007,932 | 3,363,792 |
| Norwegian | 232,820 | 345,522 | 362,199 | 402,587 |
| Swedish | 423,200 | 615,465 | 643,203 | 683,218 |
| Danish | 122,180 | 178,944 | 187,162 | 183,844 |
| Dutch | 102,700 | 133,142 | 136,540 | 126,045 |
| Flemish | 31,900 | 42,263 | 45,696 | 25,780 |
| French | 359,520 | 523,297 | 466,956 | 528,842 |
| **Central Europe:** | | | | |
| German | 1,589,040 | 2,188,006 | 2,267,128 | 2,759,032 |
| Polish | 801,680 | 965,899 | 1,077,392 | 943,781 |
| Czech | 159,640 | 201,138 | 234,564 | 228,738 |
| Slovak | 171,580 | 240,196 | 274,948 | 166,474 |
| Magyar (Hungarian) | 241,220 | 250,393 | 290,419 | 229,094 |
| *Serbian* | *18,060* | *30,121* | *40,669* | *27,289* |
| *Croatian* | *52,540* | *79,802* | *85,175* | *78,380* |
| *Slovenian* | *75,560* | *77,671* | *80,437* | *123,631* |
| **Eastern Europe:** | | | | |
| Russian | 356,940 | 315,721 | 392,049 | 57,926 |
| Ukrainian | 35,540 | 58,685 | 55,672 | 25,131 |
| Armenian | 40,000 | 51,741 | 37,647 | 23,938 |
| Lithuanian | 122,660 | 165,053 | 182,227 | 140,963 |
| Finnish | 97,080 | 124,994 | 133,567 | 120,086 |
| Rumanian | 43,120 | 56,964 | 62,336 | 42,277 |
| Yiddish | 924,440 | 1,222,658 | 1,091,820 | 1,051,767 |
| **Southern Europe:** | | | | |
| Greek | 165,220 | 189,066 | 174,658 | 118,379 |
| Italian | 1,561,100 | 1,808,289 | 1,624,998 | 1,365,110 |
| Spanish | 428,360 | 743,286 | 556,111 | 258,131 |
| Portuguese | 83,780 | 110,197 | 105,895 | 72,649 |
| **All Other:** | | | | |
| Arabic | 50,940 | 67,830 | 57,557 | 32,868 |
| All Other | 63,880 | 57,808 | 30,631 | 49,521 |
| Not reported | 248,500 | 42,233 | 7,166 | 116,272 |

*Source:* Bureau of the Census, *Sixteenth Census, Mother Tongue,* p. 51.

TABLE 34—(*Continued*)

| | Foreign-Born White | | | | | |
|---|---|---|---|---|---|---|
| | Increase | | | | | |
| | 1930–1940 | | 1920–1930 | | 1910–1920 | |
| Mother Tongue | Number | Per cent | Number | Per cent | Number | Per cent |
| Total | 2,873,785 | – 20.6 | 270,651 | 2.0 | 367,209 | 2.8 |
| **Northwestern Europe:** | | | | | | |
| English | –590,601 | – 19.1 | 89,089 | 3.0 | –355,860 | – 10.6 |
| Norwegian | –112,702 | – 32.6 | – 16,677 | – 4.6 | – 40,388 | – 10.0 |
| Swedish | –192,265 | – 31.2 | – 27,738 | – 4.3 | – 40,015 | – 5.9 |
| Danish | – 56,764 | – 31.7 | – 8,218 | – 4.4 | 3,318 | 1.8 |
| Dutch | – 30,442 | – 22.9 | – 3,398 | – 2.5 | 10,495 | 8.3 |
| Flemish | – 10,363 | – 24.5 | – 3,433 | – 7.5 | 19,916 | 77.3 |
| French | –163,777 | – 31.3 | 56,341 | 12.1 | – 61,886 | – 11.7 |
| **Central Europe:** | | | | | | |
| German | –598,966 | – 27.4 | – 79,122 | – 3.5 | –491,904 | – 17.8 |
| Polish | –164,219 | – 17.0 | –111,493 | – 10.3 | 133,611 | 14.2 |
| Czech | – 41,498 | – 20.6 | – 33,426 | – 14.3 | 5,826 | 2.5 |
| Slovak | – 68,616 | – 28.6 | – 34,752 | – 12.6 | 108,474 | 65.2 |
| Magyar (Hungarian) | – 9,173 | – 3.7 | – 40,026 | – 13.8 | 61,325 | 26.8 |
| *Serbian* | – 12,061 | – 40.0 | – 10,548 | – 25.9 | 13,380 | 49.0 |
| *Croatian* | – 27,262 | – 34.2 | – 5,373 | – 6.3 | 6,795 | 8.7 |
| *Slovenian* | – 2,111 | – 2.7 | – 2,766 | – 3.4 | – 43,194 | – 34.9 |
| **Eastern Europe:** | | | | | | |
| Russian | – 41,219 | 13.1 | – 76,328 | – 19.5 | 334,123 | 576.8 |
| Ukrainian | –23,145 | – 39.4 | 3,013 | 5.4 | 30,541 | 121.5 |
| Armenian | – 11,741 | – 22.7 | 14,094 | 37.4 | 13,709 | 57.3 |
| Lithuanian | – 42,393 | – 25.7 | – 17,174 | – 9.4 | 41,264 | 29.3 |
| Finnish | – 27,914 | – 22.3 | – 8,573 | – 6.4 | 13,481 | 11.2 |
| Rumanian | – 13,844 | – 24.3 | – 5,372 | – 8.6 | 20,059 | 47.4 |
| Yiddish | –298,218 | – 24.4 | –130,838 | 12.0 | 40,053 | 3.8 |
| **Southern Europe:** | | | | | | |
| Greek | – 23,846 | – 12.6 | 14,408 | 8.2 | 56,279 | 47.5 |
| Italian | –247,189 | – 13.7 | 183,291 | 11.3 | 259,888 | 19.0 |
| Spanish | –314,926 | – 42.4 | 187,175 | 33.7 | 297,980 | 115.4 |
| Portuguese | – 26,417 | – 24.0 | 4,302 | 4.1 | 33,246 | 45.8 |
| **All Other:** | | | | | | |
| Arabic | – 16,890 | – 24.9 | 10,273 | 17.8 | 24,689 | 75.1 |
| All Other | 6,072 | 10.5 | 27,177 | 88.7 | – 18,890 | – 38.1 |
| Not reported | 206,267 | 488.4 | 35,067 | 489.4 | –109,106 | – 93.8 |

## TABLE 34—(*Continued*)

### Native White of Foreign or Mixed Parentage

| Mother Tongue | 1940 | 1920 | 1910 |
|---|---|---|---|
| Total | 23,157,580 | 22,686,204 | 18,897,837 |
| **Northwestern Europe:** | | | |
| English | 12,181,040 | 6,721,433 | 6,673,628 |
| Norwegian | 344,240 | 658,589 | 607,267 |
| Swedish | 374,040 | 841,589 | 762,651 |
| Danish | 95,460 | 274,150 | 257,524 |
| Dutch | 103,240 | 233,959 | 198,885 |
| Flemish | 17,840 | 42,194 | 19,026 |
| French | 533,760 | 823,154 | 828,327 |
| **Central Europe:** | | | |
| German | 2,435,700 | 5,896,983 | 6,058,239 |
| Polish | 1,428,820 | 1,359,503 | 763,859 |
| Czech | 279,040 | 388,232 | 310,654 |
| Slovak | 283,520 | 344,918 | 117,970 |
| Magyar (Hungarian) | 198,600 | 205,426 | 91,799 |
| *Serbian* | *18,300* | *16,074* | *3,424* |
| *Croatian* | *58,980* | *58,503* | *20,161* |
| *Slovenian* | *97,300* | *105,808* | *59,800* |
| **Eastern Europe:** | | | |
| Russian | 214,160 | 339,900 | 37,211 |
| Ukrainian | 45,280 | 39,786 | 10,228 |
| Armenian | 26,440 | 15,193 | 6,083 |
| Lithuanian | 140,620 | 154,373 | 70,272 |
| Finnish | 118,460 | 131,905 | 80,602 |
| Rumanian | 20,340 | 29,347 | 8,847 |
| Yiddish | 773,680 | 951,793 | 624,995 |
| **Southern Europe:** | | | |
| Greek | 102,140 | 47,110 | 12,000 |
| Italian | 2,080,680 | 1,740,866 | 786,312 |
| Spanish | 714,060 | 294,737 | 190,067 |
| Portuguese | 120,500 | 109,833 | 68,619 |
| **All Other:** | | | |
| Arabic | 52,760 | 46,582 | 13,859 |
| All Other | 34,520 | 9,766 | 18,756 |
| Not reported | 264,060 | 13,170 | 196,772 |

# Index

Actors and actresses, moving picture, 275-276; radio, 276; stage, 274-276; television, 275-276

Adamic, Louis, 17-18, 22, 126, 138, 152, 161, 163, 194, 208, 210, 227-232, 262, 269, 282

Adamovich, Etheleen P., 128

Adult education, and the immigrants, 53, 198, 209, 228

Adventure, motive for emigration, 1, 4, 7, 22, 54

Agriculture, Europe, Yugoslavs in, 4, 9-11, 16, 36; United States, Yugoslavs in, 37, 39, 52, 70-71, 83, 84, 91-93, 127, 260, 263-264; see also Laborers, farm

Aircraft workers, 91

Akron, Ohio, Yugoslavs in, 74, 78

Alabama, Yugoslavs in, 75

Alaska, Yugoslavs in, 116, 202, 209, 277

Albania, 298

Albanians, in the United States, 198

Alcoholic beverages, consumption of, 190-192; sale of, 178-179, 183

Alexander, king of Yugoslavia, 7, 269, 308, 309

Allegheny City, Yugoslavs in, 40, 41, 76, 105, 116, 204-206

Amalgamated Association of Iron and Steel Workers, 86

American Association for Reconstruction in Yugoslavia, 125, 133, 135

American Association of Foreign-Language Newspapers, 155-156

American Federation of Labor, 99, 244

American Fraternal Union (Ameriška Bratska Zveza), 117, 121, 127, 144; see also South Slavonic Catholic Union (Jugoslavanska Katoliška Jednota)

American Protective Association, 49

American Revolution, Yugoslav role in, 27, 37

American Serbian Committee for Relief of War Orphans in Yugoslavia, 133

American Slav Congress, 126, 132, 133, 161

American-Slovene Communist Bureau, 248

American Tamburitza Orchestra, 122

American Yugoslav Humanitarian Club, 131

American Yugoslav Legion, 123

*Americki Hrvatski Glasnik*, 144, 167

*Amerikanski Slovenec*, 143, 144, 167

*Amerikanski Srbobran*, 143, 144, 159, 165, 166

*Ameriška Domovina*, 144, 159, 161, 169

Andrich, Spiro, 122

Angelinović, B., 271

Antonovich, Colonel Emil, 277

Arbre Croche, Michigan, missionary center, 31, 33

Arizona, Yugoslavs in, 75, 82, 90, 263

Artists, 40, 272-274

Artuković, Andrija, 211

Assimilation (Americanization), 56, 59, 73-74, 111-112, 124, 140-142, 148, 167, 191, 197-199, 209, 212-215; see also Immigrant adjustment, problem of

Atalić, Mandica, 163

Athletes, 225, 276, 277-280

Yugoslav American Home
in New York City